Reading Astrological Charts
– A Practical Guide

John Gumbs

Published by John Gumbs

ISBN 978-1-78222-874-5

Book design, layout and production management by Into Print
www.intoprint.net
+44 (0)1604 832149

Contents

Contents continued

Reading astrological charts

If you have some common sense, you can understand simply how astrology works. It is your eyes that are looking down at the symbols; and soon you are able to understand what they mean.

1: The Wheel

We are going to get know all about the wheel and how it is made up. How many degrees are in it, and how it is divided into houses. The Jewish historian Flavius Josephus wrote that Adam and Eve knew about the workings of the *"Heavenly Bodies."* We are given in the bible that on the fourth day, the sun, moon and stars were brought forth. They are for signs, for seasons, for days and for years. It is from them that the early Astrologers got to make the Calendar. Astrology and Astronomy at one time were the same until they parted company. The ancients have given us information on what they have found. We can test it and throw out what does not make sense, but hold on to what is true.

I will be mentioning some astronomical names but will not go too deeply into it. First I want you to understand that the wheel is fixed. It has 360 degrees. It is divided into twelve sections which are called *"houses."*

There is a narrow band in the sky which the zodiac occupies; and the ancients gave them these names:

Aries
Taurus
Gemini
Cancer
Leo
Virgo
Libra
Scorpio
Sagittarius
Capricorn
Aquarius
Pisces.

I used to wonder how they knew all this when I first started to research astrology. I don't think about it any more. You have to learn the zodiac names and how the symbols are written. Did you learn your ABC? Well you can learn these 12 signs. When I said that the wheel is fixed, I mean that Aries is the first sign on the wheel, and it is always found on the left hand side where the sun rises. Then the rest of the signs follow anti-clockwise. All this is very important to know. Every sign carries 30 degrees.

Here are the planets in our solar system:

The Sun
Moon
Mercury
Venus
Mars
Jupiter
Saturn
Uranus
Neptune
Pluto

We accept the sun and moon in our workings as if they were planets. Everyone knows or should know that the sun is a star, and the moon is neither a planet nor a star.

Here is something you have to remember. *The wheel starts turning when a time of birth is calculated.* People can also be born with the fixed wheel depending on what time they were born.

This fixed wheel with Aries as the first sign is the beginning of the year starting on or about the 21st of March. That is when the sun comes for the first time in the sign of Aries.

So you have 12 houses each with 30 degrees making the wheel 360 degrees.

What I want you to do now is to draw a big circle on a paper. From the top of the circle down through the middle, draw a line. From the left side, draw a line through the middle over to the right side. Now you have a cross in your circle. This cross are the four angles in the wheel. The left side is where the sun is rising and is known as the *Ascendant* or you yourself – this is around 06.00 am.

The top angle is what is known as the *Mid-heaven*, I normally refer to it as the Mid. It is noon 12.00 pm. Opposite the left side is the right angle, this is 18.00 pm, the sun sets here. This angle is known as your *partner* or the *public*. The bottom angle is *Midnight*. This angle is known as your home, your roots, the grave, your country and your parents.

So we have the first angle or the first house, your personality, how others see you. The sign there and planets will give more information.

We read the wheel anti-clockwise. Down to Midnight, the 4th house, up to the setting sun, the 7th house. At the top, noon, the 10th house, the career, outside world, your boss, your fame, and your parents.

Now make your wheel to have 12 sections big enough to place the symbols in later.

These sections are *houses*. The first house, on the left, is an angular house. It is you, yourself, your personality. It is you coming into this physical world. It is the way others see you. Any planet in this position will give you more energy, positive or negative.

The second house, that is moving anti-clockwise, is the second house. It has to do with money, your body and your possessions.

The third house is the house of communications, travel, brothers and sisters, neighbours, environment, close family, and everything to do with writing, talking, reading and signing contracts.

The fourth house is the house of your roots, your parents, your country, the grave, and real estate.

The fifth house is the house of children, love affairs, romance, speculation, sports and entertainment.

The sixth house is the house of sickness, health, work, colleagues, pets and hygiene.

The seventh house is the house of your marriage partner, your business partner, the public, open enemies.

The eighth house is the house of the other world, other people's money and possessions, legacies and the goods of the dead.

The ninth house is the house of higher education, philosophy, religion, law, foreign countries, long distance travel.

The tenth house is the house of your career, the outside world, your fame, your boss, your parents or those in authority.

The eleventh house is the house of your hopes and wishes, your friends and clubs and groups.

The twelfth house is the house of isolation, prisons, hospitals, working behind the scenes for the good of others, it is the house of secrets, the past, and enemies.

Remember that the wheel you're looking at now is the *fixed wheel*.

The sign of Aries (the ram) is at the ascendant or first house.
The sign of Taurus (the bull) is at the second house.
The sign of Gemini (the twins) is at the third house.
The sign of Cancer (the crab) is at the fourth house.
The sign of Leo (the lion) is at the fifth house.
The sign of Virgo (the virgin) is at the sixth house.
The sign of Libra (the scales) is at the seventh house.
The sign of Scorpio (the scorpion) is at the eighth house.
The sign of Sagittarius (the centaur) is at the ninth house.
The sign of Capricorn (the goat) is at the 10th house.
The sign of Aquarius (the waterbearer) is at the eleventh house.
The sign of Pisces (the fishes) is at the twelfth house.
You have to know what planet or planets are in charge of which house.
Mars is ruler of Aries and the first house.
Venus is ruler of Taurus and the second house.

Mercury is ruler of Gemini and the third house.

The Moon is ruler of Cancer and the fourth house.

The sun is ruler of Leo and the fifth house.

Mercury is ruler of Virgo and the sixth house.

Venus is ruler of Libra and the seventh house.

Mars and Pluto are rulers of Scorpio and the eighth house.

Jupiter is ruler of Sagittarius and the 9th house.

Saturn is ruler of Capricorn and the tenth house.

Saturn and Uranus are rulers of Aquarius and the eleventh house.

Jupiter and Neptune are rulers of Pisces and the twelfth house.

The planets in our solar system makes aspects to each other, these aspects could be positive or negative. The aspects are:

Conjunction, having two planets close to each other.

Semi-sextile, a distance of about 30 degrees, with a two degrees orb.

Semi-square, a distance of 45 degrees, with an orb of 2 degrees.

Sextile, a distance of 60 degrees, with 8 degrees orb.

Square, a distance of 90 degrees, with a 8 degrees orb.

Trine, a distance of 120 degrees, with 8 degrees orb.

Sesqui-quadrate, a distance of 135 degrees, 2 degrees orb.

Quincunx, a distance of 150 degrees, 2 degrees orb.

Opposition, a distance of 180 degrees, 8 degrees orb.

When the planets are passing through the signs of the zodiac, they will give the individual energies to work with according to the sign.

The sun in Aries makes an individual a part of the Arian group; in Taurus, of the Taurian group; in Gemini, of the Geminian group; in Cancer of the Cancerian group; in Leo of the Leonian group; in Virgo of the Vigoan group; in Libra of the Libran group; in Scorpio of the Scorpian group; in Sagittarius of the Sagittarian group; in Capricorn of the Capricornian group; in Aquarius of the Aquarian group; in Pisces of the Piscean group. These are the sun signs. You will get information from the sun sign about an individual, but that is not all. You have to read the whole chart. And that is what we are going to do later on. First, I want you to do some more extra wheels and have them ready.

2: Planets in Signs and Houses

First, let us get to know that when the planets are in certain signs, they're said to be *exalted* and give the individual more power to work with.

The Moon is exalted in the sign of Taurus
Mercury is exalted in the sign of Virgo.
Venus is exalted in the sign of Pisces.
Mars is exalted in the sign of Capricorn.
Jupiter is exalted in the sign of Cancer
Saturn is exalted in the sign of Libra.
Uranus is exalted in the sign of Scorpio.
Neptune is exalted in the sign of Leo.
Pluto is exalted in the sign of Pisces.

The sun is the life force. Without it nothing lives.
The moon is the emotions, the response, the feelings.
Mercury is the communicator.
Venus is love and beauty.
Mars is energy, action, war.
Jupiter (the biggest planet in the solar system) expansion, kind and protective.
Saturn (destiny) discipline, slow, power, restriction, cold.
Uranus, unexpected, disruptive, scientific.
Neptune, mysterious, psychic, dreamy, strange, see-through.
Pluto, political, dark, deep and penetrating, criminal, transformation.

The sun in Aries, the person is active, assertive, fiery.
The sun in Taurus, stubborn and a lover of possessions, loving.
The sun in Gemini, versatile, love of travel and environment.
The sun in Cancer, sensitive, protective, love home and country.
The sun in Leo, like a lion, powerful, loves entertainment and children.
The sun in Virgo, critical and analytical, interested in work and health.
The sun in Libra, harmonious relationships, togetherness, peaceful.
The sun in Scorpio, interested in deep thinking, sex, and other people's money.
The sun in Sagittarius, interest in freedom, foreign countries and higher education.
The sun in Capricorn, ambitious, wanting power, climbing to the top, cautious, patient.
The sun in Aquarius, interested in friendships, clubs and groups.
The sun in Pisces, kind, showing sympathy to others, soft and dreamy.

So, if you saw a chart with the sun in Pisces, you already have some information about what that person is like.

The moon in Aries is impulsive, active, can have a temper.

The moon in Taurus, is exalted giving more opportunities to the individual. Forceful. Loving, thinking about money and goods.

The moon in Gemini is clever, likes to communicate with others.

The moon in Cancer is homely, sensitive and protective.

The moon in Leo likes entertainment, children, and sports, thinking above love.

The moon in Virgo is looking for all the small details, sees everything that is happening around them. Works well with colleagues. Interested in health and hygiene.

The moon in Libra, the responses are harmonious and balanced. There is always kindness shown.

The moon in Scorpio could be jealous, vindictive, sometimes seeking revenge. Deep emotions.

The moon in Sagittarius, interest in freedom for self and others. Contact with foreign people. Could be philosophical and religious.

The moon in Capricorn, very cautious, ambitious, works hard. Not satisfied with low position.

The moon in Aquarius, interest in scientific and unusual subjects. Shy, in a sort of strange way.

The moon in Pisces, soft, kind, sympathetic and dreamy .

Mercury in Aries, full of ideas, impulsive, likes to thrash things out.

Mercury in Taurus, business minded, practical, loving, obstinate.

Mercury in Gemini, clever, good reasoning, communicative, writing, travel.

Mercury in Cancer, quick to remember past things, likes to be with family.

Mercury in Leo, confident, strong will, good with children.

Mercury in Virgo, good intellect, versatile, analytical.

Mercury in Libra, good companion, communicates harmoniously, peaceful.

Mercury in Scorpio, intuitive and secretive, make good spies and detectives.

Mercury in Sagittarius, believes in freedom for all, prophetic, high education.

Mercury in Capricorn, ambitious, practical, careful, good organizer.

Mercury in Aquarius, interest in science, mathematics, humanitarian.

Mercury in Pisces, telepathic, psychic, poetic, sympathetic, strong imagination.

Venus in Aries, impulsive, good with art, singing, forceful.

Venus in Taurus, strong feelings for loved ones, affectionate. Loves money.

Venus in Gemini, good for travel, writing and social contact.

Venus in Cancer, sensitive when in love, strong attachment to home, loving and kindhearted.

Venus in Leo, generous, entertaining, strong love for art.

Venus in Virgo shows the quiet and shy type. Interested in personal appearance and hygiene.

Venus in Libra, very sociable, strong feelings for others, good for art and music.

Venus in Scorpio, strong passionate nature, love of pleasure, can be jealous and secretive.

Venus in Sagittarius, interest in religion, and higher education, travel, foreign countries, and freedom.

Venus in Capricorn, ambitious, responsible, dignified, friends in high places.

Venus in Aquarius, social life, popular, get along with friends, taste for the unusual.

Venus in Pisces, sensitive, romantic, strong feelings for the other sex, caring, kind, helpful.

Mars in Aries, active, lots of energy, impulsive.

Mars in Taurus, stubborn, busy thinking about ways to make money, lovable.

Mars in Gemini, communicative, clever, active and alert.

Mars in Cancer, dress strange, a bit sloppy, busy around the home front. Sensitive and protective.

Mars in Leo, good for sports, entertainment, powerful, creative.

Mars in Virgo, hard worker, discriminative, analytical, interested in colleagues and pets.

Mars in Libra, active in love and partnerships, forceful.

Mars in Scorpio, jealous vengeful, sexy, deep thinking.

Mars in Sagittarius, active in travel, foreign contacts, freedom, long distance travel, religion and higher education.

Mars in Capricorn, ambitious, interested in the career lots of energy.

Mars in Aquarius, active for humanitarian causes, scientific, strong with friendships.

Mars in Pisces, secretive, works behind the scene, isolated, kind, helpful.

Jupiter in Aries, can be a leader, full of ideas, generous, interested in philosophical subjects.

Jupiter in Taurus, generous, loves justice, possibility for making money.

Jupiter in Gemini, humanitarian feelings, interested in high education and travel.

Jupiter in Cancer, protective, sensitive, homely, powerful energies here.

Jupiter in Leo, lots of energies, ceremonial, good leadership, strong love for children.

Jupiter in Virgo, analytical, interested in helping others, seeking out small details. Likes to have things in order.

Jupiter in Libra, interested in justice, marriage and partnerships. Working with the public, honest and truthful.

Jupiter in Scorpio, very deep and penetrating, can make good detectives. Interested in secret organizations, mystical telepathic. Can get secret information from others.

Jupiter in Sagittarius, love of philosophy and higher education. Interested in travel and foreign peoples.

Jupiter in Capricorn, much integrity, ambitious, reaching for the top in their careers. Traditional values, patient, ability to accumulate and get great wealth. Do not like waste.

Jupiter in Aquarius, universal, friendly, interested in unusual subjects, accepts other people's way of life. Scientific and occult wisdom. Attracts friends and could be involved in group activities.

Jupiter in Pisces, sensitive, soft, kind. Like to help those who are in great need. Intuitive with strong feelings. Spiritual.

Saturn in Aries, energetic. Ambitious, lots of ideas.

Saturn in Taurus, stubborn, prudent and diplomatic.

Saturn in Gemini, literature and study. Intellectual. Love of travel.

Saturn in Cancer, moody, love to be at home, love the family, protective and sensitive.

Saturn in Leo, strong-willed, determined and bold, interested in children.

Saturn in Virgo, serious, likes to investigate, analytical and critical, cautious.

Saturn in Libra, good for relationships and responsibilities, social awareness, and social responsibility. Powerful energies here.

Saturn in Scorpio, can be jealous, deep concentration, psychic, likes perfection. Works hard to gain position in life.

Saturn in Sagittarius, loves philosophy, religion and high education.

Saturn in Capricorn, ambitious, good organizers. Likes to be in power.

Saturn in Aquarius, deep penetrating intellect, friendly, scientific, could be good in mathematics. Interest in groups and clubs.

Saturn in Pisces, soft and kind and sympathetic to others, psychic, good for deep meditation. Isolation or work behind the scene.

That then were the classical planets. Uranus, Neptune and Pluto are generation planets, they stay long in one sign.

Now I shall give you the orbits of the planets:

Mercury takes 88 days to travel around the sun.

Venus takes 225 days to make its journey. Notice how strange Venus is: it goes around the sun quicker than it goes round itself. If anyone was living on Venus, they would be a year old before they're a day old. Then 18 days later, they're a day old. . Venus is odd, it turns backward, and is the slowest rotating planet in our solar system.

Mars takes 687 days.

Jupiter takes 11.86 years.

Saturn takes 29.5 years.

Uranus takes 84 years.

Neptune takes 165 years.

Pluto takes 248 years. Don't forget, Pluto has been relegated to a dwarf planet.

THE PLANETS IN THE HOUSES

The sun in the first house will give energy to the individual. He should feel strong. The chance is there to enjoy life if one looks after the self.

The sun in the second house has to do with money and how you go about using it.

The sun in the third house gives the energy to be interested in your close family, the environment and travel, and communicating.

The sun in the fourth house shows that you are interested in the home and your family, You want solid roots.

The sun in the fifth house shows a powerful and determined individual. Love of life and all it has to give. Lover of children, sports, speculation and love affairs and romance.

The sun in the sixth house shows that you have interest in work, colleagues, health, hygiene and pets.

The sun in the seventh house shows that you have the chance to enter into a marriage partnership of standing, or some business partnership. Social contact with some publicity.

The sun in the eighth house shows that you may be interested in the other side of this world and all the deep mysteries. A strong powerful will, passionate.

The sun in the ninth house shows that you are interest in foreign countries and peoples and long distance travel, high education, of course, religious and philosophical subjects.

The sun in the tenth house shows that you have the chance to hold a good career, very ambitious, seeking power.

The sun in the eleventh house shows that you are interested in friendships, clubs and groups, unusual scientific matters, universal and humanitarian.

The sun in the twelfth house shows that you can be a leader behind the scenes working for the benefit of humanity. Isolation, prisons, hospitals, taking a break, recuperating.

Remember that the aspects of the planets must be taken into consideration. The aspects will come later on.

The Moon in the first house is sensitive, moody, protective, something here to do with the mother.

The Moon in the second house is thinking about money matters, Good organizers.

The Moon in the third house could be busy with the environment, travel, brothers and sisters, and communications.

The Moon in the fourth house is good for making home and thinking of the family, real estate is shown here. Changes in the home.

The Moon in the fifth house is interested in children, life and romantic affairs.

The Moon in the sixth house, one must watch out for the health. Do not ignore it. Changes in work habit. Interested in hygiene and pets.

The Moon in the seventh house is good for publicity, marriage and business partnerships.

The Moon in the 8th house will give you insight, knowing things before hand. Has to do with legacies and goods of the dead.

The Moon in the ninth house is good for travel, especially, long distance. Interest in higher education, and freedom.

The Moon in the tenth house could bring publicity in the career and the outside world. Help from women in authority.

The Moon in the eleventh house could be very sensitive when it comes to friends, there's a need to be involved with groups and clubs. Interest also in scientific subjects.

The Moon in the twelfth house could give psychic abilities. Strong sensitive feeling, strange imaginations.

Mercury in the first house can give intellectual energies. Clever, good at reading and writing.

Mercury in the second house can show that one is always busy with ways of making money. Education is important to them.

Mercury in the third house can give great intellectual ability. This is a position for communicating well. Good for writing, debating, travel.

Mercury in the fourth house could find you with many books in the home, your own personal library. Possibility of working at home. Interests in real estate.

Mercury in the fifth house can show creative and artistic ability. They make sure that their children have a good education. They like to speculate.

Mercury in the sixth house can be very skilful in their work. Very analytical and critical. Produce good product.

Mercury in the seventh house like to be in harmony with the partner. Good sales people. Work well with the public.

Mercury in the eighth house shows that one is interested in deep and dark things. The mysteries of the other world. Interest in other people's money and taxes.

Mercury in the ninth house can give energies for philosophy, religion, law, and all the high education. They love travel and like to communicate with others.

Mercury in the tenth house gives good organizing ability. Very intellectual in the career. Can communicate well.

Mercury in the eleventh house shows those who are interested in communicating their ideas with their best friends. They communicate well in scientific matters.

Mercury in the twelfth house can be secretive, sensitive, easily hurt. This position can give psychic ability.

Venus in the first house is very good for art, music and all things that are graceful. It will give beauty to the individual.

Venus in the second house should not be short of money and possessions. Wants to gain wealth. Likes to spend on goods.

Venus in the third house shows a love for literature, the environment, brothers and sisters, art and travel.

Venus in the fourth house shows harmony with those in the family. Spends lots of time decorating the home. Beauty is important to these individuals. Venus is strong in this house. Possibility of gain.

Venus in the fifth house shows a strong love for children, love affairs and romance, entertainment and speculation and sports.

Venus in the sixth house shows love for colleagues and works well with them, love for pets. One should keep an eye on the health.

Venus in the seventh house is a powerful position. Good for working with the public and partners. Harmonious and loving. There should be happiness here ; and gain.

Venus in the eighth house shows legacies and other people's goods. Love is very deep and passionate.

Venus in the ninth house shows a love of travel, especially long distance. Contact with foreigners. High education. Good contact with in-laws.

Venus in the tenth house is a strong position. Artistic and musical abilities Get on well in the career with much publicity. Gets on well with those in authority.

Venus in the eleventh house shows good contact with friends and probably help from them.

Venus in the twelfth house shows a love of isolation. Good at art and music, . Very compassionate, kind and helpful.

Mars in the first house. Here we have Mars in its own house. There'll be much energy and assertiveness here. Lots of energy to do sports or in the workplace. Must be able to control these energies. Hard workers.

Mars in the second house shows that the individual puts all the energies in gaining possessions, impulsive. Must be careful of overspending.

Mars in the third house is very clever, intuitive, good for writing and reading and travel.

Mars in the fourth house. Mars can cause trouble to the parents if it is negatively aspected. Some difficulties can come about.

Mars in the fifth house is good for sports, entertainments. Possibility of working with children. Love to chase love.

Mars in the sixth house shows hard worker. Very good at work. Clever. Very determined, analytical and critical.

Mars in the seventh house is very powerful and can cause harm if the energies are not used properly. Very assertive and aggressive.

Mars in the eighth house is interested in other people's possessions, strong passionate love. Deep and penetrating.

Mars in the ninth house shows an interest in travel, high education. If Mars is negative there could be problems with religious and philosophical thinking.

Mars in the tenth house shows much aggressiveness here like in military affairs. Putting all their energies into their career.

Mars in the eleventh house is deeply interested in friends and clubs and groups. Much energy spent in scientific pursuit.

Mars in the twelfth house is secretive. People like to be alone, working behind the scene. There can be problems with enemies. Constantly thinking of past events.

Jupiter in the first house gives energies to be jovial, lovable. This position is like a king or queen. Jupiter makes the personality big; and one must be careful not to overeat.

Jupiter in the second house is sure to make you wealthy. Good for business enterprises. Be careful of overspending.

Jupiter in the third house has energies for teaching, writing, travelling. Interest in religion and philosophy.

Jupiter in the fourth house is very strong and can put you in a high position.

Good for the home, family and real estate.

Jupiter in the fifth house has energies for being creative, sportive and entertaining. Very good with children.

Jupiter in the sixth house shows one to be active in serving others, especially in the work place and with colleagues. Deeply interested in health. Love pets.

Jupiter in the seventh house. This is another strong position for Jupiter. Good relations in marriage and the public, are honest and seek good justice. The person is like a king or a queen.

Jupiter in the eighth house has to do with legacies and the goods of the dead. Possibility of inheriting from others. Deep in matters of the other world. Energies here to know what others don't know.

Jupiter in the ninth house. Here Jupiter is in its own house and the individual has energies to use for long distance travel, contact with foreign peoples, religion, philosophy, law, high education. Seeking freedom for self and others. Good for publishing, and teaching.

Jupiter in the tenth house. Here, we have Jupiter in a strong position, can make you a king or queen in your career. Expansive. Publicity. Good contact with superiors.

Jupiter in the eleventh house shows that you'll be joined to some large organization or club or group. Many friends who will help you.

Jupiter in the twelfth house shows a sensitive, sympathetic nature. Loves to meditate. Could be a mystic. Loves isolation.

Saturn in the houses. The ancients said that Saturn is the destiny planet. So whatever house it fall in, that is where your destiny lies. In my chart, it shows it to be true.

Saturn in the first house. This could have to do with early training in life. Heavy duties fall upon them. Sometimes they have to look after the rest of the family. Sometimes they appear cold and uninterested to others. Saturn holds a strong position because it is in an angular position.

Saturn in the second house. These people work hard and look after their money. Can be good in business.

Saturn in the third house. These people have the energies here to be good at maths, very clever, practical, slow but delivers in the end. Good for publishing, teaching, and travel.

Saturn in the fourth house. This is a position where the individual has to get out of the poverty of the family. Must strive that much harder. Disciplined parents. Heavy duties around the home front.

Saturn in the fifth house. I read that Saturn in this house does not like children. Some women have problems giving children when Saturn is in this house. It has to be very well aspected for the woman to bring forth a child. Saturn denies children. In an old mythological story, Saturn *"eats his children."* Saturn has energies here for good organization. Interested in structural buildings. A bit cold in love affairs.

Saturn in the sixth house shows energies for hard work, much responsibilities. Very serious when it comes to work, health, pets and colleagues.

Saturn in the seventh house. A strong sense of justice. Is serious when it comes to dealing with the law and justice. They take partnerships seriously. Sometimes it come early or late, and there's a difference in age.

Saturn in the eight house. This position could find one handling the partner's money or other people's. Strange occurrences, strange dreams. There's something magical when Saturn is in this house. The thinking is deep and penetrating.

Saturn in the ninth house. Here, you find that your destiny has to do with long distance travel, philosophy, religion, high education, publishing and foreign peoples. The ninth house has to do with in-laws and grandparents.

Saturn in the tenth house. This is the house where Saturn is in its own domain. It feels powerful here. On top of the world. There's always a power struggle going on. People with this position have to make sure that they do not act unfairly, for there is a big drop, and they will never get back to the top again.

Saturn in the eleventh house. This house is also owned by Saturn. Friends can be serious and loyal. A good sense of responsibility in clubs and groups. Interested in scientific and unusual subjects. Humanitarian principles.

Saturn in the twelfth house. Here, Saturn is working behind the scenes for others. This could be a leader or a president of a country. Saturn has to have good aspects coming to it for one to be in charge. The destiny can be a lonely one, even though one is in charge.

I will deal with the three outer planets later. They are Uranus, Neptune and Pluto.

3: Aspects, Calculation

Getting your aspects right is one of the main things in astrology. If the sun is trine with Jupiter, you already know that this is a positive aspect and that things would work out easy for the individual. If the sun is not good with Jupiter, you know that the individual would have to put more effort into what he or she is doing.

I shall start with the sun first seeing that it is the source of all life on earth.

The sun in good aspect to the Moon will give good health, and the person should feel good within themselves.

If the sun is negative to the moon, it will be much difficult to let your feelings flow.

The sun positive to Mercury. This combination is very good for the intellect. If the sun and Mercury are in conjunction, we check the conjunction up to 8 degrees. If the conjunction is very close, say about 1 degree apart, Oh! what great intellect, but who is the individual who can control such energies. Not everyone is capable of doing so.

This sun and Mercury then, is good for studying, writing and researching. But you do not need to have this in order to research or to write – you can have some other combination.

If the sun and Mercury are negative, you can still use this energy depending on who you are. Other individuals would find it hard to use the negative energies of sun and Mercury. It could make one nervous, and not concentrating properly.

The sun positive to Venus is just a very good contact. Love energies will flow freely, artistic and musical ability is there too. Good feelings.

If the sun is negative with Venus, you can still use these negative energies, but the love is not from the inside, it could be overbearing and show-off.

The sun positive with Mars, you had better get out my way. Courageous, ooh! Very active, hard worker. All the energies of sun and Mars forcing their way out. This combination, if it has connection with the ascendant, could give the chance of long life, and good health.

If the sun is negative to Mars, people can act in a way to cause arguments, too hasty and impulsive. A clever person can use these energies in a good way.

The sun positive to Jupiter is awesome. The sun being the giver of life and Jupiter being the biggest planet of all, gives power and expansion in all that you undertake to do.

If the sun is negative with Jupiter, over indulgence, overeating, bad health, overspending, getting too fat.

The sun positive with Saturn will give energies to be responsible, disciplined and organized.

If the sun is negative to Saturn can cause depression, not trying your best, going round thinking that everyone is against you.

If the sun is positive to Uranus, this can make you deeply interested in science. Inventive and creative. The mind is very good.

If the sun is negative to Uranus, this could cause one to be restless, troublesome. Yet, one could still benefit from these negative energies and become a brilliant scientist.

The sun positive with Neptune, gets energies to be very sensitive and intuitive, probably a mystic, psychic. Can tell of the future.

If the sun is negative to Neptune, keep away from drugs and alcohol. Dreamy, negative, mind confused.

If the sun is positive with Pluto, great and mighty powers here. Occult forces, physics and maths. Ability to see things that are hidden from others.

If the sun is negative to Pluto, may cause others to move away from them, underground activities. Wants things to change drastically. People can still use the energies for deep insight.

If the Moon is positive to Mercury, the feelings and communicating abilities are working good. There's good common sense. good in speech and writing.

If the Moon is negative to Mercury, there's nervousness, and people become uneasy, and moody and worry over small details.

If the moon is positive with Venus, the feelings and the love energies come out well. Very harmonious and gentle. There's energies for artistic and musical ability.

If the Moon is negative with Venus, doesn't really care about the feelings of others, overdoing things. Problems could easily crop up.

If the Moon is positive with Mars, lots of energies to do one's work. Always on the go. Good for study.

If the Moon is negative to Mars, one could get angry quickly and cause problems. An aggressive nature. Problems at home.

If the Moon is positive to Jupiter, this is a lucky aspect, generous, harmonious, good business sense. Can be wealthy.

If the Moon is positive to Saturn, honest with lots of common sense, strong person. Good at organizing, and careful.

If the Moon is negative to Saturn, bound to be a unfair when dealing with others, depressed, not good for speculating.

If the Moon is good to Uranus, people can be scientific, interest in astrology. Interested in making friends and joining clubs.

If the Moon is negative to Uranus, sudden changes, and disruption. Troubles with the home and friends and clubs.

If the Moon is positive to Neptune, poetic, artistic and musical. Very sensitive.

Can be psychic.

If the Moon is negative to Neptune, deceptive feelings. Best to keep away from drinks and drugs. Problems with the opposite sex. Must face reality.

If the Moon is positive to Pluto, deep and penetrating insight. Good for working and researching deep subjects.

If the Moon is negative to Pluto, moody, and thinking everyone is against them. Must be careful in meddling in magic and things that are dangerous, that are unseen.

If Mercury is positive to Venus, there's energies here for writing, cheerful, artistic, nice feelings.

If Mercury is negative to Venus, lacking the real power to learn, messing about, conceited, not really serious.

If Mercury is positive to Mars, the intellect is good, sharp, quick in response to others, communicates well.

If Mercury is negative to Mars, nervousness, teasing, not pleased with what's happening, like to argue.

If Mercury is positive to Jupiter, interest in philosophy and probably teaching, honest, the mind works good.

If Mercury is negative to Jupiter, like to tell things that are not true, Always in a hurry. Want things done quickly. No solid plans.

If Mercury is positive to Saturn, good organizer, serious, would make a good teacher or writer. Takes life seriously.

If Mercury is negative to Saturn, not steady, obstinate, undisciplined, worry a lot, takes time to understand certain things.

If Mercury is positive to Uranus, inventive, scientific, unusual ideas, high intellect. Like to find how things work.

If Mercury is negative to Uranus, gets very nervous, confused, the negative energies here can still work in scientific fields. A bit stubborn.

If Mercury is positive with Neptune, Very intuitive and sensitive Can feel when things are not right. Listening to other people's point of view. Psychic.

If Mercury is negative to Neptune, one should keep away from strong drinks and drugs. Nervous and forgetting quickly what was told to them. Like to tell fibs.

If Mercury is positive to Pluto, deep penetrating intellect. Interest in scientific subjects. Physics. Good concentration.

If Mercury is negative to Pluto, always hurrying, a secret planner. This contact is still powerful depending on who is using it.

If Venus is positive to Mars, artistic, friendly, will fall in love, harmony and togetherness.

If Venus is negative to Mars, there could be trouble in forming a real relationship, just flirting, not satisfied with the way things are going. Don't know what true love is.

If Venus is positive to Jupiter, you have the chance to become popular. Good contact with others, generous, Artistic and easy going.

If Venus is negative to Jupiter, over spending. Going from one love to the other. Wasteful.

If Venus is positive to Saturn, this aspect is good for being loyal, dealing with one's duties. Good and positive feelings.

If Venus is negative to Saturn, can be jealous, not showing real feelings. Never satisfied with the way things are going.

If Venus is positive to Uranus, don't waste time when on a date, exciting. Unusual and interesting, will definitely attract the other sex.

If Venus is negative to Uranus, relationships can be short, moody, gets bored. Sometimes people often go astray with this aspect.

If Venus is positive to Neptune, people are romantic, artistic, mystic, musical, Great compassion and understanding.

If Venus is negative to Neptune, love feelings are not real, strange feelings in love. Sometimes there are secret love affairs, gets hurt easily.

If Venus is positive to Pluto, deep powerful love. If partners tune in, they could go through barriers of time. This aspect is good for science, music and art.

If Venus is negative to Pluto, some people would have to control themselves when it comes to sex, they can go too far, thinking it has to do with love. There could be secret love affairs. The negative energies here can be dangerous when used by the wrong person.

If Mars is positive to Jupiter, powerful personality, energetic, enjoys life. Interest in philosophy, religion and travel.

If Mars is negative to Jupiter, can quickly get themselves into trouble. Not accepting orders. Always in the middle of disputes.

If Mars is positive to Saturn, a very hard worker, always on the go. Likes things to be perfect. Good organizer, appear cold at times.

If Mars is negative to Saturn, tough, obstinate, wilful. Overdo things.

If Mars is positive to Uranus, a courageous person, enormous energies here, unusual and sudden events.

If Mars is negative to Uranus, likes to get the self into trouble, restless, disruptive, a fighter, yet the energies are good for pursuing scientifical subjects.

If Mars is positive to Neptune, the energies here are good for art, music, dancers, films, healing, helping others, People are very sensitive, interested in helping others.

If Mars is negative to Neptune, while a disciplined person will use these negative energies for some good, others will misuse them, causing self deception, and probably leading others astray. It is best to keep away from drugs and alcohol.

If Mars is positive with Pluto, here, the energies could lead you into doing great things, very deep and penetrating thinker. Great powers, possibility of discovering something that was hidden, transforming from old to new.

If Mars is negative to Pluto, there could be criminal activities here, don't think of the feelings of others. Careless.

If Jupiter is positive to Saturn, good business sense, good at organizing, energies for philosophical and religious subjects.

If Jupiter is negative to Saturn, problems are bound to come about to do with money. Bad planning, not satisfied, One can still get somewhere with this contact.

If Jupiter is positive to Uranus, long distance travel, many friends, occult science, good organizing energies. Very intelligent, religious and philosophical subjects.

If Jupiter is negative to Uranus, obstinate, overdoing things, not good for gambling. Misleading others. Unusual occult meetings.

If Jupiter is positive to Neptune, energies here to help others, a real mystic, energies for healing. Good for art and music. Great love given to others.

If Jupiter is negative to Neptune, too much waste, can deceive self and be deceived by others. Best to keep away from alcohol and drugs.

If Jupiter is positive to Pluto, great power here when it comes to philosophy, religion and education. People have a deep insight into the mysteries. Very psychic.

If Jupiter is negative to Pluto, can be fanatical, underground activities, love of other people's money or possessions. This contact whether positive or negative gives insight, and people can tell things which turn out to be true.

If Saturn is positive to Uranus, strong will power. Great scientifical work. Involved with friends and groups, dependable. The chance is here to be good with maths. Thinking in the future.

If Saturn is negative to Uranus, although this aspect can be good for scientifical subjects, there can be sudden misfortune. Unusual and dangerous ideas. Not steady.

If Saturn is positive to Neptune, lots of visions and dreams. Very sensitive. Compassionate and like to help others.

If Saturn is negative to Neptune, must be aware, and keep oneself away from strange things of the occult and magic. Drugs and alcohol must be avoided. Worry too much.

If Saturn is positive to Pluto, strong powerful forces at work here. This contact has something to do with magic. Hard work and endurance.

If Saturn is negative to Pluto, criminal activities are possible. Planning and scheming or messing about with dark forces. Sometimes cold with no feelings for others.

I will leave the outer planets' aspects seeing that they're so slow. Maybe you can find something when you come to understand them.

Now we are going to do some calculating. It is important that you understand how the chart came to be made. I am doing it by hand and I do hope that you have lots of paper, pen and pencils nearby.

CALCULATING THE CHART

We already know that the first house or the ascendant is ruled by Aries with Mars as the planet in charge. This stays like that until the sun should burn itself out. This is the fixed wheel. Get it into your head; *the fixed wheel.*

Because of the circle, there is no end, for the sun goes round and round without stopping. But for us on earth, the sun starts off in zero degree in the sign of Aries.

Aries starts off the time in zero hours, zero minutes, and zero seconds – this is sidereal time, and this is the first day.

On the second day we find the time to be zero hour, 3 minutes and 56 seconds, we round it off and call it 4 minutes.

Every four minutes is another day, and when we work with astrology, this day becomes one year of your life.

Without going too deep, I'll just say that the sun is our solar day, and the first point of Aries is sidereal day.

Solar time is from the sun, sidereal time is from the stars, and this is according to the rotation of the earth to the first point of Aries which is called: the **VERNAL EQUINOX.**

From this point, we go along the ecliptic in **RA – RIGHT ASCENSION.**

The earth rotates on its axis in 23 hours and 56 minutes of Mean time known as Civil time. You can always read more on the internet if you're deeply interested.

The first point of Aries in the Celestial Sphere is where the Ecliptic (the path where the sun and planets travel) and the Equator cross.

An *ephemeris* is a big or little booklet with astronomical places of the planets for a given year. You can always get one from an astrological bookshop, should you wish to do the chart by hand.

Have your blank chart wheel ready. Later, we are going to fill it in.

Someone is born on the 17th June 1987.

We need to look into an ephemeris for the year 1987, and look for the month of June.

The first column down gives us the date.

The second column gives the day

The third column gives the sidereal time.

Once you see the date, 17th, then you see in the next column, the letter showing what day it is.

Moving to the third column, you see the sidereal time in hours, minutes and seconds. We are dealing now with simple maths, but if you go deeper in astrology, the maths become harder.

For any year in the ephemeris, you just look for the 17th June, and the third column will give you the sidereal time.

Here is an example:

If some one is born on the 17th June 2000, at 10.00 am, in London, England, we find that the sidereal time is 5 hours, 44 minutes, and 12 seconds.

H- M-S

5 -44-12

GMT is noon at London (Greenwich Mean Time).

The UK is one hour behind GMT.

This 1 hour is taken away from the birth time of 10.00 am.

That leaves us with a birth time of 09.00 am.

Now the difference between the birth and GMT is 3 hours.

We take away the 3 hours from the sidereal time of 5 hours, 44 minutes and 12 seconds, we are left with 2 hours, 44 minutes, and 12 seconds.

Before I go on I must make it clear to you that the birth depends on where the person was born.

You can also get a booklet of longitudes and latitudes of places.

These places are important. It is important to know if the country is running on time *"before"* or *"after"* GMT.

The 3 hours is known as the interval. Each hour must be multiplied by 10 seconds of interval giving us 30 seconds. This must be taken away from 2 hours, 44 minutes and 12 seconds.

We are left with 2 hours, 43 minutes, and 42 seconds.

Now we come to the tricky part. We have to look at the back of the ephemeris, and there we'll see tables of houses for London, Liverpool and New York.

We need to take the tables for London 51 degrees and 32 minutes North.

Ok! we have come this far. Hope you have your wheel drawn and ready, for I will be giving you the signs and degrees to fill in for the example chart of 17th June 2000 at 10.00 am, London, UK.

You're going to find that the houses in your wheel are not any more equal with 30 degrees for each house. Only in the Equal wheel does this happen. The reason for this is because our clever mathematicians have all come up with different house systems. The one I'm using is called the Placidean system. There are many more. The reason I picked this one is because he used a time system method to get his houses, and it made some sense to me. Again, you can find out more on the internet.

I will now give you the signs and degrees to fill in by hand in your wheel that you have ready. Later, we shall deal with the ephemeris and how to read it.

You should now know where the first house is and so on. . .

At your first house, I want you to put the sign of Leo with 25.17 (25 degrees, 17 minutes).

At the second house (remember that we are going anti-clockwise). I want you to put the sign of Virgo with 15 degrees.

At the third house, I want you to put the sign of Libra with 10 degrees.

At the top of your wheel, (the Midheaven) I want you to put the sign of Taurus with 13 degrees.

At the 11th house, I want you to put the sign of Gemini with 22 degrees.

At the 12th house, I want you to put the sign of Cancer with 27 degrees.

Now you have to put the sign of Aquarius on the 7th house with the same degrees as the ascendant or first house.

You have to put the sign of Pisces on the 8th house with the same degrees as is on the 2nd.

You have to put the sign of Aries on the 9th house with the same degrees that is on the 3rd.

Have you seen where the fixed sign of Aries is? This is because of the time and place where our example person was born.

You have to put the sign of Scorpio on the 4th house with the same degree as the Mid.

You have to put the sign of Sagittarius on the 5th house with the same degrees as the 11th.

You have to put the sign of Capricorn on the 6th house with the same degrees as the 12.

Asc	25.17	Leo
2nd	15.00	Virgo
3rd	10.00	Libra
4th	13.00	Scorpio
5th	22.00	Sagittarius
6th	27.00	Capricorn
7th	25.17	Aquarius
8th	15.00	Pisces
9th	10.00	Aries
10th	13.00	Taurus
11th	22.00	Gemini
12th	27.00	Cancer

Your wheel is now ready for the planets. *This must be done carefully.*

In the ephemeris we are going to look for the month of June for year 2000. We take the date of 17th. We are going to run our finger across both pages, noting as we go along, the information.

We move our finger, and we come to the sidereal time, we move our finger to the next column and we come to the sun's longitude. We need this. The sun is 26 degrees, 35 minutes and 21 seconds. Don't worry about the seconds, just 26 degrees and 35 minutes. Look up to the top of the column and you'll see the symbol for the sun. While you're going up, take the first sign that you come to. In this case we come to Gemini. So the sun is 26 degrees and 35 minutes in Gemini.

Back to the 17th, we move from the sun's longitude column, and move to the next one which is that of the sun's declination. We are not using that. Move to the next column and we come to the moon's longitude. We see that there is a sign exactly on the 17th day for the moon and that is 2 degrees, 44 minutes and 36 seconds, . Forget the seconds. The sign there is Capricorn.

You must be careful when you're looking for the sign the moon is in. Always take the sign that is exactly on the date, or look up the column and take the first sign that you see.

Some ephemeris are for Midnight, and some are for midday. That mean that we have to bring the moon to its proper place for the time of 10.00 am.

I shall show you how that is done later.

Go across to the page on the right, and look for the date 17th. The next column sometimes start with Mercury when you look up at the top, or Neptune, depending how old the ephemeris is.

The ephemeris that I'm using for the year 2000, has Mercury at the top (the symbol is there).

Keeping our finger or some pointer at this column, we note the degrees and minutes. 18 degrees and 40 minutes. Look up the column and always take the first sign you come to. We see the sign of Cancer.

Move to the next column. We have 28 degrees and 15 minutes in Gemini for the planet Venus which is at the top of the column.

Move across to the next column and we see that a sign is there with 0 degree and 39 minutes of Cancer. We do not have to look up the column for the sign because it is right there on the date. We look up only to see the symbol of the planet Mars.

We move to the next column and we get the degrees of 27, and 14 minutes. We look up the column and we see the sign of Taurus, and above, the symbol for Jupiter.

The next column gives us 25 degrees and 8 minutes of Taurus, Saturn's symbol is above.

These are the classical planets but we shall add the three outer planets and see where they fall inside the wheel.

We move to the next column and we get 20 degrees and 37 minutes of Aquarius. When you look up slowly at the minutes, you see that they are increasing, and at the top, or sometimes anywhere in the column, you see the R, this tells you that the planet Uranus is going backwards (retrograde). The symbol of Uranus is at the top.

Move to the next column and you see 6 degrees and 10 minutes. Look up the column and you see the sign Aquarius and the R. The symbol for Neptune is at the top.

The last column we come to for the planets is that of Pluto. In some ephemeris, Pluto is a couple of pages at the back.

Here we see the degrees of 11 and 7 minutes in the sign of Sagittarius with the R. The symbol of Pluto is at the top. ;

So we have:

Sun	26.35	Gemini
Moon	02.44	Capricorn
Mercury	18.40	Cancer
Venus	28, 15	Gemini
Mars	00.39	Cancer
Jupiter	27.14	Taurus
Saturn	25.08	Taurus
Uranus	20.37 R	Aquarius
Neptune	06.10 R	Aquarius
Pluto	11.07 R	Sagittarius

We are now going to place the planets in the wheel. If you put our example chart through a programme on the internet, you'll see that those ancients weren't far off doing it by hand.

Ready? Got your drawn chart with all the signs and degrees filled in. With your ascendant as the starting point with Leo rising with 25 degrees and 17 minutes?

Go to the 11th house. You see that it is holding 22.00 of Gemini.

The sun is in 26.35 of Gemini so we place the sun in the 11th house close to the 11th house line.

Go the the 6th house. You see that it has 27 00 of Capricorn.

Place the moon in the 5th house close to the 6th house line. The moon is in the fifth house because it only has 2 degrees of Capricorn, it is less than 27 degrees of Capricorn.

Go to the 12th house. You see the sign of Cancer with 27.00

Set the planet Mercury in the 11th house near to the 12th house line.

Go to the 11th house. Place Venus in this house near to the 11th house line.

Stay in the 11th house. Place the planet Mars in this house close to the 12th house line.

Go to the 10th house (the Mid). You see 13.00 degrees of Taurus there. Place Jupiter in the 10th house near the 10th house line.

Stay in this house. Place Saturn in this house near to the 10th house line.

Go to the 6th house. Place the planet Uranus in this house near to the 7th house line.

Do the same with Neptune and Pluto.

Now our example chart for 17th June 2000 at 10.00 am, London UK is calculated and ready to be interpreted.

Before I start interpretation, some more information for you.

If the birth is pm west of Greenwich, you add, and if the longitude is east for am, you add.

You need to know about North and South Latitudes, East and West Longitudes.

You must always look and see the difference in time between where a person is born and GMT, how many hours before or after.

You have to know when the UK is on double time or I hour.

You can always look on the internet to see all this information.

When dealing with South Latitude, you must add 12 hours, and reverse the ascendant.

4: Interpretations of Charts

You have seen that calculating a chart by hand can be very difficult if you don't know what you're doing. It is easy to make mistakes. It is important not to make any mistake, and always double check your work. Once you get to know how astrology works, it is best to make a collection of charts of people who are close to you such as family, friends, and loved ones. In this way, you'll be able to see and understand more clearly what it's all about.

Now with the chart before you whether drawn by hand or done with the computer, you can examine it with your eyes. When you get to know what you're looking at, you can quickly jot down some information.

The ascendant is LEO; don't you know what the lion is like?

The ruler of the ascendant is the sun. We find the sun in the 11th house in the sign of Gemini. The sun sign is Gemini. The person has the energies to communicate and is versatile. Interested in friends and clubs and groups.

The sun is in conjunction with the 11th house, makes it more solid that friendship is important.

The sun is in conjunction with Venus, very close. This shows that the life and love energies are working together in the 11th house.

The sun is conjunct Mars in the 11th house. This conjunction gives lots of energies.

The sun is sextile to the ascendant. Here we get more energies and the chance of prolonging life.

The sun is semi-sextile Jupiter in the 10th house. This is an easy positive aspect and is helpful to the individual.

The sun is trine Uranus in the 6th house. This aspect has to do with science and work and many colleagues .

Now we see that the ascendant ruler, the sun has many good contacts, and in the areas concerned, it should go well for the individual.

The moon is in the 5th house in the sign of Capricorn. Here the individual is ambitious, wants to be in love, likes to speculate, loves children and sports. Although the moon is in the 5th house, it is taking on energies from the 6th house, and one must not neglect the health.

The moon is opposing Mars in the 11th house giving some negative energies. Here, you see that Mars is in the sign ruled by the moon, Cancer. How would you like to be in your friends home when both of you are not talking to each other. A rather difficult situation.

The moon is making a trine aspect to the ascendant. Very sensitive with strong feelings, could be close to the mother.

We find two powerful planets up in the 10th house – Jupiter and Saturn. The tenth house is angular, and planets are very strong here.

Jupiter will be like a queen or a king in that position.

Saturn is the ruler of the 10th house, he sits powerful here, a real leader. But he must make sure he deals fair, and not to be untrue, because the fall is great, and he will never get back there again.

The two planets Jupiter and Saturn are good for religious and philosophical and educational purposes.

They will surely bring the individual in some high position in life.

Venus in the 11th house is good for help from friends.

Venus is semi-sextile to both Jupiter and Saturn in the 10th house. This is positive, and will work out in the career, the workplace and partnerships.

Venus is sextile the ascendant, this is just a beautiful aspect, gives grace and beauty to the personality with the ability for art or music.

Venus is just about trine with Uranus, and is good for friendships and work colleagues.

When planets in angular positions are square to an angle, this is a negative force, but because of being angular, they are powerful. So we see that both Jupiter and Saturn are square to the ascendant.

Mars in the 11th house will give energies towards friendships and clubs and interest in unusual scientific subjects.

Venus and Mars are in conjunction in the 11th house. There's lots of power here, and one should be careful not to go astray in the love-life.

Mars is just making a sextile to the ascendant, giving more energies to the individual to be active and assertive.

Mercury in the 11th house is sextile to the Mid, this is good for the career, for friends, for writing and communicating.

In the 6th house we have the three outer planets in the sign of Aquarius which is the 7th house sign. Uranus is conjunct the 7th house, while Neptune and Pluto are square to the Mid.

These three outer planets would influence the individual very much and make him acting like an Aquarian with much humanitarian principle.

We see also that two planets are in the sign of Taurus, and two in Gemini, and two in Cancer.

So that was a quick interpretation of the example chart.

Our next chart is of *Annie Oakley*. Her story is very interesting, and she had been through a lot. She was born 13th August 1860 at 12.00pm, North Star, Ohio, U.S.A.

Ascendant	11.25	Scorpio
2nd	10.35	Sagittarius
3rd	14.13	Capricorn
4th	19.58	Aquarius
5th	22.36	Pisces
6th	19.31	Aries
7th	11.25	Taurus
8th	10.35	Gemini
9th	14.13	Cancer
10th	19.58	Leo
11th	22.36	Virgo
12th	19.31	Libra.
Sun	21.06	Leo
Moon	07.45	Cancer
Mercury	15.07 R	Leo
Venus	18.32	Cancer
Mars	19.28 R	Capricorn
Jupiter	09.50	Leo
Saturn	28.25	Leo
Uranus	11.31	Gemini
Neptune	28.56 R	Pisces
Pluto	09.29 R	Taurus

I do hope that you'd be able to fill in the information and get it right. Get the planets in the right houses. Now for a quick interpretation.

She has Scorpio rising on the ascendant. Mars, one of the rulers of Scorpio is in the third house and is exalted in the sign of Capricorn. Pluto, the other ruler, the last outer planet, is in the 6th house in the sign of Taurus.

There are some quick things that we can see. Her sign is Leo, she has four planets in Leo, we call this a stellium. She is a strong Leo, fiery, powerful.

We see that the planet Venus is in the 9th house. This has to do with travel and foreign peoples.

The sign on the 7th house is Taurus and it is ruled by Venus. This tells us that she has some connection with the 9th house. Her partner is from another country.

Back to her ruler Mars. It is exactly square to the 12th house. We know what the 12th house represents. But we must not forget that Mars is exalted in that third house. The third house is brothers and sisters, neighbours, the environment, travel, close relatives. The 12th house is institutions, isolation, secret enemies. You see too, that Mars is conjunct the third house.

Mars is opposing Venus. They are tugging against each other. Mars, because it is exalted in Capricorn, gives much energy and one is very ambitious.

Mars is quincux to the Mid, this is a negative aspect, but you see Mars is strong in its exaltation sign.

Quite a lot of energy is put into the career. Mars is not a soft planet.

We see that Uranus is conjunct the 8th house, involvement here with other people's money, and deep insight.

Her moon is in the 8th house in the sign of Cancer. Cancer is the sign of the home and family. She is very sensitive and protective. She likes her home and family.

The Moon is conjunct the 9th house showing travel and foreign countries. The moon is trine with the ascendant, homely and close with the mother. Publicity.

It's interesting to know that she had no children. Her moon is square to Neptune in the fifth house – that of children.

Her moon is sextile Pluto in the 6th house. This gives deep insight, and to know things before hand.

Notice that Neptune is co-ruler of the fifth house.

She has Venus also in Cancer with the Moon there. Anyone with planets in Cancer are attracted to their home and country.

Venus is semi-sextile the Mid, square the 12th, and just about making a trine to the ascendant. This would make her having a pleasant personality, full of grace, and appreciate beauty.

Mercury we see is in the 9th house and is making contact with the 9th. This is also travel.

Jupiter is also in the 9th house and making a square aspect to Pluto in the 6th house.

Any aspect with Jupiter and Pluto gives insight. One can be psychic.

We see too, that Jupiter is sextile the 8th house, but square to the ascendant. Jupiter is sextile to Uranus, making it good for her second and fifth houses.

The second house is that of money and possessions, the fifth house is that of sports, and entertainment.

Her sun is in the tenth house, this is because she was born around Midday. Still she has the chance to be in a high position in her career. And the sun is ruler of the 10th house. The sun is making contact with the 11th house, showing her hopes and wishes and friends, all to do with her career.

Saturn too, is in the 10th house, and as you already know, this is a position to hold a top job, or as a leader.

Both sun and Saturn are in conjunction with the Mid.

You'll see that Saturn is quincunx to Neptune in the fifth house, and that probably is the reason why she had no children.

That was a quick interpretation of Annie Oakley's chart.

Our next chart is that of *Princess Diana*. She was born on 1st July 1961 at 19.45 pm, Sandringham, England.

Ascendant	18.24	Sagittarius
2nd	29.48	Capricorn
3rd	18.21	Pisces
4th	23.03	Aries
5th	16.03	Taurus
6th	03.18	Gemini
7th	18.24	Gemini
8th	29.48	Cancer
9th	18.21	Virgo
10th	23.03	Libra
11th	16.03	Scorpio
12th	03.18	Sagittarius
Sun	09.39	Cancer
Moon	25.02	Aquarius
Mercury	03.12. R	Cancer
Venus	24.23	Taurus
Mars	01.38	Virgo
Jupiter	05.05 R	Aquarius
Saturn	27.48 R	Capricorn
Uranus	23.20	Leo
Neptune	08.38 R	Scorpio
Pluto	06. .02	Virgo

Sagittarius is on the Ascendant and the ruler Jupiter, is in the 2nd house in what we call an intercepted sign of Aquarius (my pet word is a loop). Because of the latitude and the maths involved, some houses will have intercepted signs in them. You will understand what's going on as we go through many different charts.

What you have to do is draw a little loop outwards inside the second house. Make sure there's room to place planets inside of it, and also in the second house itself.

Do the same over in the 8th house.

Now we find that our biggest planet, Jupiter is in the sign of Aquarius. This is someone with big humanitarian principles. She will have unusual friends.

Jupiter in the second house gives the chance to become wealthy. But Jupiter is semi-square the ascendant. This is a negative aspect, and one must be careful not to over eat. It could lead to overspending.

Jupiter is conjunct the second house making it more concrete that she'll be wealthy.

Jupiter is also conjunct Saturn. These two planets are good for philosophy and high education and religion.

Jupiter is quincunx Pluto. Remember, I told you that any aspect with Jupiter and Pluto gives insight? Diana, at times could tell before hand certain things that would happen.

Jupiter is square to Neptune in the 10th house. This could have something to do with brothers and sisters, travelling, her own self and isolation and enemies. If Jupiter was in an angular position like Neptune, it would then be in a stronger position.

Her sun is in the sign of Cancer in the 7th house in conjunction with Mercury. This conjunction of sun and Mercury is always good for the intellect, depending on how close they are, and who is using them. She is very sensitive and protective.

The sun in the 7th house gives the chance of partnership with someone of high birth, or business partnerships.

The sun is sextile to Pluto in the 8th house. Pluto is ruling the 11th house along with Mars. Pluto is in its own house, and this is the house of legacies and other people's possessions.

The sun is semi-square Uranus in the loop in the 8th house. This is negative and is sure to cause some problems.

The sun is trine Neptune in the 10th house. This is a good positive aspect but still with some strangeness.

The moon is in the 2nd house in the loop in the sign of Aquarius. Here, we find that she is interested in friends, and clubs and is a humanitarian person.

The moon is just making a sextile aspect to the ascendant.

The moon is opposing Uranus and shows that she would have interest in scientifical things, also astrology.

The moon is square to the planet Venus in the fifth house. There is some sort of shyness here, and must be careful not to be led astray.

People of Aquarius always act as if they are shy, sort of unattached, but not meaning to. Don't forget that the moon is in Aquarius.

The moon has a very good aspect to the Mid. This is good for the career, much publicity in the outer world. This aspect is a trine.

The moon is trine Mercury in the 7th house. The moon is ruler of the 8th house which is the partner's possessions. Mercury is ruling the 6th, 7th and 9th houses.

Saturn is in the first house conjunct the second house. Saturn is in its own sign Capricorn. It is square the Mid. One can still hold a high position, but there's always a chance of a fall, if one misbehaves.

Capricorn is the sign of power, and Saturn is strong in this first house. Probably an early start in life. A structural frame to the body. The conjunction to the second house could have something to do with antiques or old buildings. Cautious and secure.

Venus in the 5th house in the sign of Taurus. Here, she likes beautiful things. She likes sport and entertainment, and love affairs (if Venus has a negative aspect). Most of all, she love children. Any chart with Venus in the fifth house should have a love for children even with negative aspects.

Venus is square to the sun in the 7th house. Venus is also square to Uranus in the 8th house in the loop, in the sign of Leo. Remember that Leo is the sign of the fifth house in the fixed wheel.

Some problems will crop up in the area of the fifth house and the 8th house.

Venus is trine to Saturn in the first house. This is a good aspect and leads to loyalty. Venus is quincunx the Mid. This could make one artistic and lover of music and fashion. This aspect though, is a negative one, but Venus is not a troublesome planet like Mars. But still it is negative.

Venus is square Mars and Pluto in the 8th house and is bound to bring some trouble.

Mercury has a trine aspect to Neptune, this is very sensitive, and is good for art or music. Mercury is also quincunx to the 12th house. This shows some problems in the 9th house, servants, public and partners.

Mars is conjunct Pluto in the 8th house, and both are making a sextile aspect with Neptune. Here, we are dealing with other people's possessions, and political friends. Interest in the other side of this world. Mars is also conjunct Uranus. Lots of energy.

Uranus is exactly sextile the Mid. The career is unusual, exciting, humanitarian. Things happening suddenly. Notice that Uranus is in the 8th house, the house of legacies, the other world, and other people's possessions.

Neptune is in the 10th house. Neptune is ruling the 3rd house and has to do with much travel and communications.

That was a quick interpretation of the chart of Princess Diana.

There is lots more information in the wheel but it takes a long time to interpret it.

The next chart is of the sleeping prophet of America, *Edgar Cayce*. He was born 18th March 1877 at 15.20 pm, Hopskinville, Kentucky, U.S.A.

Ascendant	24.30	Leo
2nd	17.57	Virgo
3rd	16.12	Libra
4th	18.59	Scorpio
5th	23.24	Sagittarius
6th	25.43	Capricorn
7th	24.30	Aquarius
8th	17.57	Pisces
9th	16.12	Aries
10th	18.59	Taurus
11th	23.24	Gemini
12th	25.43	Cancer
Sun	28.24	Pisces
Moon	12.23	Taurus
Mercury	11.43	Pisces
Venus	15.43	Pisces
Mars	11.13	Capricorn
Jupiter	02.02	Capricorn
Saturn	12.49	Pisces
Uranus	21.15 R	Leo
Neptune	03.39	Taurus
Pluto	22.55	Taurus

In this chart you see that the fifth sign of the fixed wheel is at the ascendant, the sign of Leo. Uranus is in the 12th house and in conjunction with the ascendant. These people has a mission and nothing will stop them. They are not easily overpowered. Uranus in the 12th has to do with occult and secrets.

Uranus is ruler of the 7th house. It is square the Mid and Pluto in the 10th house. Two outer planets Uranus and Pluto negative, but they are holding on to angular points. Some deep scientific things here.

The sun is the ruler of the ascendant sign of Leo. The sun is in the 8th house in the sign of Pisces. So we can say his sun sign is Pisces. People are soft, kind and compassionate.

The sun is semi-square the moon in the 9th house. This is negative and can cause some inner conflict. Remember, this is the sun and moon combination.

The sun is sextile Pluto i the 10th house. This is really a powerful aspect. It can give a striving for power. Deep and penetrating. Sees and feels things that others doesn't see and feel.

There are four planets in the sign of Pisces, we call this a *stellium*. This makes the person a very strong Pisces.

The moon is in the 9th house in the sign of Taurus. Taurus is a money sign and the person is responding to that as well.

The moon in the 9th house has to do with travel and higher subjects such as religion, philosophy and education. Even if people do not travel to foreign countries, they can do it mentally.

The moon is conjunct the Mid. This is bound to bring outside publicity.

The moon is sextile to Mercury in the 7th house. This is a real positive aspect and shows that the responses and the intellect are working good. Communicative. Writing. Talking. Getting to know what is true.

The moon is sextile Venus in the 7th house. This is a positive aspect and shows an affectionate and nice person. A person who likes to function on love. Likes to help others.

The moon is sextile Saturn in the 7th house. This is positive and shows a serious person who has control over the feelings. Very careful.

Mercury is in the 7th house in the sign of Pisces. In the sign of Pisces, can show someone who has psychic powers. Able to ferret out things that are hidden.

Mercury is conjunct Venus. This is a good combination for a disciplined person. The intellect and love are joined in harmony; good for art and writing.

Mercury is conjunct the 8th house. People will know about secret things. Interest in the public and partnerships because Mercury is in the 7th house.

Mercury conjunct Saturn. People are serious. Good concentration and good at organizing.

Mercury is sextile Mars in the 5th house. Here we find that these two planets being positive could make one very clever. Love of partnerships and children. Quick thinking.

Venus is in the 7th house in the sign of Pisces. Love is at its highest here. Venus is exalted in the sign of Pisces and should bring out all the love and compassion and kindness and helpfulness.

And because Venus is in the 7th house it shows what his partner is like.

Venus is making contact to the 9th house. This is like Venus in the 9th house and has to do with high thinking, foreign countries and peoples, religion, travel philosophy and education.

Venus is sextile the Mid. Musical, artistic, lovable. A good sociable person.

Venus is conjunct Saturn. There is solidness in love and loyalty as well.

Venus is exactly at the orb limit for a sextile with Pluto. if it is working, love could be very deep.

It is important to find out how negative a planet is in a chart.

In this chart we see that the planet Venus is exalted in Pisces, and have good aspects from around the chart. The person is a very loving person with deep compassion for others.

Venus is sextile Mars. Here we have the 7th house and the 5th house. Partnerships and children and entertainment all are positive with this person.

Inside the fifth house we see the planet Mars in the sign of Capricorn, and I would like to say that it is in conjunction with Jupiter. Our orb is up to 8 degrees

Mars is exalted in the sign of Capricorn, so all its energies are there to be used by the individual. And notice, Mars is the ruler of the 9th house, and also of the fourth. It is the ruler of the first in the fixed wheel.

So here we have the person deeply interested in religion, and all the high subjects. The fifth house is a creative house, so we can say that the person is very creative, and as I have already said, fond of children.

Now for those of you who are very fearful, take care and understand what you are about to read.

The fourth house has to do with the home, the country, real estate and the Grave. I just stated that Mars is the ruler of 9th house and of the fourth. This same Mars also has good contact with the moon in the 9th house. And the moon is the ruler of the 12th house, isolation, meditation, mystic, etc. You must always associate yourself with Neptune, the ruler of the 12th house in the fixed wheel.

I do hope that you know the fixed wheel by now, and have studied it deeply because it is going to help you with interpretations of the chart. It makes it more easier for you when you know the fixed wheel works. And remember, it is fixed.

Mars is also trine to the mid giving energy to the career – staying power.

Mars is sextile to Saturn. Again, we are dealing with the 7th and the 5th houses. And we find that Saturn is the ruler of the 6th and 7th houses. We can say that there is something good going on here to do with health, hygiene, colleagues and work. And also to do with partnerships and the public.

Jupiter is in the fifth house in the sign of Capricorn. Have you noticed anything here? Jupiter is in the sign known as its fall, because the opposite sign of Cancer is where the planet is exalted. So we are losing some energy here. But Jupiter is trine to the ascendant, trine to Neptune up in the 9th house, and it has Mars helping it out.

Jupiter in the fifth house is in a position to be interested in teaching – especially children. The contact to the ascendant makes the person to be kind, helpful and generous. Notice the two signs that are in trine – Capricorn and Leo. Capricorn is the 10th sign in the fixed wheel while Leo is the 5th sign in the fixed wheel. The tenth house is the career, the fifth house is creative and children etc. The chance is there to be working with children.

Saturn is in the 7th house in the sign of Pisces. I have met many people with Saturn in Pisces, and I saw how they acted towards others – very compassionate and helpful. In the 7th house, they are interested in partnerships and the public, and sometimes there could be a partner who is younger or older than the individual.

Saturn is sextile to the Mid. (10th house). Saturn owns this house. The person could be a leader or a boss, or doing well in the career.

We have Neptune in the 9th house making a 110 degree contact with the ascendant. If the trine is working here, then we have a very sensitive person. Musical or artistic. Neptune is semi-square Venus. With a disciplined person this aspect could be used for art or music.

Pluto in the 10th house holds a very strong and powerful position, and it is co-ruler with Mars over the fourth house.

Pluto is semi-sextile 11th house, square the ascendant. Remember, planets squaring angular points are strong, yet negative, and it depends on who is using these negative energies. For negative energies can be turned into good.

That was also a quick interpretation of Edgar Cayce's chart.

Our next chart is of *Jean Charon* born 25th February 1920 at 09.00 am, Paris, France.

Ascendant	12.15	Taurus
2nd	11.20	Gemini
3rd	01.06	Cancer
4th	19.39	Cancer
5th	11.52	Leo
6th	15.52	Virgo
7th	12.15	Scorpio
8th	11.20	Sagittarius
9th	01.06	Capricorn
10th	19.39	Capricorn
11th	11.52	Aquarius
12th	15.52	Pisces

Sun	05.28	Pisces
Moon	14.25	Taurus
Mercury	20.52	Pisces
Venus	02.42	Aquarius
Mars	07.07	Scorpio
Jupiter	10.22 R	Leo
Saturn	08.30 R	Virgo
Uranus	01.52	Pisces
Neptune	09.29 R	Leo
Pluto	05.46 R	Cancer

This chart has intercepted signs (*loops*). They are found in the 6th and 12 houses. They are Libra, intercepted 6th house, Aries, intercepted 12th house.

Make sure that when you draw your chart it is big enough to place the intercepted signs in.

The ascendant is Taurus with the moon in Taurus conjuncting the ascendant.

We should know by now how to interpret the moon in Taurus and in the first house.

The moon has to do with women or the mother. Probably attached to the mother and also the home. Taurus is a money sign and is stubborn and loyal and loving. Taurus belongs to the second house in the fixed wheel.

Notice that the moon is ruler of the third and fourth houses.

Here we see how planets make contact to each other negatively, but holding strong positions being angular. The moon in the first square both Jupiter and Neptune.

Another thing you must know is that the planets comes in pairs, trebles, fours, fives, and sixes etc.

The moon is trine to Saturn in the 5th house. This Saturn is the individual's destiny planet. It is in the sign of Virgo, the sign for analytical critical, looking for small details, it also has to do with work and colleagues and health. The 5th house is that of creativity sports, entertainment, children etc.

Saturn is ruling the 9th house which has to do with far-reaching things, space, foreign countries and peoples, high education, philosophy and publications.

Saturn is also ruling the 10th house which has to do with the outside world and the career, and parents and authority.

Saturn is co-ruler with Uranus of the 11th house. This house is scientific, friends, clubs groups, hopes and wishes.

The moon in the first house is sextile Mercury in the 12th house. Mercury is ruler of the second and sixth houses. This contact between the moon and Mercury is a good one. The response and emotions mixed with the intellect positively.

The moon is also sextile the 12th house.

The Moon is trine the Mid. This is bound to bring publicity in the career.

The ascendant sign Taurus is ruled by Venus. We find Venus in the 10th house in the sign of Aquarius. Venus is in an angular position and is good for the career, people could use Venus for music or art. The sign Venus is in has to do with unusual and scientific subjects. Venus is also ruler of the intercepted sign in the 6th house.

You probably want to know a bit about interceptions. Many astrologers think they have to do with energies that are held back, and are released at a certain time. I think they have to do with something extra. I am still researching them.

The moon in the first house is opposing the planet Mars in the 6th house. Mars is in conjunction with the 7th house (angular). Mars is co-ruler of the 7th house, and the intercepted sign of Aries in the 12th house.

Understand this carefully: the sun is in the 11th house in the sign of Pisces conjunct Uranus also in the 11th house, and also in the sign of Pisces.

Pisces is a water sign and people will be very sensitive with lots of feelings. This 11th house is ruled by both Saturn and Uranus in the fixed wheel. In this wheel, it is ruled by them as well. So we have Uranus in its own house. How do you feel when you're in your own house? Uranus is the planet of science, suddenness and disruptiveness, and things that are unusual. Notice that the sun is conjunct Uranus. Many scientists normally have some sort of connection with the sun and Uranus. And being in the 11th house, the individual will have many friends who are like him, and probably part of some scientifical group.

The sun is just about sextile with the ascendant giving energy to the personality. The sun is the ruler of the 5th house of creativity.

The sun is trine Mars in the 6th house. Giving lots more energy to do whatever the individual takes on for work.

The sun is opposing Saturn in the 5th house. Some slight problems in the areas ruled by the sun and Saturn.

Then we have the sun trine Pluto in the third house. This is a positive aspect and would give much deep and penetrating insight to the individual. Both sun and Pluto are in water signs.

Don't forget that the third house has to do with writings, travel, thinking reading, close family etc.

Mercury is in the 12th house in the sign of Pisces and conjuncting the 12th house.

Mercury in Pisces has psychic abilities, can easily feel and understand what's going on around them. In conjunction with the 12th, shows isolated study, very sensitive, mystical and strange.

Mercury is sextile the Mid. Communications in the career. Mercury is ruling the 2nd house and the 6th.

He has three planets in the sign of Pisces, two in Leo. A strong Pisces will show more than the Leo, and the ascendant Taurus. They'll all mix up like when a chef is in the kitchen making soup.

The ascendant ruler Venus is square to Mars, opposing Jupiter and Neptune, and quincunx to Pluto. Keep your eyes on Venus, Jupiter and Neptune – they're all in angular positions, only Pluto is not.

Pluto is co-ruler of the 7th house, that of partnerships and marriage.

Mars is in the 6th house in the sign of Scorpio, conjunct the 7th house. There is energy for deep insight here. Much energy into the work along with colleagues. There could be some confusion to do with marriage.

Mars is sextile Saturn and will bring the houses ruled by Saturn in a positive position.

Mars is square Jupiter and Neptune. Again, we are dealing with planets in angular positions but can still give some problems.

Jupiter is ruling the 8th and 12th houses, Neptune is ruling the 12th.

Mars is opposing the ascendant.

Jupiter is in the 4th house but in the sign of the 5th house, Leo. This is like a king, could be a teacher, creative, like sports and entertainment.

Jupiter is conjunct the 5th house, trine the 8th house. Here you see that Jupiter is making contact to the house of Pluto, this gives very deep insight to know hidden things.

Jupiter is conjunct Neptune. Both these planets are ruling the 12th house, and both are square to the ascendant.

Uranus is in the 11th house in the sign of Pisces. There's something definitely here to do with scientifical things.

Uranus is semi-sextile Venus in the 10th. This has to do with self, friends and work and career.

Uranus is exactly sextile the 9th. Even a child would be able to work this one out.

Uranus trine Mars. Enormous energy here.

Neptune is conjunct the 5th house.

Pluto is conjunct the 3rd house.

A quick interpretation was given here on the chart of *Jean Charon*.

The next chart is *Charles Darwin* born 12 February 1908 at 03.00 am, Shewsbury, UK.

Ascendant	04.37	Sagittarius
2nd	09.29	Capricorn
3rd	24.43	Aquarius
4th	03.18	Aries
5th	29.58	Aries
6th	19.10	Taurus
7th	04.37	Gemini
8th	09.29	Cancer
9th	24.43	Leo
10th	03.18	Libra
11	29.58	Libra
12th	19.10	Scorpio

Sun	22.01	Aquarius
Moon	25.08	Gemini
Mercury	10.02	Pisces
Venus	27.35	Pisces
Mars	22.21	Aries
Jupiter	06.52 R	Leo
Saturn	25.38	Pisces
Uranus	15.00	Capricorn
Neptune	12.31 R	Cancer
Pluto	22.53 R	Gemini

In this chart the ascendant is rising with the 9th sign of the fixed wheel. This sign in its positive way is seeking freedom for self and for others. It is the sign of long distance travel, and foreign countries. It is the sign of all high education. One thing you mustn't forget, this sign has to do with space.

The 9th sign of the fixed wheel, of course is Sagittarius.

I'd like to drum it in your head that the biggest planet in our solar system is Jupiter. It may seem strange to you now why I keep saying that, but later, you yourself will come to understand the reason. Think about it carefully, it will help you understand when you are interpreting charts. Our earth can go into Jupiter about 1300 times. Now you see how big Jupiter is.

What about someone who falls under the powers of Jupiter, positively or negatively? In some charts you will find these powers.

The ruler of Sagittarius is Jupiter. We need to go over to the 8th house and we find it there with 6 degrees and 52 minutes of the sign Leo and retrograde.

When I first started astrology, I saw the 8th house as a dark house. Mars and Pluto are rulers of this house. I wrote earlier that any connection with Jupiter and Pluto whether positive or negative, gives the ability to know things that others do not know. You're like a psychic.

Jupiter and Pluto are brothers in mythology, if we add Neptune, then we get the three brothers. What would you then say if you were to come across a chart with the three brothers in the 8th house?

Jupiter is the sky, Neptune, the sea, and Pluto, the underworld.

So we have Jupiter in the 8th house. He is going to know what's going on in this house of Pluto, his brother. Jupiter is going to make this house big, he's going to know the secrets of this house.

And notice, he is in the 5th sign of the fixed wheel, Leo.

The sun is ruler of Leo, which has to do with life power, creativity, and this fifth house, don't forget is where children are born. When a woman is having a child we look to the 5th house, then other points.

This Jupiter then, is making a trine to the ascendant. This is very positive.

Jupiter will give all its kindness and power to the individual. The individual will be generous, fortunate and lucky, and of course deeply interested in all the 9th house business.

Not only is Jupiter in the 8th house, but it is in the sign of Leo which is the sign of the 9th house. Are you with me so far? Study your 9th house properly then you'll understand more clearly when someone talks about the 9th house.

Jupiter is sextile the Mid (Midheaven). This is the point where the planets climb up to, then drops down. We shall talk more about that later.

This sextile then is a positive aspect for the outside world and the career.

Jupiter is also ruler of the intercepted sign Pisces in the third house. There are no planets in the first house.

His sun is in the sign of Aquarius in the second house but conjuncting the third house. Does this tell you anything?

He is an Aquarian and will be interested in unusual and scientific subjects, friends and groups.

Because the sun is conjunct the third house, he'll be interested in his environment, travel, close family, writing and reading.

Notice that the sun is ruler of the 9th house. Does that mean anything to you? By now you must know what the 9th house represents.

The sun has a sextile aspect with the planet Mars in the 4th house. These are positive energies and will make him active and assertive in whatever he does. Mars is ruler of the 4th and 5th house, and also co-ruler of the 12th.

The sun is trine Pluto in the 7th house. This is a deep penetrating aspect. He will be interested in things that are hidden. Pluto is co-ruler of the 12th house, house of isolation, secrets, study, meditation.

Notice the sign Pluto is in, it is the sign of the third house in the fixed wheel, Gemini.

The sun has no bad aspects, bear this in mind. It has a very good aspect with the moon.

The moon is in the 7th house in the sign of Gemini conjunct Pluto.

Whether Pluto is a dwarf planet or not, we know that it is working in the charts. In this chart, with the moon, deep insight is shown here.

The moon in the 7th house is good for publicity and partnerships.

The moon is sextile the 9th house. This has to do with travel and contact with foreign peoples. The moon is in an angular position.

The moon is sextile Mars, ideas galore, energetic, creative, strong feelings.

The moon is square to Venus. Moodiness, with slight problems in the work place and the career.

The moon is square Saturn, some slight problems with money and possessions and travel.

The Moon is square the Mid. Now you see that the moon is in an angular position, and is square to the Mid. Angle to angle, we could only say that there'll be some publicity in the career, but also some negative ones.

His Mercury is in the third house in the sign of Pisces. The third house is owned by Mercury itself, and in the fixed wheel, we find the sign of Gemini there. Very much interested in writing, talking travelling, communicating and studying.

In the sign of Pisces, Mercury is like a psychic, strong feelings and very sensitive.

Mercury is square the ascendant. Must be careful when speaking, and to think carefully before they utter something that could offend others.

Notice that Mercury is in a water sign ruled by Jupiter and Neptune. Mercury is trine to Neptune in the 8th house. Mercury is clever, alert, communicative, thinking. Neptune is sensitive, mystic, compassionate, intuitive. Just think if these two planets were in an undisciplined person chart, and being negative. They would probably be causing trouble with drinking alcohol and doing strange (Neptune) things. But as we see, in this chart, they are *positive*, and Mercury is ruler of the 7th house, and the intercepted sign of Virgo, its own sign, in the 9th house.

Neptune is ruling the opposite intercepted sign of Pisces where Mercury is stationed.

So we have Mercury in a intercepted sign of Pisces in the third house.

My theory is that something extra is happening here which has to do with the third house.

I once heard of someone who like a curry dish. I invited them to come and try some that I had made. I am not a very good cook, but I can assure you, in my company, you'll not starve.

So I went out and got all the ingredients. I made sure that everything was right; the rice not too soggy, and not too hard. The curry sauce must just be right, and taste delicious.

When the guests came, they sat down and I dished out the food, then we started eating. Every now and then, I saw the guest taking out his handkerchief, and wiping his forehead. I knew that the curry was good and it was doing its job. I was pleased.

Astrology is something like that. There are lots of combinations between the planets. It is up to you to get the right interpretation.

And when you do, you'll be pleased with yourself. But it's not an easy task. For if you were to look back at some of the old interpretations that were given long back in the past, you would not pursue astrology at all. There are some great astrologers who gets it absolutely right, and their writings make sense. Others would lead you into foolishness.

We find the planet Venus in the intercepted sign of Pisces in the 3rd house.

In this sign, Venus is exalted. Venus is ruling the 6th house which is work, colleagues, health and hygiene and pets. Venus rules the 10th and 11th houses as well.

Everything that Venus stands for should work in a good way for the individual. I said in a good way because the planet is exalted. Even when a planet is exalted, it could still be receiving negative aspects from around the chart, so you have to be careful with your interpretation.

And it is also important to know that we as human beings use the powers of the planets according to our heredity, our upbringing, and our environment.

You might find a chart with all negative aspects and hoping to give your interpretation negatively. But if you know a little about who the person is that is using the negative aspects, you'll have no problem at all with your interpretation. Sometimes you find planets in the first house making square contact to the Mid or planets in the 7th house making contact to the Mid. Also from the first house to the 4th, and the 7th to the 4th.

So we have Venus exalted in the 3rd house in interception. This Venus is also trine to the ascendant.

Venus is always good for music and art when it is making good contact.

Venus is also conjunct Saturn in the 3rd house. This can make a disciplined person loyal and responsible, patient.

Mars is in the 4th house in the sign of Aries, its own sign. There'll be lots of energy here, and there are no real negative aspect to it except the sesqui-quadrate to the ascendant. Normally, we find Mars in the fourth house giving trouble to the home and family. If Mars is very much negative, then problems with parents and family.

Saturn is in the 3rd house in the sign of Pisces intercepted.

Saturn is in the house of Mercury and it is possible that some serious study could take place. Also travel and writing. Saturn in Pisces is kind and compassionate, interested in helping others.

Saturn is square Pluto in the 7th house. This could bring problems in the second and 12th house.

Uranus is in the second house in the sign of Capricorn with a square aspect to Mars. These energies can be sudden and disruptive. Working themselves out in the third, 5th and 12th house.

Neptune is in the 8th house in the sign of Cancer, a water sign. Neptune is conjunct the 8th. It is also opposing Uranus in the second house. Neptune is co-ruler of the intercepted sign in the 3rd house.

Strange, dark, psychic experiences, very full of feelings and sensitive.

The intercepted sign of Pisces in the 3rd house is showing that something extra is happening in this third house.

The opposition to Uranus could bring out something strange and scientific, and we see that Uranus is co-ruler of the third house, while Neptune is co-ruler of the intercepted in that same house. And don't forget that Neptune is associated with the sea.

Pluto, ruler of the 12th house is in the 7th in the sign of Gemini. This is deep penetrating intellectual force. Searching, trying to unravel things. Dark writings. Contact with the public, Political.

We have gathered some quick information from this chart of Charles Darwin.

.

5: Progressing the Chart to the Future

God told Ezekiel that He has given him a day for a year. In astrology as the sidereal time moves along each day at the rate of 3 minutes and 56 seconds (call it 4 minutes).

This 4 minutes then is 1 year of your life.

Our example chart was born on the 17th June 2000 at 10.00 am, London UK.

Hope you have lots of blank charts at hand.

You can progress backwards or forwards.

If we want to know of the planets position for 2008 (example chart was born 2000).

We add the 8 years to the date of 17th june. This makes it 25th June 2000 at 10.00 am, London, UK.

The 8 years are really 8 days forward.

We are going to look at the chart of *Katey Sagal*. A lot has happened in her life. We shall see if we can spot them.

Here is her natal chart. Born 19th January 1954 at 14.37 pm, Los Angeles, California, U.S.A.

Her mother died in 1975. We take 1954 from 1975 and we get 21. This 21, is 21 days or years.

We add it to 19th January. There are 12 more days for January to end, then we have 9 days in February to make up 21 days. So our progressed date for 1975 is 9th February 1954 at 14.37 pm, Los Angeles, California, U.S.A.

Progress chart for 1975:

Ascendant	15.28	Cancer
2nd	06.50	Leo
3rd	00.59	Virgo
4th	00.31	Libra
5th	05.54	Scorpio
6th	12.40	Sagittarius
7th	15.28	Capricorn
8th	06.50	Aquarius
9th	00.59	Pisces
10th	00.31	Aries
11th	00.54	Taurus
12th	12.40	Gemini

Sun	20.39	Aquarius
Moon	15.18	Taurus
Mercury	08.01	Pisces
Venus	23.17	Aquarius
Mars	00.04	Sagittarius
Jupiter	16.24 R	Gemini
Saturn	09.18	Scorpio
Uranus	19.52 R	Cancer
Neptune	26.00 R	Libra
Pluto	23.52 R	Leo

There are a number of things you have to know when dealing with the progressive chart. In this chart the moon is the fastest moving body. It moves at about 1 degree per month. It is wise to note this down. The moon will be going through signs and houses as it makes its way anti-clockwise around the wheel.

This progress chart of Katey Sagal is showing an ascendant of Cancer. The moon is the ruler and is in the sign of Taurus, passing through the 11th house.

Uranus is in the first house in the sign of Cancer. Uranus is co-ruler of the 8th house. This 8th house has to do with dead things, legacies, the other world, deep dark secrets, taxes, the partner's possessions.

In progressive aspects we shall keep only to 1 degree orb.

You need to know that the wheel can turn.

If the first house is you, and the second house is your money, your body and your possessions, then you must know that the 10th house is your mother, and the 11th house is her body and her money and her possessions.

You have to understand the whole wheel and get to know it well.

The 9th house is your grandparents, and also your in-laws.

The 10th house is their body or their money, and possessions.

Your friends is shown by the 11th house, and the 12th house shows their body, money or possessions.

Your children is shown by the 5th house. Their bodies is the 6th house, and also what they own.

Don't forget that the third house is your close family, and will show events happening. Your brothers and sisters falls under this house, and also your neighbours. So that the fourth house will show their body and what they own.

The 7th house is your partner. The 8th house is his body and what he owns.

So then, if the fourth house is your home or the grave, then your first house must be the home or grave for your mother.

Is it getting complicated? You have to know all this if you want to understand what is going on in the progressive chart.

The 10th house is the home or grave of your partner.

The 8th house is the home or grave of your children.

The 7th house is the home or grave for your father.

The 12th house is the home or grave of your grandparents or in-laws.

We normally speak of the 9th house of religious people and foreigners, and long distance travel.

God is represented here, but the signs or planets here does not belong to God, for God is only Spirit. But we do take the 9th house for all things religious.

Uranus is about 4 degrees away from the ascendant, but we work to 1 degree.

Whenever you see any house holding 0 degree, or any planet, something is happening there.

At the 10th and 4th axis we see that the degree is 00.31.

And at the 3rd and 9th axis we see that the degree is 00.59.

The planet Mars is in the 5th house in the sign of Sagittarius holding 00.04 degree.

Mars is ruler of the 5th and 10th house.

The 5th house is the 8th house for the 10th.

In the 8th house we see the sun with 20.39 Aquarius.

It is quincunx to Uranus in the 1st house.

Uranus is ruling the 8th house, while the sun is ruling the 2nd.

We find the planet Venus in the 8th house with 23.17 Aquarius exactly opposing Pluto in the 2nd house.

Venus is the ruler of the 4th and the 11th houses. Pluto is ruling the 5th.

Notice that Mars in the 5th is making exact contact with the 3rd and 9th, and with the 4th and 10th houses.

9th February 1954 start off the progressive year for Katey Sagal. This would last until the next year when it starts on the 10th February 1954.

Quite a lot could take place inside one progressive year.

We just need to check carefully all the points of the chart.

We see that her moon is in 15.18 degrees of Taurus. This is for the month of February.

March	16.18	Taurus
April	17.18	Taurus
May	18.18	Taurus
June	19.18	Taurus
July	20.18	Taurus (add 1 degree for every month.)

To get the moon's true position we must go back to the 8th February and note down the moon's longitude. This is 1 degree and 5 minutes in Taurus.

The 9th of February is showing 15 degrees and 18 minutes. The difference between the two dates is 14 degrees and 13 minutes. This must be divided by 12 which gives us about 1 degree and 11 minutes for the exact monthly motion of the moon. The moon then for February is exactly sextile her ascendant, and the moon is ruler of the ascendant.

Around May/June the moon is in a sextile contact with Uranus in the first house.

The moon is semi-sextile Jupiter in the 12th house. Jupiter is ruling the 6th and 9th houses.

So there we are! We have seen in this progressed wheel, the energies that are there to cause certain events to take place.

Three years later, Katey Sagal got married. We add three days to the 9th of February making it 12th February 1954 at 14.37pm, LA, California, U.S.A.

Ascendant	17.59	Cancer
2nd	09.24	Leo
3rd	03.50	Virgo
4th	03.45	Libra
5th	09.12	Scorpio
6th	15.36	Sagittarius
7th	17.59	Capricorn
8th	09.24	Aquarius
9th	03.50	Pisces
10th	03.45	Aries
11th	09.12	Taurus
12th	15.36	Gemini
Sun	23.41	Aquarius
Moon	26.22	Gemini
Mercury	11.47	Pisces
Venus	27.03	Aquarius
Mars	01.44	Sagittarius
Jupiter	16.25	Gemini
Saturn	09.20	Scorpio
Uranus	19.46 R	Cancer
Neptune	25.59 R	Libra
Pluto	23.47 R	Leo

Note: You must always check the progress chart along with the natal for more information. When something is happening to one house, it is happening to the opposite house as well.

Now let's have a look to see what we can find for Katey Sagal's marriage.

Whenever you see planets or houses holding 9 degrees, they're telling you of an ending or a beginning.

At the 11th/5th axis we see that 9.12 is there. The 11th house is friendship, while the 5th house is love affair or romance.

At the 7th house we see the sign of Capricorn ruled by Saturn.

We find Saturn in the 5th house exactly conjunct the 5th house and holding 9.20 degrees of Scorpio.

Notice that Saturn is also making contact to her body (2nd house), and to his body (8th house). We find the degrees at this 2nd/8th axis are 9.24.

We pick up the planet Neptune in the sign of Libra in the 4th house.

This Libra is the 7th house sign in the fixed wheel.

The moon, ruling the ascendant (herself), is in the 12th house in the sign of Gemini, and making a trine aspect to Neptune.

Neptune is co-ruler of the 9th house. The 9th house remain what it stands for but it is also the house of ceremony (Jupiter).

This next wheel is of Katey Sagal when she lost her father and got divorced. The progress date is 15th February 1954 at 14.37 pm, LA, California, U.S.A.

Ascendant	20.28	Cancer
2nd	11.59	Leo
3rd	06.43	Virgo
4th	06.58	Libra
5th	12.28	Scorpio
6th	18.29	Sagittarius
7th	20.28	Capricorn
8th	11.59	Aquarius
9th	06.43	Pisces
10th	06.58	Aries
11th	12.28	Taurus
12th	18.29	Gemini
Sun	26.43	Aquarius
Moon	05.28	Leo
Mercury	14.32	Pisces
Venus	00.48	Pisces
Mars	03.23	Sagittarius
Jupiter	16.27	Gemini
Saturn	09.21	Scorpio
Uranus	19.40 R	Cancer
Neptune	25.57 R	Libra
Pluto	23.43 R	Leo

Have you found anything? I have. The first thing I saw was the planet Venus in the 8th house in 00.48 of Pisces.

Venus is the ruler of the 4th house; and if you count from the fourth house, always anti-clockwise, you get the 8th house for the 4th.

Venus rules the 11th house.

Notice Saturn still holding on to 09 degrees (starting/ending). Saturn is a slow planet and will stay long in those degrees.

What about Uranus conjunct the ascendant. This is something sudden or disruptive. This mean that it will affect the 7th house as well.

Remember that you cannot look for the same things in another chart. For the combinations of the planets and the aspects would be different.

But you can still look at the houses to do with the event, and find the planet or planets ruling that house. Then you find what aspects they are making to the rest of the chart.

Notice that Mercury is in the 9th house with 14.32 Pisces, it is square to Jupiter in the 11th house by about 2 degrees orb. We are working with 1 orb. If the 2 orb is working, it will bring the third house in, which is her thinking, the sixth house also, and the 9th house. We normally call the 3rd house, the low house of thinking. The 9th house we call the high house of thinking.

Now the progressed moon is in the 1st house, it is ruler of the first house.

It is making a trine contact with the MId, but quincunx to the 9th. The moon is in Leo, and this is the sign of children, love affairs and romance.

Uranus is semi-sextile the 12th house, and opposing the 7th.

The moon is semi-sextile the 3rd house.

What about the sun in the 8th house making a trine aspect to Neptune in the fourth house.

The sun is ruler of the second house while Neptune rules the 9th. There's something here to do with legacies (other people's money coming to her).

Have you noticed that Venus is in its exalted sign?

8 years later (8 days) 23rd February 1954 at 14.37pm, LA, California, U.S.A, Katey Sagal has a miscarriage.

Ascendant	27.04	Cancer
2nd	18.53	Leo
3rd	14.26	Virgo
4th	15.30	Libra
5th	20.56	Scorpio
6th	25.58	Sagittarius
7th	27.04	Capricorn
8th	18.53	Aquarius
9th	14.26	Pisces

10th	15.30	Aries
11th	20.56	Taurus
12th	25.58	Gemini
Sun	04.47	Pisces
Moon	12.19	Scorpio
Mercury	15.02 R	Pisces
Venus	10.49	Pisces
Mars	07.43	Sagittarius
Jupiter	16.43	Gemini
Saturn	09.18 R	Scorpio
Uranus	19.26 R	Cancer
Neptune	25.21 R	Libra
Pluto	23.31 R	Leo

You will come to know that the 8th house comes under operations, and we see that the planet Uranus is in the 12th house, and is semi-sextile to the second house (body, money, possessions). It is quincunx the 8th.

Jupiter, the ruler of the 6th and 9th houses is sextile the Mid. When a woman is having a child, the Mid often shows up along with the fifth house, plus other houses.

Mercury in the 9th house in Pisces is square to Jupiter in the 11th house. Mercury is ruling the 12th and 3rd houses.

When a woman is having a child, the 3rd house which is close family most of the times comes into play along with the 5th house.

Mercury is exactly semi-sextile the Mid. It is conjunct the 9th house.

We have Neptune in the 4th house making an exact trine aspect with the 12th house.

We have Saturn in the 4th house still holding 9 degrees, and is in the sign of Scorpio which is the 5th house sign.

The progress Moon is with Saturn. The moon is ruler of the ascendant. Saturn is ruler of the 7th and 8th houses.

Venus is in the 8th house, it is trine Saturn in the fourth house. Venus is ruler of the 4th and 11th houses.

Remember that Saturn doesn't like children. According to mythology, he always eats his children. When Jupiter was born, Rhea, his wife gave him a stone to eat while she hid Jupiter.

Remember too, the opposite of the 5th house is the 11th.

When checking for birth of children, we check the 5th house, planets inside the fifth house, other aspects coming from planets to the 5th house, and the ruler of the 5th house, where it is located, and the aspects it is making.

Some charts will show the 11th house instead of the 5th. That is why you must check very carefully for what you're looking for. It is there, you just need to find it.

Mars in the 5th house is holding 7 degrees, telling you that something is wrong in that house.

Notice that if we take 3 degrees away from the moon, it will end up exactly conjunct Saturn. It will put it back to the month of November 1953.

So we have seen that there was something wrong to do with the 5th house, the third house, the 8th house, and of course, the 10th house is the Mid, announcing what has happened.

In her next chart, we see the loss of a child. This chart is for 25th February 1954 at 14.37pm, LA, California, U.S.A.

Ascendant	28.42	Cancer
2nd	20.37	Leo
3rd	16.23	Virgo
4th	17.38	Libra
5th	23.01	Scorpio
6th	27.48	Sagittarius
7th	28.42	Capricorn
8th	20.37	Aquarius
9th	16.23	Pisces
10th	17.38	Aries
11th	23.01	Taurus
12th	27.48	Gemini

Uranus in the 12th house but in the ascendant sign is still semi-sextile to the second house (her body).

Pluto is in the second house in the sign of Leo, and is square to the 11th house, and to the fifth.

Mars in the 5th house is semi-sextile Saturn.

The progress moon is with Mars in the sign of Sagittarius. Around the month of April it would be in exact conjunction with Mars. The moon is ruler of the ascendant. Mars is ruler of the 5th and the 10th houses.

For the month of February the moon is exactly square to the sun in the 8th house.

Jupiter in the 11th house is semi-sextile to the 10th, exactly square to the 9th.

Inside the 8th house we see Mercury and Venus exactly conjunct in the sign of Pisces. Mercury rules the 3rd and the 12th house, Venus the 4th and 11th.

In 1994 Katey Sagal got her first child with out much problem. It was a girl. The progress date is 28th February 1954 at 14.37 pm, Los Angeles, California, U.S.A.

I want you to look carefully at this chart.

Ascendant	01.09	Leo
2nd	23.14	Leo
3rd	19.18	Virgo
4th	20.48	Libra
5th	26.05	Scorpio
6th	00.31	Capricorn
7th	01.09	Aquarius
8th	23.14	Aquarius
9th	19.18	Pisces
10th	20.48	Aries
11th	26.05	Taurus
12th	00.31	Cancer

Sun	09.48	Pisces
Moon	14.29	Capricorn
Mercury	10.46 R	Pisces
Venus	17.04	Pisces
Mars	10.22	Sagittarius
Jupiter	16.58	Gemini
Saturn	09.14 R	Scorpio
Uranus	19.18 R	Cancer
Neptune	25.46 R	Libra
Pluto	23.24 R	Leo

This wheel has intercepted signs. In the 5th and 11th houses. She is now on the ascendant of Leo, and is a strong Pisces, with sun, Mercury and Venus in that sign. We see that axis 6th and 12 are holding 0 degree. This shows that there is something here to do with sickness or work. The 12th house showing isolation or hospital.

The intercepted sign in the 5th house is telling us that there is something extra going on.

Mars is in the loop in the sign of Sagittarius, and is ruler of the 5th house and the 10th. Remember I said that when a child is born, the Mid or the 10th house is announcing it.

The third house is ruled by Mercury. This is the house of close relatives.

Mars in the 5th house (loop) is making contact with Mercury, It is also making contact with the sun also in the 8th house. Mars is semi-sextile Saturn.

Mercury is also ruler of the 11th house.

The sun is ruler of herself (ascendant) and her body (2nd house).

We have Pluto exactly conjunct the 2nd house, and is co-ruler of the 5th house.

Jupiter in the loop in the 11th house is in contact with Venus in the 8th house. Venus is ruler of the 4th and 11th houses.

Uranus is square to the Mid, trine to the 9th house. Uranus is co-ruler of the 7th and 8th house.

You can always test to see among your family or friends who have had pregnancies, see what you find. Make sure you always get the right time.

The sun is conjunct Mercury in the 8th house.

The moon is passing through the 6th house. It will make aspects as it moves along. It is in the sign of Capricorn.

So that was it then.

A child is born.

Our next progressed chart is for the 2nd March 1954 at 14.37 pm, Los Angeles, California, U.S.A.

This chart is showing the birth of a second child – a son.

I have done some research on a queen who had 15 children, and it was amazing to see what the fifth house and its ruler were doing. When one planet had its run aspecting the 5th house, another planet took over, or another sign took over and so on etc.

Ascendant	02.46	Leo
2nd	24.58	Leo
3rd	21.15	Virgo
4th	22.54	Libra
5th	28.07	Scorpio
6th	02.19	Capricorn
7th	02.44	Aquarius
8th	24.58	Aquarius
9th	21.15	Pisces
10th	22.54	Aries
11th	28.07	Taurus
12th	02.19	Cancer
Sun	11.49	Pisces
Moon	11.57	Aquarius
Mercury	08.40	Pisces
Venus	19.34	Pisces
Mars	11.24	Sagittarius
Jupiter	17.06	Gemini
Saturn	09.11 R	Scorpio
Uranus	19.16 R	Cancer
Neptune	25.44 R	Libra
Pluto	23.21 R	Leo

Remember to keep your eyes on those slow planets, they hold on to the same degree for a long time. See what house they're making contact with, and what planets. Check them carefully.

In this chart we have Pluto now in the first house for the first time and conjuncting the second house. Pluto is co-ruler of the 5th house.

Inside the loop in the 5th house we have the planet Mars, co-ruler of the same house, making an exact square to the sun in the 8th house. The sun is ruler of ascendant and the second house.

Pluto is trine the Mid.

Venus is in the 8th house trine Uranus in the 12th. Venus is ruler of the 4th and 11th houses.

Neptune is co-ruler of the 9th house, it is in the 4th and sextile the second.

The moon is in the 7th house, a very good position to have the progressed moon. It is exactly semi-sextile the sun for the month of March. It is also exactly sextile Mars. The moon is ruler of the 12th house.

Mercury you see is holding 8 degrees, this is something that cannot be explained. Mercury is in the 8th house and is ruler of the loop in the 11th house, and the 3rd. Mercury has a trine aspect to Saturn.

In 1993 Katey Sagal got married. It is important to see what the planets are doing at that time, for the following year 1994, she had a daughter.

The progressed chart for 1993 is 27th February 1954 at 14.37 pm, Los Angeles, California, U.S.A.

Ascendant	00.20	Leo
2nd	22.22	Leo
3rd	18.19	Virgo
4th	19.44	Libra
5th	25.04	Scorpio
6th	29.37	Sagittarius
7th	00.20	Aquarius
8th	22.22	Aquarius
9th	18.19	Pisces
10th	19.44	Aries
11th	25.04	Taurus
12th	29.37	Gemini

Sun	08.48	Pisces
Moon	01.25	Capricorn
Mercury	11.46 R	Pisces
Venus	15.49	Pisces
Mars	09.50	Sagittarius
Jupiter	16.55	Gemini
Saturn	09.15 R	Scorpio
Uranus	19.20 R	Cancer
Neptune	25.47 R	Libra
Pluto	23.26 R	Leo

What do you see that's interesting in this chart?

What about the ascendant changing from Cancer to Leo?

What about the zero degree at the ascendant?

It is telling you that something is happening with the ascendant (Katey Sagal) and the descendant (7th house partnership).

Uranus, the ruler of the 7th and 8th houses is in a loop in the 12th house.

Don't forget that my pet word for interception is *"loop."*

We see that Pluto is in the second house, ruler of the fifth (romance, love affair, children), is conjunct the second house.

Notice that Uranus is exactly square to the Mid, and trine to the 9th.

Notice that the sun is in the 8th house holding 8 degrees and is ruler of the ascendant and the second house.

The sun is trine to Saturn, and square to Mars.

Both Mars and Saturn are still holding 9 degrees.

Saturn will be holding these 9 degrees for a long time.

The 9 degrees tell you that something is ending or starting.

Neptune we see is in the fourth house and is exactly semi-sextile the fifth.

Venus in the 8th house is square to Jupiter in the 11th house.

Always take into consideration the signs the planets are in.

The moon is in the sign of Capricorn, in the loop in the 6th house.

It is never a good position for the moon passing through the sixth house.

If it has good aspects, then that is even better.

We see that while the moon is in the loop in the 6th house in the sign of Capricorn, it is semi-sextile to the 7th house.

Our next progressed chart is of Katey Sagal getting a divorce. The progressed date is 6th March 1954 at 14.37 pm, Los Angeles, California, U.S.A.

Ascendant	06.01	Leo
2nd	28.28	Leo
3rd	25.09	Virgo
4th	27.04	Libra
5th	02.07	Sagittarius
6th	05.53	Capricorn
7th	06.01	Aquarius
8th	28.28	Aquarius
9th	25.09	Pisces
10th	27.04	Aries
11th	02.07	Gemini
12th	05.53	Cancer
Sun	15.49	Pisces
Moon	11.18	Aries
Mercury	04.51 R	Pisces
Venus	24.33	Pisces
Mars	13.28	Sagittarius
Jupiter	17.23	Gemini
Saturn	09.05 R	Scorpio
Uranus	19.11 R	Cancer
Neptune	25.40 R	Libra
Pluto	23.16 R	Leo

You should know by now that every individual chart is different from the other. It is going to be hard to find what you are looking for unless you're all keyed up.

And that is one reason why the interpretation of the progressed wheel is so difficult.

Our progressed moon is in the 9th house in the sign of Aries for the month of March. Around November, it would be square to Uranus. Uranus is co-ruler of the 7th house.

Another indication is Neptune in the 3rd house semi-sextile the 3rd house. I think later, you'll get to understand that the 3rd house has to do with her close family, and contracts and signing papers and all that. The 9th house, which is the opposite has to do with lawyers and ceremonies.

The third house is owned by Mercury and with Neptune in that house could make one very sensitive, and some times act strangely, depending who the individual is.

Neptune is in the sign of partnerships, and it is quincunx the 9th house.

Venus in the 8th house is exalted in Pisces but is quincunx Pluto in the first house.

Mars in the 5th house would be square the sun in the 8th house. There is a 2 degrees difference here. We work close with 1 degree. If the 2 degrees are working, then we see clearly that Mars in the 5th house, the house of romance is negative to the sun ruler of the ascendant and the body.

We have Mercury in the 8th house making a trine contact with the 12th house. Mercury rules the 11th house, and also the third.

Some charts are hard while others are very easy to interpret.

Notice that Saturn is still holding 9 degrees which means end or beginning. It is in the loop in the 4th house, and is co-ruler of the 7th house, making a square to the ascendant, but this with about 3 degrees.

Katey Sagal got married in 2004. The progressed date is 10th March 1954 at 14.37 pm, Los Angeles, California, U.S.A.

Ascendant	09.16	Leo
2nd	01.59	Virgo
3rd	29.04	Virgo
4th	01.12	Scorpio
5th	06.03	Sagittarius
6th	09.25	Capricorn
7th	09.16	Aquarius
8th	01.59	Pisces
9th	29.04	Pisces
10th	01.12	Taurus
11th	06.03	Gemini
12th	09.25	Cancer
Sun	19.49	Pisces
Moon	09.38	Gemini
Mercury	02.25 R	Pisces
Venus	29.32	Pisces
Mars	15.29	Sagittarius
Jupiter	17.44	Gemini
Saturn	08.57 R	Scorpio
Uranus	19.07 R	Cancer
Neptune	25.35 R	Libra
Pluto	23.11 R	Leo

This progressed chart is easy to read.

9 degrees is rising at the ascendant, this has to do with Katey Sagal and some sort of partnerships.

The sun, ruling the ascendant is in the 8th house with a trine to Uranus in the 12th house. Uranus is ruler of the 7th house. Isn't that clear enough?

Mercury, ruler of her body or money is in the 8th house conjunct the body or money of the partner.

Mercury is also ruler of the 11th house of friendships.

The axis of the 6th and 12 houses is holding 9 degrees.

Saturn is now out of the 9 degrees and is in the 4th house holding 8 degrees and making contact to the ascendant, is sextile to the 6th house.

Mercury is exactly sextile the Mid.

The moon is in the 11th house holding 9 degrees for the month of March. Is semi-sextile the 12th house, sextile the ascendant.

Venus is exactly conjunct the 9th house. Venus is ruler of the loop in the third house, and also ruler of the 10th house.

The moon is quincunx Saturn.

6: Celebrity Charts

This chart is of *Grace Kelly* born 12th November 1929 at 05.31 am, Philadelphia, Pennsylvania, U.S.A.

Ascendant	04.41	Scorpio
2nd	03.18	Sagittarius
3rd	06.03	Capricorn
4th	11.11	Aquarius
5th	14.09	Pisces
6th	11.58	Aries
7th	04.41	Taurus
8th	03.18	Gemini
9th	06.03	Cancer
10th	11.11	Leo
11th	14.09	Virgo
12th	11.58	Libra
Sun	19.34	Scorpio
Moon	21.50	Pisces
Mercury	10.42	Scorpio
Venus	28.51	Libra
Mars	25.37	Scorpio
Jupiter	14.05 R	Gemini
Saturn	28.06	Sagittarius
Uranus	07.56 R	Aries
Neptune	03.25	Virgo
Pluto	19.31 R	Cancer

This chart of Grace Kelly has Scorpio rising. There are three planets in the first house – sun, Mercury and Mars. The sun is in conjunction with Mars. These three planets are all in the sign of

Scorpio. This makes her a strong Scorpion. This Scorpio sign is at the 8th house in our fixed wheel, and of course, by now, you should know what the 8th house is all about.

The sun and Mercury being about 8 degrees apart is good for the intellect. Good for speaking and writing.

Saturn is in the second house. This has to do with structure, antiques, old buildings.

Her moon is in the sign of Pisces. In the fifth house.

Jupiter is in the 8th house.

Venus is in its own sign of Libra in the 12th house. It is conjunct the ascendant. You find people with Venus making contact with the ascendant always has something to do with beauty.

Neptune is in the 10th house. It is sextile with Venus and the ascendant.

We also see that Venus is exactly sextile with Saturn. The sun is trine the moon. Mars is also trine the moon. Mercury is sextile Neptune.

Pluto is in the 9th house and getting a trine aspect from the sun and Mars.

Uranus is in the 5th house and trine to the Mid.

The moon is trine Pluto.

There is lots more information in the chart.

The next chart is *Philip Johnson* born 8th July 1906 at 15.00 pm, Cleveland, Ohio, U.S.A. Was known as the greatest architect in the world.

Ascendant	24.03	Scorpio
2nd	24.42	Sagittarius
3rd	00.43	Aquarius
4th	07.30	Pisces
5th	08.53	Aries
6th	03.44	Taurus
7th	24.03	Taurus
8th	24.42	Gemini
9th	00.43	Leo
10th	07.30	Virgo
11th	08.53	Libra
12th	03.44	Scorpio
Sun	15.44	Cancer
Moon	21.34	Aquarius
Mercury	11.19	Leo
Venus	21.34	Leo
Mars	17.50	Cancer
Jupiter	25.15	Gemini
Saturn	14.54 R	Pisces
Uranus	06.06 R	Capricorn
Neptune	10.20	Cancer
Pluto	22.47	Gemini

Scorpio is at the ascendant in this chart. The rulers are Mars and Pluto. Mars is in a loop in the 8th house in the sign of Cancer conjunct the sun and Neptune, all in Cancer.

Mars is trine the ascendant. It is trine Saturn.

Pluto is in the 7th house in the sign of Gemini, conjunct the 8th house. Pluto is quincunx the ascendant, and square Saturn (both planets in angular position). Pluto is trine the moon in the 3rd house. Pluto is conjunct Jupiter. Remember, I told you these two planets give insight, no matter what contact they have with each other.

Notice that both the rulers of the ascendant are also rulers of the 8th house and are making contact or is in the 8th house.

You see Uranus in the loop in the 2nd house in the sign of Capricorn. This sign Capricorn is a cold, hard structural, ambitious sign. It is normally at the 10th house in the fixed wheel. Uranus is trine the Mid. Uranus is co-ruler of the third house. It is opposing the sun and Neptune.

The moon is square the ascendant, trine Jupiter, exactly oppose to Venus.

Venus and Mercury are in conjunction in the sign of Leo in the 9th house.

Venus is sextile Jupiter and Pluto.

The sun is conjunct Neptune, trine Saturn.

Jupiter is exactly semi-sextile the 7th, quincunx the ascendant.

Mercury is semi-sextile Neptune.

Neptune is sextile the Mid.

This next chart is of *Hedy Lamarr* born 9th November 1914 at 19.30 pm, Vienna, Austria. Known as the most beautiful woman in motion pictures. An only child. Loves her dad more than any other man.

Ascendant	09.35	Cancer
2nd	26.41	Cancer
3rd	15.45	Leo
4th	10.24	Virgo
5th	15.25	Libra
6th	00.19	Sagittarius
7th	09.35	Capricorn
8th	26.41	Capricorn
9th	15.45	Aquarius
10th	10.24	Pisces
11th	15.25	Aries
12th	00.19	Gemini
Sun	16.31	Scorpio
Moon	02.03	Leo
Mercury	11.19 R	Scorpio
Venus	12.08 R	Sagittarius
Mars	28.47	Scorpio
Jupiter	14.02	Aquarius
Saturn	01.45 R	Cancer
Uranus	07.53	Aquarius
Neptune	00.26	Leo
Pluto	01.58	Cancer

Looking quickly around the chart, we see that she has three planets in the sign of Scorpio, all in a loop in the fifth house. So she's a strong Scorpion. Then we see she has a double in the sign of Aquarius. She has a double in Cancer, and also a double in Leo.

She has Cancer at the ascendant. They are lovers of the home and family, very sensitive and protective. You can have a chart with only one planet in Cancer, and you can bet your life that the person likes his home and family. We all like our home and family, but Cancer people more than anything else.

She has two planets in the 12th house. Saturn and Pluto. They are exactly in conjunction with each other, and in conjunction with the ascendant. The 12th house is ruled by Neptune in the fixed wheel, but by Mercury in this wheel.

The moon as her ruler is in the second house in the sign of Leo. Do you know what that mean? Of course, you do. She's interested in money and earning.

The moon is conjunct Neptune. Both the moon and Neptune are semi-sextile Saturn and Pluto. Saturn is ruler of the 7th, 8th, and 9th houses. Pluto is ruler of the intercepted (loop) sign in the 5th house. The fifth house is always creativity and entertainment etc.

Saturn and Pluto is pushing for a trine to the Mid with about 110/111 degrees.

Saturn is her destiny planet and it is in the house of Neptune (fixed wheel). In this wheel, we have Neptune in the second house and exactly sextile the 12th.

Saturn is the ruler of the body (the skeleton). So he will give some structure to her body even though it is in Cancer, a sign opposite to the one that he rules.

Notice that Venus is in her husband's house, and in the sign of Sagittarius. Jupiter rules Sagittarius and is in the 8th house conjuncting the 9th in the sign of Aquarius.

Venus is making contact with the ascendant. A sextile to Uranus in the 8th house. A semi-sextile to Mercury in the loop in the 5th house. This Mercury rules the 4th house (parents), and also the 12th house.

It is easy to see that this chart has something to do with the 9th house, foreign countries. And with Jupiter in the 8th house, she has deep insight, very intuitive.

Uranus is making contact with the ascendant.

Venus is making contact with the Mid. It is about 132 degrees from Neptune. This would be a sesqui-quadrate aspect.

Jupiter is sextile the 11th house.

The sun in the loop in the 5th house is making contact with the 9th house. The sun is ruler of the 3rd. The sun is square Jupiter. Jupiter is ruling the 6th and 10th houses.

Notice that Neptune is ruling her career along with Jupiter.

Saturn and Pluto are both in contact with the 12th.

Mars is trine Neptune and the moon.

The sun is semi-sextile the 5th house, trine the Mid.

Mercury is trine the Mid, square Uranus and Jupiter.

Our next wheel is *Bertrand Russell* born 18th May 1872 at 17.45 pm, Trellek, Wales. A British/Welsh writer, mathematician, logician, philosopher and Social critic

Ascendant	05.09	Scorpio
2nd	03.06	Sagittarius
3rd	08.31	Capricorn
4th	17.47	Aquarius
5th	21.01	Pisces
6th	16.07	Aries
7th	05.09	Taurus
8th	03.06	Gemini
9th	08.31	Cancer
10th	17.47	Leo
11th	21.01	Virgo
12th	16.07	Libra
Sun	28.01	Taurus
Moon	03.30	Libra
Mercury	03.24	Taurus
Venus	12.11	Taurus
Mars	27.45	Taurus
Jupiter	25.38	Cancer
Saturn	20.59 R	Capricorn
Uranus	27.58	Cancer
Neptune	25.01	Aries
Pluto	19.32	Taurus

Look over to the 7th house, You'll see the sun, Venus, Mars and Pluto in the 7th house. Mercury is in the 6th house. They are all in the sign of Taurus. This tells you straight away that the person is loving but stubborn, and is not short of a penny or two.

The ascendant is Scorpio and both its rulers are in the 7th house. Mars as we already know is the planet of war, lots of energy. In this chart with Mars in the 7th house, you can say that there could be trouble with partnerships. It is possible to have Mars in the 7th house without getting into trouble if you use your head and turn the energies to some type of sport. But if you use them on your partner, it is no good.

Mars is in conjunction with the sun. It is semi-sextile Neptune in the 6th house. It is trine Saturn in the 3rd house. It is exactly sextile Uranus in the 9th house, and Jupiter as well. It is trine the moon in the 11th house.

Pluto is conjunct with Venus in the same house. It is trine Saturn. It is sextile Jupiter, and leaving a sextile contact with Uranus. It is square the Mid, and sesqui-quadrate to the moon.

We see then that he's a strong Taurus.

His moon sign is Libra. It is semi-sextile the ascendant. Exactly sextile the 2nd house. Making a sextile with Uranus, and leaving a sextile aspect with Jupiter. It is exactly quincunx with Mercury. It is trine with the sun.

Mercury is conjunct the 7th house. Exactly semi-sextile the 9th. It is conjunct with Neptune. Opposing the ascendant.

Venus is square the Mid. Venus is trine Saturn.

The sun is sextile Jupiter and Uranus. It is trine Saturn. Semi-sextile Neptune.

Jupiter and Uranus are in conjunction.

Uranus square to the ascendant, Jupiter with 99 degrees.

Saturn is on the opposite side of them. Saturn is quincunx the Mid.

His mother and sister died in 1874

His Father in 1876.

His grandfather died in 1878.

Six months prison in 1918

1920 travelled to Russia.

Nobel prize for literature 1950

Death of brother 1931

1961 imprisoned for a week anti-nuclear protests.

Married 1894. Divorced 1921 to marry Dora Black.

Divorced 1934/5

In 1936 married Patricia "Peter" Helen Spense.

Divorced 1962 married Edith Finch.

Died peacefully 1970.

Some of you might be thinking why I don't write anything about the moon's nodes or the planet Chiron. This I will do later, when I have more insight into what they are actually doing.

The next chart is of *Prince William* of the UK.
Born 21st June 1982 at 21.03 pm, London, UK.

Ascendant	27.30	Sagittarius
2nd	12.45	Aquarius
3rd	00.22	Aries
4th	02.28	Taurus
5th	24.11	Taurus
6th	11.19	Gemini
7th	27.30	Gemini
8th	12.45	Leo
9th	00.22	Libra
10th	02.28	Scorpio
11th	24.11	Scorpio
12th	11.19	Sagittarius
Sun	00.06	Cancer
Moon	04.57	Cancer
Mercury	08.58	Gemini
Venus	25.39	Taurus
Mars	09.12	Libra
Jupiter	00.29 R	Scorpio
Saturn	15.30	Libra
Uranus	01.29 R	Sagittarius
Neptune	25.32 R	Sagittarius
Pluto	24.09 R	Libra

The ninth house sign in the fixed wheel is on the ascendant here. It is Sagittarius.

Notice that there are two planets in the sign of Sagittarius. They are Uranus and Neptune.

Neptune is the nearest planet to the ascendant. It is in the 12th house only two degrees away.

Uranus is about 26 degrees away and is in the 11th house.

Neptune is ruler of the loop in the third house. Neptune is sextile Jupiter in the 10th house. This Jupiter is the actual ruler of the ascendant sign.

Neptune is also sextile to Pluto. Pluto is in the 9th house in the sign of Libra and is ruler of the 10th and 11th houses.

With Neptune in the 12th house people could be very sensitive and seeking privacy. They could be musical and artistic, mystic psychic, interested in travel and freedom for others. This comes because Neptune is in that 9th sign which is Sagittarius. Contact with foreign peoples.

Uranus in the 11th house shows interest with clubs and friends of a scientific and unusual kind.

Jupiter, as ruler of the ascendant is in the 9th house just starting off its journey in Scorpio. It is sextile the ascendant and Neptune.

This aspect makes one to be very kind, and sympathetic to those who needs help, they are very musical and artistic.

Jupiter is in the 9th house but in the 10th house sign. This shows that the person can hold a top job, and maybe like a king or queen. Interested in ceremonies and religious things. Jupiter is conjunct the Mid.

In the sign of Scorpio, the energies are deep and penetrating. Remember too, that this sign belong to Pluto. Don't forget what I told you about Jupiter and Pluto.

Jupiter is semi-sextile Uranus.

There are three planets in the sign of Libra in the 9th house. They are Mars Saturn and Pluto. The Libran energies are strong.

Venus is in the 5th house just like his mother. Venus is conjuncting the 5th house.

Mercury is in the 5th house conjunct the 6th house.

The sun is in the 7th house in a loop in the sign of Cancer. The sun is ruling the 8th house.

The moon is also in the 7th house in the loop in the sign of Cancer and conjunct the sun. Both of them are trine to the Mid. . The sun is exactly square the 9th house.

Mercury is trine both Mars and Saturn in the 9th house.

Pluto in the 9th house is conjunct Jupiter also in the 9th house. Pluto is conjunct the Mid. Pluto is sextile the ascendant, and Neptune. Pluto is exactly semi-sextile the 11th house.

Saturn, as we see, is in the 9th house. It is the destiny planet and will have to do with lots of travel to foreign countries. And as we see too, Saturn is exalted in the sign of Libra.

Saturn is ruler of the loop in the first house, and co-ruler of the second.

Venus is quincunx Pluto. It is quincunx the ascendant as well.

Venus is sesqui-quadrate Mars in the 9th house.

Uranus in the 11th house is sextile the 9th, and semi-sextile the Mid.

The moon is square to Mars.

Saturn and Uranus are in conflict. They are 46 degrees apart.

Mercury is opposing Uranus.

The next chart is *Camilla Parker Bowles* (Duchess of Cornwall).
Born 17th July 1947 at 07.10 am, London, England.

Ascendant	04.54	Leo
2nd	21.36	Leo
3rd	13.01	Virgo
4th	12.32	Libra
5th	22.08	Scorpio
6th	03.13	Capricorn
7th	04.54	Aquarius
8th	21.36	Aquarius
9th	13.01	Pisces
10th	12.32	Aries
11th	22.08	Taurus
12th	03.13	Cancer
Sun	23.47	Cancer
Moon	10.02	Cancer
Mercury	19.55	Cancer
Venus	10.35	Cancer
Mars	11.17	Gemini
Jupiter	17.42	Scorpio
Saturn	09.57	Leo
Uranus	23.50	Gemini
Neptune	08.14	Libra
Pluto	12.23	Leo

The Duchess would have made a good Queen of England because she has the energies in her chart, but unfortunately, it is the British people who decide who will be their next king or queen. This is the one thing I found about the British people, if they don't like you, you cannot be on the top.

The Duchess is a real Cancer having four planets in that sign. We call it a stellium. She loves her home and her country very much.

She has two planets in the sign of Leo – Saturn and Pluto.

Her ascendant, as you see, is Leo. The sun is the ruler of Leo and is in the 12th house in the sign of Cancer in conjunction with Mercury. Her intellect is good.

Saturn is the nearest planet to the ascendant and it is in the first house. This position has to do with early training and upbringing. Responsibilities.

Saturn is ruling the 6th, 7th, and 8th houses.

Saturn is conjunct with Pluto also in the first house and also in conjunction with the ascendant.

Notice the big planet, Jupiter, in the 4th house in the sign of Scorpio. This is an angular position for Jupiter. This is the position where Jupiter is king or queen or someone in a high position.

The sign Scorpio is deep and penetrating.

Saturn is semi-sextile the moon in the 12th house.

Saturn is trine the Mid.

There's a loop in the 5th and 11th houses – Sagittarius and Gemini.

Saturn is sextile Mars in the loop in the 11th house.

Saturn is semi-square to Uranus in the loop in the 11th house.

Saturn is sextile Neptune in the 3rd house.

Saturn is square Jupiter in the 4th house, both planets are angular.

Saturn is semi-sextile Venus in the 12th house.

The sun is semi-sextile Uranus.

The moon is exactly conjunct Venus. Both are conjunct the 12th. Both are square to Neptune.

Mercury is trine Jupiter. Mars is trine Neptune. Neptune is sextile ascendant. Neptune is sextile Pluto. Neptune is conjunct the 4th house.

Moon and Venus semi-sextile to Mars. Mars is sextile Mid.

The next chart is of my *Queen Elizabeth* II born 21st April 1926 at 2.40 am, London, England.

Ascendant	21.23	Capricorn
2nd	18.25	Pisces
3rd	00.17	Taurus
4th	25.33	Taurus
5th	14.06	Gemini
6th	01.05	Cancer
7th	21.23	Cancer
8th	18.35	Virgo
9th	00.17	Scorpio
10th	25.33	Scorpio
11th	14.06	Sagittarius
12th	01.05	Capricorn
Sun	00.12	Taurus
Moon	12.07	Leo
Mercury	04.39	Aries
Venus	13.57	Pisces
Mars	20.51	Aquarius
Jupiter	22.30	Aquarius
Saturn	24.26 R	Scorpio
Uranus	27.21	Pisces
Neptune	22.02 R	Leo
Pluto	12.42	Cancer

The ascendant is Capricorn. The ruler is Saturn and we find it in the 9th house in the sign of Scorpio.

So here we have her destiny planet ruling the whole chart.

The 9th house is foreign countries and long distance travel, high education and religion. The 9th house is ruled by Jupiter in the fixed wheel. Jupiter likes ceremonies and bands playing. If you were to read some mythology, you'll get some insight to all that.

Saturn is conjunct the Mid. This can show a leader who is very religious.

Notice that Saturn is not in the 10th house.

The ancients had Saturn as the destiny planet and as the planet of old age.

Saturn is sextile the ascendant.

Saturn is square Mars in the first house in the loop, and also Jupiter in the same loop.

Remember, planets in angular position making square to angular points seems to be strong, yet things can still go wrong.

Saturn is square Neptune in the 7th house in the loop.

Saturn is trine Uranus in the second house.

In the first house we find a loop with the sign of Uranus.

This loop or intercepted sign is holding two planets – Mars and Jupiter. They are both in conjunction.

Mars is ruler of the loop in the second house, and co-ruler of the 10th house.

Jupiter is co-ruler of the second house, and ruler of the 11th.

Mars is the nearest to the ascendant and shows that there is a lot of energy for the queen to use. Very active and assertive.

Mars is square the Mid.

Mars is semi-square Mercury in the loop in the second house.

Mars is opposing Neptune.

Mars is semi-sextile the ascendant.

Jupiter is semi-sextile the ascendant.

Jupiter is just about 67 degrees away from the sun.

Jupiter is square the Mid.

Jupiter is opposing Neptune.

Mars and Jupiter are in the sign of Aquarius. This sign is normally at the 11th house in the fixed wheel; and it stands for universal love, humanitarian principles, friends and clubs and one's wishes. Don't forget that both Saturn and Uranus are rulers of Aquarius.

In the first house, close to the second, we see the planet Venus in the sign of Pisces and conjuncting the second house. In an angular house, Venus is strong. It is exalted in the sign of Pisces, all its energies for love and beauty will come to the fore. Venus is ruler of the third, fourth, and the loop in the 8th house.

Venus is semi-square the sun. Notice that it is not making any contact to the Mid, but is trine Pluto, one of the rulers of the 10th house.

That is one of the reasons we find it so hard to understand the workings of astrology. Later on we shall deal with that part.

Venus is quincunx the moon in the 7th house in the loop of Leo.

Venus is in the same sign as Uranus but Uranus is in the second house, and they are about 14 degrees apart. Uranus is the ruler of the loop in the first house.

Uranus is semi-sextile the sun. It is conjunct with Mercury. Mercury is ruler of the fifth and 8th houses.

Uranus is sextile the ascendant, trine the Mid, sesqui-quadrate the moon.

Mercury is in the loop in the second house. It is square Pluto in the 6th house. It is trine the moon in the 7th house in the loop. It is sesqui-quadrate Neptune.

The queen is a Taurus by the sun The sun is in the sign of Taurus in the second house and exactly conjuncting the third. The sun is the ruler of the loop in the 7th house. It is trine with Neptune.

Neptune is co-ruler of the second house.

Pluto is in the 6th house making an exact semi-sextile with the moon. Both moon and Neptune are in the sign of Leo in the loop in the 7th house. The moon is good for the public, to work with the public and brings publicity. It seems that the partner could have something to do with the sea, and is connected with her career. The 10th house is the career (the outside world).

The next chart is of *Princess Catherine* (Duchess of Cambridge). Born 9th January 1982 at 08.00 am, Reading, England.

Ascendant	14.44	Capricorn
2nd	09.00	Pisces
3rd	23.05	Aries
4th	20.00	Taurus
5th	09.11	Gemini
6th	25.59	Gemini
7th	14.44	Cancer
8th	09.00	Virgo
9th	23.05	Libra
10th	20.00	Scorpio
11th	09.11	Sagittarius
12th	25.59	Sagittarius
Sun	18.44	Capricorn
Moon	11.51	Cancer
Mercury	05.33	Aquarius
Venus	07.23 R	Aquarius
Mars	10.17	Libra
Jupiter	07.12	Scorpio
Saturn	21.49	Libra

Uranus	03.06	Sagittarius
Neptune	25.26	Sagittarius
Pluto	26.48	Libra

Princess Catherine has Capricorn as her ascendant sign. Saturn as ruler is in the 8th house exalted in the sign of Libra It is with two other planets – Mars and Pluto. All three planets are in the sign of Libra. So Libra will show very much in her personality.

Her sun is in the first house conjuncting her ascendant. She is a sunny person, very ambitious and practical.

The sun is sextile the Mid, semi-square Uranus in the 10th house, square Mars and Saturn in the 8th house, opposing the moon in the 6th house.

Saturn is conjunct Pluto in the 9th house.

Saturn is semi-sextile the Mid. Saturn is square the ascendant. Remember, that Saturn is exalted in Libra.

It is amazing to see that she has a loop in the first house with the sign of Aquarius. There are two planets in the loop – they are Mercury and Venus. They conjunct each other. They both are sextile with Uranus, co-ruler of Aquarius.

Mercury is square Pluto.

Both Mercury and Venus are trine to Mars in the 8th house. Both square to Jupiter in the 9th house. Venus is quincunx the moon in the 6th house.

Her moon sign is Cancer. Cancers like their home and family and country. The moon is conjunct the 7th house. This is good to work with the public. Much publicity. And good for partnerships.

The moon is square Mars. It is trine the Mid with about 128 degrees. It is trine Jupiter.

Mars is in Libra in the 8th house. It is sextile the 11th house. It is ruler of the third, co-ruler of the 10th. It is square to the ascendant. It is semi-sextile the 8th house.

Jupiter, the big planet, is in the 9th house but in the 10th house sign of Scorpio. Here, Jupiter is still showing that it is powerful. Good for a top job.

Jupiter is semi-square Neptune in the 11th house. It is just about making a sextile contact with the ascendant. It is square Mercury, exactly square Venus.

Uranus is in the 10th house in the sign of the 11th house, Sagittarius. it is sextile Mercury and Venus. .

Neptune we see is in the 11th house also in the sign of Sagittarius, exactly conjuncting the 12th house. We must not forget that Neptune is co-ruler of the 12th house in the fixed wheel. It is sextile Pluto in the 9th house. Sextile Saturn in the 8th house.

7: Houses Contact

In the fixed wheel we are going to get the first house contact as being 1-1

The second house as being 2-2

The third house as being 3-3 and so on.

In the *natal chart* or the progressed chart, we can see what the houses contacts are.

When we have the ruler of the ascendant in the first house, we say that the person is interested in his or herself, and then others.

When we see that the ruler of the first house (ascendant) is in the second house, we say that the person is interested in money and how they could spend it. You have also to take the opposite, other people's money.

When the ruler of the first house is in the third there's something here to do with communications and travel, reading or writing. Interests with brothers and sisters.

When the ruler of the first is in the fourth house, we say that the person is interested in home, country, parents and real estate.

When the ruler of the first house is in the fifth house, this could mean that you are interested in children, love affairs, creativity, speculation, sports and entertainment.

When the ruler of the first is in the 6th house, this could have to do with work, health, sickness, pets, colleagues and hygiene.

When the ruler of the first house is in the 7th house, this could turn out that you are interested in partnerships and the public.

When the ruler of the first house is in the 8th house, you're interested in other people's money or their possessions, legacies and taxies, and the other side of this world.

When the ruler of the first house is in the 9th house, this has to do with travel to foreign countries, space, high education, and philosophy and religion. The 9th house is also the in-laws and your grandparents.

When the ruler of the first house is in the 10th house you'll really be thinking about your career, and what you can achieve. You will also be thinking about your parents.

When the ruler of the first house is in the 11th house, it shows that you're interested in friends and clubs and groups. Also your hopes and your wishes.

When the first house is in the 12th house, you want to be left alone so that you catch up on yourself. This could also be a lonely position placed on you. Like Prime Ministers and Presidents.

This position has to do with prisons and hospitals and institutions.

One of the things you have to look for is when house 1 is in 2, and house 2 is in 1. This is something that will definitely come about. It is the same with house 3 in 1, or house 1 in 3, and so on etc.

Get to know your houses well, and you'll get to understand how they work and the information that they give out.

We know that the second house has to do with money and the body. When the ruler of the second house is in the second house You're definitely interested in money and your body. (You are probably thinking, *"second house as the body?"*) I will show you later on why that is so. So then, we are dealing with money when it comes to the second house, and of course, your body.

When the second house is in the third house, it has to do with money either received, or handed out to do with the 3rd house. This could be education, writing, reading, brothers and sisters, neighbours, contracts and travelling.

It is wise to check your chart, your family and friends' charts to verify what has been told to you.

When the second house is in the fourth house, this has to do with real estate, your home or your parents.

When the planet ruling the second house is in the fifth house, this could mean that there is money spent or received to do with the fifth house.

When the planet ruling the second house is in the 6th house, this could mean that money is used or received to do with that house. Like on pets, or work, or colleagues, or sickness and hygiene.

When you have the ruler of the 2nd house in the 7th, you are either spending money on partner or partnerships or receiving money through them.

When the ruler of the second house is in the 8th, this could have to do with you receiving some kind of inheritance or involved in paying money back to others, such as taxes. Remember that the 8th house is also the partner's money.

When the ruler of the second house is found in the 9th, this could have something to do with money from institution, or grandparents or inlaws or paying out to some lawsuit. Or you could be paying out money for travel or education.

When you have the ruler of the second in the 10th, this has to do with your career, and your parents.

Having your ruler of the second house in the 11th, this has to do with money coming from or going to friends, groups or clubs.

If you have the ruler of the second house in the 12th, this could mean money coming from some organization or pension.

Whatever it is, you know that the second house has to do with money or your body.

Now for the ruler of the third house:

When you find the planet of the third house in the third, this has to do with all the third house matters.

When you see the planet of the third house in the fourth house, this could show that there's some sort of communications going on in the home, like some sort of group or club. Everything to do with the home is important.

When the planet ruling the third house is in the fifth, you could be busy with children, entertainment and sports; not forgetting speculation and love affairs. Third house is communication.

The third house ruler in the sixth house, you could be busy with 6th house matters.

The 3rd house ruler in the 7th, this could be some sort of partnership formed through communications. It could also be a business partnership, or become very close to brothers and sisters.

The third house ruler in the 8th, shows interest in taxes, other people's money and legacies. Remember that this 8th house is the sickness house for your brothers and sisters and close family.

The third house ruler in the 9th. Both these house has to do with travelling, short or long distances. Both these houses has to do with education, low school, high school. There is also foreign countries here. Publishing material.

The third house in the 10th, here, we are dealing with your career, your parents and boss, and communications or writing and study.

The third house in the 11th, this is the time when you might meet up with friends through study, travelling or writing. Close family can also become friends.

When you find the ruler of the 3rd house situated in the 12th house, This is a strange connection and one must always take care. Can find yourself in seclusion writing or travelling. Slight problems with close family.

Remember that the contact with the houses has to do with the planets. If both planets are positive, and getting other positive contact, then you have something to laugh about But if they are negative, watch out for yourself.

Ruler of the fourth house in the fourth house. This all has to do with the home front, parents, real estate or the country. But it has to do with quite a number of things as well. The fourth house is your own end. Moving of houses. The fourth house is also partnerships of the parents. And it is the fifth house of your enemies.

I have already said to you earlier on that you must master the fixed wheel. Get to know all about the houses and who they relate to.

If you find that the ruler of the fourth house is in the 5th, something here to with entertainment, pleasure, children or love affairs and sports. The fifth house is your parents possessions.

You find that the ruler of the 4th house is in the sixth, this has to do with all 6th house matters, for positive or negative.

When the ruler of the 4th house is in the 7th, this has to do with property or real estate in connection with partner or partnerships.

The ruler of the 4th house is in the 8th, this has something to do with magic, something we don't really understand. There's a connection here to do with home, real estate and other people's possessions.

When the ruler of the 4th house is in the 9th. Here we find some contact to do with foreign countries. This could also be a move to another place.

When the 4th house is in the 10th ouse, this could have something to do with your career, holding a job in connection with the home or with the country. Working at home in your career.

When the ruler of the 4th house is in the 11th, this has to do with friends and clubs and groups.

The ruler of the of the 4th house in the 12, this could have something to do with study, the parents or something to do with isolation.

The ruler of the 5th in the 5th. You must know by now what the matters of the fifth house are. So you should have no problem understanding the contact positions. There's a lot of creativity going on. Entertainment, pleasure, love affairs or romance, speculation and children and sports.

When the ruler of the 5th house is in the 6th, this has to do with some sort of speculation to do with work or pets, sickness and hygiene and colleagues connected with all the 5th house matters, The result comes out according to the good aspects of planets involved.

The fifth house ruler is in the 7th house. This is a good combination for forming relationships. Children become interesting to you along with the partner and the public.

If you keep in the back of your head that the sun is the ruler of the 5th house, and is the power we live by, and that Venus is the ruler of the 7th house and has to do with love and beauty, you'll get a little more information of what is going on between these two houses.

The ruler of the 5th house in the 8th, this could have something to do with too much pleasure being had here. Overdoing it. If you"re going to speculate, check carefully what the planets as rulers of the houses are doing. Are they in good aspect to each other? Are they getting other good aspect from other parts of the chart? For this contact could bring you loss when speculating or difficulties with children.

When the 5th house ruler is in the 9th house, this could have something to do with teaching. Something to do with foreign peoples, or even a romance with someone from another country. This connection has also to do with travel.

When the 5th house is in the 10th, this is a good contact to do with creativity and your career or to do with children. This connection has to do with your children's work. And when we are dealing with the progressive wheel, the 10th house announces the birth of a child.

The fifth house ruler is in the 11th house. This is good for children, friends and groups and clubs and your own hopes and wishes. May gain through these.

When the fifth house ruler is in the 12th house, this could have to do with secret love affairs, trouble through children, and through enemies. Only if there are good aspects between the planets would things turn out well.

We are now at the sixth house. The natural ruler is Mercury, so keep this in mind. Everything to do with the 6th house will work out here.

When the ruler of the 6th house is in the 7th, this has to do with the public or the partner in relation to the sixth house. Something to do with the health or pets or hygiene.

When we haven the ruler of the 6th house in the 8th house, this 8th house has to do with taxes and legacies and insurances, and things that are hard to comprehend. Mars and Pluto are rulers of the 8th house. So you have a combination of Mercury/Mars. Pluto. This 8th house has to do with other people's money. The 6th house has to do with work and service and sickness; and all other 6th house business.

When the 6th house is in the 9th house, this could have something to do with work in a foreign land. Something here to do with travel, high education. One must be careful not to overwork.

When the ruler of the 6th house is in the 10th, this connection has to do with your career, your boss or your parents. This combination is Mercury and Saturn.

Having the 6th house ruler in the 11th house is very good unless it has negative aspects. This is many friends at the work place. Your hopes and your wishes come as you want them.

The ruler of the 6th house in the 12th, this has to do with work, secrets, isolation, health and pets.

With the 7th in the 7th, we are dealing with the planet Venus. You are bound to have some sort of partnership or some contact with the public.

When the ruler of the 7th is in the 8th, this has to do with your partner's body or his possessions. This has to do with Venus/Mars and Pluto. This combination is very powerful.

When the ruler of the 7th is in the 9th, this has to do with high education philosophy religion and law. It has to do with foreign countries; and your partner could be from a foreign country or from another place. Lots of travelling. The 9th house is also your in-laws and your grandparents, and your children's children.

The ruler of the 7th house in the 10th, this has to do with your partner and their parents, and also your career. the 7th house in the 11th, your partner can turn out to be your friend, or you may join friends in partnerships.

The 7th house in the 12th, this has to do with secret partnership. Because of Neptune, ruler of the 12th in the natural wheel, there could be something strange here. If the planets involved are good, then the outcome is different.

House 8 in 8. This area is ruled by Mars and Pluto. This is the house of taxes, legacies, insurances and inheritances. This is the house where dark things takes place. Or things that were hidden and then came to light – by revelation.

I can see now why many people are against astrology. This 8th house is also the house of death in connection with the fourth house, the second, the fifth and the 9th.

When the ruler of the 8th house is in the 8th house, this has to do with partner's resources, legacies or joint finances.

When the 8th house ruler is in the 9th house, this could have something to do with the other world, other countries, higher educational training and philosophy.

When the 8th house ruler is in the 10th house, this could have something to do with your parents, your career or your boss. Always check to see if the two planets in charge are in good aspect to each other, or are getting good aspects from somewhere around the chart.

When the ruler of house 8th is in the 11th house, it is quite possible that you will have some sort of luck through friends. Friends could be unusual or scientific.

When the ruler of the 8th house is in the 12th house, you have to be aware of your enemies. This could also have to do with some sorrow or isolation. Remember that the 8th house is other people's money, and the 12th house is behind the scenes, institutions, prisons and hospitals.

The ninth house in the 9th house. People with this contact could be interested in religion, philosophy, high education, travel and foreign countries.

The 9th house in the 10th, this could be something to do with your career, and your parents. Some sort of promotion and travel.

When the 9th house is in the 11th, this has to do with friends, travel and foreign countries. This could show long distance flight, like in space.

When the ruler of the 9th house is in the 12th, this could have to do with working behind the scenes, study, isolation, or can be that publishing of works is delayed. Some problems are shown.

We are now at the top of the chart where the ruler of house 10 is in house 10. Don't forget that this area is ruled by Saturn in the fixed wheel. This 10th house has to do with power, career, your boss, and your parents.

When the ruler of house 10 is in house 10, this is probably the time when it would go well with your career whatever it is. And also with the outside world and your parents.

When the ruler of the 10th house is in the 11th, this is a good contact to do with friends and your hopes and your wishes.

When the ruler of house 10 is in the 12th, this is a time when you have to be on the lookout, for there are your secret enemies who would do anything to try and get you smeared. Difficulty in the career.

We are at the 11th house The rulers here are Saturn and Uranus. This is the house of universal love; the house of friendships; the house of your hopes and wishes; the house of groups and clubs. The 11th house is also the house of many other things according to how you turn the chart.

When the ruler of house 11 is in house 11, it could turn out that you find yourself with many friends, and your hopes and wishes coming out as you wanted them to.

When the ruler of house 11 is in house 12, this placement brings secret enemies. It turns out that your friends are really your enemies. This is also the time when you want some peace and quiet. Interest in secret things.

We come to the last house, the 12th. Neptune is in charge here. This is a watery place, flimsy, see-through, glassy, strange, artistic.

When the ruler of the 12th is in the 12th, there could be a great love for pets, interest in secret things, joining secret groups, working behind the scenes. There's a watchful eye on your enemies.

8: Astrological Gossip

We're going to get into all sort of gossip here. We're going to talk about the chart and picturing it in our minds. This way, you'll be able to learn more and understand the astrological language better. You have to test astrology by doing charts for people who you know. For your families and friends.

Time is involved, along with space in the workings of astrology.

I just had a look at a chart of a girl who got killed by a serial killer. The report said that she was pretty. I picked up Venus in her ascendant in Leo. Venus is sextile Jupiter in the 11th house in the sign of Gemini. Venus is conjunct Pluto in the ascendant sign of Leo. She was involved with drugs and prostitution.

Her home front was not a happy one. She blamed her step-dad for her problems.

In her natal chart, she has the moon in the fifth house in the sign of Scorpio square to Mercury in her second house in the sign of Leo. Notice that none of these two planets are in an angular position.

This square really causes trouble, especially to those who are not disciplined.

Mercury is ruler of the 4th house and of the 12th. The moon is ruling her ascendant in the natal chart. The moon is in a loop in the 5th house.

Mercury is conjunct Mars also in Leo and in the second house.

Mars is ruler of the 11th house, and co-ruler of the loop in the fifth house.

She was jailed for for drugs and prostitution, but finished her high school there. She escaped and met with her killer. At age 20 she had a daughter, then later at 22 she got married, had a son, then a daughter.

In astrology, we see in charts a pattern that we call the **FINGER OF GOD**. This is three planets forming a trine and two sextiles.

Sometimes when I see some beautiful charts, then read the awful things that happened to the individual, it leaves me thinking, *'what's going on?'*

This girl has Jupiter in the 12th house in Gemini, and Saturn in the 4th house in Libra. Saturn is exalted in Libra.

Saturn is square Uranus, conjunct Neptune, square the ascendant and sextile Pluto.

Jupiter is semi-sextile Uranus, trine Neptune, sextile Pluto.

Her sun is sextile Jupiter, Saturn and Neptune and conjunct Pluto.

Her moon is trine the ascendant and Venus.

Her Venus is square Saturn, conjunct Uranus and square Neptune. Venus is trine the Mid.

We see that she has some good energies but with Uranus in the first house squaring her destiny planet which is exalted, didn't help her much. The fact is, anyone with Uranus in or around the ascendant, always want to have their own way. They're after something and nothing will stop them getting what they want. They just don't give up.

Both Uranus and Saturn are holding strong positions being stationed in angular houses.

We read that she was blaming her father-in-law for all her problems.

Her destiny planet, Saturn is in conflict with Uranus. Uranus being a planet of suddenness and disruptiveness is right there in her first house.

And it is unfortunate that she could not control the energies of Venus and Pluto in her progressed chart. Pluto was in her second house. It has now found itself in her first house along with Venus. These two planets could cause penetrating deep love. Too much, in fact.

I have been looking at the moon nodes but I'm not completely satisfied of what they are actually doing. I have been researching many charts of people who I know, and I'm still trying to see what is happening. The moon nodes comes from when the moon is moving from south to north across the ecliptic, and vice versa. It leaves a point which we take to be its nodes – **North** and **South**.

I've been looking at Chiron as well to see if I can pick up anything. I give Chiron to be ruler of Sagittarius, only as a test.

I give the North node to be ruler of Cancer along with the moon, as a test to see if I can get any information from it.

Looking at some charts, I see that Jupiter is in the second house. Here, the individual has the chance of becoming rich.

Because the second house has to do with the body, the individual can become very big if they do not take care.

Looking at the chart of *Kareem Abdul-Jabbar* born 16th April 1947 at 18.30 pm, New York, New York, U.S.A, we find that he has Jupiter in the second house in the sign of Scorpio.

What's also interesting is that he has Venus exalted in Pisces in the fifth house; this house has to do with sports. Venus in this house shows that he must have been a lover of all the fifth house matters.

You cannot become rich unless it is from other people's money. All the celebrities who are rich, becomes so, from their fans.

We see that the ruler of the 8th house is Venus, other people's money. Venus is trine with Jupiter in the second house. Do you see how beautiful that is?

He has Saturn in the 10th house in the sign of Leo. It is exactly sextile to the 12th house.

The sun is in Aries in the 7th house. It is square the Mid; Conjunct the 7th; Sextile the 9th; Quincunx Jupiter.

Jupiter is trine the Mid.

Pluto is in the 10th house conjunct Saturn, both in Leo.

Mars is in the 6th house conjunct Mercury in the 5th, conjunct the 6th, semi-sextile the moon in the 5th house in Pisces.

So we see, with just a little information from some planets we can tell something about a person. But you must remember that you cannot see all that is going on in the individual's life, only from the natal. And you must remember too, that there are many different ways of determining a person's future.

Bill Gates has Jupiter in the second house, and he did something about it by becoming a computer multi-millionaire.

Bill Gates was born on 28th October 1955, at 10.00 pm, Seattle, Washington, U.S.A.

In his chart, Jupiter is square Saturn; sextile Neptune; and conjunct Pluto.

His moon is in Aries in the 10th house, which is the career and publicity, outside world. Aries is the sign of action, impulsive, ideas.

His sun is in the fourth house in the sign of Scorpio, with Venus and Saturn in that sign too but in the fifth house.

Again, we see a chart with Venus in the fifth house. He must have some love for children.

I myself have a great love for children but I do not have Venus in the 5th house, this is shown somewhere else.

He has Mercury and Mars in the fourth house in the sign of Libra.

We find the planet Uranus in his first house. This position shows that he will pursue whatever he takes up and see it through. It is hard to stop Uranus in this position.

We have the President of America *Donald Trump* born 14th June 1946 at 10.54 am, Jamaica hospital, Queen's County, New York, U.S.A.

He has Jupiter in the second house in the sign of Libra square Saturn in the 11th house in the sign of Cancer. Venus is also in the 11th house conjuncting Saturn.

The President has his moon in Sagittarius sextile Jupiter.

The President has a Gemini sun trine Jupiter. The sun is in the 10th house, a high position.

The President has Mercury in the 11th house in the sign of Cancer making him to be a strong Cancer with three planets in Cancer. People love their home and their country.

The President has Mars in the 12th house conjunct the ascendant.

The ascendant is in its last stages in the sign of Leo.

Mars in the 12th house is secretive. Hanging round the ascendant angle is powerful. Lots of energy here. Warry. Don't give up easily.

Madonna was born 16th August 1958 at 07.05 am, Bay City, Michigan, U.S.A.

She has Jupiter in the second house in the sign of Libra conjunct Neptune, sextile Pluto.

She has a Virgo ascendant with the moon, Mercury and Pluto in that sign.

She has the sun in Leo square Mars in the 9th house in the sign of Taurus. Her sun is conjunct Pluto, sextile Jupiter, trine Saturn.

Her moon is conjunct Mercury, trine Mars, semi-square Jupiter, square Saturn, conjunct Pluto, conjunct ascendant, square Mid.

Britney Spears was born 2nd December 1981 at 01.30am, McComb, Mississippi, U.S.A.

She has Libra rising for her ascendant with Venus the ruler in the 4th house.

Saturn and Pluto is in her first house. Saturn is exalted in Libra.

Jupiter is in the second house in the sign of Scorpio. (This connection makes people very deep and penetrating in whatever they do.)

The sun, Mercury, Uranus and Neptune are all in the sign of Sagittarius. This makes her a strong Sagittarian.

Venus is in the sign of Capricorn in the 4th house.

The moon is in the 5th house in Aquarius. 5th house is the house of creativity etc.

Jupiter is semi-sextile Uranus; conjunct Pluto; trine Mid; semi-sextile ascendant.

She has the sun sextile the moon; conjunct Mercury; semi-square Venus; conjunct Uranus; semi-square Pluto.

Her moon is trine Saturn; trine the ascendant.

Her Mercury is semi-square Saturn; conjunct Uranus; sextile ascendant.

Her Venus is trine Mars; square Jupiter; square Saturn; sextile Uranus; semi-sextile Neptune; square Pluto; trine ascendant.

Her Mars is square Neptune; conjunct ascendant; square Mid.

Her Saturn is sextile Neptune; conjunct Pluto.

Her Uranus is sextile ascendant; quincunx Mid.

Her Neptune is sextile Pluto; square ascendant; opposing Mid.

Her Pluto is trine Mid.

Princess Diana was born 1st July 1961 at 09.45 pm, Sandringham, UK.

She has Jupiter in the second house in the sign of Aquarius.

9: Simple Medical Astrology

The planet Mars is the ruler of the head. If you have something wrong with your head, it will show up in your chart.

The planet Venus is ruler of your throat and your waist. If something is wrong there, it will show in your chart.

The planet Mercury rules your hands and your stomach. If you have something wrong with these, it will show in your chart.

The moon rules the breasts and will definitely show in the chart what is taking place.

The sun rules the heart, and in you chart, you'll see what is happening.

Pluto rules the sexual or private parts, and in your chart, you'll see what is taking place.

Jupiter rules the thighs and you'll be able to see in your chart what is happening.

Saturn rules the knees and you'll be able to see what is happening in your chart.

Uranus rules the calves and also the back, and you can see what is taking place in your chart.

Neptune rules the feet, and of course it will show up in your chart.

*

I was just looking at a chart which is an event chart of a day when I had a terrible headache.

The ascendant is Virgo. The ruler, Mercury is in the loop in the 11th house exactly conjunct Venus also in the loop.

The axis 6th and 12th houses are in 0 degree.

I find Mars in the 8th house exactly conjuncting the 8th.

The 8th house has its opposite which is the second house – my body.

But Jupiter is in the first quincunx Uranus in the 6th.

So you see already how difficult medical astrology is.

*

Looking at a chart of someone who got shot in the head, the ascendant is Taurus.

Jupiter and Saturn are both inside the 12th house and exactly conjunct in Taurus.

Venus, the ruler of the ascendant is in the fifth house in the sign of Virgo.

Uranus is in the first house conjunct the ascendant.

Venus is square Uranus. Venus is sextile Mercury in the 6th house in the sign of Scorpio. Venus is trine the two planets in the 12th house – Jupiter and Saturn.

This Scorpio sign belongs to Mars, but it has nothing to do with the head.

Mercury is the ruler of the body represented by the second sign Gemini.

Mercury is opposing the two planets in the 12th house. Mercury is square Pluto in the fourth house in the sign of Leo. Mercury is square the moon in the 10th house in the sign of Aquarius.

In this position, we know that the moon is publicity, outside world, high people.

But now we find that Mars is ruler of the 12th house.

The moon is exactly sextile the 12th.

Mars is in the 5th house, but in the 6th house sign of Libra, the opposite sign is Aries (the head).

Mars is semi-sextile Venus, conjunct Neptune.

Mars flares up when in conjunction or square or negative to Neptune. There is always danger.

Mars is trine Uranus, and trine the moon.

So from all this again, you'll see how difficult it is to get your information in medical astrology. But it is all there.

The chart is showing that the individual was in the hospital, got operated on his head, and it all went well.

The planets would have shown another picture had it gone wrong.

*

This individual has broken her back. She has Capricorn as the ascendant.

The sun is in the first house in Capricorn.

The ruler Saturn is in the 11th conjunct 12th house.

Uranus, co-ruler of the second house is in the 7th in Leo, square Neptune in Scorpio in the 10th house.

The sun in the first is also square Neptune. The sun is square to Jupiter in the 10th house.

Jupiter is ruler of the 12th house, co-ruler of the third.

Her progressed moon in passing through the 12th in the ascendant sign of Capricorn. It is semi-sextile to Venus in the first house in the sign of Aquarius (the back).

Mercury, ruler of the 6th and 9th houses is in the 12th in the sign of Capricorn, trine Pluto in the 8th house in the sign of Virgo.

It is quite obvious that an operation took place on her back and it went good.

*

In another chart we find the progress ascendant is 13 degrees and 38 minutes of Sagittarius.

We find the ruler Jupiter in the 8th house conjunct the planet Venus. Both are

— 91 —

in the sign of Leo. Both are making a trine aspect to the ascendant.

Leo happens to be the 9th sign. And I'm sure you know by now that the 9th sign has to do with travelling, even the 3rd house.

The moon is passing through the second house in he sign of Capricorn and is in conjunction with Mars in the same house and same sign.

Uranus is in the 6th house conjuncting the 7th in the sign of Gemini. Uranus is ruler of the 3rd house.

Saturn, the ruler of the second house is in the 9th in the sign of Virgo. Saturn is semi-sextile Mercury also in the 9th house but in the 10th house sign of Libra.

Mercury is conjunct the Mid. Mercury is ruler of the 7th house, and the loop in the 9th.

Saturn is exactly semi-sextile the Mid.

Do you see what's happening? Something to do with the public or partner? And Uranus conjuncting the 7th?

Mars is ruler of the 4th, 11th and 12th houses. It is exactly sextile Neptune in the 3rd house in the sign of Pisces. Neptune is here in the loop in the 3rd house. Aquarius is the sign at the third house.

The individual is working with her partner and the public. Suddenly (Uranus) there is a train crash, many animals got killed. The individual was taken to the hospital with internal damage, left side paralyzed.

The sun is in Libra in 0 degree in the 9th house and is ruler of the 9th.

Something wrong with the back. The hair later went white.

While researching, I do come across some strange charts that are very hard to interpret. If you know the person, that is not so hard; but if you do not know the person, you have to look up and find some information about them.

Many people, without even checking astrology quickly state that it is all nonsense. I have to say quite clearly here that I know astrology is true, because I see it in the faces of human beings.

Before you open your mouth and make yourself look stupid, do some homework – check it out.

No one has explained to us what *"time"* is. We know that time and space work together. Astrology works on time and space and that is why it is so difficult to pinpoint. That is why it has baffled so many people.

It is there and it is working.

Would you sit down and try to calculate every ray that comes from the sun? That is crazy work!

10: The Part of Fortune, Moon's Nodes & Chiron

The Arabs knew a lot about astrology. From their writings we get information about the part of fortune. This is done by adding the ascendant position to the moon's position, and then subtracting the sun's position.

So if the ascendant was in Scorpio 6 degrees and 20 minutes, we would write this as: **7 signs   6 degrees   20 minutes.**

If the moon was in Sagittarius 13 degrees and 43 minutes, we would write it down as: **8 signs   13 degrees   43 minutes.**

If the sun was Aquarius 19 degrees and 9 minutes, we would write it as:
10 signs 19 degrees 9 minutes.

We are going to add the 7 signs and the 8 signs, we get 15 signs.

We are going to add 6 degrees and 13 degrees, we get 19 degrees.

We are going to add 20 minutes and 43 minutes, we get 63 minutes; out of this we get 1 degree and 3 minutes. This will make our total to be 15 signs 20 degrees and 3 minutes.

Now we have to take 10 signs 19 degrees and 9 minutes from 15 signs, 20 degrees, and 3 minutes.

15	20	3
10	19	9 we are left with
05	00	54

So our part of fortune would be 5 signs, 0 degree, 54 minutes.

We count, Aries, Taurus, Gemini, Cancer, Leo for five signs, then we go to Virgo to get 0 degree and 54 minutes. Part of fortune is Virgo 0.54.

Here is a chart of a woman who lived to be 122 years old in 1997.

Jeanne Calment was born 21st February 1875 at 07.00 am, Arles, France.

In the chart you'll see the positions of parts of fortune, the moon's nodes and Chiron.

Ascendant	04.14	Pisces
2nd	23.23	Aries
3rd	24.31	Taurus
4th	16.54	Gemini
5th	07.04	Cancer
6th	29.54	Cancer
7th	04.14	Virgo
8th	23.23	Libra
9th	24.31	Scorpio
10th	16.54	Sagittarius
11th	07.04	Capricorn
12th	29.54	Capricorn

Sun	02.16	Pisces
Moon	13.26	Virgo
Mercury	16.40 R	Pisces
Venus	15.33	Capricorn
Mars	04.50	Sagittarius
Jupiter	01.36	Scorpio
Saturn	18.34	Aquarius
Uranus	12.25 R	Leo
Neptune	28.33	Aries
Pluto	20.47	Taurus
Chiron	19.13	Aries
N Node	19.57	Aries

Part of Fortune........15.24   Virgo

The 12th sign of the fixed wheel, Pisces, is the ascendant here. The two planets ruling it are Jupiter and Neptune. Jupiter is in Scorpio in the 8th house making a trine aspect to the ascendant.

Neptune is in the second house in the sign of Aries conjunct the second. It is about 9 degrees away from the node and Chiron.

We see that Jupiter is in the 9th house sign. This position gives deep and penetrating insight.

She has the sun in the 12th house and conjuncting the ascendant, lots of energy here.

She has Mercury in her first house in Pisces. This position is good for being a psychic with strong feelings of knowing when things are not right.

Mercury is exactly square the Mid. It is sextile Venus in the 11th house.

Inside the first house but in the second house sign we see the node and Chiron exactly in conjunction. Both are in conjunction with the second house.

The planet Pluto is in he second house in the sign of Taurus conjunct the third. It is sextile to Mercury in the first house. It is semi-sextile the node and Chiron. It is trine the moon and fortune in the 7th house.

The planet Uranus is in a loop in the 6th house. It is ruler over the loop in the 12th.

You see that the moon is in the 7th house, something to do with the public, partnerships and publicity.

Fortune is in the 7th house. Shall we for now say that her fortune lies in the 7th house? We do not know yet!

Notice Mars in the 9th house in the 10th house sign of Sagittarius. There's a lot of energy here. Mars is exactly square to the ascendant.

Venus we see, is in the 11th house in Capricorn.

Her destiny planet, Saturn, is in the 12th house in the sign of Aquarius. Both

Saturn and Uranus rules this sign; and Saturn is opposing Uranus in the 6th house. Something interesting here.

Anyway, we have the sun, Jupiter and Mars all making aspect to the ascendant. This is a chance of having much energy. Jupiter with its trine, is protecting.

She has the moon trine to Venus, and semi-sextile Uranus. Venus is semi-sextile the Mid.

Our next chart is of *David Berkowitz* born 1st June 1953 at 16.52 pm, Brooklyn, New York, U.S.A.

He was very good with a rifle in the army. he worked in the postal area. he kept his body clean. Torched about 2,000 fires on city property. Claimed God spoke to him through the neighbour's dog.

Was sentenced to 365 years in jail.

Ascendant	00.35	Scorpio
2nd	29.12	Scorpio
3rd	01.41	Capricorn
4th	06.43	Aquarius
5th	09.50	Pisces
6th	07.57	Aries
7th	00.55	Taurus
8th	29.12	Taurus
9th	01.41	Cancer
10th	06.43	Leo
11th	09.50	Virgo
12th	07.57	Libra
Sun	11.02	Gemini
Moon	03.32	Aquarius
Mercury	21.01	Gemini
Venus	27.15	Aries
Mars	21.43	Gemini
Jupiter	05.26	Gemini
Saturn	20.56 R	Libra
Uranus	16.28	Cancer
Neptune	21.21 R	Libra
Pluto	21.00	Leo
Chiron	20.16	Capricorn
N Node	04.29	Aquarius
Fortune	23.25	Gemini

When the moon is crossing the ecliptic from south to north, it leaves a point, this point is called the *"North Node."*

When the moon is crossing the ecliptic from north to south, it leaves a point, this point is called the *"South Node."*

In the wheel above, we find the node in the third house in the sign of Aquarius. It is conjuncting the fourth house. It is in conjunction with the moon.

The moon is square the ascendant. It is 83 degrees away from Venus. I think we can call this a square with an orb of 7 degrees.

The moon is 127 degrees away from the sun. This should be a trine or not? A trine goes up to 8 degrees orb.

If it is a trine and working, it would mean that the responses and emotions are working well. Why is the sun intercepted? And in the sign Gemini? This sign is a double sign.

We must not forget the upbringing of individuals, and their environment and heredity.

This individual was doing well until 1974 when things went wrong. You have to look into the progressed chart and to see what was taking place. Work it with the natal chart to see clearly what went wrong.

He has what we call a stellium (four or more planets in a sign). He is a strong Gemini.

Notice Jupiter in his brothers house. Remember, I told you any connection with Jupiter and Pluto gives insight.

Then we see Mars in the 8th house. Mars is exactly conjunct Mercury and exactly sextile Pluto. The position of Mars alone in Gemini is very intellectual.

Four planets locked up in the loop in the 8th house. The ruler of the house is Venus. The ruler of the loop is Mercury, and it is there in its own loop.

Mars, co-ruler of the ascendant along with Pluto is sextile Pluto. Mars is in the loop, but Pluto is in the sign of Leo in the 10th house.

We have Mars making 128 degrees to the ascendant. Mars is trine the destiny planet, Saturn in the 12th house. Mars is also exactly trine Neptune in the 12th house.

Now we find Mars with many good aspects but it is negative to the Mid. This is the career and the outside world.

Mercury has a very good aspect to Saturn. I have known many people with this aspect, and have functioned normally.

Mercury is negative to the Mid. Mercury is exactly trine Neptune, trine Saturn.

Like Mars, Mercury is also trine the ascendant.

I am still looking at Fortune to get some more information before I can say anything positive about it.

We find it here in this chart in the 8th house in the sign of Gemini, conjunct Mars and Mercury. Trine Saturn and Neptune, trine ascendant, sextile Venus in the 6th house, sextile Pluto. Fortune is about 42 degrees from the Mid. I think we could say it is near a semi-square aspect.

From reading mythology, I see Mars as a criminal in the 8th house. But not everyone who has Mars in the 8th house would end up in prison. We find the disciplined ones are always doing something good with these energies of Mars. But we must not forget that this house of Pluto is a dark one.

We see the destiny planet in the 12th house and is exalted in the sign of Libra. Saturn is conjunct Neptune also in Libra.

Uranus in the 9th house has to do with travel and high learning, dreams and visions.

I don't know yet how to accept Chiron. The astrologers say that it is the wounded healer. Chiron was a healer and teacher but he couldn't heal himself.

In our chart here, we find Chiron in the third house in the sign of Capricorn. This sign belongs to Saturn.

Chiron is square both Saturn and Neptune in the 12th house. Even though Saturn is exalted, it is still negative to Chiron in the third house.

The third house we know has to do with the way we communicate and go about with our siblings and environment.

I got the feeling that this has to do with things that were said against him in early life that has hurt him.

I have given Chiron as ruling Sagittarius (doing this as a test).

Sagittarius is in a loop in the second house. Jupiter is the ruler of the loop and is in the 8th house.

I am still working on the loops (intercepted signs) and feel that they have to do with something extra. Time will tell.

There's quite a lot to be said about this chart, and we can see that both moon and node are square to the ascendant, and Chiron squaring his destiny planet. The chart has many good aspects, but we must not let that fool us. We can only get into the house by the front door, there are no windows and there is not another door. The ascendant is the door to the chart. And even though the sun is trine with the moon and the node, we're still left with the ascendant being negative by the same two – moon and node.

A whole book could be written about this one chart. It is really baffling.

The next chart has to do with a premature birth for seven months. The baby lived just five hours.

19th April 1932 at 00.32 am, 41N38, 79W43.

Ascendant	06.48	Capricorn
2nd	17.58	Aquarius
3rd	29.52	Pisces
4th	02.04	Taurus
5th	26.10	Taurus
6th	16.28	Gemini
7th	06.48	Cancer
8th	17.58	Leo
9th	29.52	Virgo
10th	02.04	Scorpio
11th	26.10	Scorpio
12th	16.28	Sagittarius
Sun	28.56	Aries
Moon	05.17	Libra
Mercury	14.42 R	Aries
Venus	14.32	Gemini
Mars	12.20	Aries
Jupiter	12.46	Leo
Saturn	04.13	Aquarius
Uranus	19.53	Aries
Neptune	05.23 R	Virgo
Pluto	20.00	Cancer
Chiron	21.46	Taurus
N Node	24.30	Pisces
Fortune	13.09	Gemini

We know that this chart is of a baby who only lived for five hours. Do we look at the fourth house and its ruler? Yes.

The fourth house is ruled by Venus in the fifth house in Gemini conjunct the 6th.

Venus is also ruler of the fifth. Didn't you know that the fifth house is also the house of life. The sun is ruler of this house in the fixed wheel. By the way, the ancients called the fixed wheel – a frozen wheel. It cannot turn.

Don't start trembling with fear but the fourth house is the grave. When you are checking charts of people who have said goodbye (not with us anymore), you must also check the 8th house and its ruler. Of course the tenth house.

There are only six houses. The above six are just opposites.

We know that the third house is short travel, while the 9th is long travel. You must always look to the opposite houses as well.

Fortune is in the fifth house conjunct Venus. For the time being, I give Leo to fortune. Just a test for now.

And you will see that Leo is at the 8th house. Fortune is also sextile Jupiter in the 7th house but in the 8th house sign of Leo.

Fortune is sextile Mercury and Mars in the loop in the third house in the sign of Aries.

The astrologer Ivy M Goldstein-Jacobson gave the 29 degrees in the chart as a crying degree.

So I think when you look at charts and you see planets or cusps or the nodes and fortune in 29 degrees, then you know something is wrong.

If I were you I would have a small note book where you could write in all those degrees that you can look at .

The ascendant is Capricorn. The ruler is Saturn. Saturn is in the first house in the sign of Aquarius which is the second house sign.

Saturn is trine the moon up in the loop in the 9th house in the sign of Libra.

The moon is ruling the 7th house. It is exactly semi-sextile Neptune in the 8th house retrograde in the sign of Virgo.

Remember, Saturn is ruler of the ascendant and the second house.

Neptune is ruler of the third.

The fact that the child lived for 5 hours, the chart belongs to it. If it was still in the mother's womb, it would be the chart of the mother, and you would have to be looking at the fifth house and the 12th house, and of course the 8th house.

The 12th house would have been the 8th for the child (5), while the 8th would have been the fourth for the child (5). It sounds all confusing to a new comer, but later on, it will come very easy to you.

Let's have a look at *Helene Boucher*'s progressive chart for the year she crashed. The date is 18th June 1908 at 11.00 am, Paris, France.

Ascendant	16.23	Virgo
2nd	09.14	Libra
3rd	08.02	Scorpio
4th	12.44	Sagittarius
5th	18.57	Capricorn
6th	20.30	Aquarius
7th	16.23	Pisces
8th	09.14	Aries
9th	08.02	Taurus
10th	12.44	Gemini
11th	18.57	Cancer
12th	20.30	Leo

Sun	26.46	Gemini
Moon	19.42	Aquarius
Mercury	17.16	Cancer
Venus	21.34 R	Cancer
Mars	17.22	Cancer
Jupiter	11.59	Leo
Saturn	09.13	Aries
Uranus	15.40 R	Capricorn
Neptune	13.54	Cancer
Pluto	24.21	Gemini
Chiron	23.09	Aquarius
N Node	05.30	Cancer
Fortune	09.19	Taurus

Don't forget your degrees! 8 degrees. . . . . something that you can't do anything about.

9 degrees. . . . . . . something starting or ending.

The 3rd and 9th house has to do with flying or travelling.

We pick up Chiron in the 6th house in Aquarius trine to Pluto in the 10th house in Gemini. Pluto is co-ruler of the 3rd house. Chiron is also trine to the sun, but we are working to a 1 degree orb.

Notice that Fortune is in the 9th house and conjunct the 9th. Exactly semi-sextile the 8th, and Saturn.

Notice that the ruler of the 8th house, Mars, is in the 10th in the sign of Cancer exactly conjunct Mercury.

Mercury is ruler of the ascendant and the 10th house. Mars is co-ruler of the third. If you have 10, the opposite is 4. If you have 8, the opposite is 2.

Jupiter is in the 11th house in Leo sextile the Mid.

Both Mercury and Mars are conjunct the 11th and sextile the ascendant.

Uranus in the 4th house in the 5th house sign of Capricorn is trine the ascendant.

Neptune is in the 10th house in Cancer and semi-sextile the Mid.

Her destiny planet Saturn, is in the 7th house exactly conjunct the 8th in the sign of Aries. Saturn is holding 9 degrees. It is also semi-sextile the 9th. Saturn is ruler of the fifth and sixth.

The moon is in the 5th in the sign of the 6th, Aquarius and conjunct the 6th. The moon is semi-sextile the 5th.

This girl was found dead. Her progressive date is 27th April 1972 at 09.12 am, Boston, Massachusetts, U.S.A.

Ascendant	17.59	Cancer
2nd	07.03	Leo
3rd	29.07	Leo
4th	27.22	Virgo
5th	03.49	Scorpio
6th	13.44	Sagittarius
7th	17.59	Capricorn
8th	07.03	Aquarius
9th	29.07	Aquarius
10th	27.22	Pisces
11th	03.49	Taurus
12th	13.44	Gemini
Sun	07.25	Taurus
Moon	27.10	Libra
Mercury	10.31	Aries
Venus	21.26	Gemini
Mars	20.23	Gemini
Jupiter	08.19	Capricorn
Saturn	05.41	Gemini
Uranus	15.23 R	Libra
Neptune	04.36 R	Sagittarius
Pluto	29.46 R	Virgo
Chiron	14.41	Aries
N Node	00.24	Aquarius
Fortune	07.44	Capricorn

We have Chiron in a loop in the 10th house in the sign of Aries conjuncting Mercury in the loop and same sign. This conjunction is about four degrees apart.

Chiron is sextile the 12th house with the sign Gemini there.

The node is in the 7th house in the 8th house sign holding 0 degree. The node is ruling the ascendant sign of Cancer.

Fortune is in the 6th house in the 7th house sign of Capricorn.

Fortune is exactly semi-sextile the 8th. It is in conjunction with Jupiter in the same sign and house. It is trine the sun in the 11th house in the sign of Taurus. The sun is ruler of the second and third houses. Fortune has ruler over the same.

The second house ruling the body and possessions is ruled by the sun in the sign of Taurus in the 11th house. The sun is exactly square the 8th house.

We find the moon as ruler of her ascendant in a loop in the fourth house in the sign of Libra exactly semi-sextile the fourth.

Neptune in the fifth house in the sixth house sign is semi-sextile the fifth.

Venus is conjunct mars in the 12th house in the sign of Gemini. Venus is ruler of the loop in the fourth, and also ruler of the 11th.

Mars is ruler of the fifth, and the loop in the 10th.

Pluto in the fourth house in Virgo holding 29 degrees is semi-sextile to the third.

Keep your eyes on planets and cusps in 7 degrees????????????

Keep your eyes on planets and cusps in 21 degrees??????????

In this chart you see that the sun is in 7 degrees in Taurus. After reading a bit about her case, I learned that she was stabbed in the throat (Taurus).

I wonder if you can find out anything about this next chart.
22nd February 1918 at 06.30 am, Alton, Illinois, U.S.A.

Ascendant	26.05	Aquarius
2nd	12.37	Aries
3rd	16.02	Taurus
4th	10.31	Gemini
5th	01.55	Cancer
6th	24.51	Cancer
7th	26.05	Leo
8th	12.37	Libra
9th	16.02	Scorpio
10th	10.31	Sagittarius
11th	01.55	Capricorn
12th	24.51	Capricorn
Sun	03.05	Pisces
Moon	25.43	Cancer
Mercury	18.33	Aquarius
Venus	14.05 R	Aquarius
Mars	00.50 R	Libra
Jupiter	02.40	Gemini
Saturn	09.24 R	Leo
Uranus	24.14	Aquarius
Neptune	04.59 R	Leo
Pluto	03.32 R	Cancer
Chiron	27.50	Pisces
N Node	29.38	Sagittarius
Fortune	18.43	Cancer

Fortune is in the loop in the first house in the sign of Pisces. Fortune is ruling the descendant sign of Leo. Fortune is semi-sextile to the ascendant.

Fortune is square the node in the 10th house in the sign of Sagittarius. It is trine the moon in the 6th house in the sign of Cancer.

The node is in 29 degrees of Sagittarius. It is sextile the ascendant. It is square Mars in the 7th house.

Mars is in 0 degree in the sign of Libra. Mars is ruler of the second house, and co-ruler of the 9th. Mars is square to the 11th house. Mars is sextile the moon. Mars is trine Jupiter in the third house in the sign of Gemini.

Fortune is quincunx Mercury in the 12th house in the ascendant sign of Aquarius.

The ascendant is Aquarius with its rulers Saturn in the 6th house in the sign of Leo holding 9 degrees, and Uranus in the 12th house in the ascendant sign.

Uranus is the closet to the ascendant. Something unusual? Scientifical?

Saturn is trine the Mid. Uranus is exactly semi-sextile the 12th.

The sun is in Pisces conjunct the ascendant, square the Mid, square Jupiter, trine Pluto, quincunx Neptune.

The sun in Pisces, Neptune is ruler of Pisces, and yet the sun is negative to Neptune. The sun is ruling the 7th house, Neptune is ruling the loop in the first.

The moon is conjunct the 6th house, semi-sextile the 7th, quincunx the ascendant.

Jupiter in the third is semi-sextile the fifth, square the ascendant.

Mercury and Venus are in conjunction in the 12th house. Mercury is conjunct Uranus, and the ascendant.

Venus is sextile the Mid, opposing Saturn. Saturn is conjunct Neptune.

You should now know that this chart belongs to Robert Wadlow the tallest human in recorded history.

You should learn about the signs and their opposites.

Do you know that the sign of Sagittarius is known as far reaching (tall).

It is also known as travelling, (long distance). It is known as space. It is known as moving (like when a bullet is moving). It is also known as falling.

This next chart is of a Saint. My God! Is she beautiful! She is a virgin.

Her name is *Catherine Laboure*, the ninth of eleven children.

Born 2nd May 1806 at 18.00 pm (when the evening angelus was ringing).

She was born at Fain-les-Moutiers, but you can take Bourgogne, France.

I hope you see where she got her beauty from. Remember Hedy Lamarr?

Ascendant	28.49	Libra
2nd	26.12	Scorpio
3rd	29.50	Sagittarius
4th	07.32	Aquarius
5th	11.22	Pisces
6th	08.06	Aries
7th	28.49	Aries

8th	26.12	Taurus
9th	29.50	Gemini
10th	07.32	Leo
11th	11.22	Virgo
12th	08.06	Libra
Sun	11.35	Taurus
Moon	10.47	Scorpio
Mercury	06.59 R	Taurus.
Venus	27.43	Pisces
Mars	23.49	Aries
Jupiter	08.11 R	Capricorn
Saturn	23.51 R	Libra
Uranus	22.52 R	Libra
Neptune	29.25 R	Scorpio
Pluto	11.51	Pisces
Chiron	27.33	Capricorn
N Node	29.06	Sagittarius
Fortune	28.01	Aries

Chiron is in the third house in a loop in Capricorn. It is square the ascendant, sextile the second house, sextile Neptune in the second house, square Saturn and Uranus in the 12th. It is exactly sextile Venus in the 5th house, square Mars and Fortune in the sixth house, square Mercury.

The node is exactly conjunct the third house, exactly semi-sextile Neptune, sextile the ascendant, sextile Saturn, and just about making a sextile with Uranus. It is trine Fortune and Mars.

Fortune is in the 6th house in the sign of the 7th, conjunct Mars, exactly conjunct the 7th. Conjunct Mercury in the 7th house, square the Mid. Opposing Saturn and Uranus and the ascendant.

Her ascendant is Libra with Venus the ruler in the 5th house exalted in the sign of Pisces. Venus is making a quincunx to the ascendant, semi-square the sun in the 7th house, trine Neptune.

Her sun sign is Taurus, and she shows it well in her face. The sun is conjunct Mercury also in Taurus. The intellect should be good.

The sun is exactly sextile Pluto in the 5th house in the sign of Pisces. The sun is trine Jupiter in the loop in the third house. The sun rules the 10th house, Jupiter rules the third and the fifth. The sun is square the Mid.

The sun is exactly trine the 11th house.

The sun is opposing the moon in the first house.

Her moon sign is Scorpio. It is sextile the 11th house. It is sextile Jupiter, trine Pluto, square the Mid.

Mercury is square the Mid. It is trine Jupiter. It is opposing the moon.

Mars is conjunct the 7th.

I have found lots of charts with Saints or virgins with either Uranus or Mars making contact with the 7th house. They probably know before hand that there'll be problems in the marriage, so they prefer to stay away from that.

In the year 1830, she had a vision of Mary.

On the 11th May 1806 (progressive date) her mother said "goodbye" (passed away).

When she herself said "goodbye" and her body exhumed in 1933, it was found as fresh as the day she was born. It was not corrupted.

When I checked the progressive chart for 1933, I saw what was happening.

Now this next chart is an event chart of the Third Reich. It was started on the 30th January 1933 at 11.07 am, Berlin, Germany.

Ascendant	22.19	Taurus
2nd	17.35	Gemini
3rd	05.14	Cancer
4th	22.30	Cancer
5th	14.13	Leo
6th	20.03	Virgo
7th	22.19	Scorpio
8th	17.35	Sagittarius
9th	05.14	Capricorn
10th	22.30	Capricorn
11th	14.13	Aquarius
12th	20.03	Pisces
Sun	10.05	Aquarius
Moon	05.08	Aries
Mercury	04.05	Aquarius
Venus	19.59	Capricorn
Mars	19.42 R	Virgo
Jupiter	22.28 R	Virgo
Saturn	07.29	Aquarius
Uranus	19.53	Aries
Neptune	09.33 R	Virgo
Pluto	21.59 R	Cancer
Chiron	23.34	Taurus
N Node	07.59	Pisces
Fortune	17.22	Cancer

In an event chart, there are the 12 houses just as in the individual chart.

The first house represents the country, the 10th house represents the ruler, the fourth house represents the land and the home. The 7th house will have to do with treaties and partnerships of all kinds. the 8th house has to do with death and all the goods thereof. Dealing with compensations and legacies.

The ninth house has to do with travel by road, air or the ocean. Passports, customs, regulations. The 11th house has to do with the social and public side of affairs. Interest in scientifical things. The 12th house to do with prisons, hospitals, crime, drugs, mystical and psychic matters. The second house of course to do with financial and money matters. The fifth house to do with speculations, stock exchange, lotteries, children and birth control. The 6th house to do with health and hygiene, food, animals and servants.

The ascendant sign rising is Taurus and it is ruled by the planet Venus which is up in the 9th house in the sign of Capricorn. Venus is conjunct the Mid, square Uranus in the loop in the 12th house. Venus is sextile the 12th house. Venus is opposing Pluto in the third house in the sign of Cancer, and also opposing Fortune in the third house, in the same sign. Venus is trine Jupiter in the 6th house in the sign of Virgo, trine Mars in the 5th house in the sign of Virgo. Venus is trine to the ascendant.

Have we noticed Chiron in the first house in conjunction with the ascendant? Chiron is ruling the 8th house (my test). Some astrologers suggest Virgo or Libra.

Chiron is trine the Mid, semi-square the moon in the 12th house in the loop of Aries.

Chiron is trine Mars in the fifth house, trine Jupiter in the sixth house.

Chiron is sextile Pluto in the third house, is about 53 degrees to Fortune.

The node is in the 11th house but in the sign of the 12th. It is exactly semi-sextile Saturn in the 10th house. It is semi-square Venus in the 9th house. It is sesqui-quadrate to Pluto. It is opposing Neptune in the fifth house.

Fortune in the third house in the sign of Cancer conjunct Pluto. The only thing I can say about fortune is to take it by its house position and sign and the aspects it makes. In the his chart, it has to do with the home and family and land. In the third house, to do with travel, talking, reading and writing. Neighbours and contracts.

Fortune is about 54 degrees from the ascendant. We could call it a sextile. It is conjunct the fourth, sextile Mars in the fifth and Jupiter in the 6th house. It is square Uranus in the 12th house in the loop of Aries. It is exactly semi-sextile the second house.

What I want you to do is check for charts with Mars in Virgo. These people are very hard working. They can work themselves into the dirt.

This chart has Mars in the fifth house in the sign of Virgo and conjunct the 6th house. This shows a lot of hard work going on to do with the servants and social workers.

The moon we find in the loop in the 12th house in the sign of Aries. It is about 14 degrees away from Uranus in the same sign. This shows clearly that there's a lot of secret scientific things going on.

The moon is sextile Mercury in the 10th house. It is sextile the sun in the 10th house. It is sextile Saturn in the 10th house.

The moon is exactly square the 9th house.

While the 12th house is the house of enemies and secret things, the 9th house is that of long travel and foreign countries, and it will not go well because of the square aspect.

The moon is semi-square the ascendant.

The sun sign here is Aquarius it is in the 10th house, the house of high authority. It is conjunct Mercury and Saturn all in the same sign and in the tenth house. It is quincunx Neptune. This connection always bring some sort of scandal or confusion.

Consider that the sun is the natural ruler of the fifth house in the fixed wheel. Neptune is the natural ruler along with Jupiter of the 12th house in the natural wheel. So we get 5 and 12. if these planets are not good with each other, things would not work out well.

The sun is sesqui-quadrate Jupiter in the 6th house. Trouble would come through the 5th, 8th and 12th houses.

Mercury is semi-sextile the 9th house.

Jupiter is in the 6th house in the sign of Virgo conjunct the 6th. It is in conjunction with Mars in the 5th house and in the same sign.

Jupiter is exactly trine the Mid. Exactly trine the ascendant. It is quincunx to Uranus in the 12th house in the loop in the sign of Aries. Jupiter is sextile Pluto in the 3rd house.

The destiny planet is Saturn and it is in the 10th house in its own sign of Aquarius. Saturn is ruling the 9th, 10th and 11th houses.

We could then say it has something to do with foreign countries, long distance travel, structure, architecture, hard, cold and solid. Also for Aquarius, friends, clubs and groups. Scientific subjects. Unusual happenings.

The planets that are in the 10th house has to do with the boss, he or she who is ruling the country. Or is in charge of the event chart.

We see the chart with a triple Virgo – Mars, Jupiter and Neptune. A triple Aquarius – Sun, Mercury and Saturn. A double Aries – moon and Uranus.

Remember to hold on to the degrees that I have given you; use them when you are looking at the charts.

11: Duplicate Cusps and Planets

Uranus in the 7th house is ruler of the 9th. One year I went to London on holiday. I looked around to try and find somewhere cheap to stay. I was informed of a place where the students go away, and I go stay there until they returned. I found the place called Angel. At the building, the number was 5. A statue of an angel was above the main door. For some unknown reason, I started thinking about number 5 and the angel deeply. Then I looked at the charts and started seeing the cusps and planets holding 5 degrees. I decided to call it an *"Angel degree"*.

We shall look at some charts with 5 degrees within them.

This first chart is of *Tad Dameron* a Jazz musician, composer arranger and pianist. Born 21st February 1917 at 11.15 am, Cleveland, Ohio, U.S.A.

Ascendant	05.00	Gemini
2nd	28.16	Gemini
3rd	18.34	Cancer
4th	10.37	Leo
5th	09.03	Virgo
6th	18.57	Libra
7th	05.00	Sagittarius
8th	28.16	Sagittarius
9th	18.34	Capricorn
10th	10.37	Aquarius
11th	09.03	Pisces
12th	18.57	Aries
Sun	02.29	Pisces
Moon	01.21	Pisces
Mercury	07.59	Aquarius
Venus	16.26	Aquarius
Mars	04.02	Pisces
Jupiter	01.29	Taurus
Saturn	24.35 R	Cancer
Uranus	20.25	Aquarius
Neptune	02.44 R	Leo
Pluto	02.26 R	Cancer
Chiron	24.25	Pisces
N Node	17.38	Capricorn
Fortune	03.52	Gemini

You'll see in this chart duplicate signs of Gemini – ascendant and the second house. Of Sagittarius – 7th and 8th houses. Loops (intercepted signs) come about in the 6th and 12th houses.

Mercury is the ruler of the ascendant and of the second house. We find Mercury in the 9th house in the sign of Aquarius.

Travel is shown and money can come through it.

Mercury has Venus and Uranus in the same sign but not in the same house.

A strong Aquarian. Mercury is conjunct the Mid, trine ascendant, trine Fortune.

We find fortune as the nearest body to the ascendant. Fortune is in the 12th house conjunct the ascendant, semi-sextile Pluto in the second house, sextile Neptune in the 3rd house, semi-sextile

Jupiter in the 12th inside the loop of Taurus. Fortune is square the sun in the 10th house, square moon and Mars in the same house, sesqui-quadrate the node in the 8th house.

Notice that he has the sun, moon, Mars and Chiron in the water sign of Pisces. He also has Saturn and Pluto in the water sign of Cancer. Very sensitive and intuitive.

This 5 degrees that we see rising is pointing to himself and others which has to do with partner or partnerships and the public. In numerology, Mercury has that number.

Venus, you see is holding a very strong position in the 10th house.

Our next chart is of *Jacee Dugard* born 3rd May 1980 at 22.52 pm, Anaheim, California, U.S.A.

This girl was kidnapped and kept in captivity for 18 years.

Always make sure that the time you have been given is correct.

Ascendant	25.53	Sagittarius
2nd	00.44	Aquarius
3rd	08.54	Pisces
4th	13.26	Aries
5th	11.17	Taurus
6th	04.23	Gemini
7th	25.53	Gemini
8th	00.44	Leo
9th	08.54	Virgo
10th	13.26	Libra
11th	11.17	Scorpio
12th	04.23	Sagittarius

Sun	13.54	Taurus
Moon	29.15	Sagittarius
Mercury	03.31	Taurus
Venus	25.31	Gemini
Mars	00.02	Virgo
Jupiter	00.20	Virgo
Saturn	20.28 R	Virgo
Uranus	23.58 R	Scorpio
Neptune	22.15 R	Sagittarius
Pluto	19.44 R	Libra
Chiron	13.36	Taurus
N Node	25.34	Leo
Fortune	11.14	Leo

Duplicate signs come to the ascendant and the second house.

To the second and third houses; to the second and third houses; to the third and fourth houses; to the fourth and fifth house; to the fifth and sixth houses; to the sixth and seventh houses; to the seventh and eighth houses; to the eighth and ninth houses; to the ninth and tenth houses; to the tenth and eleventh houses; to the eleventh and twelfth houses, and to the twelfth and first house.

This chart we're now doing has the twelfth and first as duplicate signs.

It is important to understand that the 12th house is that of your enemies, of isolation, behind the scenes, imprisonment, hospitals, meditating and all sorts of other things which are of the 12th house.

The first house as you already know is to do with yourself. Your enemies can know what you're doing, and where you are at a certain time.

I have done some serious research on this and found it to be true.

Duplicate signs is also in the progressive chart.

Sagittarius is the sign which is doubled here. 12/1.

Jupiter is the ruler of both ascendant and the twelfth. We find it in the 8th house in the sign of Virgo holding 0 degree giving you more information.

Jupiter is exactly conjunct with Mars also in the 8th house and in the same sign.

Notice that Mars is ruling the 4th and 11th houses.

Both Mars and Jupiter are trine to the ascendant. Both are sextile to Venus in the 7th house. And they are both trine to the moon and Neptune in the first. They are square to Uranus in the 11th house.

Venus is ruler of the 5th and 10th houses. Venus is exactly semi-sextile the node in the 8th house. Venus is in a double sign – Gemini. Venus is square Saturn in the 9th house. Saturn is her destiny planet and it is ruling the loop in the first house, and co-ruler of the second.

While Venus is exactly conjunct the 7th house, it is also exactly opposing the ascendant. Venus is also opposing the moon and Neptune in the first house.

Mercury in the fourth house is conjunct the fifth, and trine the ascendant.

The axis 2/8 is in 0 degree. Something to do with her body and other people's body or property.

Mercury is about 111 degrees to the node in the 8th house. I think we could call this a trine. Not a close one though.

Mercury is trine to both Mars and Jupiter. Mercury is ruling the 6th, 7th and 9th houses. Jupiter ruling the ascendant, the third house and the 12th.

Venus is making a trine to Pluto in the 10th house.

The axis 3/9 is holding 8 degrees. This is something that cannot be explained.

And there in the first house we see the moon holding 29 degrees and in conjunction with Neptune.

Pluto is sextile to the ascendant, and to Neptune in the first house. It is semi-sextile to Saturn.

Fortune in the 8th house is sextile the Mid. It is exactly square the 11th.

Her destiny planet Saturn, is square the ascendant.

Here we see that Mars has just entered Virgo. This gives her lots of energy, tough.

In the fifth house we see that her sun is in the sign of Taurus and is exactly conjunct Chiron, both conjunct the fifth. Mercury is also in Taurus. In her face, Taurus comes out very much.

She has a triple in Taurus and a triple in Virgo, and a double in Sagittarius.

Both sun and Chiron are quincunx to the Mid.

I think that you'll see that this girl was lucky having both Jupiter and Mars and even Mercury making good aspects to her ascendant. Other charts that I have looked at weren't so lucky. The owners got killed.

This next chart is the progressive chart of *Adolf Hitler* for the year 1945. The date is 15th June 1889 at 18.30, Braunau am inn, Austria.

There is a lot of information in this chart. Hitler got defeated, he got married, and he killed himself along with his wife.

I will not be staying long with this chart, just pointing out certain things.

Ascendant	07.16	Sagittarius
2nd	11.48	Capricorn
3rd	24.12	Aquarius
4th	01.51	Aries
5th	29.27	Aries
6th	20.06	Taurus
7th	07.16	Gemini

— 111 —

8th	11.48	Cancer
9th	24.12	Leo
10th	01.51	Libra
11th	29.27	Libra
12th	20.06	Scorpio
Sun	24.43	Gemini
Moon	25.10	Capricorn
Mercury	00.22 R	Cancer
Venus	12.00	Taurus
Mars	25.23	Gemini
Jupiter	04.32 R	Capricorn
Saturn	16.37	Leo
Uranus	17.54 R	Libra
Neptune	02.52	Gemini
Pluto	05.53	Gemini
Chiron	11.37	Cancer
N Node	12.07	Cancer
Fortune	07.43	Cancer

Jupiter is the ruler of the ascendant, it is in the first house in the sign of Capricorn.

It is quincunx Pluto in the 6th house but in the 7th house sign. Pluto is holding 5 degrees. It is co-ruler of the 12th house. Something is happening there.

The duplicate signs are 10 and 11, and the opposite, 4 and 5.

The fifth axis is holding 29 degrees.

Mercury in the 7th house in the sign of Cancer is holding 0 degree. Giving information about the 7th house, and also about the loop in the 9th house.

Mercury is retrograde and is square to the Mid. This shows that the career is not going good. And there is trouble in the 9th house.

Venus is in the 5th house in Taurus and is sextile the 8th. It is sextile Chiron in the 7th house, and sextile the node in the 8th.

Venus is ruling the 6th, 10, and 11th houses.

We see Chiron exactly conjunct the 8th. I give Chiron to be ruling Sagittarius. But you can also check Libra or Virgo.

Mars is in the 7th house in conjunction with the sun. The sun is ruler of the 9th house, Mars is ruling the 4th, 5th and 12th.

Fortune is in the 7th exactly semi-sextile the 7th.

The moon is in the second house in the sign of Capricorn quincunx the sun and Mars in the sign of Gemini in the 7th house.

Both sun and Mars are sextile to the 9th. The ninth has to with ceremony, travel etc.

The 9th has also to do with foreign countries.

There is a story going around that his body ended up in Russia.

The node is conjunct the 8th, and I have given the sign of Cancer to the node (testing).

The planet Neptune is in the 6th house in the sign of Gemini and making a trine aspect to the Mid. Neptune is co-ruler of the loop in the third house, the sign of Pisces.

Saturn in the 8th house in the sign of Leo is sextile Uranus in the 10th house in the sign of Libra.

The 7 degrees of Sagittarius rising is showing that there is something to do with partner or partnerships.

Have you noticed Venus in the fifth house? He loved children.

If you study this progress chart carefully, you'll get the correct answer of what happened to Hitler.

This next chart is of the *Titanic* when it hit the iceberg. This is not the chart of when the Titanic sank – this happened later on the 15th.

Hitting the iceberg on 14th April 1912 at 23, 40pm, Atlantic Ocean, 41N44, 49W57.

Ascendant	15.01	Sagittarius
2nd	24.00	Capricorn
3rd	11.07	Pisces
4th	17.05	Aries
5th	11.25	Taurus
6th	29.30	Taurus
7th	15.01	Gemini
8th	24.00	Cancer
9th	11.07	Virgo
10th	17.05	Libra
11th	11.25	Scorpio
12th	29.30	Scorpio
Sun	24.39	Aries
Moon	24.35	Pisces
Mercury	25.32 R	Aries
Venus	02.55	Aries
Mars	05.11	Cancer
Jupiter	15.00 R	Sagittarius
Saturn	19.45	Taurus
Uranus	03.14	Aquarius
Neptune	21.02	Cancer
Pluto	27.09	Gemini

Chiron	09.29	Pisces
N Node	21.30	Aries.
Fortune	14.57	Scorpio
Sedna	11.20	Aries

The duplicate signs are 11/12. Scorpio at the 11th, and also at the 12th houses. The opposite are 5/6. Taurus at the 5th, and again at the 6th.

Sagittarius is rising with its ruler Jupiter exactly conjunct the ascendant, and in the 12th house.

Jupiter is square the moon in the 3rd house in the sign of Pisces.

The third house is travel/passengers. The sixth and 12th axis are holding 29 degrees.

Mars ruler of the 4th, 11, and 12th houses is in the 7th in Cancer holding 5 degrees.

There is a loop in the second house with the planet Uranus in the sign of Aquarius. Uranus is sextile Venus in the third house in the sign of Aries. Venus is ruler of the 5th, 6th and 10th houses.

Venus is square Mars. Uranus is quincunx Mars. Uranus is semi-square the ascendant.

What I want you to do if you have the time, is to read the mythological story about the minor planet Sedna.

It is doing something to this chart that you would see for yourself. I don't know if it's coincidence.

I will add it to the list above.

Venus is square Pluto. Pluto is co-ruler of the 11th and 12th houses.

The sun is ruler of the loop in the 8th house, it is in the fourth in the sign of Aries and is exactly square the 8th.

The moon is ruler of the 8th, it is in the 3rd house in the sign of Pisces and exactly trine the 8th.

The node in the fourth house in the sign of Aries is square Neptune in the 7th house in the 8th house sign of Cancer.

Mercury conjuncting the sun in the fourth house in the sign of Aries is semi-sextile the moon in the third house, sextile Pluto in the 7th, and square the 8th.

Fortune is semi-sextile from the 11th house in the sign of Scorpio to the ascendant.

Sedna is in the third house in the sign of Aries, and exactly semi-sextile the third.

Our next chart is that of the *mother of Jesus*. Born on 8th September BC 19 at Midnight, Nazareth, Israel.

You have to tick in -18 to get BC 19.

I used the midnight time because I do not know the time of her birth. A midday or midnight time will still give you good results.

Ascendant	02.24	Cancer
2nd	24.07	Cancer
3rd	17.16	Leo
4th	15.04	Virgo
5th	19.28	Libra
6th	27.31	Scorpio
7th	02.24	Capricorn
8th	24.07	Capricorn
9th	17.16	Aquarius
10th	15.04	Pisces
11th	19.28	Aries
12th	27.31	Taurus
Sun	14.17	Virgo
Moon	28.31	Libra
Mercury	08.00	Libra
Venus	29.46	Leo
Mars	24.17	Leo
Jupiter	14.14 R	Pisces
Saturn	27.05	Libra
Uranus	14.06 R	Capricorn
Neptune	07.52	Libra
Pluto	13.58	Leo
N Node	23.00	Sagittarius
Fortune	16.38	Leo

This midnight chart has an ascendant of Cancer rising. The ruler is in the fifth house in the sign of Libra.

We know that Cancer is a sensitive sign. It is water. It has to do with the home or the country. With this sign there's a love of home and family and country.

The moon in the sign of Libra is showing that the person is interested in partnerships and togetherness. Harmony is shown here.

The moon in the fifth house is showing that the person is interested in children and is creative. Love all that the fifth house has to give.

The moon is conjunct Saturn in the fifth house. It makes a semi-sextile contact with the sixth house. The moon is sesqui-quadrate Jupiter in the 9th house.

Saturn is exalted in the sign of Libra. And although it is exalted, it can still deny children, giving only one or two. It also depends on how strong Saturn is in the fifth house.

Saturn is the ruler of the 7th, 8th and 9th houses. Saturn is exactly semi-sextile the sixth.

Remember that the fifth house will show her children.

There are two other planets here in the sign of Libra but they are not in conjunction with the moon or Saturn. They are Mercury and Neptune, both in the 4th house.

So we see that she has four planets in the sign of Libra. She's a real Libran. Have you ever met a real Libran? The moon is trine the ascendant.

This shows that her mother will play a very important role in her life.

Of course, the moon is ruler of the duplicate signs 1/2. Saturn rules the opposite duplicate signs 7/8.

Her 7th house is her children's 3rd house.

Her 8th house is her children's 4th house.

Her ninth house is her children's 5th house.

Her sun sign is Virgo. In some charts, because of midnight, the sun will be close to the fourth house. It is semi-sextile Pluto in the second house. It is exactly trine Uranus in the 7th house. It is exactly opposing Jupiter.

To study one chart properly, it would take a long time. If you go through all the houses contact you'll soon see what I mean.

Here, we see that her 6th house has something to do with the children's money or income. Saturn is making contact to the 6th. I don't know what it is but I never like the moon and Saturn. Or the moon passing through Capricorn.

Notice that Jupiter is in a high position even though it is not in an angular house. It is conjunct the Mid and exactly sextile Uranus in the 7th house.

Jupiter is in the sign of Pisces which is the sign of itself and of Neptune. Jupiter is in the 9th house. This is a position for being really religious and philosophical, travel, compassionate, kind, helping others.

You must also look at the loops in the 6th and 12th houses. Mercury is holding 8 degrees and is ruler of the fourth house, and of Gemini in the loop in the 12th house. You should know by now what the 12th house mean. You must also notice her node in the sign of Sagittarius in the loop in the sixth house. This sign of Sagittarius belongs to the 9th house. And in the loop in the 12th, the sign of Gemini belongs to the 3rd house.

Saturn is trine the ascendant, and being ruler of the 7th, the chance s there to make partnerships. She loves children and will be close to them.

Both Mercury and Neptune in the fourth house are square to the ascendant. They hold a strong position being angular. They both are also square to Uranus in the 7th house.

Neptune is a strange planet even when people can use it for singing, painting, meditating, getting strange feelings, psychic and working behind the scenes.

There are some energies that certain human beings are not capable to handle. Mercury and Neptune can cause confusion in other people's chart, especially if they're not disciplined. And being square to the ascendant as well. There still will be trouble in the areas ruled by Mercury and Neptune.

Now we shall look at her progress chart for BC 6. What I want you to do is check your own chart by moving the time to 12:00 pm. Like if you know when you got married. When you have children. When you moved house. Check all these to get a good idea what your own chart is telling you.

Here is the chart for Mary when she was 13 years old.
Progress date is 21st September BC 19 at Midnight, Nazareth, Israel.

Ascendant	13.41	Cancer
2nd	05.16	Leo
3rd	29.30	Leo
4th	29.00	Virgo
5th	04.15	Scorpio
6th	10.53	Sagittarius
7th	13.41	Capricorn
8th	05.16	Aquarius
9th	29.30	Aquarius
10th	29.00	Pisces
11th	04.15	Taurus
12th	10.53	Gemini
Sun	27.11	Virgo
Moon	11.27	Aries
Mercury	03.38 R	Libra
Venus	16.01	Libra
Mars	02.37	Virgo
Jupiter	12.31 R	Pisces
Saturn	28.24	Libra
Uranus	13.59 R	Capricorn
Neptune	08.21	Libra
Pluto	14.20	Leo
N Node	21.43	Sagittarius
Fortune	28.07	Capricorn

Duplicate signs are 2/3, 8/9.

Let's start off with the ascendant and its ruler. The ascendant is Cancer, the ruler is the moon. We find the moon in a loop in the 10th house in the sign of Aries. As soon as the Mid finishes, Aries takes over and the moon is out of the loop.

— 117 —

While the moon is in the loop in the 10th house, it is making a semi-sextile contact with the 12th house. The 12th house is that of behind the scenes or isolation.

The moon is semi-sextile to Jupiter in the 9th house in the sign of Pisces, the sign of the 10th house. Jupiter is also ruler of the 6th house.

The moon is squaring Uranus with a 2 degrees orb but we are working with 1 orb. So what if we move the moon a month by adding 1 degree, then we would get October where the moon is exact with Jupiter, and is then square with Uranus.

Are we saying that her son was born in October?

What about the axis 2/8 holding 5 degrees?

If the moon plays an important part when the woman is having a baby, then we could say that she must have had it in the month of September or October.

Her progress date we see is September 21st. The moon moves about 1 degree per month. So we see the aspects it makes as it moves along.

Let's go to the fifth house – the house of children.

The sign of Scorpio is there ruled by Mars and Pluto.

Mars is in the 3rd house in the sign of Virgo, Pluto is in the second house in the sign of Leo.

Mars is semi-sextile Mercury in the loop in the fourth house in the sign of Libra. Mercury is ruler of the 4th house and the 12th. Mars is also ruler of the loop in the 10th house.

Pluto is semi-sextile the ascendant. It is quincunx Uranus but this has being there for sometime. That's what the outer planets do; hold their degrees and position for a long time.

Mercury in the loop in the fourth house is making a semi-sextile contact with the 5th.

Uranus is exactly conjunct the 7th. Uranus is ruler of the 8th and 9th houses.

The 3/9 axis is in 29 degrees, so is the 4/10 houses.

So from all this we know she gave birth to child.

And of course, Jupiter in the 9th house is trine the ascendant, being ruler of the 6th and 10th houses.

Check your own charts, especially the women to see what's taking place there. Check the fifth house and the sixth house. the rulers of those houses. Check where they are and what aspect they are making to the rest of the chart. And if you had twins, check carefully what you see.

There are many reports about her birth and her death. The same too, about Jesus. Some reckon that Mary was 16 when she was betrothed to Joseph, and that she was 17 when Jesus was born.

I am staying with the age of 13. The Jewish custom is 12 years old.

I had to check many charts of the birth of Jesus, and some of them are way out. The fact is: his chart had to be an important one for astrologers to leave their country and come looking for him. We shall deal with that later.

We have three dates for the death of Mary. We shall look at all three and decide which one makes sense.

The first date we have come from an ancient writer, he gives AD 41. Jesus died 11 years earlier.

The progress date for AD 41 is 18th November BC 19, Midnight, Nazareth, Israel.

Ascendant	01.25	Virgo
2nd	26.33	Virgo
3rd	25.59	Libra
4th	28.33	Scorpio
5th	01.34	Capricorn
6th	02.48	Aquarius
7th	01.25	Pisces
8th	26.33	Pisces
9th	25.59	Aries
10th	28.33	Taurus
11	01.34	Cancer
12th	02.48	Leo

Sun	25.49	Scorpio
Moon	27.37	Taurus
Mercury	25.48	Scorpio
Venus	29.00	Scorpio
Mars	10.12	Libra
Jupiter	09.38	Pisces
Saturn	05.04	Scorpio
Uranus	15.13	Capricorn
Neptune	10.22	Libra
Pluto	15.11 R	Leo
N Node	17.50	Sagittarius
Fortune	03.13	Pisces

Now we are going into deep waters. I hope you can swim, and there is no fear of the big fishes.

Okay then, let's be on our way!

It seems to me that the axis 2/8, Taurus and Scorpio has something to do with when we finish our time on earth.

Planets are either in Taurus or in Scorpio or they are making some contact with the 2nd or the 8th house. In the progress chart of Adolf Hitler, you see that the planet Venus is in the sign of Taurus and making contact to the 8th house. Mars is also ruler of Scorpio and it is making contact with the moon ruler of the 8th.

It is very complicated but you will see it clearly in the long run.

I supposed to be working with the natal and the progress, but it is too much work, so I just stick with the progress. You get more solid information if you have the time to search carefully.

In the progress chart for Mary in Ad 41, we see already that the sun and Mercury are in the sign of Scorpio.

Her moon is up there at the Mid in the sign of Taurus opposing the sun, Mercury and Venus.

Here's one part of the puzzle: look for the ruler of the fourth house and the ruler of the 8th house. See what they are doing. If they are not doing anything, you have to look for planets in the fourth house and the ruler of the 8th, or look for planets in the 8th making contact to the fourth. I told you that it was complicated.

In Mary's progress chart for AD 41 you see that Mars, ruler of the fourth house is exactly conjunct Neptune ruler of the 8th.

Venus the ruler of the 10th house is conjunct the fourth. Notice that the 10th house is in the sign of Taurus. The moon is conjunct there and is ruler of the 11th house.

The ruler of the ascendant is Mercury. It is in the third house conjunct with the sun in Scorpio. They both are in a semi-sextile contact with the third house, and sextile the second. Don't forget that the second house is her body.

Fortune is making a quincunx contact from the 7th house to the 12th.

Duplicates are the first and the second, the seventh and the eighth houses.

We don't know very much about the loops, but as I go along, I'm beginning to see something.

I said that I think that the loops has something to do with *"something extra."*

Here you see loops in 4th and 10th houses.

What about her destiny planet Saturn in the third house in the sign of Scorpio and holding 5 degrees. Saturn is ruler of the 5th and 6th houses.

And do not forget that the fifth house is the house of life. The sun rules this house. In the progress, Saturn rules it.

A date has been given for 45 AD. The progress date is 22nd November BC 19(-18), Nazareth, Israel.

Ascendant	04.43	Virgo
2nd	00.11	Libra
3rd	29.49	Libra
4th	02.19	Sagittarius
5th	05.09	Capricorn
6th	06.14	Aquarius
7th	04.43	Pisces
8th	00.11	Aries
9th	29.49	Aries
10th	02.19	Gemini
11th	05.09	Cancer
12th	06.14	Leo
Sun	29.54	Scorpio
Moon	27.15	Cancer
Mercury	02.09	Sagittarius
Venus	04.02	Sagittarius
Mars	12.48	Libra
Jupiter	09.50	Pisces
Saturn	05.31	Scorpio
Uranus	15.23	Aquarius
Neptune	10.29	Libra
Pluto	15.11 R	Leo
N Node	17.51	Sagittarius
Fortune	02.04	Taurus

In this progress which was done for a midnight time, we have Virgo ascending and the ruler Mercury is in the third house in the sign of Sagittarius exactly conjunct the fourth house. Mercury is square the ascendant by two degrees.

Venus, the ruler of the second and third houses is in the fourth house and exactly square the ascendant. Venus also rules the loop in the 9th house.

Axis 2/8 is zero degree.

Up in the loop in the 9th house in the sign of Taurus we see Fortune in 2 degrees and four minutes making contact with the ruler Mercury.

Don't forget, I have given Fortune as ruling Leo as a *"test."* If it does not work then I would have to look for another sign. But Fortune comes from the ascendant, the moon and the sun.

Uranus in the sixth house in its own sign is opposing Pluto in the 12th house in the sign of Leo. The opposition is exact but these two planets are slow planets and they'll be holding those degrees for some time. Still, we keep an eye on the houses they are in and the signs they rule.

Venus is semi-sextile Saturn in the third house in the loop in the sign of Scorpio.

Venus is also semi-sextile the fifth house.

Saturn is exactly sextile the ascendant, exactly sextile the fifth house.

Jupiter in the 7th house is in contact with Neptune in the second house. Jupiter is ruler of the fourth and also the 7th, Neptune is co-ruler of the 7th.

In this 45 AD progress chart, Mars is the ruler of the 8th house while Jupiter is the ruler of the fourth.

The planets in and around the fourth house does not make any contact with Mars at all, Neither does Jupiter.

If we go to AD 41, we find what we are looking for.

What we find in this chart of AD 41 is that it has a loop in the fourth house. Inside that loop is the sign of Sagittarius ruled by Jupiter. This loop is what I call an *"Extra."* Meaning *"extra home."*

So we have Jupiter making contact with Mars, ruler of the fourth, and the 9th, and with Neptune, ruler of the 7th and the 8th.

Then we have Sun and Mercury in the third exactly in conjunction in the sign of Scorpio. They both are in contact with the third house. The third house has to do with travel.

And you will see that Saturn is holding 5 degrees in the third house also in the sign of Scorpio, and is ruler of the fifth and 6th houses.

So AD 41 is the right chart.

What we have to do now is try and find the right chart of her son. In his chart, the right one, we'll see clearly what happened to his mother in AD 41.

I have a list of most of the dates of his birth, and I just have to check them out.

The first chart that I came across was that of 25th December BC 1(0000) at 23.45 pm, Nazareth, Israel.

At the end of the last chapter I gave you the traditional date of Jesus' birth. here is the wheel.

Ascendant	00.30	Libra
2nd	27.54	Libra
3rd	28.22	Scorpio
4th	00.32	Capricorn
5th	02.41	Aquarius
6th	03.08	Pisces
7th	00.30	Aries
8th	27.54	Aries
9th	28.22	Taurus
10th	00.32	Cancer
11th	02.41	Leo
12th	03.08	Virgo
Sun	05.12	Capricorn
Moon	10.55	Gemini
Mercury	07.18	Capricorn
Venus	20.37	Aquarius
Mars	08.55	Aries
Jupiter	08.46	Libra
Saturn	11.35 R	Gemini
Uranus	26.08	Pisces
Neptune	19.32	Scorpio
Pluto	27.30	Virgo
N Node	29.02	Sagittarius
Fortune	06.13	Pisces

This chart is very interesting and then it lacks some astrological points if we are to compare it to what we have read in the gospels. The main theme is *"love"* and I expected to find the planet Venus in the sign of Pisces; there it is exalted. There are some charts with Venus in Pisces which we shall look at later.

In this chart we have Libra just rising with its ruler Venus, in the 5th house in the sign of Aquarius.

Aquarius is a universal sign, friendly, unusual, scientific, groups, clubs and associations.

Venus in the fifth has a love of creativity, children etc.

We know that Jesus loved children.

Venus has only one aspect, this one is a square going to Neptune in the second house. Neptune is co-ruler of the 6th house. Venus is also ruling the second and 9th houses.

We have duplicate signs of 1 and 2, 7 and 8.

In the first house we have the planet Jupiter, the biggest planet in our solar system.

Jupiter is holding 8 degrees telling us that there's something here that we won't be able to understand.

Jupiter is ruler of the loop in the third house with the sign Sagittarius there, and the north node inside. Jupiter is co-ruler of the 6th house.

Jupiter is square the Mid, the sun and Mercury. These squares are coming from an angular position.

Jupiter is opposing Mars in the 7th house.

Jupiter is trine the moon and Saturn in the loop in the 9th house.

The sun sign is Capricorn. Because we are using the midnight time the sun will always be around that area so we shall not use house position. Only if the person is born at midnight then we can use the 4th house.

People has written songs about Jesus being a Capricorn.

The sun is in a close conjunction with Mercury. The sun is holding 5 degrees and Mercury 7.

The sun is sextile Fortune in the 6th house in the sign of Pisces. The sun is square Mars in the 7th house, and Pluto in the 12th.

The contact with sun and Mars is coming from angular positions. But it is still negative yet strong.

The sun is semi-square Venus in the 5th house.

In the 7th house we see Mars in its own sign of Aries. There's lots of energy here, people can get angry with their partners and with the public. You will find many people with Mars in the 7th house is either divorced, or do not get married.

Mars in the 7th house will work well if it has good aspects from the rest of the chart, and even so, there'll still be some sort of conflict.

When I first saw this chart, I said to myself Jesus would not have married. Some people still take the chance.

Uranus in the 6th house is opposing the ascendant. Fortune is conjunct the 6th house, sextile the sun and Mercury, square the moon and Saturn, trine the Mid.

Mars is sextile the moon and Saturn.

Uranus is square the node in the second house in the loop.

Uranus is quincunx the second house, semi-sextile the 8th, square the Mid.

Notice that the Node is conjunct the 4th house, is square the ascendant.

Notice 0 degree on the ascendant and the Mid.

The destiny planet Saturn, is in the 9th house in a loop with the sign of Gemini and in conjunction with the moon.

The moon rules the 10th house, while Saturn rules the 4th.

The node is semi-sextile the third house.

I want you to read up a lot on the 9th house because it has to do with all religious people. It has to do with space, it has to do with foreign countries and peoples. It has to do with high education, law, philosophy, freedom for self and others.

This ninth house loop is what I call *"extra."*

In my chart, I have experienced a 5/11 loop. I know what has happened, but I'm still thinking about it.

If we do houses contact with this chart we get:

1-5. 2-5, 3-7/12, 4-9, 5-6/9, 6-1/2, 7-7, 8-7, 9-5, 10-9, 11-4?, 12-4

Notice that we have 5-9 twice. This shows that energies are there to be a teacher, and something to do with foreign countries or peoples.

Some people may be baffled by the way we could extract information from a chart with the wrong time. I will explain that in another chapter.

We are now going to progress this chart for when Jesus was 12. We have 6 more days to finish the month of December. We take 6 days from January the next year and we get 12 days (years).

The progress date is then 6th January AD 1 (0001)

Ascendant	12.55	Libra
2nd	10.56	Scorpio
3rd	11.37	Sagittarius
4th	13.57	Capricorn
5th	16.14	Aquarius
6th	16.24	Pisces
7th	12.55	Aries
8th	10.56	Taurus
9th	11.37	Gemini
10th	13.57	Cancer
11th	16.14	Leo
12th	16.24	Virgo
Sun	16.23	Capricorn
Moon	15.58	Scorpio
Mercury	26.41	Capricorn
Venus	02.41	Pisces
Mars	14.36	Aries
Jupiter	09.35	Libra
Saturn	10.52 R	Gemini
Uranus	26.23	Pisces
Neptune	19.49	Scorpio
Pluto	27.30 R	Virgo
N Node	28.58	Sagittarius
Fortune	12.30	Leo

We are told that Jesus when he was 12 went with his parents to Jerusalem.

We notice straight away that Fortune is in the 10th house, in the sign of the 11th house, and is exactly sextile the ascendant. For me, Leo comes under Fortune (a test I'm doing).

Then we have Saturn, his destiny planet in the 8th house but in the 9th house sign, is conjunct the 9th house.

The 9th or the 3rd house is travel.

We also see that Saturn is exactly semi-sextile the 8th house. Is trine the ascendant with 2 degrees, we work with 1 degree.

Jupiter in the 12th house, ruler of the third and sixth houses is trine to Saturn, and semi-sextile the second house.

The moon in January is sextile the 12th house, square the 11th, sextile the sun, quincunx Mars.

Mars is square the Mid.

Mercury, ruler of the 9th and 12th houses is sextile Uranus, ruler of the 5th.

Remember that it is the moon which is moving the fastest in a chart.

In your natal chart, it stays in the same place for all your life.

It is in the progress where it starts to move forward or backward.

Remember too that this chart came down to us from ancient times.

There were lots of messing about with the calendar, and I think that is why there was so much confusion. God knows if we are still on the right road.

I mention earlier that Jesus could be born in October because of his mothers' progress moon making aspects to other planets or points in her chart. Her progressed month starting the year was September. So Jesus could then be born either in September, October, November or even December.

There's another thing you have to remember, in the ancient days, you used to drop the 5 days, these were for celebrations.

You can look at your own progressive chart and see when certain planets are about to change houses or even signs, and see what has taken place in your life.

Remember too, that when a negative aspect is around, and you know about it, you can do something to avert real danger. I do not think that you could completely stop it, for then it would not make any sense.

We shall peep into the chart of Jesus when he was 18 to see what we can find.

The progressed date is 12th January Ad 1 (0001)

Ascendant	17.56	Libra
2nd	16.09	Scorpio
3rd	16.58	Sagittarius
4th	19.27	Capricorn
5th	21.50	Aquarius
6th	21.49	Pisces

7th	17.56	Aries
8th	16.09	Taurus
9th	16.58	Gemini
10th	19.27	Cancer
11th	21.50	Leo
12th	21.49	Virgo
Sun	22.28	Capricorn
Moon	27.15	Capricorn
Mercury	07.09	Aquarius
Venus	09.01	Pisces
Mars	17.49	Aries
Jupiter	09.52	Libra
Saturn	10.32 R	Gemini
Uranus	26.34	Pisces
Neptune	19.58	Scorpio
Pluto	27.18	Virgo
N Node	28.59	Sagittarius
Fortune	22.43	Libra

Still with a Libra ascendant. This is ruled by Venus. Librans are peace loving people. They like harmony and togetherness.

Jupiter is in the 12th house holding 9 degrees. Some times these outer planets stay long in the same degrees.

I've been tuning in to see what they mean. It takes sometime.

Fortune is in the first house conjunct the ascendant with about 4 degrees.

It seems to me wherever Fortune is, that's the house that comes into action.

Fortune is semi-sextile the 12th house, sextile the 11th.

Always check in your own charts because when planets are making contact to the 11th house, it has to do with friendships or groups and clubs.

Fortune is square the Mid 92 degrees.

Fortune is exactly square the sun.

I gave Leo to fall under Fortune as a test.

Here we see that both sun and Fortune rules the 11th house.

Notice that Mercury in the fourth house in 7 degrees is telling us something. To do with the home, the 11th house sign Aquarius, and Mercury is ruler of the 9th and 12th houses.

The moon is passing through the 4th house in Capricorn. There's always some sort of change going on. The moon is ruler of the 10th house.

Remember, the moon is in a position for January.

The moon is semi-sextile the node in the 3rd house.

The moon is sextile Uranus in the 6th house.

The moon is exactly trine Pluto in the 12th house.

Pluto is co-ruler of the 2nd house.

Uranus is ruling the fifth.

Venus in the fifth house is quincunx Jupiter in the 12th. Jupiter is ruling the third and the 6th, Venus is ruling 8th and 1st.

Venus is holding 9 degrees.

Jupiter is holding a trine aspect with Saturn.

Venus is square Saturn.

Neptune in the 2nd house in the sign Scorpio is trine the Mid in Cancer.

And now we have Mars exactly conjunct the 7th house, ruling the 7th, and co-ruler of 2nd.

By now you should know that there's something going on to do with the 11th house, the 5th, the 7th and the 2nd. Also the fourth. Much is going on.

You notice that Saturn is ruler of the 4th and fifth houses. Venus is ruler of the ascendant and 8th house.

The next chart is when Jesus is 30 years old.

The progress date is 24th January AD 1 (0001).

Ascendant	27.54	Libra
2nd	26.29	Scorpio
3rd	27.41	Sagittarius
4th	00.40	Aquarius
5th	03.13	Pisces
6th	02.41	Aries
7th	27.54	Aries
8th	26.29	Taurus
9th	27.41	Gemini
10th	00.40	Leo
11th	03.13	Virgo
12th	02.41	Libra
Sun	04.34	Aquarius
Moon	04.15	Cancer
Mercury	21.54	Aquarius
Venus	20.57	Pisces
Mars	24.26	Aries
Jupiter	10.07	Libra
Saturn	10.03 R	Gemini
Uranus	27.00	Pisces
Neptune	20.11	Scorpio.
Pluto	27.20	Virgo
N Node	28.37	Sagittarius
Fortune	27.35	Pisces

I hope you have seen that the planet Venus is in the sign of Pisces. In this sign Venus is exalted and brings out the love energies more than ever.

There is something to do with friends or a group with Pluto in the 11th house in the sign of Virgo and exactly semi-sextile the ascendant. Pluto is co-ruler of the 2nd house.

Then we have Neptune in the sign of the second house which is a water sign, Scorpio, and is square to Mercury in the 4th house in the sign of Aquarius. Neptune is in the first house.

Mercury is ruler of the 9th and the 11th houses. The sign Mercury is in belongs to the 11th house.

Pluto is square the node in the 3rd house in the sign of Sagittarius. The node itself is conjunct the third house.

Pluto is exactly opposing Uranus. These are two outer planets and they'll be in this position for some time.

Pluto is exactly opposing Fortune. 11th and 5th houses. 6th and 12th signs.

The node is square Uranus and Fortune. The node as ruler of the intercepted sign in the 9th house.

Pluto is square the 9th house, trine the 8th, quincunx the 7th.

We find Uranus is exactly conjunct Fortune in the fifth house. Both are semi-sextile to the 7th house, sextile the 8th, exactly square the 9th.

The axis 10/4 is holding zero degree. Something to do with the outside world, the career and the home and parents.

Jupiter is still holding on to that trine to Saturn in the 8th house.

We now have Saturn passing through the 8th house which actually has to do with magic, and dark things. Pluto is the son of Saturn. Pluto's brothers are Jupiter and Neptune.

The node is sextile the ascendant.

The moon in the intercepted sign in the 9th house is ruler of the sign, and is sextile to 11th house. January it is moving away.

The sun is exactly quincunx the moon. the sun is ruler of the 10th house. The sun is semi-sextile the fifth house.

Mercury is semi-sextile Venus in the 5th house.

Now we have Venus exalted in Pisces and trine Neptune in Scorpio. Pisces is ruled by Neptune. We have houses 1/5, signs 8/12.

Now we are going to look at the chart when he was 45 in AD 41 when the days of his mother ended.

The progress date we have is 8th February AD! (0001).

Ascendant	10.14	Scorpio
2nd	09.21	Sagittarius
3rd	11.22	Capricorn
4th	15.11	Aquarius
5th	17.45	Pisces
6th	16.14	Aries
7th	10.14	Taurus
8th	09.21	Gemini
9th	11.22	Cancer
10th	15.11	Leo
11th	17.45	Virgo
12th	16.14	Libra
Sun	19.35	Aquarius
Moon	24.07	Cancer
Mercury	14.41 R	Aquarius
Venus	03.52	Aries
Mars	02.57	Taurus
Jupiter	09.48 R	Libra
Saturn	09.48 R	Gemini
Uranus	27.39	Pisces
Neptune	20.21	Scorpio
Pluto	27.04 R	Virgo
N Node	28.00	Sagittarius
Fortune	14.46	Aries

There's still a bit of confusion within the astrological community over which house is the mother for the man, and for the woman. In my own chart, the 10th house is my mother. The fourth house that of my father.

So we can say that the 4th and 10th houses are the parents.

In this chart, Jesus has the sign of Leo at the 10th house. The sun is the ruler.

The sun is in the fourth house holding 19 degrees. It seems to be that this has something to do with and end, or a change. I am not absolutely sure.

There's a lot more information within that 19 degrees. It takes a long time to check it out properly.

His ascendant would be her end (4th house).

The sun is square to Neptune in the first house.

His fifth house is her 8th house.

Neptune is co-ruler of the 5th house.

Her body is ruled by Mercury with the sign of Virgo at the 11th house.

Mercury is in the fourth house in the sign of Aquarius conjuncting the fourth house, and exactly sextile to Fortune in the fifth but in the 6th house sign. Fortune has rule over Leo (my test).

Saturn, ruler of the third house and the fourth is in the 8th house holding 9 degrees; and is exactly trine to Jupiter in the 11th house (his mother second) also holding 9 degrees.

Pluto in the 11th house is still exactly opposing Uranus in the fifth house. Uranus is co-ruler of the fourth, while Pluto is co-ruler of the ascendant.

The North Node in the second house is square to Pluto and to Uranus.

Jupiter is exactly trine the 8th house.

Fortune is trine the Mid.

Jupiter is semi-sextile the ascendant. Saturn is quincunx the ascendant.

Venus in the fifth house but in the 6th house sign is semi-sextile Mars in the 6th house.

Venus is ruler of the 7th and 12 houses. Mars is ruler of the ascendant and the 6th.

Here is another natal chart for Jesus.
28th January 7 BC (-6) at 03:34 am, Bethlehem, Israel.

Ascendant	14.21	Capricorn
2nd	22.21	Aquarius
3rd	00.55	Aries
4th	03.01	Taurus
5th	28.41	Taurus
6th	21.13	Gemini
7th	14.21	Cancer
8th	22.21	Leo
9th	00.55	Libra
10th	03.01	Scorpio
11th	28.41	Scorpio
12th	21.13	Sagittarius
Sun	09.15	Pisces
Moon	19.08	Pisces
Mercury	16.29	Aquarius
Venus	19.13	Pisces
Mars	21.00 R	Virgo
Jupiter	02.49	Pisces
Saturn	11.34	Pisces
Uranus	02.16	Pisces
Neptune	05.01 R	Scorpio
Pluto	08.33 R	Virgo
N Node	09.04	Taurus
Fortune	24.14	Capricorn

This chart is powerful. It has 6 planets in the sign of Pisces the fishes.

They are the sun, the moon, Venus, Jupiter, Saturn and Uranus.

Fortune is in the first house showing that the person has to make their own way in life.

Mercury is in the second house in the sign of Aquarius.

The node is in the fourth house in the sign of Taurus.

Mars and Pluto in the loop in the sign of Virgo in the 8th house.

Then we have Neptune in the 10th house.

If we start doing house contact we are going to get house 1 in house 2

House 2 in 2, house 3 in 8, house 4 in 2, house 5 in 2, house 6 in 2, house 7 in 2, house 8 in 2, house 9 in 2, house 10 in 8, house 11 in 8 and house 12 in 2.

We now find that house 2 is very strong. This has to do with his body or with his possessions. And on the opposite side, with other people's possessions.

Have a look back in the traditional chart and you'll see that the moon and Saturn are in conjunction, in the loop, in the sign of Gemini, in the 9th house. The moon is responsible for the 10th house while Saturn is responsible for the 4th house.

In this chart we have Neptune holding a strong position in the 10th house, and is ruler of the loop in the second house. This 10th house belongs to the mother and the individual's career.

Having Mars and Pluto in the 8th house is rather dark. But in this chart they are making good contact with the ascendant. Mars is making contact with the 8th house itself. But Mars is co-ruler of the 8th along with Pluto. And here they are both in the 8th house. Pluto is holding 8 degrees and is co-ruler of the 10th and 11th houses along with Mars.

The 11th house is the individual's friends, so this gives us a contact of 11/8.

Mars is exactly square the 12th house.

Inside the loop in the second house we have Jupiter and Uranus exactly in conjunction; and they both are in trine to the Mid. Inside this same loop, we have the planet Venus and the moon in exact conjunction. By the way, Jupiter rules the loop and the 12th house while Venus rules the 4th, 5th and 9th houses. The moon rules the 7th.

The ascendant in this chart is Capricorn. Capricorn people always want to be at the top in their profession. The ruler of Capricorn is Saturn and it is in the second house in the sign of Pisces, in the loop.

Saturn is very sympathetic, and kind, wanting to help others. . it is conjunct Venus and the moon and the sun.

Both Venus and the moon are sextile to the ascendant. Have you ever found someone with Venus to the ascendant and not showing some kind of love or beauty?

Both Venus and the moon are sextile to Fortune in the first house.

The sun is sextile the ascendant; and the ascendant ruler, Saturn is sextile the ascendant.

Mercury is semi-sextile the ascendant.

The sun, Jupiter, Saturn and Uranus are all opposing Pluto.

Venus and the moon are opposing Mars.

Pluto is sextile the Mid.

The sun is trine Neptune and the Mid. We also have the ascendant ruler, Saturn, trine to Neptune and the Mid.

Mercury semi-sextile to the moon and Venus.

Saturn is sextile the node.

The sun is exactly sextile the node.

Mercury is square the node.

The node is opposing Neptune and the Mid.

The node is trine Pluto.

We see that something is happening in the 3/9 axis.

Now I will show all the dates that I have. You can look them up if you have the time.

7th January AD 3 at 04:50 am.
18th February BC 5 (-0004) at 21:04 pm.
1st March BC 7 (-0006) at 01:30 am or 01:21 am.
1st September BC 2 (-0001) at 04:30 am.
10th September BC 3 (-0002) at 00:23 am.
3rd May BC 7 (-0006) at 05:45 am.
10th August BC 3 (-0002) at 23:11 pm.
Pierre d'Ailly's chart of Jesus: 24th December BC 1 (0000) at 22:12 pm.
Jerome Cardan's chart of Jesus: 25th December BC 1 (0000) at 00:07 am.
Tiberio Russiliano's chart of Jesus:
25th December BC 1 (0000) at 00:21am.
The early classical astrologers selected the year BC 1.
According to the internet the first complete chart of Jesus was cast by French scholar and ecclesiastic Cardinal Pierre d'Ailly (1350-1420).

Those of you who are deeply interested, you can see what you make of all those dates. One thing is for sure. You have to know what the four gospels are telling you.

13: Here, There and Everywhere

In the beginning, I had my say too about this astrology business. I said that it was rubbish, ridiculous, it can't be true. How wrong I was. I spent a few years working on charts of people who I knew, especially close families. But you cannot stop some men and women from having their say. And they do so without checking anything. If you only knew how many times I have heard people ranting and raving against astrology. Not many people can swallow the truth; and I have already said many times, astrology is true. Haven't you heard of Isaac Newton? He took astrology as his life's work and not astronomy. The other scientists raved at him, he told them, "I have studied it, and you haven't."

I want you to draw a line across your paper. Put "A" at the beginning. Put "B" in the middle, and "C" at the end.

B represents yourself and now – the present. A represents the past, and C represents the future – events that are to come.

With your accurate birth time at B, you can work back to A; and also work forward to C.

Any time charted between A to C will refer to you as the individual. So if you were to take intervals of 20 minutes – each chart that you erect, will give you information, and each one would be correct. You'll be seeing different planetary combinations than what is set up for B.

I wrote about intervals of 20 minutes but this could also be years. Between B and A there are events that are long gone. You can work back from B as many years as you want, then erect a chart. You can do the same from B to C.

Remember that everything works in a circle and always finds itself back at B which is the present.

Suppose you got married at age 20, this is between B and C. All you need to do is erect a chart for 20 years from B.

If you knew for sure the exact year Adam and Eve were created, you could erect a chart for those years from B to A.

CONCEPTION MONTH

If you were born in the month of January, count four months forward to April, this is your conception month. Now you have to go back 1 year.

If you were born in February, your conception month is May.

If you were born in March, your conception month is June.

If you were born in April, your conception month is July.

If you were born in May, your conception month is August.

If you were born in June, your conception month is September.

If you were born in July, your conception month is October.

If you were born in August, your conception month is November.
If you were born in September, your conception month is December.
If you were born in October, your conception month is January.
If you were born in November, your conception month is February.
If you were born in December, your conception month is March.

Remember you move from the month you were born, counting four months forward, then you subtract one year from your birth year.

This has to do with normal births of 9 months.

Let us quickly run through a chart. This man was a poet. He has Aquarius rising with 5.43 degrees. If we take the classical ruler only, we end up with Saturn. Saturn is in the sixth house in Cancer. Mars is in the same sign with Saturn but not in conjunction. The moon is conjuncting the ascendant with 10. 29 Aquarius. The moon is semi-sextile to the 12th. There's a loop in the first house with the sign of Pisces in it. Duplicates are 4th and 5th both in Gemini. 10th and 11th in Sagittarius. In the 7th house is the loop carrying the sign Virgo. Venus is in that sign.

The sun is in the sign of Leo in the 7th house semi-sextile to the 6th. The sun is conjunct the 7th house. In the 7th house is also the node in 19.12 Leo.

Uranus as co-ruler of the ascendant is in the 8th house conjunct the 8th house. Jupiter is also in the 8th house. Both planets in the sign of Libra.

The mid axis is 5.28 Sagittarius. Mercury is in the sixth house in the sign of Leo with 02.09 degrees. Neptune is in the third in Taurus. Pluto is in the third with 04.53 Gemini.

Looking at his progress chart for the year he is no more, we find the ascendant is Pisces in 23 degrees and 18 minutes. The rulers are Jupiter and Neptune. Jupiter is in the 7th in the 8th house sign of Scorpio with 1 degree and 44 minutes. Neptune is in the second house but the third sign of Gemini with 00.04 degree. The third house axis is Gemini 08.54

The 6th and 12th axis is also in 8 degrees (8.43).

The Mid axis is 27.26 Sagittarius.

Mars and Pluto are rulers of the 8th house. Mars is in the fifth house conjunct Saturn, both in the sign of Leo. Mars is holding 00.25, and Saturn 01.08 degree.

Both Mars and Saturn are square to Jupiter.

The sun is in the sign of Virgo in the 6th house with 04.09 degrees. Pluto is in the second house but in the third sign of Gemini with 05.03 degrees. The sun is square Pluto.

Venus is still in the loop in the 7th house in the sign of Libra holding 05.58 degrees. Venus is semi-sextile to the sun, exactly trine Pluto.

The moon is in the 10th house in Sagittarius conjuncting the Mid. The degrees of the moon are 28.45. The moon is square the ascendant, quincunx Neptune.

Jupiter is quincunx Neptune. Mars and Saturn sextile Neptune.

Mercury, the ruler of the 3rd, 4th and 7th houses is in the 6th in the sign of Leo with 20.59 degrees, conjuncting the node with 3 degrees.

I don't know what you make of this but the chart is showing that there's no more life for the individual, the chart is still working and is there for anyone to check the past and the future.

The natal chart is for 3rd August 1887 at 19.30 pm, Rugby, UK.

He was no more in the year 1915.

Let's have a quick look at President *Donald Trump*'s chart.

It is for the 14th June 1946 at 10:51 am, Jamaica, New York, U.S.A.

Ascendant	29.50	Leo
2nd	23.01	Virgo
3rd	21.13	Libra
4th	24.22	Scorpio
5th	29.21	Sagittarius
6th	01.45	Aquarius
7th	29.58	Aquarius
8th	23.01	Pisces
9th	21.13	Aries
10th	24.22	Taurus
11th	29.21	Gemini
12th	01.45	Leo
Sun	22.55	Gemini
Moon	21.12	Sagittarius
Mercury	08.51	Cancer
Venus	25.44	Cancer
Mars	26.44	Leo
Jupiter	17.27 R	Libra
Saturn	23.48	Cancer
Uranus	17.53	Gemini
Neptune	05.50 R	Libra
Pluto	10.02	Leo
N Node	20.48	Gemini
Chiron	14.54	Libra
Fortune	28.15	Aquarius

Here we see this chart has Leo rising almost at its end. The ruler, the sun is up in the 10th house in the sign of Gemini conjunct with Uranus and the node. The sun is about 27 degrees from the Mid, I think we can call this a semi-sextile.

The sun is conjunct the 11th house. It is just about making a sextile aspect with the ascendant. The sun is semi-sextile Saturn in the loop in the 11th house, also Venus in the same loop. The sun is sextile the planet Mars in the 12th house in the ascendant sign of Leo. There is a semi-square between the sun and Pluto. The sun is trine Jupiter and Chiron in the second house in the sign of Libra. There's an opposition between the sun and the moon, both planets in an angular position. The moon in the fourth house in the sign of Sagittarius.

The ascendant ruler is sextile the 9th house, square to the 8th.

From all that information we can tell that the President has a chance of holding a top job. (I should say the individual because he's now president.) A chance of having many friends and groups and clubs. Connection with foreign peoples and countries. He is a talkative person, likes communications, is scientific. Has the chance to be very rich (Jupiter in the second house; and with a good aspect from the sun). Loves his home and his country. (Three planets in Cancer). Very sensitive, balanced and harmonious.

We see that he has two planets along with the moon's north node in the sign of Gemini.

He has Mercury, Venus and Saturn in Cancer in the loop in the 11th house. Something extra is happening here in this 11th house.

His destiny planet, Saturn is not very strong in the sign of Cancer but it has a conjunction with Venus. This could make for someone who is loyal (love and discipline).

Even though Saturn is not working that well in the sign of Cancer, it has a sextile to the Mid.

That is what Saturn wants: power. It is exactly trine with the 8th house. This has to do with other people's possessions. other people money will come to him. And don't for get that the 8th house is that of politics as well. This is where the home or nation speculate, or parents. A lot of energies are coming from Cancer.

In Libra at the third house, we find the planet Jupiter, Neptune and Chiron in that sign. Energies are here for being harmonious and togetherness and the public and marriage partnerships. Having Jupiter alone in Libra shows a person who is very kind and harmonious, likes to have peace.

We find Mars in the 12th house with Pluto in the same sign, which is the ascendant sign. In the 12th house, Mars is secretive. There's lots of energy here because it is connected with the ascendant. You find many people with this contact who are fighters, military commanders, but not every one who has this contact will be military commanders. They probably use the energies for something else.

The moon in the sign of Sagittarius is long-reaching. Interested in high education, travel, freedom for self and others. This person is interested in space. Sagittarius is the sign of space and of foreign countries. The moon is in its own house – the fourth. Just about conjuncting the fifth. In a sextile aspect with Jupiter. And almost a sextile with Chiron. 111 degrees to the ascendant, trine Mars. It opposes the sun, Uranus and the node. And we see it is quincunx the Mid, this aspect is negative but still gives publicity while the moon holds a strong position in the 4th. The Moon is ruler of the loop in the 11th house.

Mars is semi-sextile Saturn and Venus in the loop in the 11th house.

Notice the destiny planet Saturn is conjunct the 12th house showing that the destiny has to do with something secret or working behind the scenes for the benefit of others. Saturn is ruler of the opposite loop with Capricorn in it. Saturn rules the 6th, and 7th along with Uranus.

We find Neptune holding 5 degrees in the second house and is co-ruler of the 8th house.

Jupiter in the second is semi-square the ascendant.

Mars is square the Mid.

The node in the 10th house is sextile the 9th.

Venus is the ruler of the 3rd and 10th houses. It is sextile the Mid.

Jupiter in the second house is exactly trine Uranus in the 10th house.

Fortune is in the 6th house conjunct the 7th, trine the 11th. It is square the Mid. Fortune opposes Mars.

Looking at this chart, it is easy to tell the mother what her child would turn out to be.

I was about to let someone know that I was planning to check every ray of the sun. I held back because they would have thought of me as a mad man. But really! I wasn't planning such a thing. In astrology you can get involved in making a chart for every event – that too, is madness. But nothing stops a human being from doing so if he wants to. The mere fact though is that you are just playing with time and space. Could you imagine making a chart for when you first went to school, and when you had your first kiss? It can be done. Or when your parents move house, or when you got your first job?

Well, the planetary world knows everything. The chart that you did create when you got your first kiss, will tell you about the future, and so is all the other charts. They are all different from your own birth chart. But you see, we don't waste time doing so.

We are not looking properly at the chart and all the aspects within it. We should do so. Two planets that are not in an angular position and making a square to each other will bring trouble in the signs and houses they are in; and also the houses they rule. A person with common sense will avert some of the negative energies.

In seems to me that the node in the 10th house is a good position for the career.

I don't know yet what to say about Fortune. Try and see if you can get any insight to what it is actually doing.

We can have a quick peek into the chart of *James Dewey Watson* born 6th April 1928 at 01:23 am, Chicago, Illinois, U.S.A.

Ascendant	14.13	Capricorn
2nd	27.46	Aquarius
3rd	09.18	Aries
4th	09.51	Taurus
5th	02.53	Gemini
6th	22.58	Gemini
7th	14.13	Cancer
8th	27.46	Leo
9th	09.18	Libra
10th	09.51	Scorpio
11th	02.53	Sagittarius
12th	22.58	Sagittarius
Sun	16.14	Aries
Moon	28.58	Libra
Mercury	22.35	Pisces
Venus	23.32	Pisces
Mars	29.00	Aquarius
Jupiter	16.28	Aries
Saturn	19.04 R	Sagittarius
Uranus	04.06	Aries
Neptune	26.38 R	Leo
Pluto	14.59	Cancer
Chiron	04.26	Taurus
N Node	10.45	Gemini
Fortune	26.57	Cancer

We have to read this chart as if if we don't know who is the owner. We are not trying to find out what job he's going to do for human beings can be good at more than one job. What we are after is to find the energies in this natal chart that the individual could use as a foundation to project themselves forward. And you must not forget that energies are given in each progressive year.

I am not going to the ascendant as we should normally do but I'm going right into the loop in the second house. Because of this loop, duplicates come at the 11th and 12th houses; and the 5th and 6th houses.

Inside this loop, we have two planets in Pisces. They are Mercury and Venus. When Mercury is in Pisces the individual has the ability to be a psychic, able to feel and sense things that ordinary people cannot sense.

Venus is exalted in the sign of Pisces and the love energies could be very strong. In the loop this is something extra (my test).

Notice that Mercury is holding 22 degrees. I've been trying for sometime to get some meaning about it.

Mercury is exactly square the 12th. Mercury is also moving away from a sextile aspect with the ascendant. Mercury is square Saturn in the sign of Sagittarius in the 11th house. Mercury is trine Fortune in the 7th house. Just about making a quincunx to Neptune in the 7th house. Mercury is sesqui-quadrate to the Mid.

We see three planets in the sign of Aquarius all hanging around the third house. The sign on the third house is Aries has to do with beginnings and ideas. The planets are Sun, Jupiter and Uranus all conjunct the 3rd house. Uranus is in the second house. The sun and Jupiter is exactly in conjunction.

The individual will function more as an Aquarian, and as a Pisces, and as a Cancerian because of Pluto and Fortune in the sign of Cancer.

The moon is in Libra in the 9th house. The moon is trine the second house with Mars in there in the sign of Aquarius. This is much endurance, lots of energy. Mars is conjunct the second house, this is scientific and much energy. Notice that Mars is in 29 degrees and is ruler of the third and tenth houses. Mars is sextile to Chiron in the third house in the sign of Taurus.

Chiron is conjunct the fourth house.

Notice that the sun is in the same sign with Uranus, and you always find this contact with scientists; the sun making some sort of contact with Uranus.

The sun is square Pluto in the 7th house. Jupiter is also square Pluto. Both Sun and Jupiter are square to the ascendant.

Uranus is exactly semi-sextile Chiron, sextile the node in the fifth house.

Don't forget this fifth house is ruled by the sun and is the house of life and creativity etc. If we go up to 10 degrees then the sun and Jupiter would be trine to Neptune in the 7th house.

Venus is trine Fortune. Fortune is semi-sextile the 8th house. Fortune is exactly semi-sextile Neptune.

Pluto is exactly conjunct 7th house, trine the Mid; and is ruler of the 10th house. Opposing the ascendant.

Neptune is conjunct the 8th house, sextile the moon. Opposing Mars.

The node in the fifth house is trine the 9th, and quincunx the Mid. The node is given ruler of the 7th house by me as a test.

So we see with all the energies in this chart, the individual has the ability to do some secret work, or something strange to do with the 8th and 12th houses, and the fifth and third. We must not forget that the third is ruled by Mercury.

Note: You must take time checking the chart properly. If you progress it, always check it with the natal one.

As I have already told you the 22 degrees seems to me as if it is working magically or disruptively or even scientifically. I would need to have lots of charts and to know the individuals who are owners of the charts. But sometimes that's not possible.

What I'm trying to do as well is to use the numbers and try to work them in the chart. So that when any point or planet is holding a certain number, we get information straight away why it is holding that number.

And you must not forget too, that when you're looking at a chart, keep at the back of your mind, the fixed chart. I always see the ascendant as energetic with Mars as ruler, finding where it is and what it is doing. Of course the ascendant could be weak according to what aspects it is receiving.

A quick look at the chart of *Sigmund Freud* born 6th May 1856 at 18:30 pm, Freiberg/Mahren, Czech Republic.

Ascendant	10.10	Scorpio
2nd	08.58	Sagittarius
3rd	14.55	Capricorn
4th	23.39	Aquarius
5th	26.16	Pisces
6th	21.04	Aries
7th	10.10	Taurus
8th	08.58	Gemini
9th	14.55	Cancer
10th	23.39	Leo
11th	26.16	Virgo
12th	21.04	Libra
Sun	16.19	Taurus
Moon	14.40	Gemini
Mercury	27.47	Taurus
Venus	26.11	Aries
Mars	03.22 R	Libra
Jupiter	29.34	Pisces
Saturn	27.32	Gemini
Uranus	20.35	Taurus
Neptune	19.51	Pisces
Pluto	04.26	Taurus
Chiron	05.41	Aquarius
N Node	23.27	Aries
Fortune	08.31	Sagittarius

In 1886 he married and had six children.

1907 became friends with Carl Jung.

1923 diagnosed with cancer. He had 33 operations.

1938 he fled to London.

1939 upon his request a friend administered a lethal dose of morphine, ending his life.

The ascendant sign is Scorpio with the rulers being Mars and Pluto. Mars is in the 11th house in the sign of Libra conjunct the 12th house. Pluto is in the 6th house in the sign of Taurus conjunct the 7th house.

Pluto is in the same house sign as the sun, Mercury and Uranus. So we have four planets in the sign of Taurus. We can say that he will show these energies more than the Scorpion ascendant; and more than the two planets in the fifth house – Jupiter and Neptune, in Pisces. More than the two planets in the 8th house – the moon and Saturn, in the sign of Gemini; and more than the node and Venus in the sign of Aries in the sixth house.

Mars is about 53 degrees from the Mid. About 95 degrees from Saturn; about 125 degrees from Mercury; and 133 degrees from Uranus. It is about 175 degrees from Jupiter; about 150 degrees from Neptune.

Pluto is sextile Saturn; square the Mid;conjunct the node and Venus; semi-sextile Jupiter

We see that the sun is conjunct Uranus in the 7th house. People with sun and Uranus contact can work in the scientific field. And we see also that Mercury is conjunct Uranus.

The destiny planet, Saturn is in the house of Pluto. The moon sign is Gemini in the 8th house conjunct the 8th.

People with the moon in the 8th house has great insight. The moon is sextile the Mid. It is semi-square Venus; square Neptune.

Mercury is semi-sextile Venus; exactly semi-sextile Saturn.

We get about 82 degrees from the sun to the Mid.

The sun is sextile Neptune. Uranus sextile Neptune. Saturn square Jupiter.

Both the node and Venus are sextile to Saturn.

The node and Venus shows a deep love. In the sign of Aries, assertive, energetic, full of ideas.

The contact between Venus and Saturn is very good, shows loyalty in love.

If you do house contact you'll get more information.

Note: I have two charts of Sigmund Freud, one giving 09.39 degrees of Scorpio with 09:39 Leo as the Mid heaven; this was from the Equal house system.

The next one is the Placidus system giving 10.10 degrees of Scorpio as the ascendant and 23.39 degrees of Leo as Mid heaven.

Now to have a quick look at the chart of *Roger Federer* born 8th August 1981 at 08:40 am, Basel, Switzerland.

Ascendant	11.00	Virgo
2nd	03.32	Libra
3rd	01.55	Scorpio
4th	06.08	Sagittarius
5th	12.21	Capricorn
6th	14.25	Aquarius
7th	11.00	Pisces
8th	03.32	Aries
9th	01.55	Taurus
10th	06.08	Gemini
11th	12.21	Cancer
12th	14.25	Leo
Sun	15.37	Leo
Moon	20.44	Scorpio
Mercury	13.27	Leo
Venus	17.41	Virgo
Mars	13.56	Cancer
Jupiter	07.18	Libra
Saturn	06.12	Libra
Uranus	26.03	Scorpio
Neptune	22.15 R	Sagittarius
Pluto	21.55	Libra
Chiron	22.40	Taurus
N Node	00.54	Leo
Fortune	16.07	Sagittarius

In this chart Virgo is on the ascendant; it is in the 11th house in the sign of Leo. The 11th house in the fixed wheel is ruled by both Saturn and Uranus.

We see that Mercury is conjunct the sun which is in the 12th house and also in the sign of Leo. This combination of the sun and Mercury is good for the intellect.

The node is also in the 11th house with Mercury about 12 degrees and some minutes away.

Inside the first house and in the ascendant sign, we see the planet Venus.

Already, we see that the person is a bit shy, likes things to be pure, and he is fiery because of Mercury in the sign of Leo. And he likes friendships and groups and clubs.

To have Venus in an angular position is very good; the person is full of love and can be an artist or a singer or anything to do with Venus.

Venus has a sextile coming to it from the moon in the third house in the sign of Scorpio.

So we see that the ascendant is Virgo, with a Leo sun, and a Scorpio moon.

Seeing that the moon is responses and feelings and emotions, and it is in good aspect with Venus, it tells us that things will go well where it has to do with love and his feelings towards it. There'll be lots of travelling – short and long.

Venus is getting a square aspect from the fourth house from both Fortune and Neptune. They're all in an angular position and will not cause much problems.

Notice his destiny planet in the second house, is exalted in the sign of Libra; and is exactly trine the Mid.

Saturn making contact with the Mid is good for the career, even if it is negative. It is up to the person to behave themselves and act in a good way. For Saturn always bring the individual down if he acts negatively. You will find in the charts of many leaders that Saturn is doing something. If not natally, it will find its way progressively to make some sort of contact with the Mid or with a planet ruling the Mid.

Saturn is in conjunction with Jupiter in the second house also in the sign of Libra.

These two planets could lead to 9th house energies

In the chart, Jupiter rules the fourth and the 7th, while Saturn is ruler of the 5th and the 6th houses. Remember that in this chart Saturn is powerful.

The 5th house has to do with sports, children, entertainment and speculations. The 6th house is work and colleagues and pets and sickness.

Saturn is semi-square the moon.

We find Mercury as ascendant ruler is conjunct the 12th house while in the 11th. Is semi-sextile the 11th. Is 27 degrees from the ascendant. Exactly semi-sextile Mars also in the 11th house but in the sign of Cancer. Mercury is just about making a sextile to the Mid.

It is said that when planets are leaving a contact that they are strong. We find Mercury leaving a contact with Pluto. Now these two planets would give deep insight.

If we use an eight degree limit for a sextile we would find that Mercury is sextile Saturn, and also sextile Jupiter.

Mercury is square the moon, trine Fortune.

Notice Jupiter in Libra in the second house. This placing can give the opportunity to become rich. Jupiter in Libra is nice feelings, togetherness, kind.

Jupiter is also trine the Mid.

Mars in the sign of Cancer is not so powerful but it is in the 11th house which is the house of Saturn and Uranus and so turns out to be powerful. Try and find someone with Mars and Uranus, then you'll see what I mean.

Mars is conjunct the 11th and also semi-sextile the 12th. It is sextile the ascendant, sextile Venus, square Jupiter and Saturn, trine the moon, quincunx Fortune, sesqui-quadrate Uranus, square Pluto.

The sun is in the 12th conjunct the 12th. This position is of someone who has to work behind the scenes, sometimes to help others. They like privacy. The sun is semi-sextile Venus.

The sun is sextile Pluto and this is a power house with deep insight and plenty of energy, ability to change. The sun is square the moon. The sun is trine Fortune and Neptune.

When dealing with astrology remember that upbringing and heredity and the environment are important factors.

Be very careful about the aspects because they could be very misleading. A negative aspect could work out for good in a person who doesn't give up, while a positive aspect could be detriment. I mean you could see a positive aspect in a chart, and you think it's good; while it could be showing the death of someone.

Always remember too that Mars represents yourself and the first house; and you coming into this physical world. The sun is life. Always keep the fixed wheel in the back of your head when looking at a chart. And don't forget your house contacts.

For those of you who are fearful do not check the next two charts.

This progress chart is of a woman who died of Melanoma.
The progress date is 7th March 1963 at 22:00 pm, Washington, DC, U.S.A.

Ascendant	04.34	Scorpio
2nd	03.12	Sagittarius
3rd	05.46	Capricorn
4th	10.37	Aquarius
5th	13.22	Pisces
6th	11.32	Aries
7th	04.34	Taurus
8th	03.12	Gemini
9th	05.46	Cancer
10th	10.37	Leo
11th	13.32	Virgo
12th	11.32	Libra
Sun	16.49	Pisces
Moon	21.57	Leo
Mercury	28.15	Aquarius
Venus	04.13	Aquarius
Mars	05.48 R	Leo

Jupiter	23.29	Pisces
Saturn	17.38	Aquarius
Uranus	02.40 R	Virgo
Neptune	15.33 R	Scorpio
Pluto	10.43 R	Virgo
N Node	27.11	Cancer
Fortune	09.42	Aries

If you want to work with the natal chart, it is the 2nd February 1963 at 22:00pm.

The progressed ascendant in this chart is Scorpio, with Neptune in the first house in the sign of Scorpio.

The rulers of the ascendant are Mars and Pluto.

Mars is in the 9th house in the sign of Leo and holding 5 degrees, squaring the ascendant; and exactly semi-sextile to the 9th, also holding 5 degrees. The sign there is Cancer. Did you get that?

Mars is opposing Venus in the third house but in the fourth house sign.

Pluto is in the 10th house in the sign of Virgo and is exactly semi-sextile the Mid. Pluto is also semi-sextile the 12th house.

Now let us look at Mercury, ruler of the 8th house. It is in the fourth.

Saturn and Uranus are rulers of the fourth house. We have Mercury with Saturn; at a distance of about 10 degrees.

We have Uranus up in the 10th house making a square to the second house (the body or possessions).

Mercury is opposing Uranus with about 175 degrees.

Venus is semi-sextile the third house; and square the ascendant, sextile the second.

We have the progress moon in the 10th house with 21 degrees and 57 minutes for the month of March. The individual died 2nd November 1996.

If we count from April to November, moving the moon about 1 degree a month, we get it to be in 29 degrees of Leo, and opposing Mercury the ruler of the 8th and 11th houses.

The moon is ruler of the 9th house. We find also the node there in the sign of Cancer making a quincunx aspect to Mercury.

The fifth house, the house of life is rule by both Jupiter and Neptune. Jupiter itself is in the fifth house and making a sesqui-quadrate aspect to the ascendant with about 3 degrees orb.

The sun is in the fifth house, ruler of the 10th, and semi-sextile Saturn in the fourth house. Do you get it?

The sun is also trine to Neptune in the first house in the sign of Scorpio. The opposite sign is Taurus. Do you get it.

When you work with the natal, you get more information.

Fortune is trine the Mid but is quincunx Pluto.

Our next chart for a quick look through is progressive date of 23rd November 1925. This has to do with an overdose so I hope you know what to look for. The time is 11:24 am, Mineola, New York, U.S.A.

Remember some charts are easy to read than others.

Ascendant	04.49	Aquarius
2nd	22.01	Pisces
3rd	29.50	Aries
4th	26.47	Taurus
5th	18.23	Gemini
6th	09.17	Cancer
7th	04.49	Leo
8th	22.01	Virgo
9th	29.56	Libra
10th	26.47	Scorpio
11th	18.23	Sagittarius
12th	09.17	Capricorn
Sun	00.53	Sagittarius
Moon	08.37	Pisces
Mercury	22.45	Sagittarius
Venus	18.02	Capricorn
Mars	06.44	Scorpio
Jupiter	20.41	Capricorn
Staurn	18.39	Scorpio
Uranus	21.35 R	Pisces
Neptune	24.47	Leo
Pluto	14.27 R	Cancer
Chiron	24.33	Aries
N Node	28.20	Cancer
Fortune	12.33	Taurus

The individual was born 13th October 1925.

In this progress wheel we have the ascendant as Aquarius, the rulers being Saturn and Uranus. Saturn is in the sign of Scorpio in the 9th house while Uranus is in the first house in the sign of Pisces.

Saturn is exactly semi-sextile the 11th house, exactly sextile Venus in the 12th house.

Uranus is conjunct the second house and square Mercury in the 11th house. Remember that this 11th house is ruled by Saturn and Uranus in the fixed wheel.

Jupiter is the ruler in this progressive chart.

Mercury is the ruler of the 8th house and it is holding 22 degrees and exactly squaring the 8th house. It is also ruler of the 5th house, the house of life.

The moon in the first house is in the sign of Pisces. It is holding 8 degrees and 37 minutes for the month of November which is the progress date. The overdose took place in August. We just have to move the moon back three degrees, 1 degree per month, and we get it about 5 degrees Pisces in the first house. Then it is semi-sextile the ascendant. The moon is ruler of the 6th house.

You notice that the axis 6/12 is holding 9 degrees. The axis 3/9 is holding 29 degrees. The axis 2/8 is holding 22 degrees.

The moon is making a trine aspect to Mars in the 9th house.

The node in the 6th house in the sign of Cancer is square to the 9th house.

Neptune is square the Mid with about 2 degrees orb. It is trine Mercury with about the same orb.

Jupiter in the 12th house is sextile Uranus in the first house.

Chiron in the second house is quincunx the Mid.

Some astrologers associate Chiron with Capricorn, Aquarius and Virgo.

And some astrologers associate the Node with Taurus.

14: Quick Look and Move On

Here's the chart of *Sir Paul McCartney* born 18th June 1942 at 14:00 pm, Liverpool, United Kingdom.

Ascendant	25.18	Virgo
2nd	18.09	Libra
3rd	17.30	Scorpio
4th	23.44	Sagittarius
5th	00.45	Aquarius
6th	01.16	Pisces
7th	25.18	Pisces
8th	18.09	Aries
9th	17.30	Taurus
10th	23.44	Gemini
11th	00.45	Leo
12th	01.16	Virgo
Sun	26.37	Gemini
Moon	17.26	Leo
Mercury	18.22 R	Gemini
Venus	19.00	Taurus
Mars	02.41	Leo
Jupiter	01.50	Cancer
Saturn	05.13	Gemini
Uranus	01.58	Gemini
Neptune	27.07	Virgo
Pluto	04.16	Leo
Chiron	12.09	Leo.
N Node	07.55	Virgo
Fortune	16.08	Scorpio

Almost everyone knows about Sir Paul McCartney from the Beatles and how famous they were.

In his chart we find Virgo rising with Neptune right there in the first house and ruler of the 7th.

The sun is in Gemini in the 10th house in a group with Mercury, Saturn and Uranus. Mercury is conjunct the sun, and Saturn conjunct Uranus.

The Saturn Uranus conjunction can bring out genius qualities. Can make one intellectual.

The sun is conjunct Jupiter.

Jupiter is exalted in the sign of Cancer and is also in the 10th house.

This is a very high position and people can do well in their career.

The moon is in the 11th house in the sign of Leo in a group with Mars and Pluto. So we see that he is a strong Gemini, followed by a strong Leo followed by the ascendant Virgo.

We see Venus in the 9th house in Taurus. This is a sign of travel to other countries, long and short.

Fortune is in the second house.

His ruling planet Mercury is conjunct the Mid.

This next chart is of *Sylvia Browne* (Sylvia Celeste Shoemaker). Born 19th October 1936 at 14:00 pm, Kansas City, Missouri. U.S.A. She was born with a caul. Psychic gifted all her life. Spirit took over her body when she was 8.

Ascendant	04.53	Aquarius
2nd	20.48	Pisces
3rd	28.34	Aries
4th	25.51	Taurus
5th	17.53	Gemini
6th	09.10	Cancer
7th	04.53	Leo
8th	20.48	Virgo
9th	28.34	Libra
10th	25.51	Scorpio
11th	17.53	Sagittarius
12th	09.10	Capricorn
Sun	26.15	Libra
Moon	14.05	Sagittarius
Mercury	08.44	Libra
Venus	25.51	Scorpio
Mars	14.22	Virgo
Jupiter	21.12	Sagittarius
Saturn	16.34 R	Pisces
Uranus	08.02 R	Taurus
Neptune	17.55	Virgo
Pluto	28.44	Cancer
Chiron	23.09	Gemini
N Node	25.53	Sagittarius
Fortune	22.43	Pisces

The ascendant is Aquarius. Saturn and Uranus are the rulers. Saturn in the first in Pisces conjunct the second house. This shows an early start in life. very kind, compassionate and helpful. Interest in old things.

Uranus is in the third house in the sign of Taurus which is the fourth house sign. Notice that Uranus is holding 8 degrees. Inside the third house, Uranus could be scientific, unusual and communicative.

The sun sign is Libra. The sun is in the 8th house conjunct the 9th house, and having Mercury in the same sign.

Notice that Mercury too, is holding 8 degrees.

After reading some mythology about Mercury being in the domain of Pluto, I came with the theory that people with Mercury in the 8th house, or conjuncting the same or making any contact with Pluto has some sort of deep insight; and can ferry out things that others can't do. Remember, I am not working out any aspects with these quick charts.

The moon sign is Sagittarius. The moon is in the 10th house with Jupiter and the node in the same.

Notice the planet Venus exactly conjunct the Mid.

Mars and Neptune conjunct in the 7th house; both conjuncting the 8th house.

Mercury is ruler of the 5th and 8th houses.

Fortune is in the second house conjunct the second and Saturn.

Mars is exactly square the moon.

This next chart is very interesting. It is an event chart. It is of the *Chernobyl Explosion* on 26th April 1986 at 01.30 am, Chernobyl, Ukraine.

Ascendant	22.49	Sagittarius
2nd	05.20	Aquarius
3rd	22.49	Pisces
4th	26.31	Aries
5th	19.18	Taurus
6th	06.51	Gemini
7th	22.49	Gemini
8th	05.20	Leo
9th	22.49	Virgo
10th	26.31	Libra
11th	19.18	Scorpio
12th	06.51	Sagittarius
Sun	05.22	Taurus
Moon	24.26	Scorpio
Mercury	10.58	Aries
Venus	28.53	Taurus
Mars	13.08	Capricorn
Jupiter	14.23	Pisces
Saturn	08.35 R	Sagittarius

Uranus	22.00 R	Sagittarius
Neptune	05.43 R	Capricorn
Pluto	05.59 R	Scorpio
Chiron	11.55	Gemini
N Node	29.59	Aries
Fortune	11.53	Cancer

The 22 degrees is rather puzzling. I'm trying to get a good hold on what it is saying. I have seen it so often in charts.

In this event chart you see 22 degrees of Sagittarius rising. Uranus is exactly conjunct and is in the 12th house. Jupiter is the ruler of the ascendant.

Jupiter is in the second house but in the third house sign of Pisces. And notice, the third house is also holding 22 degrees.

There is a loop in the first house with the sign of Capricorn. In this loop are Mars and Neptune.

I don't know if you know this, but Mars and Neptune are really two dangerous planets. I must say when they are in conjunction and negative.

Saturn is the ruler of the loop in the first house, and is in the 12th house in the sign of Sagittarius holding 8 degrees. This is something that is out of our power.

Jupiter, the ruler of the ascendant is sextile Mars.

The node is in the fourth house holding 29 degrees.

Venus ruler of the 5th and 10th houses is in the fifth and semi-sextile the node.

Uranus is exactly square the 3rd house.

The sun in the 4th is holding 5 degrees. The sun is ruler of the 8th.

Uranus is ruler of the second along with Saturn.

Neptune in the loop is also in 5 degrees.

Pluto in the 10th house is in 5 degrees.

There's a loop in the 7th house with Fortune in it and it is square to Mercury in the 3rd house.

Duplicate at 12/1, 6/7.

2/8 axis in 5 degrees.

This chart is of *Jean Migures* born 11th May 1940 at 23:00 pm, Alger, Algeria.

He claimed he was kidnapped and used for experiments aboard a flying saucer. His mission began 11th August 1969.

Ascendant	03.23	Capricorn
2nd	11.03	Aquarius
3rd	20.57	Pisces
4th	24.23	Aries

5th	20.23	Taurus
6th	12.11	Gemini
7th	03.23	Cancer
8th	11.03	Leo
9th	20.57	Virgo
10th	24.23	Libra
11th	20.23	Scorpio
12th	12.11	Sagittarius
Sun	21.02	Taurus
Moon	13.29	Cancer
Mercury	09.37	Taurus
Venus	03.45	Cancer
Mars	26.18	Gemini
Jupiter	28.59	Aries
Saturn	06.33	Taurus
Uranus	21.56	Taurus
Neptune	22.51 R	Virgo
Pluto	00.47	Leo
Chiron	16.10	Cancer
N Node	18.34	Libra
Fortune	25.50	Aquarius

What I'm trying to do as I go along is to incorporate numbers into the chart. Sometimes it may not work, so be careful, only theoretical. I had the idea that numbers in the chart especially if held by houses and the planets must be telling us something.

In this chart we see 3 degrees of Capricorn rising. 3 could be a magical number. Anyway, the ruler of the ascendant is Saturn. We find Saturn in the fourth house in the sign of Taurus which is the 5th house sign.

Saturn is in a group with the sun, Mercury and Uranus. This makes a strong Taurus.

Jupiter in the fourth house is in the sign of Aries is conjuncting Saturn.

The sun sign is Taurus, the moon sign is Cancer.

Notice that Venus is exactly conjunct the 7th house. Venus holding 3 degrees.

This is a good sign that the individual could get married, be involved with the public or some partnership.

The sun and Uranus in the 5th house exactly in conjunction.

In any chart, this conjunction is good to pursue scientifical subjects.

Both are also in conjunction with the 5th house.

Notice that Saturn, the ruler of the ascendant is conjunct with Mercury, and that Mercury is ruler of the 6th and 9th houses.

Notice Neptune in the 9th holding 22 degrees.

Fortune in the second house in Aquarius trine the Mid.

Pluto in 0 degree in the 7th house in the sign of Leo, the 8th house sign.

This chart is of conjoined twins. Born 10th December 1927 at 07:30 am, Derby, UK. They both died 12 days later.

Ascendant	08.51	Sagittarius
2nd	15.31	Capricorn
3rd	02.15	Pisces
4th	09.51	Aries
5th	05.15	Taurus
6th	23.42	Taurus
7th	08.51	Gemini
8th	15.31	Cancer
9th	02.15	Virgo
10th	09.51	Libra
11th	05.16	Scorpio
12th	23.42	Scorpio

Sun	17.14	Sagittarius
Moon	08.32	Cancer
Mercury	01.20	Sagittarius
Venus	01.34	Scorpio
Mars	01.18	Sagittarius
Jupiter	24.19	Pisces
Saturn	10.59	Sagittarius
Uranus	29.29	Pisces
Neptune	29.10 R	Leo
Pluto	16.38 R	Cancer
Chiron	01.55	Taurus
N Node	18.41	Gemini
Fortune	00.09	Cancer

Let me just say that if you are a professional astrologer, you should have no problems sorting this one out. Those who are just learning will still be scratching their heads, but never mind, it will come to you in the end.

The twins died 12 days later. The chart can still be progressed but not for the twins.

First, we see that 8 degrees is at the ascendant with Sagittarius rising. Jupiter being the ruler and is in the third house conjunct Uranus.

The closest planet to the ascendant is Saturn. Saturn is ruler of the body and co-ruler of the loop in the second house.

The next is Mercury then Mars and then the sun.

The moon in the 7th house in Cancer is also holding 8 degrees and is ruler of the 8th house.

Fortune is 0 degree.

Pluto is conjunct the 8th ruler of the duplicates 11/12.

Axis 10/4 is holding 9 degrees.

Axis 11/5 holding 5 degrees.

Chiron is exactly opposing Venus, ruler of the 5th and 10th.

Chiron is quincunx Mercury and Mars in the 12th house.

I've been looking at the 15th degrees, and soon I'll have to make up my mind what's it all about.

Remember the outer planets will hold their degrees for a long time. Here you see Neptune in the loop in the 8th house in the sign of Leo quincunx Uranus in the third house in Pisces.

Chiron is trine the 9th house.

Venus is sextile the 9th, semi-sextile Mercury and Mars.

Mercury and Mars are in exact conjunction in the 12th house.

Notice that Jupiter, the ruler of the ascendant sign Sagittarius is making a sextile contact with the 6th house.

Fortune is quincunx Mercury and Mars, trine Venus, sextile Chiron.

Our next chart is that of *Condeleezza Rice* born 14th November 1954 at 11:30 am, Birmingham, Alabama, U.S.A.

Ascendant	03.09	Aquarius
2nd	15.13	Pisces
3rd	22.38	Aries
4th	21.24	Taurus
5th	14.56	Gemini
6th	07.18	Cancer
7th	03.09	Leo
8th	15.13	Virgo
9th	22.38	Libra
10th	21.24	Scorpio
11th	14.56	Sagittarius
12th	07.18	Capricorn
Sun	21.49	Scorpio
Moon	18.45	Cancer
Mercury	02.38	Scorpio
Venus	22.45	Scorpio
Mars	16.14	Aquarius

Jupiter	29.56	Cancer
Saturn	13.14	Scorpio
Uranus	27.38	Cancer
Neptune	26.45	Libra
Pluto	26.45	Leo
Chiron	24.20	Capricorn
N Node	07.55	Capricorn
Fortune	00.5	Libra

Aquarius is rising with the rulers as Saturn and Uranus. Saturn is in the 9th house in Scorpio. Uranus is in the 6th house in Cancer. Cancer is the sign of home, and family and country, Scorpio is deep, penetrating insight. Saturn is in the house of travel, Uranus is in the house of work, colleagues, servants, sickness, service.

Inside her first house is the planet Mars in Aquarius. Mars gives lots of energy.

Her sun sign is Scorpio, with Venus, Saturn and Mercury in the same sign. We say that she is a strong Scorpio.

Her Mercury is conjunct with Neptune. There are some human beings who cannot control this combination.

Both sun and Venus in the 10th house are good positions for the career.

Venus itself rules the fourth house which is the home or the country.

Notice that the Node is in the 12th house exactly conjunct the 12th, and would be ruler of the 6th house (in my test).

Chiron is in the 12th and could be ruler of the ascendant or the 12th according to some astrologers. For my test, it would be the 11th house.

Notice that Jupiter is exalted in the sign of Cancer and has a trine aspect to the Mid, the sun and Venus.

Fortune is in the 8th house in the sign of Libra.

She is not married and she has no children. Work that one out.

What have you come up with?

You see that Mercury is in Scorpio in the 9th house; and is square to the ascendant. Mercury is ruler of the 5th and 8th houses.

Venus holds a strong position in the 10th house, but has drop some of its energies because of being in Scorpio which is opposite Taurus.

Notice that Jupiter is exalted in Cancer but is in 29 degrees and is conjunct the 7th. Jupiter is ruler of the second and 11th. The person will have a big partnership and would not be short of money. I think she can still get married if she wants to. But being a scorpio, she has the insight that it won't work as she wants it to.

The following chart is of a Male born 21st June 1894, at 12:57 pm, Calcutta, India.

Three weeks old, fingers and toes broken. The nurse threw him at a dog in self defence.

One year feet badly scalded.

At 8 nearly died of pneumonia.

At 12 he fell over a slope with his horse which was killed, he broke his ribs.

At 14 broke both arms at roller skating.

In 1917 got caught between the footboard and platform and was rolled round and round, almost every bone was broken. His viscera crushed and smashed, pelvis broken, and bladder injured.

Ascendant	12.41	Libra
2nd	11.49	Scorpio
3rd	12.00	Sagittarius
4th	12.39	Capricorn
5th	13.40	Aquarius
6th	14.14	Pisces
7th	12.41	Aries
8th	11.49	Taurus
9th	12.00	Gemini
10th	12.39	Cancer
11th	13.40	Leo
12th	14.14	Virgo
Sun	29.50	Gemini
Moon	02.40	Aquarius
Mercury	26.00	Cancer
Venus	20.16	Taurus
Mars	28.41	Pisces
Jupiter	17.44	Gemini
Saturn	18.24	Libra
Uranus	11.36 R	Scorpio
Neptune	13.53	Gemini
Pluto	10.44	Gemini
Chiron	16.04	Virgo
N Node	06.06	Aries
Fortune	15.31	Taurus

Libra is on the ascendant with Saturn there in the first house. Saturn is exalted in Libra. Things happen to the individual early in life.

Venus is the ruler of Libra, it is in the 8th house in its own sign Taurus. It is conjunct with Fortune.

Uranus is also in the first house but in the sign of the second house. Notice that Uranus is exactly conjunct the second house (the body, and possessions).

Uranus is the planet of unexpected things. Scientific, suddenness, unusualness.
Chiron is in the 12th conjunct the 12th.

The individual is a strong Gemini with four planets in that sign. They are the sun, Jupiter, Neptune and Pluto.

Mars is in the 6th house conjunct the Node.

Neptune in Gemini in the 9th sign is semi-sextile the Mid, exactly sextile the 11th, quincunx its own house, the 12th. Neptune rules the sixth.

Neptune is also conjunct the 9th, trine the ascendant.

You see that the sun is holding 29 degrees.

Uranus is semi-sextile the ascendant, trine the Mid.

The Moon is in the fourth house in the sign of Aquarius.

Pluto in the 8th house in Gemini is semi-sextile the 8th.

The next chart is of *Alan Bean* born 15th March 1932 at 15:10 pm, Wheeler, Texas, U.S.A. An Aeronautical engineer, Navy Pilot. Travel to the moon 14th November 1969.

Ascendant	10.59	Leo
2nd	03.29	Virgo
3rd	00.29	Libra
4th	02.41	Scorpio
5th	07.44	Sagittarius
6th	11.13	Capricorn
7th	10.59	Aquarius
8th	03.29	Pisces
9th	00.29	Aries
10th	02.41	Taurus
11th	07.44	Gemini
12th	11.13	Cancer

Sun	25.04	Pisces
Moon	29.09	Gemini
Mercury	10.54	Aries
Venus	07.44	Taurus
Mars	15.35	Pisces
Jupiter	13.28 R	Leo
Saturn	02.00	Aquarius
Uranus	17.57	Aries
Neptune	06.06 R	Virgo
Pluto	20.01 R	Cancer
Chiron	19.48	Taurus
N Node	26.19	Pisces
Fortune	15.08	Scorpio

Have you had a good look around with your eyes?

The ascendant is Leo with Jupiter in the first and conjuncting the ascendant.

The ruler of the ascendant is the sun in the 8th house in the sign of Pisces. Mars and the Node is also in this sign.

Neptune, is co-ruler of the 8th together with Jupiter.

Neptune is in the second house in the sign of Virgo conjunct the second. Neptune is trine to the Mid, and to Venus.

Fortune is in the fourth house in Scorpio.

Saturn is in the sixth house in its own sign Aquarius exactly square the Mid. Saturn is conjunct the 7th, semi-sextile the 8th.

Mars is in the 8th house in Pisces trine Pluto, exactly trine Fortune.

The Node is in the 8th house in Pisces conjunct the sun, square the moon in the 11th house.

Mercury is in the 9th house conjunct Uranus, exactly trine the ascendant, square the 12th, trine Jupiter.

Uranus is in the 9th house in Aries trine the ascendant. Notice that Aries gives energies for ideas.

Venus in the 10th house is a very good position for the career. In this angular house, Venus is strong. It is ruler of the 10th house and also of the third. This Venus position is good for artists and musicians. Venus is square the ascendant and Jupiter. But notice, this is all from an angular position.

The moon sign here is Gemini with the moon holding 29 degrees. The moon is semi-square Jupiter, square the Node, and the sun.

The third ninth axis is holding 0 degree.

This next chart you have to tear apart by jotting down every thing that you see. Checking your ascendant, and what the ruler or rulers are doing. Check where the rulers are; the aspects they are making to the rest of the chart. Check the planets in the first house and which planet is nearest the ascendant. The aspects they are making.

Do your house contacts. Look around for the other planets in the houses and what they are doing. Check the degrees the houses and planets are holding.

Now you have to decide what you think the chart is telling you positive and negative.

Ascendant	03.08	Pisces
2nd	16.15	Aries
3rd	18.35	Taurus
4th	13.29	Gemini
5th	05.59	Cancer
6th	00.28	Leo

7th	03.08	Virgo
8th	16.15	Libra
9th	18.35	Scorpio
10th	13.29	Sagittarius
11th	05.59	Capricorn
12th	00.28	Aquarius
Sun	20.39	Virgo
Moon	15.57	Libra
Mercury	27.13 R	Virgo
Venus	04.55	Virgo
Mars	21.56	Scorpio
Jupiter	00.07 R	Pisces
Saturn	22.25	Virgo
Uranus	09.02	Cancer
Neptune	16.06	Libra
Pluto	18.49	Leo
Chiron	16.08	Sagittarius
N Node	28.33	Pisces
Fortune	28.26	Pisces

Remember, if you see a planet holding 0 degree, note the house and sign its in; it is giving you information. Do the same with the rest.

For a start we have Jupiter and Neptune as rulers of the ascendant. Jupiter is retrograde and in Pisces, holding 0 degree; and in the 12th house. Jupiter is conjunct the ascendant, also ruler of the 10th house.

The 12th house we all know is a strange house, for positive or negative. The fact that Jupiter is holding 0 degree points to the ascendant, the person himself. It points to the sign of Pisces and it points to the career, or the parents, and to the 12th house.

The 6th and 12th axis is holding 0 degree. We know the energies that are in those houses. Work, sickness, pets, colleagues, and health. The 12th house, isolation, hospitals, prisons, working behind the scenes for the benefit of others.

We have the node in the first house in Pisces exactly conjunct Fortune also in Pisces. In my test, the node gets to rule the fifth house, Fortune we give to the sixth house, Leo. Remember, these are only tests.

The 5th house you already know is the house of children, love affairs, speculation etc.

The other ruler of the ascendant is Neptune and we find it in the 7th house in the sign of Libra exactly conjunct the 8th house.

Neptune is also the natural co-ruler of the 12th house. Neptune is conjunct the moon who is ruler of the 5th house.

We have the 5th and 11th axis holding 5 degrees. Neptune happen to be exactly sextile Chiron in the 10th house in the sign of Sagittarius.

You see Pluto ruler of the 9th house is exactly square the 9th house. I'm working on an idea that the 9th house has to do with birth as well.

The sun in the 7th house, in the sixth sign is sextile Mars in the 9th house in the sign of Scorpio. Mars is ruler of the 9th and also of the second house.

Mercury in the 7th house in the sign of Virgo is opposing the node and Fortune in the first house. in Pisces.

Venus is conjunct the 7th house and is ruler of the third and 8th houses. Venus is trine the 11th.

Jupiter is exactly semi-sextile to the 12th. The moon is conjunct the 8th.

If you check the second house and its ruler and sign you'll get a clue.

The second house is the body. Mars is the ruler of the body. Mars is in the 9th house; this house has many energies. Mars is in the sign of Scorpio which has to do with sex or other people's possessions or the other world. Mars is also ruler of the 9th house itself, and natural ruler of the ascendant and 8th houses.

I only did this chart to let you see that if you take your time and examine a chart properly, you can come close in extracting information. But this is not usually my way of testing a chart. Hope you came close with your interpretation.

The chart is of *Lynn Harris* born on 13th September 1950 at 18:10 pm, Orange, California, U.S.A Born with penis and vagina.

This next chart is of *Fatima Bernardes* born 17th September 1962 at 07:00 am, Rio de Janeiro, Brazil.

She had triplets on the 21st October 1997.

Ascendant	16.46	Libra
2nd	20.18	Scorpio
3rd	17.10	Sagittarius
4th	11.38	Capricorn
5th	07.33	Aquarius
6th	08.40	Pisces
7th	16.40	Aries
8th	20.18	Taurus
9th	17.10	Gemini
10th	11.38	Cancer
11th	07.33	Leo
12th	08.40	Virgo

Sun	24.01	Virgo
Moon	09.53	Taurus
Mercury	19.38	Libra
Venus	09.19	Scorpio
Mars	16.06	Cancer.
Jupiter	05.34 R	Pisces
Saturn	05.10 R	Aquarius
Uranus	02.22	Virgo
Neptune	11.31	Scorpio
Pluto	10.21	Virgo
Chiron	07.43	Pisces
N Node	07.55	Leo
Fortune	03 38	Gemini

Some charts show in the natal more information than others. But we must always progress the chart to a certain year when an event took place.

Having a quick look at this chart we see in the 5th house Chiron holding 7 degrees and in the sign of Pisces. Also in the 5th house is the planet Jupiter holding 5 degrees and is in the sign of

Pisces. Then we have Saturn in the 4th house holding 5 degrees in the sign of Aquarius. Saturn is exactly semi-sextile Jupiter. Jupiter is ruler of the 3rd house which is that of the close family etc. Chiron we see is exactly semi-sextile the 5th house.

Libra is rising in this chart with Mercury there in the first house conjuncting the ascendant. Venus is ruler and is in the first house in the second house sign of Scorpio.

This woman is a strong Virgo with three planets in the sign. They are sun, Uranus and Pluto. She has energies to be scientific in some way. The sun and Uranus is always good for scientifical subjects.

Her moon sign is Taurus. The moon is in the 7th house sextile the 6th house. It will also trine the 12th, trine Pluto in the 12th. It is exactly opposing Venus. Venus is sextile the 12th, sextile Pluto.

Mercury is semi-sextile the second house.

Mars in the 10th house in Cancer is exactly square the ascendant, semi-sextile 9th house.

Neptune is exactly trine the Mid. Fortune is square Uranus in the 11th house. Uranus is conjunct the 12th.

The node is exactly conjunct the 11th house, semi-sextile the 12th, quincunx Chiron.

15: Returns

Returns are getting the planets back to their original positions in the natal chart. It takes a lot of time, but is worth it. I will deal with it very clearly so that you'll understand it. We take the sun first because it is the giver of life. It moves one degree per day which is equal to one year. Note the sun's position in your chart. The degrees and minutes it is holding; the sign it is in. All you have to do is take a year forward or backward from your own chart. So if you were born in 1974, you could go to a year forward to 1975 or backward to 1973. You can go as many years forward and backward as you want.

Let's start with you putting your date, month, and the year that you want into the computer; using the same time of your birth.

I will be using *Lillian Smith* the Californian trick shooter's chart, who was rival to Annie Oakley as an example.

She was born 4th August 1871 at Coleville, California, U.S.A. I am using a Midnight time.

In the chart you'll see that the sun is in 11 degrees and 27 minutes, and is in the sign of Leo.

She is 4 years old and we want to see her sun return chart. We tick in 4th August 1875, Midnight in the computer. We find that the sun is 11 degrees and 29 minutes.

The minutes are too many. We need to bring them down to 27. We have to change the date to 3rd August 1875 at 23.25 pm, then we'll see that the sun is holding 11 degrees and 27 minutes. This is the sun return chart for four years old. We can now begin to read the chart but we must remember that it is for a whole year. From one date to the next.

She was 10 when she started shooting seriously. Let's have a look at her solar return chart.

We tick in the computer 4th August 1881, Midnight. We find her sun at 12 degrees and 1 minute. We have to bring it to 11 degrees and 27 minutes. We change the date to 3rd August and find that the sun is now 11 degrees and 3 minutes. We need to bring the minutes up to 27.

You have to play around with the Midnight time by adding to it. I've added 10 hours making it 10 am. And believe it, the sun is there holding 11 degrees and 27 minutes.

The sun return for 1881 is 3rd August, 10:00 am

Ascendant	10.04	Libra
2nd	07.12	Scorpio
3rd	08.03	Sagittarius
4th	11.27	Capricorn
5th	14.32	Aquarius
6th	14.29	Pisces
7th	10.04	Aries
8th	07.12	Taurus
9th	08.03	Gemini
10th	11.27	Cancer
11th	14.32	Leo
12th	14.29	Virgo
Sun	11.27	Leo
Moon	18.14	Scorpio
Mercury	22.47	Cancer
Venus	27.11	Gemini
Mars	29.51	Taurus
Jupiter	23.27	Taurus
Saturn	12.03	Taurus
Uranus	12.06	Virgo
Neptune	16.30	Taurus
Pluto	29.12	Taurus
Chiron	22.23	Taurus
N Node	16.36	Sagittarius
Fortune	16.51	Leo

I hope that you had no trouble understanding how to get the sun back to its natural position for any year that you want.

Lillian Smith is only 10 and her father is confident that no one could beat her. Have you seen what is inside her 8th house? She has 6 planets in this 8th house. Taurus is on the 8th house ruled by Venus in the 9th house in the sign of Gemini. It so happen that Venus is also ruler of the ascendant.

Her sun is Capricorn; and you should no what a Capricorn is like by now. Bottom place is not for the Capricorn.

You should also know this Venus position in the 9th house. It has to do with travelling. She's a Californian girl, that Lillian Smith. She had to travel a lot in order to get competition.

Her moon sign is Scorpio. Scorpios can sting if they want to. They have energies for deep insight. Can be jealous and sexy.

We see that 7 degrees is at the second and 8th axis.

8 degrees is at the 3rd and 9th axis.

The node in the third house in the sign of Sagittarius is sextile her ascendant.

Fortune in the 11th house is also sextile her ascendant. Uranus is in the 11th conjunct the 12th.

The moon is trine the Mid. The node is quincunx Neptune in the 8th house. Fortune is square Neptune. Inside her 8th house we find Mars and Pluto both exactly in conjunction; and both are natural rulers of the 8th house. Both are in conjunction with Chiron, and Jupiter. This conjunction of Jupiter and Pluto is very psychic. Jupiter is conjunct Chiron and Neptune. Chiron is conjunct Neptune.

Saturn is conjunct Neptune, sextile the Mid, trine Uranus. This trine aspect could also make one a genius in whatever subject they study.

Saturn is trine the sun. The sun is trine Neptune.

We see Mercury in the 10th house in the sign of Cancer ruled by the moon. The moon is trine Mercury.

Mercury is sextile Mars and Pluto. It is sextile Chiron, Jupiter and Neptune.

Our next step is the moon's return. This is for every month.

We are going to use a chart.

This chart is of *Dorothy Dandridge* born 9th November 1922 at 22:35 pm, Cleveland, Ohio, U.S.A.

We shall take the year 1965 to get a moon return.

She died mysteriously from an overdose, known as a rare embolism. The date is 8th September 1965.

For the moon return. If we take her birth month November and the year 1965; and her birth time of 22:35 pm, we are going to end up with her moon in another position. If we use the 2nd November 1965 with the time of 15:25 pm we end up with her moon in the same place as when she was born. But the month is November; we want the month she died which is September.

If we take the 8th September 1965 we are also going to be out with the moon position. If we take the 9th September 1965 01:10 am, we are going to get her moon in 26 degrees and 36 minutes of Aquarius, just what we want.

Ascendant	05.45	Cancer
2nd	25.12	Cancer
3rd	16.16	Leo
4th	12.29	Virgo
5th	17.12	Libra
6th	28.29	Scorpio
7th	05.45	Capricorn
8th	25.12	Capricorn
9th	16.16	Aquarius
10th	12.29	Pisces
11th	17.12	Aries
12th	28.29	Taurus

Sun	16.18	Virgo
Moon	26.36	Aquarius
Mercury	00.48	Virgo
Venus	24.34	Libra
Mars	12.47	Scorpio
Jupiter	28.44	Gemini
Saturn	13.37 R	Pisces
Uranus	15.18	Virgo
Neptune	17.41	Scorpio
Pluto	16.06	Virgo
Chiron	20.24 R	Pisces
N Node	08.38	Gemini
Fortune	16.03	Sagittarius

I hope it wasn't too hard for you and that you now see how it works.

We know in this moon return, she didn't make it. The moon itself is the ruler of the ascendant and is in the 9th house in the sign of Aquarius. This moon position is exactly as that in her natal chart.

We have a duplicate of 1st and second houses; 7th and 8th houses.

Mercury in the third house holding 0 degree, in its own sign, and ruler of the 4th house, and also the intercepted 12th. In her fourth house, the sun is conjunct Pluto exactly, conjunct Uranus. The sun is ruler of the third house, Uranus ruler of the 9th, and Pluto ruler of the 6th.

The sun is in an exact contact with the third house, so is Pluto. Uranus is in a semi-sextile contact with the third house. .

The sun is semi-sextile the fifth house. Pluto is semi-sextile the fifth house.

Did you notice the ascendant is holding 5 degrees? Here it has to do with the person herself and the partner or the public.

The sun is sextile Neptune in the 5th house and in the sign of Scorpio.

Neptune is exactly semi-sextile the fifth house, square the third. Don't forget when aspect is at one house it is also at the opposite.

Venus in the 5th house in the sign of Libra is square the second. Mars in the fifth house in Scorpio is exactly sextile the fourth house.

We have Fortune in the loop in the 6th house in the sign of Sagittarius exactly square the sun and Pluto, square Uranus. Exactly trine the third, sextile the fifth, and semi-sextile Neptune.

Mars in the fifth house is exactly trine the Mid, trine Saturn.

The return moon, ruler of the ascendant is semi-sextile the 8th. Saturn in the 10th house is conjunct the Mid.

Jupiter inside the loop in the 12th house in Gemini is exactly semi-sextile the 12th. The node is holding 8 degrees in the loop in the 12th in the sign of

Gemini. The node is ruling the first and second houses.

We move on to Mercury. This planet has a period of 88 days. We are going to bring it back to its original position in the natal chart. You have to work back and forth, using your senses to get the planet in its correct position.

Let us use the chart of *Catie Ball* the American swimmer who won a gold medal in 1968. She was born 30th September 1951 at 13:58 pm, Jacksonville, Florida, U.S.A.

Remember the Mercury return is for a period of 88 days. If you were to tick in 30th September 1968 at 13:58 pm, you would see that Mercury is in the 10th house in 0 degree and 50 minutes of Scorpio. We want it to be in Virgo.

For 26th August 1968 we pick it up in 20 degrees and 39 minutes of Virgo, still in the 10th house.

We finish off the day with 23:58 pm, Mercury is in 21 degrees and 20 minutes of Virgo.

On the 29th August we have Mercury in 26 degrees and 06 minutes of Virgo. On 30th August at 09:45 am, we get Mercury back to its natal position.

Ascendant	11.39	Libra
2nd	09.54	Scorpio
3rd	10.27	Sagittarius
4th	12.20	Capricorn
5th	14.17	Aquarius
6th	14.34	Pisces
7th	11.39	Aries
8th	09.54	Taurus
9th	10.07	Gemini
10th	12.20	Cancer
11th	14.17	Leo
12th	14.34	Virgo
Sun	07.13	Virgo
Moon	01.49	Sagittarius
Mercury	26.44	Virgo
Venus	26.40	Virgo
Mars	15.57	Leo
Jupiter	14.20	Virgo
Saturn	25.04 R	Aries
Uranus	28.11	Virgo
Neptune	23.55	Scorpio
Pluto	22.05	Virgo
Chiron	02.08	Aries
N Node	10.02	Aries
Fortune	06.15	Capricorn

This Mercury return chart has Libra rising with the ruler Venus in the 12th house in the sign of Virgo exactly conjuncting Mercury. This will lead us to the 1st, 8th, 9th, and 12th houses.

Venus is in a 2 degrees conjunction with Uranus, the co-ruler of the fifth house. It is in a 4 degrees conjunction with Pluto, co-ruler of the second house. You notice that Venus is in Virgo along five other planets, they are Sun, Mercury, Jupiter, Uranus and Pluto. She is a strong Virgo.

Both Mercury and Venus are quincunx to Saturn in the 7th house in Aries.

Jupiter in the 12th house is exactly conjunct the 12th.

Both Mercury and Venus are in a sexttile contact with the moon. This will bring the 10th house into operation, also herself, the first house. Not forgetting the 8th house which has to do with other people's possessions. This 8th house is actually the goods of the public or partner.

Uranus is sextile the moon bringing the 5th house into play. This 5th house is the house of creativity, sports and speculation and children.

Jupiter is also exactly semi-sextile with 11th house. The node in the sixth house is conjunct the 7th, sextile the 9th. The moon in the second house in Sagittarius is trine Chiron in the sixth house.

The sun is in the 11th house in Virgo holding 7 degrees. The 2nd/8th axis holding 9 degrees.

Mars in the 11th house in the sign of Leo conjunct 11th.

Our next task is to bring Venus back to its natal position. This return is 225 days.

We shall use the *President of America*'s chart... born 14th June 1946 at 10:45 am, Jamaica Hospital Queens (Queens County) New York, U.S.A.

His natal Venus position is 25 degrees and 44 minutes of Cancer.

Taking the date of 10th June 2018 at 10:54 am, we find Venus at 26 degrees and 8 minutes of Cancer.

We need to bring Venus down to 25 degrees and 44 minutes of Cancer.

Messing about with the time we get 10th June 2018 at 02:40 am, and find Venus in 25 degrees and 44 minutes of Cancer.

Ascendant	25.03	Aries
2nd	29.06	Taurus
3rd	22.38	Gemini
4th	13.35	Cancer
5th	06.46	Leo
6th	08.11	Virgo
7th	25.03	Libra
8th	29.06	Scorpio
9th	22.38	Sagittarius

10th	13.35	Capricorn
11th	06.46	Aquarius
12th	08.11	Pisces.
Sun	19.21	Gemini
Moon	01.29	Taurus
Mercury	24.31	Gemini
Venus	25.44	Cancer
Mars	07.34	Aquarius
Jupiter	14.42 R	Scorpio
Saturn	07.05 R	Capricorn
Uranus	01.14	Taurus
Neptune	16.28	Pisces
Pluto	20.45 R	Capricorn
Chiron	02.09	Aries
N Node	07.00	Leo
Fortune	07.11	Pisces

Hope you had no trouble following the instructions.

This Venus return has the ascendant as Aries with Mars as ruler. Mars is in the 11th house, and has to do with groups and friends.

Mars is semi-sextile to the 12th house, exactly semi-sextile to Fortune in the 11th house, in the sign of Pisces.

Mars is exactly semi-sextile to Saturn in the 9th house in the sign of its own, Capricorn.

Mars is exactly opposing the node in the 5th house in the sign of Leo. The node, in my test, is ruling the fourth house. Mars is co-ruler of the 8th.

Chiron will act before Mars because it is the nearest planet to the ascendant; and it is ruler of Sagittarius. Keep in mind that there are also the sign of Virgo, Capricorn and Aquarius, not yet confirm if they make any sense.

Chiron is making a square contact with Saturn. It is semi-sextile with both the moon and Uranus in the first house in the sign of Taurus. It is trine Venus in the fourth house. The node has a trine to Chiron.

Note that Chiron is in the 12th house. Chiron is sesqui-quadrate Jupiter in the 7th house in the sign of Scorpio.

We find the moon and Uranus in conjunction exactly, in the first house in the sign of Taurus. The moon is ruler of the fourth house, Uranus co-ruler of the 11th.

Notice that 29 degrees is on the second house and eighth house.

The sun is there in the second house in the sign of Gemini with about 3 degrees conjunction. The sun is ruler of the 5th house.

The planet Mercury is in the third house, its own house, conjuncting the third house of Gemini, its own sign. Mercury is sextile the ascendant. It is semi-sextile Venus in the fourth house. Mercury is also ruler of the 6th house, while Venus is ruler of the 2nd and the 7th.

Mercury is square Neptune in the 12th house in the sign of Pisces. Neptune is in its own house and in its own sign.

The moon and Uranus are trine to Saturn.

The sixth and 12th house has 8 degrees on the cusps.

The sun is square to Neptune, semi-square both Moon and Uranus, conjunct Mercury, semi-square the node.

Venus, the return planet is in the fourth house making an exact square to the ascendant.

The node in the fifth house is square to Jupiter in the 7th house. It is exactly quincunx Saturn, exactly quincunx Fortune.

Jupiter is sextile the Mid, sextile Pluto, trine Fortune, trine Neptune.

Saturn is conjunct the Mid, semi-sextile 11th, sextile 12th.

Pluto is in a 7 degrees conjunction with the Mid and is square to the ascendant. Planets in angles and squaring angles are very strong.

Fortune is conjunct 12th.

The next chart will be the return of Mars. This will be about 687 days.

We shall use the chart of *Audrey Hepburn*, that great actress. Born on 4th May 1929 at 03:00 am, Ixelles, Belgium. Her natal Mars is in 25 degrees and 9 minutes of Cancer.

I managed to get her Mars back at its original position in the natal chart by going to the year 1955. She was married to Mel Ferrer in 1954.

On the 3rd July 1955 at 20:58 pm we found Mars at 25 degrees and 9 minutes of Cancer.

Ascendant	12.42	Capricorn
2nd	05.03	Pisces
3rd	19.37	Aries
4th	17.24	Taurus
5th	07.07	Gemini
6th	24.10	Gemini
7th	12.42	Cancer
8th	05.03	Virgo
9th	19.37	Libra
10th	17.24	Scorpio
11th	07.07	Sagittarius
12th	24.10	Sagittarius

Sun	11.06	Cancer
Moon	25.47	Sagittarius
Mercury	21.32	Gemini
Venus	24.54	Gemini
Mars	25.09	Cancer
Jupiter	04.14	Leo
Saturn	14.41 R	Scorpio
Uranus	26.54	Cancer
Neptune	25.08 R	Libra
Pluto	25.03	Leo
Chiron	04.00	Aquarius
N Node	26.26	Sagittarius
Fortune	29.23	Gemini

Her ascendant sign in this Mars return is Capricorn. There is an intercepted sign in the first house carrying Aquarius and Chiron. So we have to look for the planet Uranus as well.

Saturn is in the 9th house in the sign of Scorpio conjuncting the Mid. It is sextile the ascendant. It is trine the sun.

Uranus is in the 7th house in the sign of Cancer. Remember that this sign of Cancer has to do with the home or the country; and you will find that people with just one planet in Cancer has the energy for loving their home and family. What about people with more planets in Cancer?

Uranus is conjunct Mars in the 7th house. Mars is ruler of the third and tenth houses.

Uranus is semi-sextile to Pluto in the intercepted sign in the 7th house carrying Leo. Uranus is square Neptune in the 9th house. This is a long drawn out aspect. Uranus is almost trine the Mid with about 110 degrees. Uranus is quincunx the Moon in the 12th house in the sign of Sagittarius. It is exactly quincunx the Node also in the 12th house and in the same sign as the Moon.

Chiron in the first house in the intercepted sign is square to Neptune in the 9th house. It is semi-sextile the second. Sesqui-quadrate to Mercury in the 5th house. It opposes Jupiter in the 7th house in the intercepted sign of Leo, exactly.

Mercury in the fifth house is conjunct the 6th, conjunct Venus in the sixth, and Fortune. It is sextile Pluto, trine Neptune in the 9th. Opposing the Moon and the Node in the 12th house.

Venus is in the 6th house in the sign of Gemini exactly conjunct the 6th, conjunct Fortune, semi-sextile to Mars and Uranus in the 7th, sextile Pluto in the intercepted sign in the 7th. Trine Neptune in the 9th, opposing the Moon and Node in the 12th.

Fortune in the 6th house is opposing the Moon and Node in the 12th. It is sextile Pluto in the 7th. Trine Neptune in the 9th. Sesqui-quadrate the Mid and Saturn.

The sun is conjuncting the 7th, trine the Mid and Saturn.

Mars is conjunct Uranus in the 7th, exactly semi-sextile Pluto, exactly square Neptune. 111 degrees to the Mid. Exactly quincunx the Moon, quincunx the node in the 12th. Conjunct Jupiter.

Pluto is exactly sextile Neptune. Exactly trine the Moon, trine the Node.

The moon and Node is sextile Neptune. Saturn is conjunct the Mid, sextile the ascendant.

The next return is that of Jupiter, this takes 12 years.

Every 12 years Jupiter is back where it started. Just add 12 years to the year of your birth. For example: if you were born in the year 1987, add 12 years bringing it to 1999. Add another 12 years and you get 2011 and so forth. Do a Jupiter return for 1999, and for 2011. Add another 12 years and you end up with 2023.

We are going to work with the chart of Kate Winslet. She was born 5th October 1975 at 07:15 am, Reading, United Kingdom.

Her Jupiter position is 20 degrees and 40 minutes in the sign of Aries; and is retrograde.

We are looking for Jupiter's return for the year 2011. This is the year she got divorced. The following year 2012, she got married.

I've had fun trying to bring Jupiter back to its position. We pick it up on March 2011 at 07:15 am. Jupiter is in 14 degrees and 40 minutes of Aries.

On the 30th April 2011 at 07:15 am Jupiter is in 22 degrees and 7 minutes of Aries.

On 23rd April 2011 at 07:15 am, Jupiter is in 20 degrees and 27 minutes of Aries.

On 24th April 2011 at 09:15 am, Jupiter is in 20 degrees and 43 minutes of Aries.

On the 24th April 2011 at 11:30 am, Jupiter is 20 degrees and 44 minutes of Aries.

On 24th April 2011 at 12::30 pm, Jupiter is 20 degrees and 45 minutes of Aries.

And on 24th April 2011 at 13:40 pm, we get Jupiter in 20 degrees and 46 minutes of Aries.

Ascendant	25.43	Leo
2nd	15.00	Virgo
3rd	10.20	Libra
4th	13.40	Scorpio
5th	22.43	Sagittarius
6th	27.52	Capricorn

7th	25.43	Aquarius
8th	15.00	Pisces
9th	10.20	Aries
10th	13.40	Taurus
11th	22.43	Gemini
12th	27.52	Cancer
Sun	03.59	Taurus
Moon	27.13	Capricorn
Mercury	12.56	Aries
Venus	04.03	Aries
Mars	17.15	Aries
Jupiter	20.46	Aries
Saturn	12.20 R	Libra
Uranus	02.24	Aries
Neptune	00.30	Pisces
Pluto	07.26 R	Capricorn
Chiron	04.30	Pisces
N Node	26.17	Sagittarius
Fortune	18.56	Taurus

This Jupiter return chart is showing Leo rising with its ruler the sun up in the 9th house in the sign of Taurus. The sun is semi-sextile Venus in the 8th house in the sign of Aries. Venus is ruler of the third and tenth houses.

The sun is semi-sextile Uranus in the 8th house in the sign of Aries. Uranus is co-ruler of the 7th house.

The sun is trine Pluto in the 5th house in the sign of Capricorn. Pluto is co-ruler of the 4th house.

The sun is sextile Neptune in the 7th house in the sign of Pisces. The sun is also sextile Chiron in the 7th house in the sign of Pisces. Neptune is co-ruler of the 8th house, Chiron ruler of the 5th house (still in test research). It could also be 6th, 7th and 2nd.

The sun is trine the node in the 5th house in the sign of Sagittarius. The node is ruler of the 12th (test research).

The planet Saturn is in the 3rd house in the sign Libra. Saturn rules the 6th and 7th houses; is exalted in the sign of Libra.

Saturn is semi-square the ascendant, square Pluto, exactly opposing Mercury in the 9th house, and opposing Mars and Jupiter also in the 9th house, all in the sign of Aries.

We must not forget that Aries is the first sign in the fixed wheel; and it gives energy, is impulsive, and give ideas.

The Node is in the 5th house in the sign of Sagittarius, is semi-sextile the moon also in the 5th house but in the sign of the 6th.

The Node is sextile Neptune in the 7th house. It is square Venus in the 8th and also Uranus. The Node is trine Jupiter in the 9th. It is sesqui-quadrate the Mid.

The Moon is exactly conjunct the 6th house, semi-sextile Neptune, sextile Venus and Uranus in the 8th house. The Moon is quincunx the ascendant.

Pluto is in the 5th house in the sign of Capricorn, sextile Chiron, square Venus and Uranus, square Mercury, trine the Mid.

Chiron is conjunct Neptune in the 7th house, both in the sign of Pisces, the 8th house sign. Chiron is exactly semi-sextile Venus.

Neptune is semi-square Mars in the 9th house, opposing the ascendant.

Venus in the 8th house is in conjunction with Uranus. Venus is conjunct 9th, conjunct Mercury. Uranus is conjunct the 9th.

In the 9th house we have Mercury conjuncting Mars and Jupiter. Mars conjuncting Jupiter. Mercury and Mars conjunct the 9th. Mercury semi-sextile the Mid. Mars semi-sextile Fortune in the 10th house.

Mars and Jupiter both trine the ascendant. Fortune conjunct the Mid.

Note: There are many planets in Aries, this is called a stellium. All hanging around the 9th house. And notice that Mars is giving energy to the ascendant, while Jupiter is protecting.

I have never did a Jupiter return until I did one for 1966 when I got married. It was plain to see what the energies were doing, and in what department (house).

I will make Saturn the last return. If you want to check the rest, you can do so. But I will stop at Saturn. This return will last for 29 years.

We shall use the chart of *Sandra Bullock*. She was born on 26th July 1964 at 03:15 am, Arlington, Virginia, U.S.A.

Her natal Saturn is in 03 degrees and 44 minutes of Pisces.

On the 28th February 1994 at 21:00 hrs, we got Saturn in 3 degrees and 44 minutes of Pisces.

Ascendant	17.22	Libra
2nd	14.55	Scorpio
3rd	16.09	Sagittarius
4th	19.55	Capricorn
5th	23.01	Aquarius
6th	22.32	Pisces
7th	17.22	Aries
8th	14.55	Taurus
9th	16.09	Gemini
10th	19.55	Cancer
11th	23.01	Leo
12th	22.32	Virgo

Sun	10.15	Pisces
Moon	22.12	Libra
Mercury	23.36 R	Aquarius
Venus	20.37	Pisces
Mars	24.59	Aquarius
Jupiter	14.39 R	Scorpio
Saturn	03.44	Pisces
Uranus	24.51	Capricorn
Neptune	22.32	Capricorn
Pluto	28.01	Scorpio
Chiron	05.48	Virgo
N Node	27.58	Scorpio
Fortune	05.24	Pisces

This Saturn return gives an ascendant of Libra with the ruler Venus, in the 5th house in the sign of Pisces. Venus is exalted in this sign. Lots of energies for love, creativity and entertainment. A love for children.

Venus is trine the Mid, sextile Uranus and Neptune in the 4th house. Venus is trine Jupiter in the 1st house, Pluto and the Node in the 2nd house.

The moon is in the first house, notice the degrees it is holding. It is ruler of the 10th house. It conjuncts the ascendant. Making a square contact with the Mid. Exactly square Neptune in the 4th house, square Uranus in the same house. Trine Mercury and Mars in the 5th house. Sesqui-quadrate the sun in the 5th house.

Jupiter in the first house in the sign of Scorpio is exactly conjunct the second. It is trine the Mid. Jupiter is square to Mercury, trine to the sun and Venus.

The nod is in the second house conjunct Pluto also in the second house, both in Scorpio. The Node is sextile Uranus and Neptune. It is square Mercury and Mars, Saturn and Fortune.

Pluto is sextile Uranus and Neptune, square Mercury and Mars, about 111 degrees from Venus, square Saturn and Fortune.

Both Uranus and Neptune are in the 4th house square the ascendant. Uranus is exactly semi-sextile Mars in the 5th house, semi-sextile Mercury also in the 5th house. Both are semi-square the sun, and sextile to Venus. They both are in conjunction with the 4th.

In the 5th, we have Mercury and Mars ion Aquarius both in conjunction with the 5th. Mars is conjunct Saturn.

The sun is in the 5th house and is conjunct Saturn and Fortune.

Venus is in the 5th house in the sign of Pisces conjunct the 6th, trine the Mid.

Mercury in the third house is square Saturn in the first. Mars in the 7th is opposing Saturn. Mercury is square Mars. The sun in the 4th house is square Uranus and Pluto in the 7th. The sun is square the Moon.

Venus in the third house is opposing Neptune in the 9th.

Jupiter in the second gives the chance of becoming rich. The sun is in good aspect with Jupiter. This is another aspect of doing well. This aspect is also a protective aspect.

We see Mars in the 7th house. The person has to be very discipline to control these energies of Mars. In an event chart, the 7th house is the house of war. In a personal chart, it is the house of the public and partnerships. There'll always be some trouble there.

After some long research, I found that Mars and Uranus is very dangerous. Enormous energy is found here. Uranus, being a sudden planet, can make things happen to shock. The Moon is conjunct Uranus and Pluto. I have always seen Pluto as a dark planet whether it is positive or negative.

16: Talking About Charts Without Drawing Them

The first chart I am going to talk on is that of *Shauna Grant*, the actress who killed herself. With this chart, I'll be using a Midnight time. She was born 30th May 1963, Bellflower, California, U.S.A. Of course, you can draw the chart. I meant that I won't be drawing the chart like I normally do.

On the 21st March 1984 around 19:10 pm, she shot herself. She died on the 23rd March 1984.

In the Midnight chart, you have to look very carefully, and only take the aspects the sun makes, but not its position. It will always be hanging near to the 4th house. Sometimes a little distance away. You have to make charts for the years that events took place, and check them carefully. You have to be sure that you see in the chart the aspects of the planets and the cusps for the event.

One thing you must never forget, and that is the upbringing of the individual; and the environment.

In the Midnight chart she has Aquarius on the ascendant. This sign is ruled by Saturn and Uranus. Read up a bit about the ascendant in Aquarius. Saturn is in the first house in Aquarius, its own sign. This shows that she started out in life very young.

The other planet as ruler, Uranus is in the 7th house in the sign of Virgo.

Note: IMD has given the date of 21st March when she died.

The sun in Gemini is always two sided. The Moon in Virgo is critical and analytical. These people when they are young, sees all what goes on around the family, and they take it all in.

Venus in Taurus is stubborn, loving, likes expensive things.

We must remember that looking at a natal chart does not immediately show us what is going to happen. It shows us the energies, positive and negative that the individual has to work with. I once came across some charts that had many negatives, and yet the individuals came out good in the society. Again, I would say, it truly depends on the early life of the individual.

Let us have a look at her progress Midnight chart when her parents moved house. This was in 1973. The progress would be 10th June 1963.

What are we looking for? To find what the 4th house and its ruler is doing. 4th house has to do with the home. We can also pick up planets in the sign of Cancer. Cancer is the sign that is fixed at the 4th house.

We find the planet Mercury in the 3rd house in the sign of Gemini, and is ruler of the 4th house with the sign Gemini there, is square her ascendant, and square Mars in the 7th house.

In 1982 she ran away from home. And from here on, the trouble started. She broke up with her boyfriend, went in as a model and ended up doing films for sex. In the early days, she was a cheerleader.

We find her ascendant holding 22 degrees, her 6th and 12th houses as well. Saturn is directly on her ascendant in 23 degrees. Her Node is in the 5th house in 22 degrees and conjuncting her 6th house.

In her 3rd house, we find Mercury and Venus both in Gemini in conjunction. Mercury is now ruler of the 4th and 5th, and intercepted 7th house. Both Mercury and Venus are square to the ascendant and to Saturn, they are also both square to Mars and Uranus.

Then we got the moon going into the 12th house exactly conjunct the 12th holding 22 degrees. It is exactly semi-sextile the ascendant.

Notice that her Mercury is in the sign of Taurus. She was warned by someone in the model office not to go into the sex business, she did not listen. Here, we see how free will works. She was free to do what she wants. Anyone is free to do what they want to do, but you'll have to pay for it later, if you've made the wrong decision.

I will talk about the chart of *Ernest C jr. Anthony* born 6th December 1964 at 20:11 pm, Boston, Massachussets, U.S.A. He committed suicide by shooting himself This happened in the year 1992.

Remember, I do skip over a lot because it's quite a lot of work to compare the progress chart with the natal chart. But I do it quickly. Professionals will go over every single thing that's going on before they make a final decision.

His progress date is 3rd January 1965 at 20:11 pm. This corresponds to the year 1992 when the event took place.

In his natal chart there are three heavy planets in the second house in the sign of Virgo. Mars and Uranus, as I have been checking them, gives enormous energy, leading to sudden action whether positive or negative.

Let's have a look at the second house. This house is the body. The sign there is Virgo. Mars is there conjunct with about 3 degrees. Uranus and Pluto are there.

The ruler of the second house is Mercury in the fourth house in the sign of Sagittarius, conjunct Venus. Mercury is square the second. Venus is exactly sextile the third.

The Node in the 10th house in Gemini is exactly square the second house. Jupiter in the 9th house in the sign of Taurus is exactly trine Pluto in the first house but in the sign of the second. Fortune in the 12th house is exactly square Jupiter, and semi-sextile Pluto. Mercury is semi-sextile Neptune in the third house but in the sign of the fourth. Neptune is co-ruler of the 8th along with Jupiter. Mars is co-ruler of the fourth with Pluto. Venus is also semi-sextile Neptune. Neptune is exactly semi-sextile the third.

Saturn in the 7th house in the 8th house sign of Pisces is semi-sextile the sixth. The Node is semi-sextile the Mid.

The sun and Moon are in a loop in the fifth house in the sign of Capricorn.

If you have time, check the natal chart with the progressed chart, and you'll get more results.

This next chart is the murder of *Joanna Yeates* born 19th April 1985, Hampshire, UK.

What I'm interested in is the progress chart; and that work out as the 14th May 1985.

The next chart was when she left the pub in Bristol around 20:00 hrs to walk 20 minutes to her home. The date is 17th December 2010 when she disappeared.

I have told you before to keep your eyes on Taurus and Scorpio as they are of the 2nd and 8th houses. Cancer as well. I had been for a long time chasing Gemini and Cancer, but I had to let go. You must also check carefully the duplicate; and don't forget that they are really one sign. Let's talk about the 14th May 1985, the progress chart. These charts, I'm sorry, are Midnight.

The ascendant rising is Capricorn in its first sign. Saturn is in the 10th house in the sign of Scorpio. It is conjuncting the South Node by about 6 degrees.

Saturn has a good aspect to the Moon in the loop in the second house. The Moon is in the sign of Pisces. When counting from the ascendant, Pisces become the third sign.

Neptune is in the ascendant. It has a trine to Mercury in the third house. Neptune would be co-ruler of the loop in the second house. Mercury would be ruler of the 6th house, and also of the loop in the 8th house.

The enemy could either be Jupiter, ruler of the 12th house – secret enemy. Or the Moon in the third sign of the loop in the second house. Jupiter has a trine to Mars in the 5th house but in the 6th house sign of Gemini. Jupiter has a square to the sun in the 4th house in the sign of Taurus.

Jupiter is also sextile to Uranus in the 12th house. This Uranus is co-ruler of the second house, of the body, It is opposing Mars, and square to the Moon.

The moon has a trine to Saturn in the 10th house in the sign of Scorpio. The Moon is square Mars and Uranus, sextile the sun.

Venus we find in the 3rd house in the sign of Aries with a good aspect to Mars and to Uranus.

Mercury is also in the third house, its own house, and opposing Pluto. Pluto is co-ruler of the duplicate 10th and 11th houses.

The third house to do with neighbours, short distances, travel, communications. Pluto is just a dark planet, co-ruler of the 8th house.

What I get from this is that her career, her friends, neighbours, her work and the loop in the 8th house; house of darkness comes to the fore.

We see that Mars in Gemini is opposing Uranus in Sagittarius. You probably want to know about this. I have seen in many charts where Mars, even when it is friendly to Uranus causes problems. And this is depending on who is using the energies. For a wise person could dig in to scientifical subjects, while a foolish person would get injured or killed.

Let's have a look at the chart when she left the pub and her friends.

This chart is the 17th December 2010 at 20:00 pm, Bristol, UK. She is walking home.

Now what I want you to notice is the Moon in the loop in the 10th house holding 13 degrees, and is exactly sextile the 12th, and square the ascendant.

The ascendant sign for this chart is Leo. Its ruler, the sun, is in the 5th house in the sign of Sagittarius.

Notice that the 5th house/11th house is holding 5 degrees. The sun is square the 3rd house. It is semi-sextile Neptune in the 7th and Chiron also in the 7th. Chiron and Neptune are exactly in conjunction both with 26 degrees in the sign of Aquarius. They both are exactly semi-sextile to Uranus in the 9th house in the sign of Pisces. Both sextile to the Mid. The sun is square Uranus and Fortune. Fortune is in the 9th house exactly conjunct Uranus in the sign of Pisces. Both Uranus and Chiron are semi-sextile to Fortune.

Once we pick out what we want we move on. On her way home she is seen by CCT cameras, picking up a pizza in Tescos. But now let's draw a chart for 20:50 pm on the same day.

We find that the planet Mercury is holding 0 degree in the 5th house in the sign of Capricorn. Mars is also in the same sign and is holding 7 degrees. Mars is ruler of the 4th house and the 9th. Mercury is ruler of the 2nd (always remember that the 2nd house has to do with money or the body), and the 11th houses.

The ascendant is Leo, and it is holding 22 degrees. Make a note of that 22 degrees because it keeps coming up, and I'm trying to get a hold on its real meaning. It is telling us something.

Notice that the 10/4th houses are holding 8 degrees. This is something that we cannot explain, but has to do with those houses. And of course you know what the fourth house represents.

The 3rd/9th houses are in 5 degrees. Fortune is in the 8th house conjuncting the 9th.

The sun is squaring Jupiter in the 8th house, and also Uranus. The sun is in the 5th house in the sign of Sagittarius. It is conjunct Pluto with about 8 degrees; conjunct the Node with about 7 degrees; conjunct Mercury with about 4 degrees.

The Node in the fifth house is conjunct Pluto also in the fifth house. The node is conjunct Mercury in the fifth house. The Node is conjunct Mars in the fifth house.

The Node, Mercury, Mars and Pluto are all in the sign of Capricorn – the sign of cold and damp, cautious, slow, taking one's time.

At the third house is the sign of Libra, its ruler is Venus. Venus is in the fourth house in the sign of Scorpio. Venus is exactly sextile to the second house, and exactly trine the 8th. Venus is also ruler of the 10th house.

Fortune is exactly square Pluto in the fifth house. . Square the Node in the same house. Mars in the fifth house is trine the Mid.

Our last chart on this subject is that of the little girl who went missing in Portugal. Everyone must have heard about it. She is *Madeleine McCann* born 12th May 2003 at 18:14 pm, Leicester, UK.

If we progressed the chart to 2007, which is 4 years, we get the following:

Progressive date is 16th May 2003 at 18:14 pm, Leicester, UK.

Libra is rising with its ruler Venus in the 7th house in the sign of Taurus and holding 0 degree. You should know by now how to check when a planet is holding 0 degree.

Venus is holding 0 degree. It is in the 7th house; in the sign of Taurus; the 8th sign. Venus is ruler of the ascendant and the 8th house.

The sun is in the 8th house in the sign of Taurus, exactly conjunct the 8th house. The sun is semi-sextile Saturn in the 8th house but in the sign of Gemini, the 9th house sign. Saturn is ruler of the intercepted sign (loop) in the 3rd house, and also co-ruler of the 4th. The sun is ruler of the 10th house.

The 4th/10th house is holding 8 degrees

The sun has a square to Uranus in the sign of Pisces in the 4th house.

In the second house, which is the body, we have the Moon's South node crying (29 degrees) of Scorpio.

The Moon is in the second house in the sign of Sagittarius with about 171 degrees from the sun.

The moon is ruling the loop in the 9th house. With my test, this is giving, extra travel or to do with the 9th house, the same way as the third house has to do with extra neighbours, travel, environment and so forth.

Inside the loop, is Chiron. We have Sagittarius which I work with, as test; and we also have Capricorn, Aquarius or Virgo.

Pluto is in the second house and is co-ruler of the second along with Mars. Pluto is in t he sign of Sagittarius, the same sign as the Moon.

Mars is in the 4th house conjunct Neptune in the sign of Aquarius. Both Mars and Neptune are semi-sextile to the 5th house.

The moon in the 2nd house is squaring Uranus in the 4th house.

We are told that the parents left the children at around 20:30 pm.

Check was made through the evening until 22:00 pm. The mother found Madeleine missing.

Looking at the chart for 3rd May 2007 at 22:00 pm, Praia da Luz, Portugal, we find:

The ascendant is in 3 degrees of Sagittarius. The ruler Jupiter is in the ascendant sign about 10 degrees away from Pluto, also in the ascendant sign, both in the first house. The second house is Capricorn and is ruled by Saturn up in the 9th house in the sign of Leo. There is an exact trine aspect from Jupiter to Saturn.

Jupiter is sextile Neptune in the 3rd house in the sign of Aquarius. Jupiter is square Mars and Uranus in the 4th house. Mars and Uranus are in the sign of Pisces. Jupiter is also square the Node in the 3rd house, in the sign of Pisces. Jupiter is sextile the 11th house, trine the 5th. Jupiter is sextile Chiron in the 3rd house in the sign of Aquarius.

We find that the third house is at the fore, and this could mean travel, close relatives, neighbours, environment. Brothers and sisters.

Lets us see what the ruler of the 12th house (secret enemies) is doing.

Inside the 12th house we see the Moon, it is crying. The Moon represents the mother or someone feminine. The Moon is ruler of the 8th house. The Moon is semi-sextile Pluto in the first house. Pluto is co-ruler of the 12th house along with Mars.

Mars is in the fourth house conjunct Uranus. Mars and Uranus is enormous energy. These two planets are dangerous, if their energies are not used properly.

We find the second house ruler, Saturn in the 9th house is sextile to the 11th.

I am getting the feeling that if the girl was taken, she must have known those who did so. They were friends. And as we see, if this is so they won't harm her because of the contact Jupiter has with Saturn, and both being good to the 11th. But we mustn't be led astray by good aspects.

In the fourth house we have Uranus exactly semi-sextile the fifth house. Uranus is co-ruler of the 3rd house. Here we see how often the third house came up.

Uranus is conjunct the 4th house. Uranus is sextile Fortune in the 6th house in the sign of Taurus.

Inside the 6th house we have the sun exactly conjunct Mercury, and both exactly sextile the Node in the third house. Taurus is the sign at the 6th house. The sun is ruler of the 9th, Mercury is ruler of the 7th and 10th.

Fortune is exactly trine the 10th.

17: Lots of Tips

You know quite well that when you see the planet Saturn in the 10th house, that the individual has a chance of holding a top Job. The same goes for Jupiter. Venus can also bring you good things in your career. Painting, singing, dancing, acting, and all the beautiful things that goes with Venus. Mars is a bit more military. Lots of energies.

If I have Jupiter in the sign of Libra, and it is making a sextile contact with Uranus in Sagittarius. Check the houses they are in. if Jupiter is in the 8th and Uranus in the 11th, then you just need to say: 8/11, and 7/9.

8　11
7　9

Start matching: **eight – – eleven; eight – – nine; eight – – seven; nine – – eleven; nine – – seven;** and **seven – – eleven.**

This can be used for all aspects and house and sign positions.

Have you ever considered a loop in the 9th house with the sign of Leo, and Jupiter in that sign and ruler of the ascendant and the 4th house?

Do you know that people with a Virgo ascendant, depending on what degree it is in, will have the next sign which is Libra to live through?

This goes for all the signs starting from Aries.

Some of us do not accept that events are there in the future in time; but time isn't the cause of the events.

You know it took the researchers a long time to crack the DNA code. The astrological workings will go on as long as the cosmic world is there and working.

I read what some philosophers said about astrology. They said it cannot explain courage and determination, and other things within the human being.

Little do they know that with a mixture of certain planets energies within us, we get the courage and determination to do certain things. But that is really hard to explain to them.

Some people write and talk about astrology without testing it first.

If you want to find the real person, go to the second house and check it out thoroughly.

What is rather interesting is reading a chart, could be your own, for a future year. Seeing all what the planets are doing before that year gets to you. Do you see now that you have all that information in front of you, and the time has not arrive yet. Amazing!

Mars in a good contact with Neptune is really powerful. It is up to the individual how to use those energies.

I am at the moment trying to get some more info on the loops, the duplicate houses. I had a loop that came in my 5th/11th houses. As I have told you before, I have the feeling that these house has something to do with extra. So I had extra 5th house energies; and extra 11th house energies. So in the 11th house, this could work out as extra friends and groups and clubs which I came across. There was one woman who liked me very much, and she told me that she was married and she didn't mind. Now, I don't mess about with married women like that so I kept out of trouble.

The trouble with these loops or intercepted signs is that they set themselves up. The next year, they just take over the house that they were waiting to take over, according to the degrees around the chart. Some loops are empty, only carrying the signs, while others can have many planets in them. They can also stay along time in the loop depending on the degrees around the chart.

Suppose you find Venus in the 11th house exactly trine Pluto in the 3rd house, Venus in the sign of Taurus while Pluto is in the sign of Virgo, what would be your interpretation? Venus is also ruling the fourth house, and Pluto co-ruling the 5th.

Venus in the sign of Taurus loves beautiful things, and in the 11th house has to do with friends or groups and clubs. Help will always come to one from women friends. The trine to Pluto, can make things easier, and the third house will also come into force. We get 11-2, 3-6.

This contact of 11-2 is good for money.

The contact 11-3 could bring friendship with neighbours, brothers and sisters or close relatives and even travel and writing or publishing.

The contact 11-6 could bring you many friends, especially in the work area.

Inside the chart the aspects make what we call *"the finger of God."* This is three planets making two sextiles and a trine. Known as positive or easy. The signs they come in can be like this:

1	3	5
2	4	6
3	5	7
4	6	8
5	7	9
6	8	10
7	9	11
8	10	12
9	11	1
10	12	2
11	1	3
12	2	4

Then we have what we call the negative finger of God, a bit stressful but can be put to good use. Three planets having an opposition and two squares. They come in these signs:

1	4	7
2	5	8
3	6	9
4	7	10
5	8	11
6	9	12
7	10	1
8	11	2
9	12	3
10	1	4
11	2	5
12	3	6

I was doing some research on people whose partners are from another country. The first chart was okay. The second chart had the moon at the descendant. The moon was in the first in 3 degrees of Aquarius. Inside the 7th house was the planet Jupiter in the sign of Cancer, Pluto in the sign of Leo. I was about to give this up as a bad job, then I looked again and saw that the 9th house was ruled by Libra. The planet Neptune is in the sign of Libra, and is making a good contact with the moon. The moon is good with Saturn and Uranus both in the fifth house in Gemini. Pisces is in a loop in the second house, but is in the third sign from the ascendant.

We must not forget that the third house is also close relatives or family, while the 5th house represents romance and love affairs. So one must check carefully when they are looking for clues. All charts doesn't show the same thing.

We do find aspects patterns in the chart such as a square – four planets. We also get an X – four planets; or an X inside of a square. We get a grand trine – three planets. We find a cross inside a diamond. And a cross. Then there is the star of David. You can pick up other patterns too.

I am getting very more interested in the loops and their duplicates. A chart with a loop in the 8th house with the sun inside the loop and is ruler of the loop, along with Mercury also inside the loop. I found the person were involved with other people's goods, and with a partner from another country. Mercury was ruler of the 7th and 9th houses.

In the opposite loop, Jupiter and Neptune were inside in the sign of Aquarius. Jupiter was ruler of the ascendant, and co-ruler with Neptune of the third house. There were lots of short distance travelling.

It is interesting to do a chart of Queen Elizabeth I of England for the time she died. This is given as 24th March 1603 at 02:15 am, London UK.

This chart is a very easy one. If you have for the ascendant 1 degree and 33 minutes, then you have the right chart. The ruler of the ascendant is Saturn, and you find it in the 11th house but in the 12th house sign of Sagittarius. It is square the planet Neptune in the loop in the 8th house in the sign of Virgo. This Neptune is exactly opposing the planet Venus in the loop in the second house in the sign of Pisces which is ruled by both Jupiter and Neptune. Saturn and Uranus are rulers of the second house.

Venus, ruler of the fourth, fifth and ninth houses is exactly semi-sextile with the sun in the second house but in the third house sign of Aries. Venus is square to Saturn.

Remember, for good results we are using a distance of 1 degree orb. I have not really checked to see up to what degree they work.

The sun is ruler of the 8th house. In the 8th house we have the moon conjunct the 8th house. The moon is ruler of the 7th. Are you baffled here? The queen wasn't married. But she was in partnership with the country, and now it has ended.

I think that's why it is so difficult to read charts. Even in your own chart, if you are married and have a career, your chart will show your 7th house planet, as being affected, but has nothing to do with your personal partnership.

The sun is in the second house, and is trine Saturn in the 11th house. The node in the 10th house in the sign of Scorpio is conjunct the 11th. The node, at the moment, in my test, is ruling the 7th house.

We could get a square from the moon in Leo in the 8th house to Jupiter in the 10th house in Scorpio.

The moon is also making a trine aspect to Mercury in the third house. Notice that Mercury is ruler of the 6th and 8th houses, while the moon is ruler of the 7th.

The sixth house is servants; the seventh house is the public.

Venus is sextile the ascendant, the sun is square the ascendant. Neptune is trine the ascendant, and exactly quincunx the sun.

We shall now take a peep in the progressive chart of ex Prime Minister *David Cameron*, and see how he fell from power.

His progressive date is 28th November 1966 at 06:00 am, London, UK.

First, let me say that there's a loop in this progressed chart, probably brought over from the last chart. This loop will end as the chart progresses.

The loop is in the third and ninth houses, In the third loop, the sign of Aquarius;and in the ninth loop, the sign of Leo. The loops in my test has to do with extra travel, talking, communicating etc. I hope I could get a more clearer insight in these loops (intercepted signs).

In the 9th house loop we have the planet Jupiter making an exact semi-sextile contact with the Mid. This is the outside world, the career.

In the 10th house there are three planets, I am wondering if I can use them seeing that they are part of the sign that Jupiter is making a contact to. If we can use them, then Mars is ruler of the ascendant, the fifth and sixth houses. Uranus co-ruler of the loop in the third. Pluto co-ruler of the ascendant.

We shall use this method as test to see if it is okay. If not, we kick it out the door.

Jupiter in the loop in the 9th house has a trine to the sun in the first house in the sign of Sagittarius, Jupiter is the ruler of this sign. But the sun is square to the Mid. Even though both are angles, it still shows some conflict here. There's something to do with travel, foreign countries, communications.

The node in the 6th house in Taurus is exactly conjunct the 7th, opposing Mercury and the ascendant. The node, in my test has rule over the 9th house. The node is also exactly semi-sextile the 8th house where we pick up the moon, ruler of the 9th.

Uranus in the 10th is sextile the 9th. Uranus is co-ruler of the loop in the third.

I hope you see that the axis 6/12 is crying. I'm picking up on this crying business that it shows that something is wrong. It seems to me that there is some good behind this.

Mercury in the first house is conjunct the ascendant, and semi-sextile the second house. Again, we see some sort of communication going on, The sign at the second house is Sagittarius, and Mercury itself is in the sign of Scorpio. Deep, political, intellectual. We see too, that Mercury is conjunct Neptune with about 5 degrees. Something is not right here Neptune is trying to make Mercury out as a fool. Communications are not clear. Neptune is co-ruler of the fourth house.

You can dig out more information.

Let's have a quick look at *Meghan Markle*'s chart who just a while ago became Her Royal Highness Duchess of Sussex, by marrying our Prince Harry, son of Prince Charles and Princess Diana.

In her chart, you'll see that she has what it takes to be a queen or royalty.

She was born on the 4th August 1981 at 04.46 am, Canoga Park, California, U.S.A.

The first thing I saw was that she has the same degree in Cancer rising just like Joan of Arc. But with Mars in the sign of Cancer, and in the 12th house. Here we have a house of secrets and Isolation. This isolation, you must remember can be of one who is in a position to serve the public. Having Mars in the ascendant sign, but not conjuncting the ascendant can still give lots of energy. Mars is supposed to be in its fall in the sign of Cancer. It is exactly square the Mid. Exactly semi-sextile the sun in the first house in the sign of Leo. Exactly sextile the third house with the sign of Virgo.

The ascendant ruler is the Moon, and it is in the thrd house but in the fourth house sign of Libra. You know what Librans are like. And Cancers are people who love their homes, country and families.

Mars is sextile Venus in the third house in the sign of Virgo. Venus is getting or I should say giving beauty through Mars in the ascendant sign, and not from the ascendant itself.

Mars is ruler of the 5th and 10th houses.

Mars is about 82 degrees from the Moon. About 84 degrees from Jupiter, and about 83 degrees from Saturn.

She is a Leo with the sun in the first house conjuncting Mercury. The node is also in Leo. Mercury is conjuncting the node. This sun and Mercury does give the ability to be intellectual. The sun is exactly trine the Mid. It is exactly semi-sextile the third house; semi-sextile Venus; about 52 degrees from thew moon; about 54 degrees from Jupiter; and about 53 degrees from Saturn.

A lion woman doesn't give in easily. They love entertainment, children and sports.

Venus is in Virgo in the third house. This position of Venus in Virgo is someone who is looking for the right partner.

She is a strong Libran with the Moon, Jupiter, Saturn and Pluto in the sign. Saturn is exalted in this sign. The Moon is conjunct Jupiter and Saturn. Jupiter is conjunct Saturn.

The Moon, Jupiter and Saturn are all in conjunction with the fourth house, from the third. Pluto is square the ascendant, both angles.

Her Uranus is in the fifth house in the sign of Scorpio with about 9 degrees conjunction to the fifth house. Uranus is trine the ascendant. Uranus is co-ruler of the 8th house. The 8th house is also her partner's body or possessions, and legacies and all that stuff. Uranus is universal and scientific, and unusual.

Mercury in the first house has a good aspect to the Mid. A sextile to the Moon in the third house; a sextile to Jupiter in the third house; and a sextile to Saturn in the third house.

She will do well if she keeps to the rules of the Royal House. there were some rules that Diana hated, and she was still well-loved.

When I was in the army, there were rules I had to keep by, if they were broken, I would have to pay. In any organization this is so.

Since I've been doing research, I never like to see Neptune in the 5th house. This house is the house of the sun, the house of life. Any contact with the sun and

Neptune is strange. I started off learning astrology by calling Neptune a strange planet, positive or negative. But mind you, if there are some good contacts from other planets, Neptune in its strangeness can be good for singing, painting dancing and all that has to do with the arts. I don't know why Neptune is in the fifth house and exactly conjuncting the 6th house in the sign of Sagittarius.

Since the house has to do with servants, work, animals; and Sagittarius has to do with foreign countries or higher education and religion. I was thinking more of servants in a foreign country. Neptune is co-ruler of the 9th house along with Jupiter. Neptune rules the natural sign in at the 12th house in the fixed wheel.

Chiron is in the 11th house in the sign of Taurus exactly semi-sextile the 12th. This could be something to do with enemies and the past; and if Chiron really is the ruler of Sagittarius, then she'll have many friends, and not forgetting the 12th house contact.

Chiron is sextile the ascendant, this contact is service, servants, colleagues, pets. We see that it is a positive aspect.

A quick look now at *Prince Harry's* Chart (Duke of Sussex).

He was born on the 15th September 1984 at 16:20 pm, London, UK.

He has a chart with Capricorn rising just like the Queen. Inside the first house is the loop of Aquarius, no planets. The Queen has the same loop of Aquarius in the first house but with Mars and Jupiter there.

The Duke of Sussex has his ruler of the ascendant which is Saturn in the 9th house conjuncting the Mid in the sign of Scorpio, just like the Queen. In the Queen's chart, Saturn is on its own. In the Duke of Sussex chart, Saturn is with Pluto.

In the Duke's chart, Jupiter is in the 12th house conjuncting the ascendant. His ruler, Saturn is sextile the ascendant. The Queen's ruler, Saturn is also sextile to the ascendant.

When you see a chart with Saturn in the 9th house, you can tell that the person is thinking about long distance travel, or will be actually doing it for real. There's also energies here for high education and religious thinking.

The Queen has her Venus in the first house exalted in the sign of Pisces, The Duke has his Venus in the 8th house in the sign of Libra.

Over the years I've been watching Virgo's and Leo's, it is not really a good combination, but we all know what human beings are like. A virgo fits much more with a Taurus or a Capricorn. But a Leo and a Virgo, well, it can work, if the Virgo is not too critical and analytical about what the Leo does. Anyway, we all know what the Lion is like.

The Duke has his Moon in the fourth house in the sign of Taurus, a bit stubborn but loving. His sun is in the 8th house about 16 degrees away from

Mercury. Very intellectual with interests of things belonging to the 8th house.

Mercury is in the 8th house holding 5 degrees, and is ruler of the fifth, sixth, and 8th houses. Mercury is square Uranus in the 11th house, trine Jupiter in the 12th, and the ascendant.

Mercury is about 54 degrees from Pluto in the 9th house in its own sign of Scorpio. Mercury is square to Chiron in the fifth house in the sign of Gemini which is owned by Mercury. Mercury is about 66 or 67 degrees from Saturn.

In his chart, the Duke has a sextile from Mars to Venus, just like the Duchess of Sussex. Mars is also semi-sextile to the Mid.

Uranus is conjuncting the 11th house, Venus the 9th, the Moon the fourth, Chiron, the fifth, and Mercury the 8th.

While the Duke has his ascendant as Capricorn, and the descendant as Cancer, the Duchess of Sussex has it the other way round. Cancer as the ascendant, and Capricorn as the descendant.

Neptune is in the 12th house conjunct Jupiter also in the same house. Jupiter is sextile the second house. Uranus is opposing Chiron. Mercury is square the 11th. Jupiter is semi-square the Mid.

Annie Oakley and her husband Frank Butler lived together for 50 years both doing the same things in life. It is up to two human beings, if they love each other, and are both doing the same things in life, to make sure that their relationship lasts.

You can tell when something is from space or long distance travel. Check the rulers of the third and ninth houses, see what they are doing. For instance, if you have Cancer on the ninth house, and the moon is in the 11th, then you know this has to do with long distance travel. Planets could also be in the 8th house but in the 9th house sign and making contact to planets in the 10th, but in the 11th house sign. You could also have the planet of the 11th house in the 9th.

Don't forget that the 9th house has to do with in-laws, grandparents etc.

18: Sidereal Charts and BTBs

I've been through thousands of charts, and I have to say that the workings of astrology is true; but there still remain a sort of mystery about it. As I have already said it is like the sun, it is there and working; and will carry on doing so until everything collapses. Real astrology cannot be accepted by everyone, for there is that truth about it that turns some people away. From what I have seen everything is connected, like a spider's web. You'll find a chart where brother and sister has to make some sort of partnership, whether personal or public. A chart where one cannot get on with their neighbours. One ends up with nothing but bad luck. In another chart, you'll find the husband killing the wife, and vice versa. There's quite a lot going on. Astrology is really not for a fearful person. But there's one thing we must stop and consider: God saw all that he made, and it was good. So then, the negatives that we come up against are good. Some of the prophets said that *good and bad comes from God."*

One thing I can say, if you are planning of studying astrology, you won't be disappointed. It will make you think quite a lot; and you will see for yourself, how hard it is to try and explain its workings.

If we look up to the Midheaven in the chart, we are looking at the highest point – Midday. This is a mean day, 24 hours. Sidereal time is 23 hours, 56 minutes and 4.1 seconds. You measure sidereal time where the star comes to the Mid, and then how long it takes to return.

So what we are actually doing is using sidereal time to erect the chart. The sun will always be hanging around the Mid. We only use its aspects to the rest of the chart.

We'll start off with the chart of *Bernard Archeriaux* born 19th March 1945 at 23:00 pm, Montoire sur le Loire, France.

Things were so bad for him that he wrote a book about his misfortunes. The details above are his normal chart. For the sidereal chart use the noon time.

Ascendant	09.38	Cancer
2nd	26.54	Cancer
3rd	16.09	Leo
4th	11.01	Virgo
5th	16.06	Libra
6th	00.39	Sagittarius
7th	09.38	Capricorn
8th	26.54	Capricorn
9th	16.09	Aquarius
10th	11.01	Pisces
11th	16.06	Aries
12th	00.39	Gemini

Sun	28.29	Pisces
Moon	11.38	Gemini
Mercury	14.50	Aries
Venus	02.52	Taurus
Mars	25.34	Aquarius
Jupiter	21.48 R	Virgo
Saturn	04.00	Cancer
Uranus	09.32	Gemini
Neptune	05.15 R	Libra
Pluto	08.07 R	Leo
Chiron	00.22	Libra
N Node	14.42	Cancer
Fortune	22.48	Virgo

In his original chart we see that Mars and Pluto are the rulers of his ascendant. Mars is in the 4th houses in the sign of Aquarius about 24 degrees away from Fortune. Mars is semi-sextile the sun in the 5th house. The sun here is exactly conjunct the 5th. The sun is square the destiny planet Saturn in the 8th house in the sign of Cancer. Saturn is in its fall in Cancer. The moon is in the 8th exactly semi-sextile the 9th. The moon is in Gemini. Pluto is square the ascendant.

In the sidereal chart the moon is ruler of the rising sign of Cancer. The moon is in the 12th house. Have you ever found a chart with the Moon in the 12th house, and the person hasn't been through some difficult times?

Neptune is the natural ruler of the 12th house along with Jupiter. This house is of isolation, prisons, hospitals, enemies, working behind the scenes, can lead to singing and dancing and the arts. If the aspects to the moon are positive, then the native could bypass certain events.

Note: Always check carefully the information given to you of a birth chart. For it is possible that you could waste precious time on a chart that is not correct.

Looking more at this sidereal chart, we find that the sun in the 10th house is negative to Saturn in the 12th house. Here we have life and the destiny planet not in a good contact. Saturn, we are told from the ancients, is the destiny planet.

We have the same sun not in good contact with Jupiter in the fourth house. And of course, the sun is also negative to Neptune. Any contact with the sun and Neptune can bring a scandal, even if the energies are used for singing, dancing, the arts and such like.

Venus in the 11th house is negative to Pluto in the second house. Remember that these two house can bring sums of money to the owner, if the energies are good. House 2 and 11.

The aspect from Saturn to Neptune is negative. Remember, some people has a chart with almost all negatives, and has made something of their lives by either being a scientist or a doctor depending on what energies they have to work with. So you see, it could be the individual, his environment, and his upbringing that comes into play as well.

Moving on to *Prince William*'s sidereal chart we see that he has the moon in the 10th house, showing much publicity. He has Mars in the first house, showing much energy. Jupiter, Saturn and Pluto are in the 2nd house. He could be a very rich man with Jupiter in the second. The conjunction of Jupiter and Pluto gives deep insight. Saturn has to do with old things, like buildings and such like.

Prince William's sidereal chart is 21st June 1982 at 12.00 pm, London U.K.

Ascendant	18.50	Virgo
2ns	11.19	Libra
3rd	10.06	Scorpio
4th	15.25	Sagittarius
5th	22.20	Capricorn
6th	23.41	Aquarius
7th	18.50	Pisces
8th	11.19	Aries
9th	10.06	Taurus
10th	15.25	Gemini
11th	22.20	Cancer
12th	23.41	Leo
Sun	29.44	Gemini
Moon	29.14	Gemini
Mercury	08.44	Gemini
Venus	25.13	Taurus
Mars	09.03	Libra
Jupiter	00.29 R	Scorpio
Saturn	15.30	Libra
Uranus	01.30 R	Sagittarius
Neptune	25.33 R	Sagittarius
Pluto	24.09 R	Libra
Chiron	25.15	Taurus
N Node	14.06	Cancer
Fortune	18.20	Virgo

Neptune is holding an angular position, and Venus in the 9th, shows a love of travel and foreign countries.

The next sidereal chart is of the richest man in the world, *Jeffrey P. Bezos* born 12th January 1964 (no natal time). But sidereal time is 12:00 pm, Albuquerque, New Mexico, U.S.A.

In the Midnight chart, you can see quite quickly where the money is coming from. The sidereal chart will give you something to talk about. If you find it, you are very good, and has a good intuitive insight.

Ascendant	29.55	Aries
2nd	01.56	Gemini
3rd	25.55	Gemini
4th	18.08	Cancer
5th	13.05	Leo
6th	15.55	Virgo
7th	29.55	Libra
8th	01.56	Sagittarius
9th	25.55	Sagittarius
10th	18.08	Capricorn
11th	13.05	Aquarius
12th	15.55	Pisces
Sun	21.36	Capricorn
Moon	28.22	Sagittarius
Mercury	05.02	Capricorn
Venus	24.41	Aquarius
Mars	29.35	Capricorn
Jupiter	11.58	Aries
Saturn	21.39	Aquarius
Uranus	09.43 R	Virgo
Neptune	17.27	Scorpio
Pluto	14.02 R	Scorpio
Chiron	11.29	Pisces
N Node	10.43	Cancer
Fortune	06.41	Aries

If we had the correct time of the individual's birth, it would have been easy to see where the energy for getting money is coming from.

In the sidereal chart we already have a clue. Mercury is holding 5 degrees in the 9th house in the sign of Capricorn. Mercury is ruler of the second and third houses, and also the 6th. If we say, the 6th house is carrying Uranus, then we find that Uranus is ruling the 11th house giving us 11-2, the money houses. But that's not enough.

We see that Mars is in the 10th house in 29 degrees, and is exalted in the sign of Capricorn. Mars is ruler of the ascendant, and is exactly square the ascendant.

Mars is trine the second house. Mars is ruler of the loop in the 7th house carrying Neptune. Neptune is ruler of the 12th house carrying Chiron. Chiron is ruler of the duplicate 8th and 9th houses.

The 8th house has to do with other people's money.

We go back to the loop in the 7th house, Pluto is there. Pluto is ruler of the loop along with Mars Both are natural rulers of the 8th house. We are not done yet.

Jupiter in the 12th house is in the sign of Mars conjuncting Fortune. Jupiter is ruler of the duplicate 8th and 9th houses, co-ruler of the 12th.

The node in the 3rd house is sextile Uranus in the fifth house. We know that the 5th house is speculation. Uranus is in contact with Mercury – the contact is good.

The moon in the 9th house in Sagittarius is trine the ascendant. The moon is ruler of the 4th house.

Neptune in the loop in the 7th house is making contact with the Mid, while Pluto is square the 11th, and trine the 12th.

Chiron in the 11th is exactly semi-sextile Jupiter, both are rulers of the duplicate 8th and 9th houses.

Venus in the 11th house is sextile the 9th. Venus is ruler in the 1st, and ruler of the 7th.

The sun is exactly semi-sextile Saturn in the 11th house. Saturn is ruler of the 10th and 11th houses. The node is trine Chiron, square Jupiter.

Are you satisfied that the individual has the opportunity here to become rich?

The next sidereal chart is of *Claude Vorilhon* born 30th September 1946 at 05.00 am, Ambert, France.

Messages were supposed to be given to him by extraterrestrial. He had his 1973 UFO experience, and that is what we are going to look at.

The sidereal progs are 27th October 1946, using noon time.

Ascendant	27.54	Sagittarius
2nd	08.29	Aquarius
3rd	22.15	Pisces
4th	25.49	Aries
5th	20.01	Taurus
6th	09.29	Gemini
7th	27.54	Gemini
8th	08.29	Leo
9th	22.15	Virgo
10th	25.49	Libra
11th	20.01	Scorpio
12th	09.29	Sagittarius

Sun	03.25	Scorpio
Moon	00.58	Sagittarius
Mercury	26.40	Scorpio
Venus	02.29	Sagittarius
Mars	22.38	Scorpio
Jupiter	06.49	Scorpio
Saturn	08.20	Leo
Uranus	21.25 R	Gemini
Neptune	09.16	Libra
Pluto	13.17	Leo
Chiron	28.02	Libra
N Node	13.36	Gemini
Fortune	25.26	Capricorn

Remember I told you about the 9th and 11th houses for long distance travel? You can bring in the third well for, although it represents short distance travel, it could also be long distance. Whether the person actually does it is something else. It could be a vision or a dream. Some people spend their lives dreaming about distant places, and never actually been there.

Notice the ruler of the 9th house which is Mercury, in the 11th house in the sign of Scorpio conjunct with the planet Mars.

There's something I have to tell you. I have been looking at 22 degrees for some time now. In Numerology both 11 and 22 are known as 'Master Numbers'.

I am trying to see if they can work themselves out in astrology. At first, I thought that 22 had something to do with magic, I still have the strong feeling.

You notice that Mercury is in a group of four. Sun, Mercury, Mars, and Jupiter all in the sign of Scorpio. I don't know if you know this, but Jupiter in Scorpio is a very deep penetrating combination. You find many people with this position and they are busy with things to do with the other world, or they can be detectives, doctors and those sort of deep subjects.

Here is a sidereal chart of a Saint, *Catherine Laboure*. Her sidereal progs is 6th September 1806, Fain-les Moutiers (close to Vassy), France. Her body had not decomposed, and her eyes were still blue.

Ascendant	25.02	Scorpio
2nd	26.22	Sagittarius
3rd	05.09	Aquarius
4th	13.35	Pisces
5th	13.58	Aries
6th	06.50	Taurus
7th	25.02	Taurus
8th	26.22	Gemini
9th	05.09	Leo

10th	13.35	Virgo
11th	13.58	Libra
12th	06.50	Scorpio
Sun	13.08	Virgo
Moon	19.36	Gemini
Mercury	08.52 R	Virgo
Venus	15.06	Leo
Mars	21.53	Cancer
Jupiter	28.37	Sagittarius
Saturn	25.43	Libra
Uranus	23.27	Libra
Neptune	27.45	Scorpio
Pluto	11.01 R	Pisces
Chiron	22.19	Capricorn
N Node	24.43	Sagittarius
Fortune	01.30	Virgo

Let's go to her body. The second house is ruled by Jupiter, and Jupiter is in this house conjuncting it. There's a loop in this house with the sign of Capricorn making Saturn ruler of the loop. Saturn is in the 11th house exalted in Libra, and is exactly semi-sextile to the ascendant.

Inside the ascendant is the planet Neptune making contact with Jupiter and the second house. It is semi-sextile Saturn.

Inside the loop in the second house is Chiron holding 22 degrees. Chiron in our test is ruling Sagittarius.

The node is in the first house in the second house sign and is conjunct the house. It is semi-sextile the ascendant, sextile both Saturn and Uranus in the 11th house.

The third /ninth houses are holding 5 degrees. Mercury in the 9th house is in Virgo and holding 8 degrees pointing us to the 8th and 10th house. The sun, ruler of the 9th is exactly semi-sextile the 11th house. Note the moon's position because it can be moved 1 degree per month, and it will be making contact with the rest of the chart.

Okay, you have seen a few sidereal charts which were done only using sidereal time for 12.00 pm. You can do your own charts, and from your friends and family as well to see what you make of it all.

Now we are going to tackle the BTB; we are going to use *King Alfred the Great* as an example. First let me tell you how it works.

BTB can be used if you have the year when someone is born, but not the day or the month. Suppose you know the date when the person has done something in his life, you can even use that date and get a BTB.

King Alfred was born in the year 849. He passed away on 26th October 899. Winchester, England. Now take 849 away from 899, and you get 50. We are now going to go back from 26th October, so that we could get the BTB. We already got 26 years in the month of October, we need another 24. The month before October is September, it carries 30 days. 24 from 30 gives us 6th September. Our BTB is 6th September 899, Winchester, England. King Alfred got married in the year 868. If we take 849 from 868 we get 19. We add this 19 to 6th September and we get a progressive date of 25th September 899, Winchester, England.

Ascendant	29.09	Cancer
2nd	15.25	Leo
3rd	05.38	Virgo
4th	04.11	Libra
5th	13.12	Scorpio
6th	25.56	Sagittarius
7th	29.09	Capricorn
8th	15.25	Aquarius
9th	05.58	Pisces
10th	04.11	Aries
11th	13.12	Taurus
12th	25.56	Gemini
Sun	01.54	Libra
Moon	03.06	Pisces
Mercury	29.43	Virgo
Venus	19.50 R	Virgo
Mars	13.46 R	Pisces
Jupiter	02.13	Leo
Saturn	20.38	Sagittarius
Uranus	25.59	Sagittarius
Neptune	16.56 R	Taurus
Pluto	23.47 R	Taurus
Chiron	03.56	Taurus
N Node	16.26	Virgo
Fortune	00.21	Capricorn

I hope that you have come to comprehend that interpreting a chart is not at all straight forward. If it was, everyone would be able to dig in and interpret a chart. You need to have some wisdom, to be intuitive, and to have insight.

This BTB chart of King Alfred progressed to the year he got married shows you that Mars, the planet of the fifth house (romance), and of the 10th house, is in the 9th in the sign of Pisces, and making an exact sextile to the 11th house. The 11th house is where we make friends, or join clubs and groups.

The Moon is in the sign of Pisces in the 8th house semi-sextile to the Mid, sextile Chiron, quincunx Jupiter.

Chiron is square Jupiter, both in angles.

Mercury in the third house is exactly sextile the ascendant, and is ruler of the 3rd and 12 houses.

Notice the sun in the sign of Libra making a sextile contact with Jupiter in the sign of Leo.

The node is in a three degrees conjunction with Venus. The node ruler of the ascendant, Venus of the 4th and the 11th. The node is trine Neptune in the 11th house. Neptune is co-ruler of the 9th with Jupiter.

The sun is sextile the ascendant, and is ruler of the 2nd house. It is square Fortune in the 6th house.

The ruler of the 7th house is Saturn, and we find it in the 5th house square Venus in the 3rd.

Uranus is exactly conjunct the 6th house, co-ruler of the 8th with Saturn.

The BTB for the *Duchess of Sussex (Princess Meghan)* can be as follows:

Her mother was born in the year 1956, but has no other information. We can find the BTB by using the Duchess of Sussex's birthdate which is 4th August 1981 at 04.46 am, Canoga Park, California, U.S.A. The wedding date of the Princess can also be used because it is an event that has something to do with the mother.

From since I was a child, I like Kings and Queens, Princes and Princesses, and of course all the other titles. But when someone marries a Prince, to me she is a Princess.

If we take 1956 from 1981 we are going to get 25 years. These 25 years has to go backwards from 4th August. So we end up with 10th July as the BTB for the mother. Remember, you have to use the year 1981, the time 04:46 am, Canoga Park, California, U.S.A.

Ascendant	03.02	Cancer
2nd	24.30	Cancer
3rd	17.25	Leo
4th	15.01	Virgo
5th	19.27	Libra
6th	27.51	Scorpio
7th	03.02	Capricorn
8th	24.30	Capricorn
9th	17.25	Aquarius
10th	15.01	Pisces
11th	19.27	Aries
12th	27.51	Taurus

Sun	18.07	Cancer
Moon	03.20	Scorpio
Mercury	28.21	Gemini
Venus	12.56	Leo
Mars	24.38	Gemini
Jupiter	03.08	Libra
Saturn	04.01	Libra
Uranus	26.18 R	Scorpio
Neptune	22.48 R	Sagittarius
Pluto	21.33	Libra
Chiron	21.44	Taurus
N Node	01.47	Leo
Fortune	18.15	Libra

All astrologers, and those who study the science, should know that planets at the angles are very powerful. And when we see Jupiter in or conjuncting an angle, we get to know that the person has energies to be of someone powerful.

Inside this chart, we see Jupiter in the fourth house in the sign of Libra, and in conjunction with Saturn. But the sign Libra belongs to the fifth house which has to do with children. We see that the mother has come through roots of kings and queens. This is because Jupiter is in the fourth house.

Jupiter is exactly square the ascendant, and Saturn is square the ascendant.

The ruler of the ascendant is the moon in the fifth house in the sign of Scorpio. The moon is exactly semi-sextile Jupiter, semi-sextile Saturn. the moon is exactly trine the ascendant.

Saturn is in the fourth house in the sign of Libra, Saturn is exalted in this sign.

Cancer people likes their home and their families and their country. With the ascendant in Cancer and the ruler in the fifth house, it shows that she loves children and is creative.

The sun in her first house is trine to Uranus and Pluto in the fifth house. Uranus rules the 9th house, showing contact with foreigners; and Pluto rules the 6th, showing contact with servants and all 6th house energies.

There's a loop in the 12th house with the sign of Gemini. There are tow planets in the loop, Mercury and Mars. I think this has something to do with the past, or some sort of Isolation, or working behind the scenes for others. It will have to do with the 11th house and the 4th house.

Neptune is in the other loop in the 6th house with Sagittarius as the sign here. This is just showing an extra 6th house with Neptune ruling 10th house.

Notice that Mercury is making contact with the 12th house; Mars exactly with the 2nd, and Uranus to the 6th.

Chiron is exactly opposing Pluto. Venus in the second shows someone who will never be short of money or possessions unless. . . they are foolish.

The sun is trine the Mid, a very good contact. It is semi-sextile the 3rd.

Do you know that the Jewish historian Josephus Flavius wrote that Adam and his family, Seth and his family all knew about the workings of the heavenly bodies? Adam predicted that the world will be destroyed at one time by fire, and at another time by the force of water.

We dig into the life of *Martha Beck*, born 1919, died by electrocution on 8th March 1951, Ossining, New York, U.S.A.

It's interesting to read her life story on biography.com. You'll read how easy it is for certain people to get into trouble, and what makes them do the things that they do.

Her BTB is 4th February 1951, Ossining, New York, U.S.A.

Ascendant	05.06	Scorpio
2nd	03.41	Sagittarius
3rd	06.43	Capricorn
4th	12.13	Aquarius
5th	15.13	Pisces
6th	12.45	Aries
7th	05.06	Taurus
8th	03.41	Gemini
9th	06.43	Cancer
10th	12.13	Leo
11th	15.13	Virgo
12th	12.45	Libra
Sun	14.34	Aquarius
Moon	15.57	Capricorn
Mercury	22.13	Capricorn
Venus	04.11	Pisces
Mars	09.57	Pisces
Jupiter	11.52	Pisces
Saturn	01.53 R	Libra
Uranus	06.01	Cancer
Neptune	19.28 R	Libra
Pluto	18.45 R	Leo
Chiron	29.34	Sagittarius
N Node	20.58	Pisces
Fortune	03.43	Sagittarius

The ascendant is Scorpio holding 5 degrees, and is trine to Uranus in the 8th house in Cancer, exactly conjunct the 9th.

Mars, co-ruler of the ascendant s in the fourth house in the sign of Pisces, conjunct Jupiter, conjunct Venus, all in the 4th house in the sign of Pisces. Mars is trine the ascendant.

Pluto, the other co-ruler of the ascendant is in the 10th house in the sign of Leo.

There are some good energies in the chart such as Venus exalted in Pisces, and Saturn exalted in Libra.

Unfortunately, Saturn is square Uranus, and 43 degrees from Pluto which is a semi-square. Saturn has a square to Chiron in the second house.

Fortune is in the second house in the sign of Sagittarius exactly conjunct the second. It is square Venus, Mars and Jupiter in the fourth house.

Venus, Mars and Jupiter are all trine to the ascendant, and to Uranus in the 8th house.

The Moon is in Capricorn in the third house conjunct Mercury also in Capricorn. Both of them are square Neptune in the 12th house.

Neptune is sesqui-quadrate Venus, semi-square Fortune. Neptune is conjunct the 12th house.

The sun is square the ascendant. The Moon is semi-sextile the sun. The moon is exactly sextile the 5th house. I am still trying to understand what this 15 degrees is all about. I have seen it in many mysterious charts, strange charts. I am still working to find out what it is.

Jupiter is semi-sextile the fourth, and semi-sextile the 12th.

Getting into deep waters we are going to do two BTBs on *Jesus's* Charts. They are of the Resurrection. Most historians has taken the date of 3rd April which was a Friday, in the year AD 33, at 15:00pm, Jerusalem, Israel. It would mean that the Resurrection took place on 5th April. If we take the BTB, we would end up with 3rd March.

It is said that he was 33 years old.

For our BTB, we need 30 days from the month of March, that leaves us with the 1st March as the BTB, AD 33, 15:00 pm, Jerusalem, Israel.

We are going to use the 3rd March as the BTB from the Resurrection day of 5th April AD 33 at 04.00 am, Jerusalem, Israel.

The Crucifixion BTB is 1st March from 3rd April.

Ascendant	24.45	Capricorn
2nd	04.46	Pisces
3rd	12.54	Aries
4th	13.16	Taurus
5th	07.46	Gemini
6th	00.14	Cancer
7th	24.45	Cancer

8th	04.46	Virgo
9th	12.54	Libra
10th	13.16	Scorpio
11th	07.46	Sagittarius
12th	00.14	Capricorn
Sun	12.46	Pisces
Moon	14.14	Virgo
Mercury	25.52 R	Aquarius
Venus	06.41	Aries
Mars	20.18	Taurus
Jupiter	11.04	Gemini
Saturn	16.09 R	Cancer
Uranus	18.30 R	Leo
Neptune	29.42	Capricorn
Pluto	14.40	Sagittarius
N Node	04.49	Aries
Fortune	26.13	Cancer

I had to go into deep waters many times while researching astrology. Some difficult areas I had to tread. But there's no harm, as long as you get back out safely. We know that ancient dates can be very misleading, but I like to dig in and see what I could find.

The ascendant here is Capricorn having Neptune in conjunction with it. There's a loop in the first house with Aquarius as the sign carrying the planet Mercury.

Neptune is ruler of the second house. Mercury is ruler of the 5th and the 8th houses. In the 8th house we see the moon in the sign of Virgo. I hope you know what that mean.

The moon is very sensitive in the 8th house, psychic, clairvoyant, knowing things before they happen. In Virgo, very critical, analytical, wants to know all the details.

The moon is making a sextile contact to the Mid. This will bring publicity. It is square Pluto in the 11th house. Pluto is co-ruler of the 10th house. The moon is square Jupiter in the fifth house, it is sextile Saturn in the sixth.

This Saturn is the ruler of the ascendant, and co-ruler of the loop in the first house. Saturn is semi-sextile Uranus in the loop in the 7th house in the sign of Leo. Saturn is sextile the moon in the 8th house, trine the Mid, square Mars in the fourth house.

Neptune in the first house is leaving a sextile aspect with Venus in the second house. Neptune is sextile the node in the second house. This Venus and node connection appears to me of people with lots of love.

Neptune is opposing Fortune in the 7th house in the sign of Cancer. Remember, our test for fortune is Leo.

As far as I'm concern, Mercury in the loop has to work itself out in the sign it is in, Aquarius, groups and friends. It also has the fifth house, children, creativity, speculation etc. Mercury has to work itself out in the 8th house. Mercury is semi-sextile the ascendant. It is square Mars, opposing Uranus.

The sun is square Pluto in the 11th house, trine the Mid, quincunx the 9th house. It is leaving a sextile aspect with Mars, square Jupiter in the fifth house, trine Saturn.

Venus is semi-square Mars, sextile Jupiter.

I said to you earlier that we are in deep waters, you are going to get wet, and may even have to swim to get yourself back to shore. Dealing with these sorts of charts can be stimulating, and you can learn a lot. But we do not really know for sure if Jesus was crucified on a Friday of a certain year. An ancient historian said that he was crucified on a certain day in the year 29 when the Geminus twins were consuls – very interesting information.

But we are dealing with what our modern historians have come up with. So you can safely get back to shore without harm.

This next chart is an eye opener. It is the BTB from 9th April the day of the Resurrection. Crucifixion took place on Friday 7th April AD 30.

Our BTB is 7th March AD 30, 04.00 am, Jerusalem, Israel.

Ascendant	28.47	Capricorn
2nd	09.26	Pisces
3rd	17.15	Aries
4th	16.57	Taurus
5th	11.08	Gemini
6th	03.38	Cancer
7th	28.47	Cancer
8th	09.26	Virgo
9th	17.15	Libra
10th	16.57	Scorpio
11th	11.08	Sagittarius
12th	03.38	Capricorn
Sun	16.26	Pisces
Moon	24.39	Virgo
Mercury	21.40	Pisces
Venus	00.43	Aquarius
Mars	17.49	Sagittarius
Jupiter	16.28	Pisces
Saturn	04.40	Gemini
Uranus	03.36 R	Leo

Neptune	23.21	Capricorn
Pluto	08.34	Sagittarius
N Node	03.09	Gemini
Fortune	07.00	Leo

I am going to dip my feet in a mysterious pool of water, hope no dangerous fishes are in it.

In the last chart we had Neptune in the first house. In this chart, it is in the 12th. It still remain co-ruler of the second house. Jupiter is also co-ruler of the second and is in the second in Pisces exactly conjunct the sun also in Pisces. While we had Mercury locked in the loop in the first house in the sign of Aquarius in the last chart, we have Venus in the loop in the first house in the sign of Aquarius. I was hoping it would be in the sign of Pisces which is more soft and compassionate and kind. But Venus in Aquarius could stand for Universal love, unusual love, Friendship love, group love etc.

My feet are still in the mysterious pool of water so I'm going to be a bit mysterious. I read somewhere, if I can remember rightly, that Jesus said that the Father is in him.

Why do we have Venus in the loop in the first house? Venus is ruler of the fourth house, the Father; and Venus is also ruler of the 9th house, the Father God.

In our charts, anything to do with God, Jesus or any great religious person or long distance travel. Heaven, all has to do with the 9th house. And as I have already mentioned, the 11th house in contact with the 9th house, has to do with space or long distance travel. There's something coincidental with this chart, it might not be the right one, and yet we get certain strange things. I'm not getting bit as yet by any fishes. If we look up to the Mid we see that it has 16 degrees and 57 minutes of Scorpio. This would represent the mother of Jesus.

Let me just explain quickly that there are two groups of historians. One group has taken the AD 30 chart as the year Jesus was crucified, the other group has taken AD 33. Now I have been doing a lot of research to try and pinpoint the correct year. It is not at all an easy task. Isaac Newton has given the year as AD 34. I think the year that Jesus died can be plotted out, but it takes some good intuitive powers to do so. We must remember Tiberius and Sejanus. Did Jesus died before Sejanus or after? He could not be active while Sejanus was alive. And before I go on, we have another problem. The days from Resurrection to Pentecost are 50 days. To get 50 days we would have to take 5th April as the resurrection date. I'll come to that after I've been through this BTB.

So the ruler then, of the Mid, would be Mars and Pluto. Mars is in the 11th house conjunct the 11th house, making us to see that his mother was friendly with Jesus's friends. Pluto, the other ruler is in the 10th house holding 8 degrees.

This is something that cannot be explained. Both planets are in the sign of Sagittarius.

The second house in this chart is holding 9 degrees.

The sun and Jupiter are both semi-sextile the 3rd. Venus is trine to Saturn and the Node.

Saturn is conjunct the Node in the sign of Gemini (the twins).

Both sun and Jupiter are trine to the Mid. Mars is semi-sextile the Mid, and square sun and Jupiter.

The moon is in the 8th in the sign of Virgo and making a trine contact to Neptune and the ascendant.

Mars is exactly sextile to the 9th. Both Saturn and node are trine the ascendant. The moon is opposing the sun, Mercury and Jupiter in the second house.

Saturn is semi-sextile the 6th, sextile to Uranus. Uranus is quincunx the 12th. The moon is 82 degrees from Mars.

To round it off, Jesus told his disciples, *"You are in me."*

If you look at the 11th house, you see the sign Sagittarius, and it is ruled by Jupiter down in the second house which is the body of Jesus.

But let us get back to dry land.

AD 33 could be the right year. The 5th of April is the Resurrection. From that date to the Pentecost are 50 days.

Something strange happened to the disciples while they were in Jerusalem. The people around heard a sound like a rushing wind. Tongues of fire came down and rested on the heads of the disciples. Immediately they started talking in other tongues.

The people around thought that the disciples were drunk. Peter stood up and told them, *"Fellow Israelites, it's only 9 in the morning."*

Here we have the time from Peter. So we can set a chart for the 25th May AD 33, 09:00 am, Jerusalem, Israel.

Ascendant	29.02	Cancer
2nd	21.30	Leo
3rd	17.48	Virgo
4th	19.18	Libra
5th	24.20	Scorpio
6th	28.26	Sagittarius
7th	29.02	Capricorn
8th	21.30	Aquarius
9th	17.48	Pisces
10th	19.18	Aries
11th	24.20	Taurus
12th	28.26	Gemini

Sun	03.00	Gemini
Moon	29.56	Virgo
Mercury	27.13	Gemini
Venus	17.20	Aries
Mars	10.03	Cancer
Jupiter	24.47	Gemini
Saturn	19.44	Cancer
Uranus	17.47	Leo
Neptune	00.33 R	Aquarius
Pluto	13.41 R	Sagittaius
N Node	03.06	Aries
Fortune	25.58	Scorpio

First we see the planet Neptune in the 7th house holding zero degree, and in the sign of Aquarius. This is pointing to the 9th house. You must also bear in mind that if there was no Neptune, we would have to look towards Jupiter.

We find Jupiter in the 11th house in the sign of Gemini exactly semi-sextile the 11th house. Jupiter is ruler of the 6th house, servants, and of the 9th house, heaven, space, foreign things. There's a 11/9 contact telling us that there is something from space, or long distance travel, or foreign country.

The ascendant is Cancer with the moon in the third house in the sign of Virgo. The moon is exactly sextile the ascendant.

Speculating a bit here with Fortune in the fifth house, the house of life, in the sign of Scorpio, dark things, hidden, other worldly.

The moon is square Mercury in the 11th house. Remember the 11th house has to do with a group or friends or a club. Mercury rules the 3rd house, travel, speech communication, environment.

Here we have mercury in the 11th house and is ruler of the 12th. Something here to do with the past, friends who are enemies. If we take the two houses we get 3/12. This could be people in the neighbourhood who are your enemies. The two planets would be Mercury/Neptune, and this is strange talk, strange communication .

Peter said that the men and women were saying that the disciples were drunk, and that's when he told them that it is only 9 in the morning and these men are not drunk.

Now we find Venus in the 9th house, conjuncting the Mid, and exactly semi-sextile to the 9th. Venus is ruler of the 4th and 11th house. Venus is square Saturn in the 12th house. Saturn is exactly square the Mid. Saturn is trine the 9th.

Mercury is conjunct the 12th, conjunct. Jupiter. Fortune is quincunx Jupiter.

The sun is exactly sextile the node in the 9th. Here we have an 11/9.

Uranus is exactly trine Venus, trine the Mid, exactly quincunx the 9th.

19: Clearing Up Some Misunderstandings

To me, astrology is a science. The reason I say so is because I can definitely see in the faces of some people, the signs; and from the actions of many people, I can see that astrology really works. Our scientists are baffled, they can't seem to get a grip on its workings. If anyone should give me an accurate time, I will give accurate information which he cannot deny. Only someone who wants to deceive, would say it's not true. It must be made clear that sometimes we are put in a group, and later, we know what group we belong to. This is done very often in places like the army and such like.

There are only 12 signs and not 13. These 12 signs the ancients knew were close to the ecliptic where the sun travels. If there are 50 billion people who falls under the sign of Libra, they all haven't got the same chart, but are a part of the Libra group. There is also an argument about twins, I don't pay any attention to that any more. You can have twins having the same chart, and one of them dies before the other. What do you want astrology to do here? Sometime we get times that are a few minutes apart. There are cases where the twins grow up and they both have a wife with the same name, both having the same jobs and so on.

Time has a lot to do with astrology, space as well. I am not hitting out at the scientists. If I wanted to hit out, I'd go and play cricket. The scientists cannot explain time. I like to watch professional football, but I enjoy kicking a ball about. Let the sun sign astrologers have their fun.

A good example is the case of *King George III*, and the commoner, *Samuel Hemmings*.

A landowner got his servants ready to plant potatoes, apples, bananas, cherries, mangoes and lime. When he blew his whistle, they all started planting. He noted the time, and made a chart. The one chart for six different things his servants planted. Who is able to read the chart and tell what's going on?

Before you attack the astrologers, take some time and study what they have studied.

There are some people too, who quote passages from the bible, trying to say that the bible is against astrology. They should read Genesis chapter 1, verse 14 to 19.

Astrology was the first science, and it is still the first science. It was pushed out its place by deception, and by people who knew the secrets, and wanted it to be hidden. We should not get ourselves wrongly mixed up with 'spiritual' and 'physical' for they are two separate things. Astrology is of moments, events in the 360 degrees chart. It is possible to see certain things in the natal chart, but some things do not present themselves until a specified time. This is where we use progressions. If the astrologer had looked at my chart, and told me I would get married in 1966, I would have said that he was crazy. The thought of marriage hadn't entered my mind as yet. If he wanted to he could have plotted the month, and he would have been correct.

There is evil in our human society, and I believe strongly that it is because of the planetary energies, that we act accordingly. It depends on the individual human being how he use these energies, and believe me, they are inside himself.

If you found 100 charts with the planet Mars in the first house, you can bet your life that every single one of them would be active doing some strenuous work. What Mars is actually doing is giving you the energy to tackle whatever work you do.

It is the same, if you meet a woman with Venus in Pisces, and having a good aspect from Saturn, she 's not likely to go and prostitute herself. Human beings are strange, and they would get up and do something that baffles the mind. So you can see how hard it is to pinpoint the actual workings of astrology. But I have seen the proof from photos, and from careful observation that astrology is true.

Some human beings doesn't need astrology. They go through life with their 'ups and downs', and seem to sort themselves out. There's no point talking to these people or trying to convince them that it was the planetary energies in their positive and negative aspects which brought about the 'ups and downs.'

There are some people who are obstinate, they've been drilled to believe only in one thing, which sometimes turn out to let them down. No one can be a President of the United States if he hasn't got the right chart. And no one can be a Prime Minister of England if he hasn't got the right chart.

The moon is there in the sky as a witness, it sees everything that's going on. We must watch ourselves if it is in a negative contact with Mars.

Any system that you use in astrology, you'll get the same result, but not the same chart. This probably has something to do with the space, open space, and the time. And if everything in our universe works on electromagnetic waves, then we can only say that is probably what astrology works on. These waves are light.

In the army, I studied astrology, and help many people. But the army is a community, and astrology has no say really because all orders comes from the big bosses. Everything is planned for you. Dates are already plotted out, all the planning is done, there's nothing you can do. It is the same in a civilian community. Letters are sent to you to do this or that, or report here or there. Astrology really has nothing to say in that area. Only if the boss listens to you, and act, and you have to be absolutely correct, then astrology can have a say.

You must remember too, that people who are deeply spiritual has no need to study astrology, they will turn against it. Of course they have the right to do what they want to do, but that doesn't mean that astrology is untrue. For these same spiritual people get their energies from astrology.

Astrology and astronomy walked hand in hand in the beginning – like two lovers. Then they argued, and there was a break between them. Astrology was accepted as a science, and people held chair in it.

Some scientists are saying that there's no known laws that would make a distant star or planet to have influence on human beings. I have studied some of the stars and their influences, and I must say that I really don't like them, but that doesn't say they don't work.

Crick and *Watson* had problems studying DNA, but they didn't give up. They finally got their breakthrough.

I don't think that an astrologer can definitely say that he has finally found how astrology work, that would be like saying he knows how may rays come from the sun. I would like to see a break through, but I don't think that is going to happen. The science is too complex. I love astrology, but I love my Creator more, who made it possible.

I still won't forget that psychologist who argued with me saying that astrology wasn't true, and that it was rubbish. Later, he spent some time and studied it, found me in a book shop, and apologized.

Okay, let's go through some more charts.

The chart we are going to look at is of *Riley Fox* born 31st March 2001, Wilmington, Illinois, U.S.A. We haven't got a time so we'll be using that of Midnight. There are two charts, that of the natal, and that of the progressed. She was only 3 years old in 2004 when her body was found. She was bound, gagged, sexually assaulted, and then drowned. It is our task to see what we can make of both charts.

Ascendant	19.31	Sagittarius
2nd	25.23	Capricorn
3rd	05.59	Pisces
4th	11.27	Aries
5th	08.35	Taurus
6th	00.09	Gemini
7th	19.31	Gemini
8th	25.23	Cancer
9th	05.59	Virgo
10	11.27	Libra
11th	08.35	Scorpio
12th	00.09	Sagittarius
Sun	10.35	Aries
Moon	25.13	Gemini
Mercury	19.54	Pisces
Venus	08.51 R	Aries
Mars	20.23	Sagittarius
Jupiter	07.29	Gemini
Saturn	27.42	Taurus
Uranus	23.27	Aquarius
Neptune	08.19	Aquarius
Pluto	15.13	Sagittarius
Chiron	28.52	Sagittarius
N Node	10.44	Cancer
Fortune	04.53	Libra

The ascendant is Sagittarius; the ruler is Jupiter in the 6th house in Gemini. Pluto is in the 12th house conjunct the ascendant, conjunct Mars in the first house. Mars is conjunct the ascendant, and conjunct Chiron in the first house in Sagittarius.

We know that Mars gives lots of energy in the first house, an angular position, very strong.

There is a loop in the second house with Uranus and Neptune in the sign of Aquarius. Neptune is holding 8 degrees.

The third house axis has 5 degrees. Mercury is there in the 3rd house exactly square the ascendant. Venus is also in the 3rd house in the sign of Aries, with 8 degrees.

The moon is in the 7th house in the sign of Gemini trine Uranus. The 5th house axis has 8 degrees Saturn is in this house in the sign of Taurus. The moon is exactly semi-sextile the 8th. The node in the 7th in Cancer is exactly square the sun. The 6th house axis is 0 degree.

We shall not spend much time with this chart because it is the foundation chart. What we are interested in is the next chart where the event took place. Then we can examine both. But I will only be looking at the progressive chart.

This progressive chart is the 3rd of April 2001, Wilmington, Illinois, U.S.A.

Ascendant	21.54	Sagittarius
2nd	29.00	Capricorn
3rd	10.00	Pisces
4th	15.00	Aries
5th	11.00	Taurus
6th	03.00	Gemini
7th	21.54	Gemini
8th	29.00	Cancer
9th	10.00	Virgo
10th	15.00	Libra
11th	11.00	Scorpio
12th	03.00	Sagittarius

You notice apart from the ascendant, all the other degrees have 00 for minutes. This was taken from a hand ephemeris.

Sun	13.18	Aries
Moon	03.37	Leo
Mercury	24.23	Pisces
Venus	07.10 R	Aries
Mars	21.23	Sagittarius
Jupiter	07.58	Gemini
Saturn	27.59	Taurus
Uranus	23.35	Aquarius
Neptune	08.23	Aquarius
Pluto	15.13 R	Sagittarius
Chiron	28.54	Sagittarius
N Node	10.49	Cancer
Fortune	12.13	Aries

Inside the 12th house which is ruled by Neptune in the fixed wheel, you'll see the planet Mars. I hope you know now a lot about Mars and its energies.

— 212 —

Mars is exactly conjunct the ascendant. And we see too, that the chart has a duplicate at the 12th and the ascendant.

Pluto is in the 12th house being co-ruler of the 11th; it is exactly sextile the Mid. The moon is over in the loop in the 8th house in the sign of Leo exactly trine the 12th.

Chiron is in the 12th semi-sextile the 2nd. Inside the second we have a loop carrying two planets – Uranus and Neptune in the sign of Aquarius. Uranus is co-ruler of this sign. Neptune is holding 8 degrees and is co-ruler of the third. You know what the third house represents?

Mercury is in the third house in the sign of Pisces semi-sextile Uranus in the loop in the second.

Do not get yourself all in a muddle because you come up with some good aspects.

Venus in the third house in the sign of Aries is exactly sextile Jupiter in the sign of Gemini in the 6th house. Jupiter is the ruler of the ascendant, and co-ruler of the third.

The north node, ruler of the 8th house is in the 7th in the sign of Cancer exactly sextile the 9th. Fortune in the third house is conjunct the sun, and quincunx the 11th.

Study the 12th house properly, the planets there, and what they are doing. The second house will give you lots more information.

This next chart you have to look at it properly, and write down what is possible for the individual. Is there a chance of becoming rich. Is it good for them to speculate? What about Marriage? Is there a chance? Remember this is only the natal chart, and things work themselves out later.

The birth time is 1st January 1943, 00.07 am, Fort Bragg, North Carolina, U.S.A.

Ascendant	23.53	Virgo
2nd	20.28	Libra
3rd	20.44	Scorpio
4th	23.17	Sagittarius
5th	25.54	Capricorn
6th	26.31	Aquarius
7th	23.53	Pisces
8th	20.28	Aries
9th	20.44	Taurus
10th	23.17	Gemini
11th	25.54	Cancer
12th	26.31	Leo

Sun	09.52	Capricorn
Moon	26.51	Libra
Mercury	26.52	Capricorn
Venus	20.54	Capricorn
Mars	11.36	Sagittarius
Jupiter	21.32 R	Cancer
Saturn	06.45 R	Gemini
Uranus	01.10 R	Gemini
Neptune	02.03	Libra
Pluto	06.40 R	Leo
Chiron	29.03 R	Leo
N Node	27.30 R	Leo
Fortune	06.54	Sagittarius

I don't know what you have down for your notes. Let's begin with the ascendant, its ruler, and the aspects it is making with the rest of the chart.

The ruler, Mercury is in the fifth house in the sign of Capricorn. Capricorn is ruled by Saturn. We find Saturn in the 8th house, and don't forget that this sign Capricorn is at the tenth house in the fixed wheel.

Mercury has a trine to both Saturn and Uranus in the 9th house both in the sign of Gemini. Gemini is the sign at the third house in the fixed wheel, and it has to do with writing, selling, travelling, close relatives and the environment.

Gemini is at the 10th house in this natal chart. Saturn is in conjunction with Uranus. The two planets makes the individual to be a genius in whatever he do. They are both trine to the planet Neptune, the only planet in the first house in the sign of Libra.

Neptune has a good aspect to Pluto in the 11th house, and another to Mercury, the ruler of the chart.

Neptune has a negative aspect coming from the sun, both are in angular position, but there could still be some confusion or scandal.

There's nothing stopping the individual of getting hitched. Neptune and Jupiter are rulers of the 7th house. If there were no Neptune, we would have to depend on Jupiter alone. Jupiter is very strong because it is exalted in the sign of Cancer, and holding an angular position in the tenth house.

It is rather difficult for someone who has just learned about astrology to interpret this chart. But they can practice and understand that astrology, well, I must say the interpretation of it is very difficult. That is because you do not know the make up of the individual, compare to another, and how they will use the same energies.

People with Jupiter exalted are sort of lucky people. The chance is there to expand.

Do you know that this chart shows an individual who love humanity and would like to help them.

In the chart you'll see the finger of God, this aspect comes from Saturn to Pluto to Neptune and back to Saturn. You have the same coming from Uranus to Pluto to Neptune and back to Uranus. These are positive fingers of God aspects.

The negative finger of God comes from Jupiter to Mercury to the Moon and back to Jupiter. We also got one from Jupiter to Venus to the moon and back to Jupiter. Then we got one from Pluto to Mercury to the Moon and back to Pluto.

The positive ones has trines and sextiles; the negative ones has oppositions and squares.

There's a grand trine between Saturn, Mercury and Neptune, also a grand trine between Uranus, Mercury and Neptune.

Remember that squares coming from angular positions are very powerful, and does not cause much trouble. It also depends on who is using them.

In this chart you'll see that the ruler of house 11 is in house 2, this is good for lots of money coming now and then. And don't forget Jupiter exalted in the 10th house, and is ruler of the fourth and tenth houses.

Venus holds a strong position being in the fourth house, ruler of the second and the ninth houses.

The sun also holds a strong position because the individual was born just after midnight.

Doing a chart for midnight, we normally do not look at the sun 's position, only the aspects it is making with the rest of the chart. But when an individual is born at midnight, we do take the sun position seriously.

Our first clue to this chart comes from the planet Mercury, the ruler of the ascendant. Mercury in Capricorn in the fifth house. The fifth house has to do with children, speculation, entertainment, sport, love affairs.

The individual is a business man, who is a dealer, and one of the wealthiest men in America. He is *Ron Perelman*.

21: Charts Of People Who Held High Positions

Looking at *Tony Blair*'s chart of 6th May 1953 at 06:10 am, Edinburgh, Scotland, we find 4 degrees and 63 minutes of Gemini rising. The ruler Mercury is in the loop of Aries in the 12th house, There are two loops in the 12th house; that of Aries; and that of Taurus. Venus is also in Aries with the ruler of the chart. In the loop of Taurus we have Jupiter and the sun. Mars is in the 12th house conjuncting the ascendant.

Ascendant	04.53	Gemini
2nd	25.00	Gemini
3rd	10.11	Cancer
4th	26.04	Cancer
5th	17.30	Leo
6th	26.21	Virgo
7th	04.53	Sagittarius
8th	25.00	Sagittarius
9th	10.11	Capricorn
10th	26.04	Capricorn
11th	17.30	Aquarius
12th	26.21	Pisces
Sun	15.22	Taurus
Moon	11.29	Aquarius
Mercury	26.23	Aries
Venus	15.01	Aries
Mars	03.27	Gemini
Jupiter	29.12	Taurus
Saturn	22.20 R	Libra
Uranus	15.16	Cancer
Neptune	21.54 R	Libra
Pluto	20.48	Leo
Chiron	20.59	Capricorn
N Node	07.26	Aquarius
Fortune	01.00	Pisces

The Moon as ruler of the third and fourth houses is in the 10th house – house of the outside world, publicity and the career.

We see that Chiron is in the 9th house conjuncting the 10th. The ruler of the 10th is Saturn, and we find it in a loop in the sixth house in Libra, exalted in this sign, conjuncting Neptune also in Libra. In this sixth house we also have the loop of Scorpio.

The ruler, Mercury, is in the 12th in Aries in the loop, exactly square the Mid. Mercury is also ruler of the second and 6th houses.

Mars in Gemini is very intellectual, and being in conjunction with the ascendant from the 12th house will give energies. Mars is ruler of the loop of Aries in the 12th house, and of Scorpio in the 6th.

Notice that Mercury is semi-sextile the 2nd house. This house can give information about the individual resources. You also see that Venus, the natural ruler of the second house is exactly square Uranus in the third house. Uranus is ruler of the 11th house in this chart. So we have a connection of 11 with 2. Remember, money keeps coming in with this combination.

You must always remember that Gemini is one sign, and is only split because of the mathematics involved. **The Placidean House System**. Notice too, that the sun in the sign of Taurus in the loop in the 12th house is sextile Uranus. Taurus belongs to the second house natural.

Always check your loops properly for mistakes can easily be made.

The node is in the 10th house and is ruler of the fourth house (in our test), and it seems to me that if the node is in the tenth house, it has to do with the career, and maybe a high position. Of course, I'm not absolutely sure of this, but still doing research on it.

Our next chart is that of *Fidel Castro* born 13th August 1927 at 02:00 am, Biran, Cuba.

Ascendant	29:14	Gemini
2nd	23.35	Cancer
3rd	19.19	Leo
4th	18.55	Virgo
5th	22.38	Libra
6th	27.12	Scorpio
7th	29.14	Sagittarius
8th	23.35	Capricorn
9th	19.19	Aquarius
10th	18.55	Pisces
11th	22.38	Aries
12th	27.12	Taurus
Sun	19.32	Leo
Moon	20.52	Aquarius
Mercury	01.31	Leo
Venus	24.02	Virgo
Mars	11.54	Virgo
Jupiter	02.53 R	Aries
Saturn	01.04	Sagittarius
Uranus	02.57 R	Aries
Neptune	26.26	Leo
Pluto	16.20	Cancer

Chiron	06.05	Taurus
N Node	26.40	Gemini
Fortune	00.34	Capricorn

Some charts are easy to read, others not. If you were given the task to tell this individual's mother, when he was born, what he'll become. You'd see straight away, the planet Jupiter in the 10th house exactly conjunct Uranus both in the sign of Aries. It would be easy to say to her that her son has the chance of holding a top job, and you won't be wrong.

The ascendant is Gemini with the node in the 12th conjuncting it. Pluto is in the first house but in the second house sign of Cancer. Here, we have a touch of Cancer. The individual likes his home and country. Pluto is conjunct the second house.

Mercury, the ruler of the ascendant is in the second house but in the third house sign of Leo along with the sun and Neptune, both in the third house. There's always some sort of confusion with these two planets – Sun and Neptune.

Mercury is semi-sextile the ascendant. Neptune is sextile the ascendant, and is co-ruler of the 10th.

Venus holds a strong position in the 4th house. We see Mars in the third in Virgo conjunct the 4th. A hard worker with some confusion in the home or the land.

The moon in the sign of Aquarius is in the 9th house conjunct the 9th. Travel and foreign countries are shown here. The sign of Aquarius has to do with friends, clubs and groups.

Saturn has good aspect to Jupiter and Uranus from out of the 6th house, the house of colleagues, work, health and hygiene.

Venus is square the ascendant, but both are angular. The sun is exactly conjunct the 3rd house, and is ruler of the third.

Bill Clinton was President of the U.S.A. A very high position. Not just anybody can get that job. He was born 19th August 1946 at 08:51am, Hope Arkansas, U.S.A.

Ascendant	05.30	Libra
2nd	03.03	Scorpio
3rd	03.37	Sagittarius
4th	05.58	Capricorn
5th	08.18	Aquarius
6th	08.37	Pisces
7th	05.30	Aries
8th	03.03	Taurus
9th	03.37	Gemini
10th	05.58	Cancer

11th	08.18	Leo
12th	08.37	Virgo
Sun	26.00	Leo
Moon	20.18	Taurus
Mercury	07.36	Leo
Venus	11.07	Libra
Mars	06.21	Libra
Jupiter	23.13	Libra
Saturn	02.08	Leo
Uranus	21.08	Gemini
Neptune	06.51	Libra
Pluto	11.51	Leo
Chiron	18.52	Libra
N Node	17.15	Gemini
Fortune	29.48	Gemini

This ex-president of the United States of America is a Libran by his ascendant. He has four planets in the first house plus Chiron, all in the sign of Libra. The planets are: Venus, Mars, Jupiter and Neptune.

Venus, the ruler of the chart, is in its own sign of Libra, in the first house, conjunct with Mars and Neptune, and with Chiron.

Venus is square the Mid, exactly sextile Pluto in the 11th house, sextile Mercury in the 10th house, conjunct the ascendant. We know that Venus will make the person handsome – man or woman. We find that he's a strong Libran, and also a strong Leo with the sun, Mercury, Saturn and Pluto in that sign.

He has the planet Uranus, the node and Fortune in Gemini, so he is a strong Gemini too.

In a chart, when I see Jupiter holding an angular position, I already know that that person has the chance of holding a top job, the person to me, is like a king or queen. If they make a mess of it, then that's their own fault.

Because of the position of Saturn too, we could tell his mother that her son has the chance to hold a top job.

We notice too, that Saturn is in the sign of Leo, the lion. It is in conjunction with Mercury, the ruler of the 9th and 12th houses. The 12th is an isolated position, behind the scenes working for the benefit of others. The 9th is foreign countries and travel.

Both Mercury and Saturn is conjuncting the 11th house. This is the house of friendships and groups and clubs.

People with Uranus in the 9th house are travellers, and can turn out to be a genius. Jupiter in the 1st is trine to Uranus, Chiron too. The sun is sextile Uranus. If he didn't become president, he had the energies to be scientific.

The sun is sextile Fortune. Both are rulers of the 11th house. Remember that my test is with Fortune, I am working with it as ruler of the 11th house, just a test. Then we have the ex-President with his moon in Taurus in the 8th house. It is semi-sextile Uranus in the 9th house, square the moon in the 11th house, quincunx Jupiter in the first.

People with the moon in the eighth has the chance of feeling when things are not right. They have deep insight.

Willy Brandt was born 18th December 1913 at 12:45 pm, Lubeck, Germany. He was a Statesman, and Leader of the Social Democratic Party in Germany. In 1969 he became Chancellor.

Ascendant	09.05	Aries
2nd	24.23	Taurus
3rd	16.16	Gemini
4th	03.07	Cancer
5th	20.36	Cancer
6th	15.13	Leo
7th	09.05	Libra
8th	24.23	Scorpio
9th	16.16	Sagittarius
10th	03.07	Capricorn
11th	20.36	Capricorn
12th	15.13	Aquarius
Sun	25.58	Sagittarius
Moon	27.31	Leo
Mercury	06.22	Sagittarius
Venus	12.43	Sagittarius
Mars	21.18 R	Cancer
Jupiter	22.05	Capricorn
Saturn	13.46 R	Gemini
Uranus	05.19	Aquarius
Neptune	27.38 R	Cancer
Pluto	00.11 R	Cancer
Chiron	10.47	Pisces
N Node	18.37	Pisces
Fortune	10.38	Sagittarius

I take it that you know that the ascendant is Aries, and that Mars, the ruler, is in the fourth house, in the sign of Cancer conjunct Neptune. Mars is not so comfortable in Cancer, in fact, it's in its fall. But Mars is holding a strong position in the fourth house. It is sesqui-quadrate to Mercury in the 8th house. It is opposing Jupiter in the 11th.

Let's look at the moon in the 6th house in Leo, ruler of the fourth. It has four signs between itself and the Mid. Those four signs are 120 degrees. The moon has about 2 degrees to go, that makes 122 degrees plus what is on the Mid, 3 degrees, giving us a total of 125 degrees. So the moon is trine with the Mid.

We find that the 10th house is the sign of Capricorn, with the 11th house also of Capricorn. As I said a long time ago, It is one sign, but split by the mathematicians, giving us two houses, and so we get a loop in the 12th and 6th houses. Note that although Jupiter is in the 11th house in Capricorn, it is still in the one sign of Capricorn, and so he has the chance of holding a big job with many big friends.

Because Mars is conjunct Neptune, and Neptune is the ruler of the loop in the 12th along with Jupiter, inside the loop we get the node and Chiron, The node is ruling the fourth house (in my test), and Chiron is ruling the 9th house (in my test).

So the chance is there to hold a job to do with the 4th house, which is the country, and to travel, foreign countries, and high education. But I don't think it will be an easy one.

Chiron is semi-sextile the ascendant. Fortune is conjunct Venus in the 8th house, and Mercury, squaring Chiron, opposing Saturn in the second house in Gemini.

Mercury is conjunct Venus, trine the ascendant.

Venus is also trine the ascendant. Saturn is sextile the ascendant, opposing Venus and Mercury.

The moon is sextile Pluto. Mercury is sextile Uranus. Uranus is sextile the ascendant.

We take the next chart which is of *John Cage* born 5th September 1912 at 05:00 am, Los Angeles, California, U.S.A. He was a composer and music theorist.

Ascendant	05.39	Virgo
2nd	00.55	Libra
3rd	00.27	Scorpio
4th	03.03	Sagittarius
5th	06.06	Capricorn
6th	07.17	Aquarius
7th	05.39	Pisces
8th	00.55	Aries
9th	00.27	Taurus
10th	03.03	Gemini
11th	06.06	Cancer
12th	07.17	Leo

Sun	12.34	Virgo
Moon	25.14	Gemini
Mercury	25.01	Leo
Venus	29.23	Virgo
Mars	01.49	Libra
Jupiter	07.15	Sagittarius
Saturn	04.00	Gemini
Uranus	29.58 R	Capricorn
Neptune	25.14	Cancer
Pluto	29.57	Gemini
Chiron	08.33	Pisces
N Node	13.57	Aries
Fortune	22.59	Scorpio

It's not hard to see that this chart is ruled by Mercury, and it is in the 12th house. The 12th house is the home of Jupiter and Neptune. Mercury is exactly semi-sextile Neptune in the 11th house. And Neptune is sextile Venus in the first house.

Venus is conjunct with its own house – the second. There we find Mars conjuncting it. Mars is sextile Neptune.

We see the moon in the 10th house exactly semi-sextile Neptune, exactly sextile Mercury. The moon is square Venus, both planets holding angular positions.

The moon in the 10th house can bring publicity. The 10th house is the career, the outside world, fame, parents, standing in the profession etc.

John Cage has what it takes to be in a top job. Unfortunately, he wasn't a leader of a country. Saturn is in the 10th in it's own house, in the sign of Gemini, the intellectual, genius position. Pluto is also in the 10th house in the same sign Gemini.

Jupiter is in the 4th house, and is ruler of the 4th and 7th houses. The sun and Venus holding angular positions in the first house. Jupiter is square the ascendant, and square Chiron in the 7th. Jupiter is exactly trine the 12th.

The next chart is of *John F. Kennedy* born 29th May 1917 at 15.00 pm, Brookline, Massachusetts, U.S.A.

Ascendant	19.59	Libra
2nd	17.19	Scorpio
3rd	19.01	Sagittarius
4th	23.46	Capricorn
5th	27.18	Aquarius
6th	26.14	Pisces
7th	19.59	Aries

8th	17.19	Taurus
9th	19.01	Gemini
10th	23.46	Cancer
11th	27.18	Leo
12th	26.14	Virgo
Sun	07.50	Gemini
Moon	17.12	Virgo
Mercury	20.35	Taurus
Venus	16.44	Gemini
Mars	18.25	Taurus
Jupiter	23.02	Taurus
Saturn	27.09	Cancer
Uranus	23.43 R	Aquarius
Neptune	02.40	Leo
Pluto	03.16	Cancer
Chiron	29.25	Pisces
N Node	12.29	Capricorn
Fortune	29.21	Capricorn

We all know about John F Kennedy and his leadership in the White House.

Libra is rising. Ruled by Venus in the 8th house in the sign of Gemini, conjunct with the sun. Venus is semi-sextile the 8th house, square the moon in the 11th house in the sign of Virgo. Venus is trine the ascendant.

The contact of Venus to the ascendant is very good. Inside the 8th house you see the planet Jupiter exactly sextile to the Mid, conjunct Mercury and Mars, sextile Saturn in the 10th house.

And of course, Saturn in its own house – the 10th, gives the chance of being in a top job. Pluto is there in the 9th house. Notice the sign they are in. Although Saturn is not functioning so well in Cancer, it holds a strong position in the 10th, an angular house. Saturn is semi-sextile the 11th, semi-sextile the 12th. Saturn is ruler of the 4th and co-ruler of the 5th houses.

Mercury is in the 8th house conjunct the 8th, conjunct Mars, sextile the Mid, trine the moon.

Mars is also in the 8th house conjunct the 8th, sextile the Mid, trine the moon.

Uranus is in the 4th conjunct the 5th, exactly square Jupiter, square Mercury, square Mars

The Moon is semi-sextile the ascendant, exactly sextile the second house, trine the 8th.

Here you see that the moon is in the 11th house and making contact with the second, this is one way of money coming to the individual. 11 and 2.

22: Observing, Understanding and Accepting

In this chapter, I'm going to be all over the place, but I'll try not to lose you. For those who are good in the subject, there'll be no problem in following me. Those who are new will probably be scratching their heads, but eventually, will understand. What I want you to do, is to make a book of charts of yourself. The time must be accurate. It is a lot of work if you have done many years in life. The work will not be too hard for people who are young. Once you've done that, you can always check it against the events that took place in your life, year by year.

For an example, if you were married in a certain year, check your chart book and see what you can read. Remember that the moon is moving the fastest in the charts. Because they are progressed charts, the planets will all be moving very slowly. Check to see what planets you have in the 12th house. They are making their way up to the Mid, and then back down to the west side. Note the moon's position in your first chart. In the second chart, your moon will move.

Once you have those charts, you can look through them as if it's a book – page for page. Every page is a year of your life. So then, events are going to happen whether you like it or not. Some, you can avoid. Others, you just have to be sensible, and try to avoid too much confusion. This can be done by using your spirit – going into the spirit.

Check the year you met your wife, and the year you got married; the year your wife became pregnant. This is important for you will see in the chart what is taking place. And the year she brought forth her first child. Check for when you got a job or was fired. Check for winning any great sum of money; for going on a long journey that year.

In the charts, you'll notice that the sun is not going to go up to the Mid like Mars, Jupiter, Uranus, Neptune and Pluto. It will stay around the place and time where you were born. It will only be at the Mid if you were born at that time which is Midday. Check the moon as it moves along, and see what aspects it is making to the rest of the chart. Check the planets carefully, and see what contact they are making to each other and the points of the chart.

All this is very important for you. An example is: If the sun in your first chart is about four houses away from Uranus, you can bet your life at some point, it will oppose Uranus, and this could bring sudden and disruptive confusion.

Talking about sudden and disruptive confusion, I am at the moment going through it. My sun is opposing Uranus, and I thought it was the end of the world for me. This were sudden, confused, disruptive, explosive, and sometimes way too quick. But I got through it. I had to move very quickly from my house to another house while they renewed my old home. I stayed away for four weeks, then I am now back in the old home which looks very nice...

So let's get back to the progressive charts.

This is very exciting. The moon can be in any sign when it starts out. It can even be changing signs as well. Keep a check on it. If it is in Aries, it will move along and go to Taurus and then the next sign and so on until it comes to the last sign of the wheel. Make sure that you check the aspects it is making to the whole wheel, and note them down. You are going to find that when the moon is entering the angular houses (first, fourth, seventh and tenth) something is going to happen, some sort of change. And keep in mind too that the moon is natural ruler of the fourth house.

Your moon could start out being in contact with many planets, I mean in the same sign, but as you will see when you check the progress charts, it will move away from them. The planets are going to the left to go up to the Mid, while the moon is going to the right, and will also come to the Mid.

This happened in the year 1946. She was 40 years old. Her perpetual date or cosmic year would be 7th April 1906 at 15:00 pm, West Bromwich, UK.

Mercury and Venus are close to the sun. The sun is not going up to the Mid. It will stay around in the same place according to the birth of the individual.

Now you have a good idea of making a book of charts for each year of your life. Make sure that you check it properly, and don't forget to check each year with the natal. That is also important.

Check it with your own family. Father, mother, grandparents, sisters, brothers, aunts, uncles and all the rest of the family. Your own wife and children and so on.

What we are going to do now is check the chart of *Madeleine Carroll*, a British actress who was well-bred, beautiful, and the first British woman to make it in Hollywood. She was married four times, and we shall check each of her progress chart to see what is happening.

Madeleine Carroll was born on the 26th February 1906, at 15:00 pm, West Bromwich, UK.

Ascendant	10.32	Leo
2nd	27.25	Leo
3rd	19.30	Virgo
4th	20.05	Libra
5th	00.17	Sagittarius
6th	10.08	Capricorn
7th	10.32	Aquarius
8th	27.25	Aquarius
9th	19.30	Pisces
10th	20.05	Aries
11th	00.17	Gemini
12th	10.08	Cancer

Sun	07.07	Pisces
Moon	14.56	Aries
Mercury	12.06	Pisces
Venus	10.06	Pisces
Mars	16.09	Aries
Jupiter	28.34	Taurus
Saturn	05.38	Pisces
Uranus	07.36	Capricorn
Neptune	07.43 R	Cancer
Pluto	20.43 R	Gemini
Chiron	09.22	Aquarius
N Node	20.07	Leo
Fortune	18.21	Virgo

Make sure that when you use a software programme that it is accurate. Don't take it for granted, you good be wasting good time. And make sure the time you work with is accurate.

This natal chart is showing 10 degrees and 32 minutes of Leo, you might get another one showing a few more minutes. She is a Leo with the node in the first house, and is exactly trine the Mid, the moon in the 9th house, and Mars also in the 9th house. It is semi-sextile Fortune in the second house.

Trying to see what Fortune is doing in the wheel is still not solid, but we can just go on the house and sign and aspects it makes.

The node is also exactly sextile Pluto in the 11th house.

The sun is the ruler of Leo, and it is in the 8th house in the sign of Pisces.

I don't think it is easy to overpower a Leo woman, even if they appear to be soft and kind. Leo is a fire sign, and there is always some go in the individual.

With the sun in Pisces, people are kind, soft, compassionate, helpful, dreamy, interested in being alone at times. The sun is exactly trine the planet Neptune in the 11th house. Note that Neptune is conjunct the 12th and is ruler of the 9th.

A lot has been written about Madeleine Carroll. Some writings had her as the most beautiful woman in the world, and she was one of the top paid actress as well. You see that she has four planets in the sign of Pisces, she is a strong Piscean. These people like to help others. They do not like to see others suffer.

I am working with the node as ruler of the 12th house (as a test). If something better shows up, I'll change to it.

The sun is conjunct Mercury, this gives a good intellect. The sun conjunct Venus, this is all about life, love and beauty. The sun conjunct Saturn, there's some seriousness here, steady, slow, patient. Saturn is Pisces are vet friendly, helpful and kind. Mercury conjunct Venus, intellect, communications, feelings, love and beauty. Mercury tends to be psychic in Pisces. Mercury conjunct Saturn, steady, serious, intellectual. Venus conjunct Saturn, study, shy, loyal, serious. Venus is exalted in Pisces, and the individual has access to all its energies.

Mercury is trine Neptune in the 11th house. Venus is trine Neptune. Saturn is trine Neptune.

We don't know yet how Fortune is actually working, but it is in the second house, in the sign of Virgo, conjunct the third, semi-sextile the node, square Pluto. Fortune and Pluto are not in angular houses, but they are in houses 2 and 11, money coming in, with some slight problems.

Venus is exactly quincunx the ascendant. I have seen in some charts the quincunx to the ascendant makes one extremely beautiful. Also if Venus is on the opposite side of the ascendant, and even conjuncting the ascendant.

We see her 5/11 houses in 0 degree. It is telling us something. We see Saturn in the 8th house with 5 degrees, it too is telling us something.

There is a loop in the 4/10 houses. The sign of Scorpio is in this loop of the fourth house. Taurus is in the loop of the 10th, carrying the planet Jupiter. Notice that Jupiter is rule of the 5th, and also co-ruler of the 9th. Uranus is in the 5th in Capricorn conjuncting the 5th, and is exactly sextile to the sun, Mercury, Venus and Saturn. Chiron is in the 6th house in the sign of Aquarius conjuncting the 7th, semi-setile Mercury and Venus. Chiron is semi-sextile to the 6th. Venus is exactly sextile to the 6th. Uranus is exactly opposing Neptune. We do not know for sure which sign Chiron belongs to. I work with Sagittarius as a test. Some think that Chiron belongs to Virgo, others, say Capricorn. If we take Sagittarius, we get a 5/6/7. If we take Virgo, we get a 3/6/7, and if we take Capricorn, we get a 6/6/7.

We know that she only had one child, a daughter born in 1951, and died in 1983. Madeleine Carroll had four marriages.

Here is the progress chart for 1951. The **Perpetual date** is 12th April 1906 at 15:00 am, West Bromwich, UK.

I always call this date the **cosmic year** for the individual.

Ascendant	11.10	Virgo
2nd	02.07	Libra
3rd	29.53	Libra
4th	04.51	Sagittarius
5th	12.52	Capricorn
6th	15.19	Aquarius
7th	11.10	Pisces
8th	02.17	Aries
9th	29.53	Aries
10th	04.51	Gemini
11th	12.52	Cancer
12th	15.19	Leo

Sun	21.47	Aries
Moon	09.12	Sagittarius
Mercury	09.11 R	Aries
Venus	06.01	Taurus
Mars	18.43	Taurus
Jupiter	05.47	Gemini
Saturn	10.48	Pisces
Uranus	08.29	Capricorn
Neptune	07.46	Cancer
Pluto	20.58	Gemini
Chiron	11.59	Aquarius
N Node	17.44	Leo
Fortune	28.35	Aries

Astrological interpretation is a hard thing, but it can be mastered, and give good results. You need to be on your own for an hour or more to sort this out. Both charts must be looked at – the natal and the progressed. We often hear that the master of the chart is the ruler of the ascendant, that is true, but I also like to take the nearest planet to the ascendant, first, and then all others nearest.

In Madeleine's natal chart, the sun is ruler but the node is there, and is ruler of the 12th house carrying Neptune, co-ruler of the 9th.

The sun is in the 8th and in the sign of the 9th.

The progressed chart for 1951 when she had her daughter is showing Virgo as the ascendant with its ruler Mercury in the 8th house in the sign of Aries.

Before we move on lets find first, what we are about. The third house is the house of close family, and a child falls under this.

Then the fifth house is the house of children. The 6th house is the house of sickness.

The 10th house suppose to be announcing the birth.

So the planet Saturn is ruler of the 5th house, co-ruler of the 6th. At the fifth, but in the 4th is Uranus. At the 6th but in the 5th is Chiron.

Saturn is in the 6th conjunct the 7th, semi-sextile to Chiron in the 5th. Saturn is semi-square the ascendant progressive ruler, Mercury, in the 8th house. Saturn is square the moon in the 4th house.

Putting Saturn in the natal chart, it would be conjuncting Venus in the 8th house. Saturn ruler of the 6th, 7th and 8th houses in the natal chart. Venus ruler of the 4th, and the loop in the 10 carrying Jupiter. This Jupiter is ruling the 5th and 9th houses in the natal chart.

Taking Mercury, the ruler of the progressed ascendant, and placing it in the natal chart, it would be in the 9th house, semi-sextile Venus in the 8th. Mercury would be ruling the 3rd and 11th houses.

Mercury would be sextile Chiron in the 6th house. Chiron (in our test) is ruling the 5th house. Mercury is also trine to the ascendant of the natal chart. It is square the 12th house.

You must always bear in mind that there are only six houses which double themselves. So if you have contact with the 11th house, it flows over to the 5th. The 6th house over to the 12th and so on.

There is an old saying, *"As above, so below."* Don't forget that.

What you must remember too, and it is very important, human beings are made up from different parents. And sometimes you will struggle to find what the chart is telling you but it is all there.

I was reading a book, and it says that the 72 degrees is a positive aspect.

Now let us move to the year when Madeleine Carroll got divorced, and married again that same year.

The progress date is 7th April 1906 at 15:00 pm, West Bromwich, UK. She is 40 years old.

Ascendant	07.45	Virgo
2nd	28.23	Virgo
3rd	25.28	Libra
4th	00.08	Sagittarius
5th	08.31	Capricorn
6th	11.31	Aquarius
7th	07.45	Pisces
8th	28.23	Pisces
9th	25.28	Aries
10th	00.08	Gemini
11th	08.31	Cancer
12th	11.31	Leo
Sun	16.52	Aries
Moon	24.15	Virgo
Mercury	12.32 R	Aries
Venus	29.50	Aries
Mars	15.11	Taurus
Jupiter	04.48	Gemini
Saturn	10.17	Pisces
Uranus	08.28	Capricorn
Neptune	07.42	Cancer
Pluto	20.54	Gemini
Chiron	11.47	Aquarius
N Node	18.00	Leo
Fortune	15.03	Aquarius

We jump in straight away at the 7th house. Saturn is there making a contact with Chiron in the 6th house. The ruler of the 7th house is Neptune. Neptune is in the 10th house conjuncting the 11th, and is sextile the ascendant.

The 4/10 axis is in 0 degree, telling us that something is happening in the home or the outside world. Sometimes this is a move or something to do with the career up in the 10th.

Venus in the 9th house is crying (29 degrees) in the sign of Aries, which has to do with the individual, and of course, the opposite sign Libra, the partner.

Venus is also making a sextile contact with the 8th house which has to do with the partner's money, or taxes, or inheritances. Remember, that crying degrees turns out to be strong in the end.

Saturn is semi-sextile the 6th house, while Chiron is exactly conjunct.

At the 5/11 axis we find 8 degrees, this is something that cannot be explained. Something that we cannot do anything about. It just happens.

The 5th and 11th houses has to do with romance and friendships.

What you must notice too, is that her Neptune has just moved into the 10th house, being ruler of the 7th and 8th in the progressive chart.

I think we have seen the energies that were working in her chart for 1946.

Uranus in the 4th house is exactly conjunct the 5th, and is trine to the ascendant. Uranus is a planet of suddenness, disruptive, and unusual. Uranus is co-ruler of the 6th.

The sun in the 8th house is semi-sextile Mars in the loop in the 9th house in Taurus. Mars is also ruler of the other loop in the 3rd

It is also important to notice that her moon, the progress one, is passing through the sign of Virgo in the first house, and conjuncting the second. This moon is semi-sextile the third house. It is ruler of the 11th.

23: Numbers

I said mix astrology with numbers. It is already filled with numbers. The 12 houses, and the 8 planets, and 12 signs. Then there's the number of all the aspects and so on. Some of the numbers are experiments so don't take them too seriously. If you find that they make sense, then okay. I hadn't a clue what was going on in school when the teacher started writing numbers on the blackboard. Numbers and me doesn't seem to get on yet, I like to mess about with them.

We are told that there are only 8 planets in our solar system, I think there are 10.

There are nine numbers that we work with. They are: 1, 2, 3, 4, 5, 6, 7, 8 and 9. Numbers of the planets goes like this:

The sun =1
Moon = 2
Mercury =5
Venus = 6
Mars = 9
Jupiter = 3
Saturn = 8
Uranus = 4
Neptune = 7
Pluto =0

There is really no 0
So here you can see that the sun and Pluto makes 10.
The beginning and the end.
Remember all this is just from myself messing about. But there is some serious stuff amongst this lot. Let us have a look at this chart below.
The date is 14th August 1944 at 12:03 am, San Francisco, California.

Ascendant	23.27	Taurus
2nd	19.39	Gemini
3rd	11.19	Cancer
4th	03.36	Leo
5th	00.56	Virgo
6th	08.17	Libra
7th	23.27	Scorpio
8th	19.39	Sagittarius
9th	11.19	Capricorn
10th	03.36	Aquarius
11th	00.56	Pisces
12th	08.17	Aries

Sun	21.20	Leo
Moon	29.59	Gemini
Mercury	18.19	Virgo
Venus	04.36	Virgo
Mars	20.36	Virgo
Jupiter	04.02	Virgo
Saturn	06.42	Cancer
Uranus	12.36	Gemini
Neptune	02.27	Libra
Pluto	08.44	Leo
Chiron	17.07	Virgo
N Node	26.12	Cancer
Fortune	14.48	Cancer

This chart has a Taurus ascendant with its ruler Venus, in the 5th house in the sign of Virgo.

Does that say anything to you?

Venus in the 5th house is exactly conjunct with Jupiter also in Virgo, and in the same house.

Jupiter is ruling the 8th and 11th houses.

Venus is also ruler of the 6th house.

The ascendant ruler is in number 5, the house of romance, creativity, gambling, entertainments children and sports.

It is quite possible that the individual is interested in all the 5th house energies. Or could settle for one or two.

It still remain that the 5th house has been brought into operation because of the ruler of the ascendant.

We see too, that number 6 and number 5 are in contact, and that is because Venus the ruler of the ascendant is in 5, and is ruler of 6.

House 6 has to do with work, pets, colleagues, health and sickness etc.

The chart we are looking at is that of *Robyn Smith*. Her father deserted her and her mother at her birth. Her mother had mental troubles. Robyn Smith became a jockey in 1969. Riding the horse 'North Sea' she became the first woman to win a major race in the USA in 1973. She retired in 1980, and married that same year, the actor Fred Astaire.

You see that she was a very strong Virgo, and her 5th house is packed.

Number 8 is ruled by Jupiter, other people's possessions, and also her partner's.

Number 11 is also ruled by Jupiter, this is the house of friends and clubs.

Inside her first house is the planet Uranus in the sign of Gemini, conjunct the second house, and is ruler of the 10th.

So we have the two planets, Uranus first, then Venus.

People with Uranus in the first house, doesn't give in easily. They go for what they set their mind upon no matter what.

I hope you have noticed that her Venus is conjunct the big planet Jupiter.

And you have seen now that numbers do work, especially with astrology.

Dane Rudhyar was an author, modernist composer and astrologer. He lived to be 90 years of age. Disabled at 12, predicted in 1972 that the age of Aquarius would start in 2062. He was married in 1930 to Maria Contento.

Dane Rudhyar was born 23rd March 1895 at 00:42 am, Paris, France.

Ascendant	13.50	Sagittarius
2nd	20.51	Capricorn
3rd	05.12	Pisces
4th	11.41	Aries
5th	07.34	Taurus
6th	27.05	Taurus
7th	13.50	Gemini
8th	20.51	Cancer
9th	05.12	Virgo
10th	11.41	Libra
11th	07.34	Scorpio
12th	27.05	Scorpio
Sun	02.08	Aries
Moon	24.37	Aquarius
Mercury	05.24	Pisces
Venus	28.47	Aries
Mars	12.07	Gemini
Jupiter	27.46	Gemini
Saturn	06.10 R	Scorpio
Uranus	19.35 R	Scorpio
Neptune	13.14	Gemini
Pluto	09.56	Gemini
Chiron	06.13	Libra
N Node	21.33	Pisces
Fortune	06.19	Scorpio

The chart has Sagittarius rising. The ruler is Jupiter. Jupiter is in the 7th house in the sign of Gemini.

There are three other planets in the sign of Gemini. They are: Mars, Neptune and Pluto, all in the 6th house. All in conjunction with each other.

This shows us that he is a strong Gemini.

I was looking for information about if he was married, I found it. Married in 1930.

If we take number 1, it has a connection with 7. Number 2 has a connection with 10.

Number 3 has a connection with 7 or 6.
Number 4 has a connection with 6.
Number 5 has a connection with 4.
Number 6 has a connection with 4.
Number 7 has a connection with 2.
Number 8 has a connection with 2(loop).
Number 9 has a connection with 2.
Number 10 has a connection with 4.
Number 11 has a connection with 6.
Number 12 has a connection with 6.

There is quite a lot of information in this chart. Axis 3/9 in 5 degrees.

Fortune up in the 10th house in the sign of Scorpio exactly conjunct Saturn, conjunct the 11th. Fortune (in my test) is ruling the loop in the 8th house.

We are beginning to get some information on the working of Fortune. The house and sign it is in. Still a long way to go.

We see that Neptune is exactly conjunct the 7th, and is ruler of the 3rd. Mars too, is conjunct the 7th, and it is in the 6th conjunct Neptune. Mars is trine the Mid. You can always do a progressive chart for the year when he was aged 12. . There you'd see what's taking place.

A progressive chart for the year 1930 would also show you what's happening, that is the year he got married.

You notice that the body of his partner or her possessions, or of the public, or business partner is in a loop in the second house. The moon is there. The sun is ruler of the loop in the 8th house.

Ok, let's see if you can find the person in this chart. The date is 26th January 1944, 12:30 pm, Goodwater, Alabama. U.S.A.

Ascendant	14.45	Taurus
2nd	13.07	Gemini
3rd	06.13	Cancer
4th	29.11	Cancer
5th	26.16	Leo
6th	01.48	Libra
7th	14.45	Scorpio
8th	13.07	Sagittarius
9th	06.13	Capricorn
10	29.11	Capricorn
11th	26.16	Aquarius
12th	01.48	Aries

Sun	05.39	Aquarius
Moon	20.59	Aquarius
Mercury	11.17	Capricorn
Venus	28.17	Sagittarius
Mars	06.28	Gemini
Jupiter	24.09 R	Leo
Saturn	20.14 R	Gemini
Uranus	04.56 R	Gemini
Neptune	04.07 R	Libra
Pluto	07.38 R	Leo
Chiron	15.09. R	Virgo
N Node	06.49 R	Leo
Fortune	00.06	Gemini

Taking the ascendant sign of Taurus, we find its ruler, Venus, in Number 8(8th house), and in the sign of Sagittarius.

Sagittarius is the sign that is normally on the 9th house in the fixed wheel.

It has to do with freedom, space, higher education, foreign peoples, long distance travel and law and philosophy, And believe it or not, things that are high, moving or falling.

Sagittarius here is at the 8th house. This 8th house is ruled by Mars and Pluto in the fixed wheel.

In this chart, Jupiter has rule over Sagittarius. We find Jupiter in the fourth house in the sign of Leo (a fire sign) The sun is ruler of Leo, and is in the 10th house in the sign of Aquarius.

Saturn and Uranus are rulers of Aquarius. Saturn is in the 2nd house in the sign of Gemini. The ruler of Gemini is Mercury in the 8th house in the sign of Capricorn. Mercury is conjunct with the 9th. The ruler of the 9th is Saturn.

Did you get lost with all that? You shouldn't. There's lots of information there. The number 2 sign of the circle tells you that the individual is very strong, loving but stubborn. Why don't you go out and push a Taurus, and see what happens? Money and possessions are very important to them.

The ruler, we see is Venus and is in the 8th house.

I used to call this house when I first started researching astrology, the dark house.

It has to do with politics, other people's possessions, taxes, inheritances, legacies, partner's money, and sex.

Jupiter is ruling the sign that Venus is in.

Jupiter is in the 4th house, so there's more information here.

Jupiter is ruler of the 9th sign in the fixed wheel. But here, it is ruler of the 8th, and the loop in the 11th.

With my test about the loops, I am still holding on for the time being, until I get more information. The loops are something 'extra.' So that the loop in the 11th house has to do with extra friends, groups or clubs.

Of course, the individual would be busy with all that Jupiter represents. Just keep to the basics, don't go over the top, and your information would be spot on.

In the fourth house, Jupiter has to do with the home or the country. And for me, this is a position where the individual can be a king or a queen. This is an angular position for Jupiter, very strong.

The chart we are looking at belong to *Angela Davis*.

Do not forget to write down properly all the aspects you find.

The sun is with the South Node in the 10th house, in the sign of Aquarius, (number 11).

The sun is trine Mars and Uranus in the first house. This is really enormous energy, and one has the chance to be a scientist. The energies between the sun and Uranus shows that.

Mars is in its own house, number 1. It is very strong here. Then we have Uranus in the first house. I think you need to see a few charts with Uranus in the first house to understand what I am saying. These people will follow what they have in mind no matter what.

I am off to another chart, hope you are not lost in finding your way around.

See what you make of this next chart. 11th December 1950, at 15:00pm, New York, New York. U.S.A.

Just like the last chart, you have to find the person, decide if they have the chance to become rich, get married, and have children.

Ascendant	25.43	Taurus
2nd	21.08	Gemini
3rd	12.01	Cancer
4th	03.38	Leo
5th	00.36	Virgo
6th	08.37	Libra
7th	25.43	Scorpio
8th	21.08	Sagittarius
9th	12.01	Capricorn
10th	03.38	Aquarius
11th	00.36	Pisces
12th	08.37	Aries

Sun	19.13	Sagittarius
Moon	23.34	Capricorn
Mercury	09.08	Capricorn
Venus	26.01	Sagittarius
Mars	27.14	Capricorn
Jupiter	01.19	Pisces
Saturn	01.29	Libra
Uranus	08.12 R	Cancer
Neptune	19.04	Libra
Pluto	19.45	Leo
Chiron	23.50	Sagittarius
N Node	23.51	Pisces
Fortune	00.04	Cancer

Just like the last chart, this chart has Taurus rising, and its ruler Venus, is in the 8th house in the sign of Sagittarius. Here we have number 8 again. This is the house of other people's money, taxes, legacies, partner's possessions etc.

We find that Venus is conjunct Chiron, and the sun. Venus is also in conjunction with the 8th.

Venus is in a sextile contact with Jupiter, the ruler of Sagittarius. Jupiter is in the 11th house in the sign of Pisces, conjunct 11th.

I will just say something here. In the beginning when I first took up the research work of astrology, I was nearly put off by things like twins, and someone having the same planetary combinations, and such like. I got over all that, and moved forward, knowing that there is more to it than that. People are different because they have different parents, different hereditary influences, different upbringing and environmental contact. You might find that they have a few energies to share, but they cannot be completely alike.

Let us take a look at the second house (number 2), the house of money. We see that the ruler is in the 8th house in the sign of Capricorn. Saturn ruling Capricorn is down in number 5 in the sign of Libra. In this sign, Saturn is exalted, and all its energies should work for the best in this house. Libra takes us back to its owner, Venus in the 8th house. We can definitely say yes, this individual won't be bad off.

Mercury in the 8th house is opposing Uranus in the 2nd house.

The moon is in the 9th in the sign of Capricorn conjunct Mars. This position of the moon shows connection with foreign peoples or much travel. Mars is exalted in Capricorn, and is ruler of the 7th and 12th house.

This chart is of *Christina Onassis*.

This next chart, you have to get the person. No guessing. Good interpretation would let you see clearly who the individual is.

Born December 16, 1901 at 09:30 am, Philadelphia, Pennsylvania. U.S.A.

The chart is of a woman. Is there any chance of her getting married and having children?

What house is very important to her?

Ascendant	26.10	Capricorn
2nd	11.17	Pisces
3rd	20.43	Aries
4th	19.19	Taurus
5th	11.43	Gemini
6th	02.27	Cancer
7th	26.10	Cancer
8th	11.17	Virgo
9th	20.43	Libra
10th	19.19	Scorpio
11th	11.43	Sagittarius
12th	02.27	Capricorn
Sun	23.58	Sagittarius
Moon	26.22	Aquarius
Mercury	14.43	Sagittarius
Venus	10.44	Aquarius
Mars	17.12	Capricorn
Jupiter	17.52	Capricorn
Saturn	15.55	Capricorn
Uranus	17.31	Sagittarius
Neptune	00.15 R	Cancer
Pluto	17.33 R	Gemini
Chiron	05.54	Capricorn
N Node	11.19	Scorpio
Fortune	28.35	Scorpio

This chart s showing a Capricorn ascendant. Saturn is the ruler. It is in the 12th house in its own sign of the ascendant.

I won't even try to tell you what Capricorns are like. I am sure you know by now.

Something is going on in this 12th house, the house that she is interested in. Saturn is in conjunction with Mars and Jupiter all in the same house. Chiron is in the same sign. She is a strong Capricorn.

Her sun sign is Sagittarius, It is in the 11th house with Mercury and Uranus all in the same sign. Here too, she is a strong Sagittarian.

How much do you know about the sign Sagittarius? It is a sign of freedom, high education, law, philosophy, religion, foreign countries, long distance travel, movement, things that are falling, space, the higher mind.

It is quite possible that she would get married. The moon is ruler of the 7th, and it is in the first. It is making a good contact with Neptune in the 5th house. Also a good contact with the sun in the 11th house.

She has Venus in the first house in Aquarius sextile Mercury in the 11th in Sagittarius. You'd think that her fifth house would be good for many children with Mercury being ruler of the fifth house. But we see that Pluto is there in Gemini opposing the sun, Mercury and Uranus.

She had three marriages, and one child. She once called in an astrologer to find out why her life was so beautiful.

The chart is of *Margaret Meade*.

24: Accurate Charts

This chart is of *Albrecht Durer* born 21st May 1471 at 10:30 am, Nuremberg, Germany. (Have you ever seen his pen drawings? I have a book of them, and I am still amazed.)

I will point out one or two things, nothing more.

Ascendant	26.46	Leo
2nd	16.52	Virgo
3rd	12.53	Libra
4th	16.19	Scorpio
5th	24.26	Sagittarius
6th	28.53	Capricorn
7th	26.46	Aquarius
8th	16.52	Pisces
9th	12.53	Aries
10th	16.19	Taurus
11th	24.26	Gemini
12th	28.53	Cancer
Sun	08.15	Gemini
Moon	24.50	Gemini
Mercury	18.15	Taurus
Venus	21.30	Gemini
Mars	14.27	Aries
Jupiter	24.38	Virgo
Saturn	01.33	Gemini
Uranus	22.15	Libra
Neptune	11.30	Scorpio
Pluto	13.00	Virgo
N Node	28.35	Sagittarius
Fortune	13.21	Virgo

We find the ascendant ruler, the sun, in the 10th house in the sign of Gemini conjunct Saturn i the 10th house, and also in Gemini. Mercury is in the 10th house in Taurus, this brings us back to Venus.

There are four planets in the sign of Gemini, the sun moon, Venus and Saturn, showing that he is a strong Gemini. There are tow planets in Virgo along with Fortune. This Virgo sign will help with the small details.

Venus in angular position is always good for beauty, art, singing, dancing etc.

Jupiter in the second house gives the chance to have much resources

The following chart is of *Joshua Reynolds* born 27th July 1723 at 10:20 am, Plympton, UK.

Ascendant	06.50	Libra
2nd	01.43	Scorpio
3rd	02.34	Sagittarius
4th	08.46	Capricorn
5th	14.07	Aquarius
6th	13.31	Pisces
7th	06.50	Aries
8th	01.43	Taurus
9th	02.34	Gemini
10th	08.46	Cancer
11th	14.07	Leo
12th	13.31	Virgo
Sun	03.21	Leo
Moon	08.24	Gemini
Mercury	22.25	Cancer
Venus	07.25	Cancer
Mars	21.58	Taurus
Jupiter	29.37	Sagittarius
Saturn	23.41	Sagittarius
Uranus	25.22	Libra
Neptune	29.07	Taurus
Pluto	25.08	Virgo
N Node	11.33	Gemini
Fortune	11.33	Leo

Libra is rising, Uranus is in the first in the ascendant sign. The ruler of the ascendant, Venus is in the 9th house in the sign of Cancer, conjuncting the Mid, and square to the ascendant.

Pluto in the 12th house is exactly semi-sextile Uranus.

The sun sign is Leo. The sun is in the 10th conjunct Fortune.

Venus is semi-sextile the moon in the 9th house. The moon is in Gemini conjunct its node. It is exactly semi-sextile the Mid.

Jupiter and Saturn in the third, sextile Uranus.

Our next chart is of *William Turner* born 23rd April 1775 at 01:15 am, London, UK.

Ascendant	17.35	Capricorn
2nd	12.29	Pisces
3rd	25.49	Aries
4th	22.05	Taurus
5th	11.00	Gemini
6th	27.51	Gemini
7th	17.05	Cancer

8th	12.29	Virgo
9th	25.49	Libra
10th	22.05	Scorpio
11th	11.00	Sagittarius
12th	27.51	Sagittarius
Sun	02.40	Taurus
Moon	05.24	Aquarius
Mercury	05.37	Aries
Venus	28.19	Taurus
Mars	26.50	Leo
Jupiter	22.40	Taurus
Saturn	03.45	Libra
Uranus	00.49	Gemini
Neptune	20.42	Virgo
Pluto	27.19	Capricorn
N Node	00.50	Virgo
Fortune	19.49	Libra

Capricorn is rising; the ruler is Saturn; it is in the 8th house in the sign of Libra, exalted, and in the same sign with Fortune.

Pluto is in the first house in the ascendant sign, and is trine to Saturn. Fortune in the 8th house is conjunct the 9th, and square to the ascendant.

The sun sign is Taurus along with Venus and Jupiter. More of a Taurus here. The moon is in a loop in the first house in the sign of Aquarius. Mercury is in the second house in the sign of Aries, the sign of ideas and assertiveness.

The sun in the third house is quincunx Saturn.

Uranus has a trine with Saturn. Venus in the fourth house in Taurus, holding a very strong position is trine with Saturn. Mars is in the opposite loop in the 7th house in the sign of Leo squaring both Venus and Jupiter. Remember that planets in an angular position is not so bad as when they are in second or third house. Still there is some negative force there.

The sun is square Pluto, Jupiter is trine the ascendant.

The next chart is of *John Logie Baird* born 13th August 1888 at 08:00 am, Helensburg, Scotland.

Ascendant	21.41	Virgo
2nd	13.17	Libra
3rd	11.51	Scorpio
4th	18.27	Sagittarius
5th	26.50	Capricorn
6th	27.47	Aquarius
7th	21.41	Pisces

8th	13.17	Aries
9th	11.51	Taurus
10th	18.27	Gemini
11th	26.50	Cancer
12th	27.47	Leo
Sun	20.56	Leo
Moon	02.51	Scorpio
Mercury	09.50	Leo
Venus	29.56	Leo
Mars	12.08	Scorpio
Jupiter	27.09	Scorpio
Saturn	11.33	Leo
Uranus	14.22	Libra
Neptune	02.12	Gemini
Pluto	05.45	Gemini
N Node	29.19	Cancer
Fortune	03.36	Sagittarius

This chart has Virgo rising, with the ruler, Mercury, in the 11th house in the sign of Leo conjuncting Saturn also in Leo. Venus is in the 12th house and is in Leo. The sun sign is Leo in the 11th house conjunct the 12th. The chart shows a strong Leo.

Mercury is sextile Uranus in the second house in Libra. Mercury is trine Fortune in the third house in the sign of Sagittarius.

The moon is in the second house in the sign of Scorpio. Mars is n this sign but in the third house. Jupiter is also in Scorpio in the third house. People with Jupiter in Scorpio has the ability to penetrate deep and to know things that others do not know.

He is a strong Scorpio as well. Neptune and Pluto are both in the sign of Gemini, and in the 9th house.

With these two signs in Gemini, quite a lot of discoveries came about.

In my early research, I had the idea that if Neptune was making contact with the Mid, or in the 10th house, that the person would become famous.

Mercury is sextile Neptune and Pluto.

This next chart belongs to *Llewellyn George* born on 17th August 1876 at 04:18 am, Swansea, Wales.

This man was an astrologer and has a nice interesting book out: *Llewellyn's New A to Z Horoscope Maker And Interpreter.*

Ascendant	18.16	Leo
2nd	06.28	Virgo
3rd	00.23	Libra
4th	02.36	Scorpio
5th	12.16	Sagittarius
6th	19.20	Capricorn
7th	18.16	Aquarius
8th	06.28	Pisces
9th	00.23	Aries
10th	02.36	Taurus
11th	12.16	Gemini
12th	19.20	Cancer
Sun	24.33	Leo
Moon	22.11	Cancer
Mercury	06.23	Virgo
Venus	16.33	Cancer
Mars	23.12	Leo
Jupiter	23.22	Scorpio
Saturn	05.30 R	Pisces
Uranus	20.38	Leo
Neptune	05.19	Taurus
Pluto	24.26	Taurus
Chiron	00.17	Taurus
N Node	21.16	Pisces
Fortune	03.52	Libra

A lion ascendant with three planets in it. The planets are: the ruler, sun, Mars and Uranus. I have already told you that with Uranus in the first house, the individual has something to do, and nothing is going to stop him.

The sun is exactly square Pluto in the 10th house. Neptune and Pluto in the 10th house are in the sign of Taurus.

Neptune is making a trine contact to the second house and to Mercury in the first in the sign of Virgo. Mercury is trine the Mid.

Jupiter in the fourth house is square to the planets in the first house. But here you see, they are all in angular positions. Jupiter is opposing Pluto.

The moon is in the 12th house in the sign of Cancer conjunct the 12th, conjunct Venus in the 11th house, sextile Pluto, trine Jupiter, semi-sextile sun and Mars in the first.

You see that Mercury is exactly conjunct the second house.

Mercury is opposing Saturn in the 5th house in the sign of Pisces. Saturn is conjunct the 8th, sextile the Mid. The moon is trine its North node in the 8th house.

Here is *Queen Victoria*'s chart. She was born 24th May 1819 at 04:15 am, London UK.

Ascendant	05.58	Gemini
2nd	26.58	Gemini
3rd	14.04	Cancer
4th	02.25	Leo
5th	27.06	Leo
6th	08.01	Libra
7th	05.58	Sagittarius
8th	26.58	Sagittarius
9th	14.04	Capricorn
10th	02.25	Aquarius
11th	27.06	Aquarius
12th	08.01	Aries
Sun	02.07	Gemini
Moon	03.37	Gemini
Mercury	08.56	Taurus
Venus	26.33	Aries
Mars	17.38	Aries
Jupiter	17.04	Aquarius
Saturn	28.38	Pisces
Uranus	23.19	Sagittarius
Neptune	28.03	Sagittarius
Pluto	27.29	Pisces
N Node	18.13	Aries
Fortune	07.28	Cancer

The ascendant in this chart is Gemini. Its ruler is Mercury, and is in a loop in the 12th house in the sign of Taurus.

When I looked at her photo, I see that she has the features of Taurus, and also of Gemini.

The fact that Mercury is in the 12th house shows that she would be in an isolated position, working behind the scenes for others. Taurus has to do with money and possessions. ; it is the second sign in the natural wheel.

It is also easy to see that she has the chance to hold a top position, Jupiter in the 10th house in the sign of Aquarius.

I noticed that Queen Elizabeth 2nd has Jupiter in Aquarius in a loop.

Victoria reigned for 63 years, and Our queen, has passed that.

Jupiter is strong in an angular house, also when it is well-aspected in the chart.

We see that Mercury is exactly semi-sextile the 12th, making what she has to do more behind the scenes, and isolated. Mercury is square the Mid, sextile

Fortune in the second house in the sign of Cancer. Note: Cancer has to do with the home or the country.

She is a Gemini because her sun is in that sign. It is conjunct the moon. Both are in the 12th house. The sun is exactly trine the Mid, and the moon is trine the Mid. She has Venus, Mars and the node in the sign of Aries in the 12th house. She has taken on a bit of the Ram. Her 12th house is packed, five planets and the node.

Here's a chart of *Antonio Vivaldi* born 4th March 1678 at 16:57, Venice, Italy.

Ascendant	14.33	Virgo
2nd	08.03	Libra
3rd	07.04	Scorpio
4th	11.07	Sagittarius
5th	16.26	Capricorn
6th	17.59	Aquarius
7th	14.33	Pisces
8th	08.03	Aries
9th	07.04	Taurus
10th	11.07	Gemini
11th	16.26	Cancer
12th	17.59	Leo
Sun	14.31	Pisces
Moon	02, 41	Leo
Mercury	25.34	Aquarius
Venus	28.06	Aries
Mars	24.25	Aquarius
Jupiter	11.08	Pisces
Saturn	03.30	Gemini
Uranus	06.40	Aries
Neptune	17.09	Aquarius
Pluto	09.40	Cancer
N Node	19.31	Scorpio
Fortune	02.43	Aquarius

Virgo is at the ascendant. This is the sign that is most important for digging into small details and being critical and analytical.

The ruler Mercury is in the universal sign of Aquarius in the 6th house conjunct Mars and Neptune. The node is also in Aquarius but in the fifth house. Mercury is sextile Venus in the 8th house.

Uranus in the 7th is conjunct the 8th, semi-sextile the 9th, sextile Saturn in the 9th in Gemini. This position of Saturn shows the ability to be intellectual. Uranus is sextile the Mid. It is trine the moon in the 11th house in the sign of Leo.

The sun sign Pisces is in the 6th house conjunct Jupiter also in Pisces. The sun is exactly conjunct the 7th, opposing the ascendant, square the Mid, trine Pluto in the 10th in Cancer.

There is something going on with Uranus in or around the 8th house. I have seen that in many charts.

The following chart is *Victor Emanuel* 2nd born 14th March 1820 at 00:30 am, Turin, Italy. He was king of Sardinia and also of Italy. A very good leader.

Ascendant	07.30	Sagittarius
2nd	11.18	Capricorn
3rd	21.44	Aquarius
4th	28.57	Pisces
5th	27.25	Aries
6th	19.11	Taurus
7th	07.30	Gemini
8th	11.18	Cancer
9th	21.44	Leo
10th	28.57	Virgo
11th	27.25	Libra
12th	19.11	Scorpio
Sun	23.21	Pisces
Moon	15.29	Pisces
Mercury	06.15	Aries
Venus	29.38	Aries
Mars	18.19	Cancer
Jupiter	05.31	Pisces
Saturn	02.09	Aries
Uranus	28.38	Sagittarius
Neptune	00.52	Capricorn
Pluto	27.10	Pisces
N Node	02.36	Aries
Fortune	29.38	Scorpio

Jupiter is the ruler of the ascendant. Uranus is in the first house in the ascendant sign of Sagittarius, Neptune is also in the first house, but in the sign of the second house which is Capricorn.

Uranus is semi-sextile with Fortune in the 12th house in the sign of Scorpio/ Uranus is exactly square the Mid, conjunct Neptune, square the sun and Pluto both in the third house in the sign of Pisces.

Note that Jupiter is in the third house in the sign of Pisces. People I have met with this position are very kind and helpful.

The chart has two groups of planets. Sun, moon, Jupiter and Pluto in Pisces; Mercury, Venus Saturn and the node in Aries.

The sun is trine Mars in the 8th house, and so is the moon. Pluto is exactly semi-sextile the 5th.

Uranus is square to Saturn and the node in the 4th house, all hiding angular positions.

Saturn is exactly conjunct the node.

You have been given a few accurate charts to look at. I do hope you get to understand a little bit more about serious astrology.

Do a lot of tests on your friends and family, and people who you know. Most of all make sure you understand the progressive chart, and its workings with the natal. You also have the transits. I am not very busy with the transits, that's not my area, but they do work.

The ancients have given Mars and Saturn as two very dangerous planets, especially when they are in negative aspect. Jupiter and Venus are helpful planets, but always remember the negative side of life.

25: Moments in Time; Where Sickness Comes From

We have to go back and check the rotation of the earth on its axis. It takes approximately 24 hours to do so. One degree is equal to four minutes of space time which works out as one year in the life.

Have you ever had anyone say to you "one minute" or "one moment"? There's a difference between the two. A minute is 60 seconds, while a moment is 30 seconds longer. But a moment could be between 1 to 90 seconds. Below 4 minutes, we cannot make a chart because all the planets are there still in the same position, except for the seconds, and that will be ridiculous. Yet we know that seconds are ticking away in our lives. So every four minutes we can make a chart. The moon is the fastest, and is moving about 2 or 3 minutes each time. With the rotation hours, we just multiply by 60 and we come out with 1440 minutes; divided by four, we get 360 charts. Some people would still go into that area. I would need to have a robot to that sort of work.

If we take the date 17th March 2019 at noon, we find that the moon is at 6 degrees and 5 minutes in the sign of Leo. Four minutes later, it is 6 degrees and 8 minutes in the sign of Leo. Another four minutes later, and it is 6 degrees and 10 minutes in the sign of Leo. So there you see what I mean.

Sometimes it is pointless to make a chart when moments are not so far from each other. And quite a lot of things can happen in the same moment.

Space and time are joined together, they cannot part, that too, is why astrology is true. If we take DNA, you must have something so that you can check it. With astrology, you don't need to have anything – only space and time. If you were there at the time God started His creation, you would have been able to make a chart for that moment in time. .

Many people have got their own theories of where sickness came from, or why we get sick. My theory is: you either get sick or you don't. There are so many germs around to make us become sick. Then you have the wind to blow and carry germs everywhere. And the make up of our bodies with all the cells, they can get damaged.

Once you know the planetary signs ruling the parts of the body, you'll soon get to know that every individual is capable of a different kind of sickness. It could be to the head, the throat, the arms or shoulders, the chest, the heart, the belly, the liver, the private parts, the thighs, the knees, the calves, and the feet.

You can catch the flue, get a headache, accidentally get a cut. These things will be registered in the individual, and someone who is good with the astrological science, would see that immediately.

To verify what I say, you only have to check it out carefully among your family, and friends, and others whom you know. Like someone had a surgery; check it out. Someone injured his head; check it out. Someone had trouble with their arms, shoulders, or with the nervous system; check it all out.

Sickness comes from above. It comes also from what is given down through the parents. It is very easy to see in the chart what is happening when someone is affected with disease. There's no doubt about that. For an example:

The 6th house shows sickness, and the planet Mercury is ruler of the 6th house. Spinal problems can be seen from the sign of Leo or the sun, and the back Aquarius. Sometimes you get a shock when you hear the news of someone who has passed away suddenly, this happens because of some contact with planets and Uranus.

Uranus, we know is a disruptive, sudden planet; and yet, it is the planet of science and astrology.

Let's take for another example: Mars in Leo, square to the moon in Scorpio; and again, Mars opposing Uranus in Aquarius. In the same chart, you have the sun square to Jupiter and Pluto. Then you have Jupiter opposing Pluto; and the moon square Uranus. This is a pretty negative chart. But depending on who has this chart, there is a chance of getting through it. Good breeding, the person will turn the negatives to positive or to some good use.

We see that Mars is in the sign of Leo. Leo is the sign that is at the fifth house in the fixed chart. It stands for children, love and romance, speculations and entertainment, and sports. We notice too, that Mars is opposing Uranus, and Uranus is in the sign of Aquarius. Aquarius is the sign on the 11th house in the fixed chart. It stands for friendship, clubs and groups, and the individual hopes and wishes.

Here we see, that problems could come about in the 5th and 11th houses, and also through their signs.

Even when Mars is positive with Uranus, it could still give some problems.

One thing we must never forget, the chart is not only for yourself alone. It is a circle of 12 houses, and refers to others as well. This will become clear when you have mastered the chart, and why the 11th house is also the education and communication and travel for your grandchildren. It is also the house of your parents body and their possessions.

With the example I have just given, and you had a child with those aspects, it would be your duty to take some sort of action, to see that the child doesn't get hurt. Mars/Uranus is sudden; active energy, used wrongly. Overdoing it. So it would be wise to talk to someone, and tell them to ease off. You notice too, that Mars is in the sign of Leo. Medical wise, Leo rules the heart, the opposite sign, Aquarius, rules the back.

I am not into Medical astrology, for I know it is very deep and interesting. It would take up too much of my time. I am pretty happy in trying to search the natal and the progressive chart. And they have brought up quite a lot of interesting facts.

Astrology is very deep and penetrating. We walk around with it within us, so it is pretty hard to try to convince people about it.

You are at the grocers, and at that moment in time, you meet the one you love. You can make a chart of that moment.

What are you going to see? Exactly at that moment, the positions of the planets in the sky. But as I have already said, we are not going to make a chart for every moment in time.

You'll be able to read what has just happened – you meeting your love – and the possibility of any solid attachment.

That moment in time, does it suddenly vanish away? Not at all It is recorded. From that moment, it can be progressed into the future, or back to the past.

Let's see what we can make of this next chart. A man is born on the 6th April 1940 at 21:30 pm, Manhattan, New York, U.S.A.

Ascendant	24.03	Scorpio
2nd	24.39	Sagittarius
3rd	00.25	Aquarius
4th	07.01	Pisces
5th	08.28	Aries
6th	03.30	Taurus
7th	24.03	Taurus
8th	24.39	Gemini
9th	00.25	Leo
10th	07.01	Virgo
11th	08.28	Libra
12th	03.30	Scorpio
Sun	17.07	Aries
Moon	09.02	Aries
Mercury	20.13	Pisces
Venus	02.27	Gemini
Mars	03.31	Gemini
Jupiter	20.40	Aries
Saturn	02.08	Taurus
Uranus	20.00	Taurus
Neptune	23.31 R	Virgo
Pluto	00.37 R	Leo
Chiron	14.15	Cancer
N Node	20.24	Libra
Fortune	02.08	Sagittarius

Who is this man? We have no biography about him. But what we can do, is read his chart and get some information.

His sun sign is Aries with the moon and Jupiter all in that sign, and in the fifth house. The sun is conjunct Jupiter. We know a little bit what Aries people are like. They are assertive, active, and it could be that this man is full of ideas.

The sun is ruler of the 9th house, and there we find Pluto exactly conjunct the 9th. The 9th house represents too, the higher mind.

Pluto is ruler of the ascendant and the 12th house.

Mars also co-ruler of the ascendant sign, and is in the 7th house in the sign of Gemini, and in conjunction with Venus also in the 7th house.

There's going to be trouble here, unless the man takes control of the Mars energy. Well, trouble with his partner or the public.

We see that the planet Neptune is in the 10th house in the sign of Virgo. In the 4th house we have the planet Mercury in the sign of Pisces. This position can make one to be psychic, or can turn out to be strange and mysterious.

Mercury is in the sign ruled by Neptune, and is opposing Neptune.

Jupiter is in the 5th house in Aries, and is quincunx Neptune.

Neptune is sextile the ascendant, but is square the second house.

Notice that Neptune is ruling the 4th house while Mercury has rule over the 8th house. Both planets are holding angular positions.

The node in Libra in the 11th house is exactly quincunx Uranus in the 6th house in the sign of Taurus. Uranus is conjunct the 7th house. It is exactly semi-sextile Jupiter in the 5th in Aries. Uranus is sextile Mercury.

The node is exactly quincunx Mercury. Mercury is trine ascendant.

Mars in the 7th house is exactly semi-sextile 6th house, semi-sextile Saturn in 5th house conjuncting 6th.

Venus is exactly semi-sextile Saturn, semi-sextile 6th.

The moon is in the 5th in Aries conjunct the 5th.

You would see straight away that this chart is not an easy one. There are energies in it for one to get married, and have problems. That's what this physical life is all about – nothing is really smooth.

These are very important. It is figuring out how to use the energies in the chart. As most of you already know, it depends on the upbringing of a child and its heredity and environment.

We are going to the next chart which is a progressed one. if you are fearful and afraid, do not look at this chart.

This chart is progressed from the one above. It is done for the year 1973 when he gassed himself.

The progressed date is 9th May 1940 at 21:30 pm, Manhattan, NY, U.S.A.

Ascendant	07.59	Sagittarius
2nd	10.57	Capricorn
3rd	19.21	Aquarius
4th	25.53	Pisces
5th	25.14	Aries
6th	18.18	Taurus
7th	07.59	Gemini
8th	10.57	Cancer
9th	19.21	Leo
10th	25.53	Virgo
11th	25.14	Libra
12th	18.18	Scorpio
Sun	19.14	Taurus
Moon	19.00	Gemini
Mercury	05.59	Taurus
Venus	02.26	Cancer
Mars	25.06	Gemini
Jupiter	28.33	Aries
Saturn	06.19	Taurus
Uranus	21.49	Taurus
Neptune	22.52 R	Virgo
Pluto	00.46	Leo
Chiron	16.02	Cancer
N Node	18.40	Libra
Fortune	08.06	Scorpio

You may not know this but the 4th house has to do with the grave. It shows where you came from. It has to do with your parents, lands and estates.

The opposite house, which is the outside world, and what is happening in your life. The energies goes from one house to the opposite. So from 4th it goes over into 10th.

The 8th house has to do with death, other people's possessions, legacies and taxes and inheritances.

Let us first look at Mercury holding the angel degree in the 5th house, and in the sign of Taurus. Remember, Taurus rules the second house with the opposite as Scorpio. Scorpio is the fixed ruler of the 8th house.

Let's have a look at the moon in the 7th house in the sign of Gemini. Remember that the moon rules the moods and emotions. Here it is in a double sign. Do you know what Gemini's are like? They are double, cannot make up their mind what they want, or they will change at the last minute. I have lived with a Gemini, nice woman, but as I just said, always changing, not saying what they actually want at that moment.

The moon is in 19 degrees of Gemini, and you see that it is exactly sextile the 9th house, and exactly semi-sextile the sun in the 6th house in the sign of Taurus.

The moon is for the month of May. If we add 2 degrees, we see that it is making contact with Neptune in the 9th house in the sign of Virgo. Another degree would bring it exactly conjunct; and another one, it would be leaving the contact. So we have the months of July, August and September.

The moon is ruler of the 8th, and Neptune is ruler of the 4th.

The moment the moon came into contact with Neptune, it triggers off the emotions and the strangeness, and caused the man to do something foolish.

Mercury is in conjunction with Saturn in the fifth house, and also in the sign of Taurus.

The sun in the 6th house in the sign of Taurus is exactly square the 9th, and quincunx the node in the 10th house in the sign of Libra. The node is sextile the 9th, and semi-sextile the 12th.

The ascendant ruler is Jupiter in the fifth house in the sign of Aries (the head), and it is square Pluto in the 8th house.

Saturn is quincunx the ascendant, and is ruler of the body (2nd house) and co-ruler of the third. The sun is conjunct the 6th.

What we have done is only the progressed chart, just a bit of it. We haven't even compared it to the natal chart.

That is a lot of work, but there are many things that we would find there giving good information.

If we should start thinking about moments in time, we would find that it becomes ridiculous. I could think of moments of yesterday, of today, and even of tomorrow.

26: Questions

It is a recorded fact that astrology works. Just think of the ancient astrologers who had to tell the king whether to go to war or not. If he got it wrong, he would lose his life. Have you read about the 700, 000 volumes of books that went up in flames in the Alexandrian library? God knows the secrets that were in those books. We are still missing something to put astrology back where it belong.

Is astrology true?

Yes, it is true. As I have already said earlier, I have seen the zodiac signs in the faces of many human beings.

Why doesn't the scientists admit then that it is true?

The scientists are looking for hard facts, astrology is not like that. You just can't grab it and say that it is true. It takes a lot of research work. It is not something that is solid to hold in your hand. This science came from the Creator.

Is astrology a religion?

Sorry, I'm afraid it's not. In some old writings, astrology was there to serve us.

Then everything is already laid out for us?

It looks that way, but we can actually refuse to accept certain things if we wanted to. That is our choice. But in reality, it would be foolish to do so. For if the astrologer says that you are going to get married, it is there in the chart. But you can say, I don't want to. You must not forget that there's another person who is waiting to hook up with you. So you can see how difficult it is.

Can I win a lot of money from astrology?

Yes, you can, if it is in your chart. But not only winning a lot of money, you can have a good stable life.

Where does sickness come from?

Sickness comes from the solar system down to everything on earth. Human beings becomes sick from inheritance, from the environment. If a chart is checked properly, when a human being is sick, it is there recorded, showing what part of the body is sick. That is why we have the 12 signs of the zodiac responsible for the parts of the body, and the 10 planets as well.

My grandmother has passed away, would it be possible to see that in the chart?

Of course! Your grandparents are shown by the 9th house, and its ruler or rulers.

Can I be religious and still use astrology?

Yes, you can. It is from the energies of astrology that you are able to be religious. To join any group that you want to whether it is positive or negative.

What can astrology really teach me?

It can teach you quite a lot. To know who you are; to see the energies that you have to work with; and the ability to control them in a useful way. There are positive and negative energies.

Are there any powers higher than astrology?

This is a very hard question, and a good one. There are powers higher or greater than astrology. The Creator, if you believe in one, is greater. The first power over all powers. All the energies of the solar system are within us. And it is through these energies that we would be able to become wise, and tap into other high energies.

Is it true that one human being can have more love in them than another because of astrology?

That's true. Divine love is from God but in our solar system, the planet Venus gives out energies, and we receive them. Venus is known as the planet of love and beauty. I have checked, and it is so. Here's an example: There's a woman born to poor parents. At the time of her birth, the planet Venus was in the sign of Pisces – in this sign, the planet is said to be exalted, giving out all its love energies. Now this woman knows nothing at all about astrology, but in her life, love was always her number one. She even had sympathy and kindness for those unfortunate ones. Even if you don"t believe in astrology, it is still working within you.

Is it not possible for a human being to control his or her own life?

According to what energies we have within ourselves from the solar system, things could go well, and again it could go wrong. Sometimes we need a helping hand; and we live in a society where we try to help each other.

Some human beings are not capable of controlling their own lives. It is done for them by some institution or medical care.

What if a prediction doesn't come true?

If the time of birth is accurate, the prediction will be true. An astrologer, a good one, will not make a prediction on a false birth time.

Can we use other times to get information from a chart?

Yes, that is so. But the planets would not be in the same position as at birth. You must remember that the birth chart does not move.

What do I do if I want to know something for a certain year?

You just have to progress your chart from its natal root to the year that you want. So if you were born the 10th May 1965, and you want to know what the energies are for when you're 30 years old, just work forward, a day for a year. So then we get the 9th June 1965 as your 30th year.

Can I refuse what's inside my chart?

I don't think so. When we are told about a storm, we prepare for it. You can ignore doing so and bear the consequences, No, you cannot refuse what has been given to you.

Are there other charts that influence me?

There are many. For an example, if you are married, the chart has influence on you. If you have a job, the chart has influence on you and so on. But there are so many, we don't get to do them, but it can be done.

You said that I mustn't speculate at this time, Why?

Your moon is passing through the fifth house in the sign of Aries, and is making a square aspect to Mars and Saturn in the second house. The sign the moon is in belongs to Mars, and the moon is negative to Mars. Seeing that the moon is the fastest body, it will take about three months before it leaves Mars. You can still do what you want, ignore the good advice, it is your choice, but believe me, it is a bad one.

Can an astrologer tell if I will have children or not?

There's no doubt about that. Yes, they can tell you if you'll have children or not. Here's an example: A woman has Saturn in the fifth house in the exalted sign of Libra. It means that the woman is very friendly, and is open to creative things and partnerships and harmony. Her ascendant ruler is Mercury in the first house in Cancer. Mercury is square Saturn. She is not Married, and she has no children. She is very old now.

I have my accurate birth time, can you make many charts with it?

You can make thousands from it, but do you want to go through all that work? Suppose there are five bus stops from where you live. With an accurate time, you can make a chart at the first bus stop, but it is going to be different from the original one, the place where you live. So for every bus stop, you can make a chart. It all refers to you. We do play with time and space, and live in time and space. Time ticks along, and events are taking place every moment.

Here's a chart that I made for Midnight. It is an event chart. Together, we shall see if we can decipher what it is telling us. For my part, I'll pretend I do not know what's it is about. I could give you the date but if I did so, you'd get a clue what's it all about.

Ascendant	07.41	Gemini
2nd	02.22	Cancer
3rd	25.34	Cancer
4th	21.09	Leo
5th	22.22	Virgo
6th	29.48	Libra
7th	07.41	Sagittarius
8th	02.22	Capricorn
9th	25.34	Capricorn
10th	21.09	Aquarius
11th	22.22	Pisces
12th	29.48	Aries

Sun	12.28	Virgo
Moon	07.41	Gemini
Mercury	12.37	Virgo
Venus	08.57	Leo
Mars	02.33	Cancer
Jupiter	02.26	Cancer
Saturn	23.17	Leo
Uranus	08.46	Scorpio
Neptune	13.24	Sagittarius
Pluto	12.51	Libra
Chiron	05.27	Taurus
N Node	16.47	Libra
Fortune	12.28	Virgo

In my research, I had to spend time reading what the astrologers have published. They are not all saying the same thing so it is rather difficult for my research, but I still plod along.

Taking the part of Fortune, which comes from one of the oldest system, the Arabian system, we find that it is in the 4th house in the sign of Virgo.

I've been keeping my eye on it for sometime now, and I could only say, to take it in the house where it is, and the sign, and its aspects.

Fortune gives us a clue. The fourth house, and the 6th house sign. The 4th house has to do with the home or the country, and the 6th sign Virgo has to do with service, work, co-workers.

Fortune is in the fourth house but in the fifth house sign. The fifth house has to do with speculating, gambling, taking chances.

We see that it is exactly conjunct with Mercury, the ruler of the sign that it is in. Mercury is also ruler of the ascendant sign of Gemini. Remember, you always use the opposite sign as well. You cannot have one and not the other.

So if we take the Gemini/Sagittarius, this shows something to do with fire, moving or falling, something tall, and of course 3rd and 9th house business.

The third house has to do with communications, the 9th house has to do with long distance travel/

Fortune is also in exact conjunction with the sun. The sun is in the sign of Virgo. In fact you see the sun, Mercury and Fortune all exactly in conjunction in the 4th house in the sign of Virgo.

At the ascendant, we see the moon in an exact conjunction with the ascendant. The moon is the ruler of the 4th house in the fixed wheel, and is ruling the second and third houses in the chart. Again, we have the fourth house coming up. So then we could say it must have something to do with this house – the home or the country – and travelling and speculation.

Inside the loop in the 12th house, we see Chiron in the sign of Taurus. This is the sign of the second house, and is a body, a product. Venus, the ruler of the loop, is in the third house in the sign of Leo and holding 8 degrees. This is something that is out of our explaining, but it has to do with communications, travel, speculation. Venus is also ruler of the 6th house, work and service.

We have Pluto in the 5th house in Libra, the sixth sign, making contact with the sun, Mercury, and fortune in the fourth house. Pluto is ruling the sign of Scorpio in the loop in the sixth house. Inside this loop we see the planet Uranus, which is a scientifical planet, and is ruler of the 10th house.

In the second house we have the planet Mars exactly in conjunction with Jupiter, and they, in excat conjunction with the second house. Jupiter is exalted in Cancer, again showing the home or country. Mars is ruler of the 12th, showing, isolation, or secret.

You notice that Chiron is in 5 degrees.

The chart was done for Midnight, and not for the actual time. This shows you that we can still know what the event is about. But it is more secure to work with accurate charts.

The chart is for the launching of Voyager I.

27: Hope You Can Follow Me

This next chapter is just me going all over the place, but still keeping within the laws of astrology. After reading the book of Virginia Woolf, and how she took her own life by filling her jacket pocket with stones, and then going into the water, I decided to draw a progressive chart. She has Leo in its 1 degree, with the ruler, the sun, up in Aries in the 9th house. Mars is in the sign of Cancer in 9 degrees. Mars is ruler of the 5th and 10th houses. The third house has 8 degrees. This is third/ninth. Mercury is in the 8th house in Pisces conjunct the 9th, semi-sextile to the 10th. Mercury is ruler of the 3rd and 12th houses. The moon is in the 11th house in Gemini, and is ruler of the loop in the 12th with Mars in there. Saturn is in the 10th in the sign of Taurus sextile to Mars. Pluto is in the 11th in Taurus semi-sextile 12th. The node is in the 5th in Sagittarius trine ascendant. The node in my test, is ruling Cancer. Then there is Uranus in the 3rd house in the sign of Virgo, sextile to the 5th.

I hope you can work that one out.

Sometimes you find a chart with planets in negative aspects. Example. Moon square or conjunct Mars. You can get a progress that is positive like moon and mars sextile, but because the natal positions of these two planets are negative, you have to be careful with your interpretation.

I have come up with an idea and have been following it through, so far, it seems as if it's working. I can only use accurate charts. It is a bit complicated, I'll let you know fully what's it all about. I am wondering if the progressive date mean anything at all except that it starts the cosmic year for the individual.

I have this deep feeling that at the conception of the child, the spirit takes over. Remember, some of us call the spirit the soul. But it is made clear that they are different.

I have spent some time trying to dig into those loops. It seems to me that the chart sets itself up, progressively, this is already taken care of, even before you pop out the womb. You can start off with a loop in your first house, this, according to my test, has something to do with an extra personality. Whether this is from the past or not, I do not know, because I see the past, only as the past. Later on, this loop in the first house will go away. You can see before hand, what loops you have coming your way, progressively, and which house they would fall in.

I myself, haven't had many loops, but the ones I've had, I'm still trying to work them out. The events took place, and I know what happened.

Many people talk about reincarnation, but it hasn't got a hold on me as yet. I am still open for all theories, and to see if there is anything in it.

I am looking at a chart with a loop in the 11th house. The sign of Pisces is in the loop; the planets Mercury and Venus and Neptune are in the loop. Neptune is ruler of the loop. The opposite loop is in the 5th house carrying the sign of Virgo with Fortune in it.

In the 12th house there is a loop with the sign of Taurus. Uranus is in the loop. The opposite loop carries Scorpio with no planet there. The ascendant of the chart is Gemini. Mars is in Gemini exactly conjunct the ascendant both holding 9 degrees.

What interpretation would you give?

Because the ascendant is rising with 9 degrees, we can say that something is ending or starting. Mercury, the ruler of the ascendant is in the loop in the 11th house. This has to do with something extra, like friends, clubs or groups. Mercury is conjunct Venus, and this will bring the 12th house loop into operation, and also the 6th house. Inside the 12th house loop we see Uranus ruler of the 11th. The sign is Taurus which is the natural 2nd house. Fortune in the loop in the 5th house in Virgo has to do with work, pets, servants etc. Fortune, in the test is ruling Leo. . Leo is on the 4th and 5th cusps, and ruled by the sun in the 12th house in Aries ruled by Mars. Mars is exactly conjunct the ascendant, and has rule over the loop in the 6th house.

Always refer to the loops as something extra. Or if you like, double.

You can have loop in the 9th house with planets inside. This loop is there waiting to take over when the 9th house cusp has come to its end. Let's say that Aries is on the 9th house cusp, the next sign we know to take over is Taurus. Taurus was in the loop, just waiting. If there was 29 degrees of Aries on the 9th house, then it would go to 0 Taurus, and out comes the loop.

And you can bet your life that something is going to happen.

Here is a chart of a woman who was an activist and author.

She was born 25th March 1859 at 06:00am, Haarlem, Netherlands.

Ascendant	05.22	Aries
2nd	21.20	Taurus
3rd	14.21	Gemini
4th	01.58	Cancer
5th	20.00	Cancer
6th	14.40	Leo
7th	05.22	Libra
8th	21.20	Scorpio
9th	14.21	Sagittarius
10th	01.58	Capricorn
11th	20.00	Capricorn
12th	14.40	Aquarius

Sun	04.03	Aries
Moon	21.17	Sagittarius
Mercury	19.22	Aries
Venus	19.36	Aquarius
Mars	08.19	Taurus
Jupiter	15.04	Gemini
Saturn	05.32 R	Leo
Uranus	00.22	Gemini
Neptune	24.57	Pisces
Pluto	06.18	Taurus
Chiron	20.44	Aquarius
N Node	27.44	Aquarius
Fortune	22.36	Sagittarius

Before I drew her chart, I was looking at her picture, and saw that she showed Taurus in her face.

Her ascendant is Aries with the sun closest to the ascendant, but in the 12th house. Mercury is in the first house. The ruler of the ascendant is Mars, and is in the first house in the sign of Taurus.

There are lots of energies here to work with. Mars in its own house, the first. Mars is conjunct Pluto also in the sign of Taurus and in the first house. Pluto is semi-sextile the ascendant. Pluto rules the 8th house along with Mars.

There is a loop in the 12th and 6th houses.

In the 12th, there is the sign of Pisces, carrying Neptune (think about that)! The opposite loop has no planets, but Mercury is the ruler of the sign that is in the loop, and the sign is Virgo.

Mercury has a sextile aspect with Venus in the 12th. It is also sextile to Jupiter in the 3rd, in the sign of Gemini. Mercury is trine the moon in the 9th house in the sign of Sagittarius.

We must not forget her destiny planet, Saturn, in the sign of Leo; this is powerful, and she did use it.

So we see here, she has Aries energies, Gemini energies, Aquarian energies, and her moon in Sagittarius in the 9th.

This next chart is her progressed chart of her last year. Maybe, we shall find something of interest.

The progressed date is: 15th June 1859 at 06:00 am, Haarlem, Netherlands.

Ascendant	22.05	Cancer
2nd	07.50	Leo
3rd	26.19	Leo
4th	22.13	Virgo

5th	00.03	Scorpio
6th	16.00	Sagittarius
7th	22.05	Capricorn
8th	07.30	Aquarius
9th	26.19	Aquarius
10th	22.13	Pisces
11th	00.03	Taurus
12th	16.00	Gemini
Sun	23.33	Gemini
Moon	21.22	Sagittarius
Mercury	13.56	Gemini
Venus	25.50	Taurus
Mars	04.29	Cancer
Jupiter	01.10	Cancer
Saturn	09.19	Leo
Uranus	04.44	Gemini
Neptune	27.06	Pisces
Pluto	08.03	Taurus
Chiron	22.35	Aquarius
N Node	23.23	Aquarius
Fortune	19.54	Capricorn

The astrologers have told us that we must look to the fourth and the 8th houses. Doing research, I have to get onto all areas, and to see if what the astrologers wrote make sense.

I read an article where an astrologer said that it is not possible to predict the death of someone. That is actually not what I'm researching, but it can be done; and has been done many times over. What I'm actually interested in is the workings of the progressed chart and the individual human being. How the two blend together.

There's a solid reason why the scientific people do not accept astrology. There's no solid evidence, they say.

Some astrologers have their own interpretations of the workings of astrology, not all follow the same rules. And as for me, I try to pick up on what's going on all the time.

I've been so far trying to work some numbers into the chart which is rather difficult. Like the number 22. This number is known as a master number in numerology. Placing it in the chart is something else. It could be on the cusp of any house; and a planet could hold its number.

I'm sensing it as being magical; twice the number of the moon with a frequency of the planet Uranus.

In this chart we are looking at, Cancer is on the ascendant. Its ruler is the moon in Sagittarius in the 6th house. The moon is square to Chiron and the Node in the 8th house in the sign of Aquarius ruled by Uranus. Uranus is in the 11th house, in the 12th house sign of Gemini. Uranus is exactly semi-sextile Mars in the 12th house in Cancer. Mars is the ruler of the 5th house, and the intercepted Aries up in the 10th house.

I must state here that the loops in 4th and 10th are known to me (in the test) as extra houses. And it may surprise you to hear that this has to do with the grave or the home. Sometimes people move to other people's home, and sometimes it has to do with their departing. It also has to do with lands and estates.

The second sign with Leo there, rules the body or possessions. The sun is in the 12th house in Gemini exactly trine the node in the 8th, trine Chiron in the 8th, is square to the Mid, and semi-sextile to the ascendant.

By now you've seen that it is not an easy task when it comes to interpreting a chart. We can make many mistakes. A good astrologer, when he looks at a chart, will know what's going on.

Here is a progress chart of someone who got hit by a car. Their age was 8 years. The date is 24 April 1960 at 11:31 am, Montreal, Canada. This is without looking at any transits.

Ascendant	01.12	Leo
2nd	19.51	Leo
3rd	12.47	Virgo
4th	12.51	Libra
5th	20.40	Scorpio
6th	29.21	Sagittarius
7th	01.12	Aquarius
8th	19.51	Aquarius
9th	12.47	Pisces
10th	12.51	Aries
11th	20.40	Taurus
12th	29.21	Gemini
Sun	04.26	Taurus
Moon	19.51	Aries
Mercury	12.29	Aries
Venus	18.42	Aries
Mars	17.14	Pisces
Jupiter	03.35 R	Capricorn
Saturn	18.25	Capricorn
Uranus	16.55	Leo
Neptune	07.52 R	Scorpio
Pluto	03.41 R	Virgo

Chiron	01.27	Pisces
N Node	22.39	Virgo
Fortune	16.37	Cancer

Anything to do with travel, we go to the 3rd or 9th houses. In this chart we see that Virgo is at the third house. There we find Pluto and the node. Pluto is in the second house making a trine contact with the sun up in the 10th house in the sign of Taurus. Pluto is ruling the fifth house. I have already told tou about the axis of Taurus and Scorpio. They belong to the 2nd and 8th houses. Neptune is there at the fifth house sign but in the 4th. Neptune is ruling the 9th house. There we find Mars and Chiron. Chiron is in the 8th house and is given Sagittarius as its sign (only in the test) because some astrologers has given Capricorn and Virgo. Sagittarius is on the 6th house. Mars is in the 9th house semi-sextile Venus in the 10th house. It is conjunct the moon in the same house. The moon is ruler of the loop in the 12th house carrying Fortune ruling the sign Leo (only as test). Leo is on the ascendant, and the second house. At the second house but in the first house, we find Uranus ruler of the 7th house. Venus, up in the 10th, is square to Saturn in the loop in the 6th house in the sign of Capricorn. Mars while in the 9th, is sextile Saturn. The moon also in the 10th is square to Saturn, while it is semi-sextile the 11th house, exactly trine the second house. . Mars in the 9th house is quincunx Uranus in the first. Fortune in the loop in the 12th house is exactly sextile Uranus Chiron in the 8th house is exactly quincunx the ascendant. Jupiter in the loop in the 6th house is trine the sun. Both Moon and Venus are sextile to the 8th house, the moon in an exact contact.

Then we look at Mercury the ruler of the 3rd and 12th houses. Mercury is in the 9th house in the sign of Aries exactly conjunct the Mid, and exactly semi-sextile the 9th which is the sign of Pisces.

28: Predictions

Predicting what is going to happen to an individual in a certain year is very hard to do, but it can be done. There's no getting away from it that the energies one reads in the chart, especially if the time is an accurate one, refers to the individual of that chart. As we already know, he or she is the first house, the ascending sign, where the ruler is, what sign and house it is in, and what aspects it is making with the rest of the chart.

I have been doing some deep research on women who gave birth, and this brought me onto the fifth house, and of course the third house which is close family. After doing many charts, I realize that it is not that easy to predict the birth of a child and especially its sex. With continuous research, I have now seen how the charts differ from each other. First, I had this idea, and it is a good one, that the 10th house should be declaring what has taken place in the fifth, house of children. Then I had the other idea, looking for Virgo which rules the belly. Then I saw sometimes that Scorpio was present. Here is an example: In one chart, I saw Saturn conjuncting the 5th house, and was ruler of the 10th. In another, I saw the moon and Jupiter in conjunction in Scorpio, but none of them were ruling the 10th house. Then I saw Mars in the first house, making good contact with both moon and Jupiter, and had rule over the 10th house.

What can we predict from the following chart?
Progressed date 4th July 1965 at 08:16am, Red Bluff, California, U.S.A.

Ascendant	11.54	Leo
2nd	03.09	Virgo
3rd	29.12	Virgo
4th	01.20	Scorpio
5th	07.29	Sagittarius
6th	12.04	Capricorn
7th	11.54	Aquarius
8th	03.09	Pisces
9th	29.12	Pisces
10th	01.20	Taurus
11th	07.29	Gemini
12th	12.04	Cancer
Sun	12.24	Cancer
Moon	27.26	Virgo
Mercury	04.45	Leo
Venus	04.31	Leo
Mars	02.50	Libra
Jupiter	16.45	Gemini

Saturn	17.11 R	Pisces
Uranus	11.38	Virgo
Neptune	17.23 R	Scorpio
Pluto	14.05	Virgo
Chiron	22.31	Pisces
N Node	12.11	Gemini
Fortune	26.55	Libra

This was a marriage that was very quick and sudden. She didn't want it to happen, but it had to be done.

Notice Uranus in the second house, as ruler of the 7th, and is exactly semi-sextile the ascendant, the ruler being the sun in the 12th house in Cancer, exactly conjunct the 12th; semi-sextile the ascendant; sextile Uranus. Uranus, we know, is the planet of suddenness, disruptive, and unusual.

We sometimes fight against certain things, and yet end up having to go through that experience.

In the 12th house is he planet Mercury exactly conjunct Venus, both in the sign of Leo.

Mercury rules the second, third and 11th house. Venus rules the loop in the third carrying Mars and Fortune in the sign of Libra. Venus is also ruler of the 10th.

I hope you'll see here that Uranus, the husband, is in the second house and exactly in contact with his wife (the woman). Uranus is conjunct Pluto ruling the 4th house.

It's interesting here, because the loops are in houses 3 and 9, and these houses has to do with travel. I remember reading something about going to another country.

Much more I will not say because the marriage wasn't a good one. The husband ended up killing 7 people, and his wife was included.

In a chart you can have the moon square to Mars. In the progress for a certain year, if the progress moon is square the progress Mars, you can bet your life, there'll be trouble.

Having Mars in the natal square Uranus, and in the progress, Mars should square the progress Uranus, this is also dangerous. And if you have children with this natal aspect, you should make sure that they are not too destructive, and to use this energy in a good way. And when the year comes in the progress, do not let them go wild.

I could have predicted Prince Charles getting married in 2005. While I was in London, I heard that they had change it to another date, but still in 2005. There was an astrologer who predicted the death of Queen Victoria 3 years before it took place.

I was in London when this woman told ne how old I would live to be.

Make sure you use an accurate time when predicting, if you are going to do so. Some astrologers know quite a lot from the chart, but they do not tell everything they see. Some people are not capable of accepting what is true. And remember, some people give false birth dates and times.

Some of you men who has got a Leo wife, that is a Leo sun, or a Leo ascendant, or groups of planets in Leo, be very careful, and don't try to overpower them. You're going to get your self into trouble if you do. Sometimes you have to let them take the lead. I have come across quite a few women who were Leo's, and I saw how they behave. Have you seen what the lion do when it's hungry? Well, don't be foolish, if you want to stay with your wife or girlfriend.

I used to think to myself when I read that 'it is written in the stars' how could that be? But years of experience has shown me that it is so. I was looking at the picture of Blanka Vlasic, the Croatian high jumper, and I saw traces of Virgo, there. When I looked at her chart, she had both Venus and Mars in Virgo. This Mars in Virgo, is a very hard -working individual. Venus in Virgo is looking for the perfect partner.

Here's a progress chart of a woman. The date is 13th October 1905 at 11:00am. She and her husband died when their ship was torpedoed.

Use your codes to get proper information.

Ascendant	13.03	Sagittarius
2nd	19.55	Capricorn
3rd	04.24	Pisces
4th	11.04	Aries
5th	06.58	Taurus
6th	26.26	Taurus
7th	13.03	Gemini
8th	19.55	Cancer
9th	04.24	Virgo
10th	11.03	Libra
11th	06.58	Scorpio
12th	26.26	Scorpio
Sun	19.25	Libra
Moon	19.20	Aries
Mercury	20.12	. Libra
Venus	19.46	Virgo
Mars	03.49	Capricorn
Jupiter	05.59 R	Gemini
Saturn	26.28 R	Aqaurius
Uranus	00.43	Capricorn
Neptune	10.25	Cancer

Pluto	22.40 R	Gemini
Chiron	01.20	Aquarius
N Node	27.20	Leo
Fortune	12.58	Gemini

Uranus holds the first code being in 0 degree in the first house and in the sign of Capricorn. Uranus rules the sign of Aquarius which is in a loop in the second house carrying Saturn and Chiron. Chiron would be ruling Sagittarius (in my test), and is pointing to the ascendant, Saturn is ruling the second house carrying Mars and Uranus. The second house is her body or possessions. Mars is ruling the 4th, 11th and 12th houses.

Now we find that the planet Jupiter is in 5 degrees and 59 minutes, almost 6 degrees. But it is still in angel degrees. It is in the sixth house, in Gemini, the sign of the husband or the public. Jupiter is ruler of the ascendant and of the third house. The third house has to do with travel. You will also see in the 9th house that Venus is exactly semi-sextile to the sun. The sun being ruler of the loop in the 8th house with the sign of Leo carrying the node which I gave as ruler of Cancer (as a test). Cancer is on the 8th house cusp. Venus is also semi-sextile Mercury. Mercury is ruler of the 7th and 9th houses.

Jupiter is square to the 9th, and is quincunx to the 11th. Neptune in the 7th house is square the Mid. The node in the 8th house in a loop is square the 12th house. Saturn in the loop in the 2nd house is exactly square the 12th. The moon in the 4th house is exactly square the 2nd house. Venus is sextile the 8th, and the sun and Mercury is square the 8th. Fortune in the 6th is conjunct the 7th.

It takes time to read a chart properly. It is complicated, sometimes tricky. Why should it be so? It is just the way things are. DNA wasn't easy to discover. It took a long time, and hard and extensive research.

I was looking in a chart where someone got married. Aries was on the cusp of the 7th house. I saw the ruler in the 11th house, but was doing absolutely nothing to the rest of the chart. It was only when I started checking carefully that I was brought to the 11th house where I could bring Mars into the picture. This has happened many times. So you see how difficult it could get.

In my chart, it is clear that the 10th house is my mother, and that the fourth house is my father.

Sometimes predictions can be out according to the time you were give.

If you have a prediction of 1-4-7, first, fourth and seventh houses. You can work it out as 1-4, 1-7, and 4-7.

1-4 is definitely something to do with the individual and the home. Possibly a move.

1-7 has to do with the individual and partnerships, Also to do with the public.

Then 4-7 has to do with home and partnerships. Probably with a partner, to do with home, real estate. Always check to see if the rulers are in good aspect. Your prediction will not be wrong.

In my own chart, there were times when the planets were negative, and I experienced what happened. There's like another person within you knowing what is going to happen, and takes it in without too much bother. For we are not alone in this world. So it seems to me that other people at some time, are responsible in a certain way, along with the negative energies, of causing you trouble. Of course, you can bring it on your own self as well.

In a chart we have the cosmic year starting on the 18th April. The cosmic year of the individual is just the Perpetual date, the Progressive date. A marriage took place in October. Let's see what we could find. The moon is passing through the 4th house with 13 degrees of Cancer exactly conjunct its node in the 4th. The node too, rules Cancer (in my test). Cancer is on the cusp of the 4th and 5th houses. So here we have the 5th house of romance in operation. The moon is ruler of the 4th and 5th houses. The moon is trine Mars in the 12th house in the sign of Pisces with 18 degrees. In order to get to October, we have to add at least one degree every month to the moon's position. In October, we find that the moon is in 19 degrees of Cancer, and that mean that it is leaving its aspect with Mars. Planets leaving aspects, is the time when things happen. They can happen too, when they are coming in to make contact, and when they are exact. So we have October as the month of the romance. The month the marriage took place. There's always some sort of changes when the moon is passing through the 4th house. Some people move, others move things around. The people of this marriage moved houses.

Mars in the 12th house is ruler of the first and of the 8th houses. Inside the first house, there are three planets in Aries. The sun, Mercury and Venus, The sun/Mercury is a conjunction of 7 degrees, while sun/Venus has a conjunction of 4 degrees. Neptune, the ruler of the 12th loop with Mars there, is exactly conjunct the 7th house. Here we find Neptune in an angular position, and square to Saturn in the 4th house, also in an angular position. Remember these angular positions, they are strong houses. So Saturn is ruler of the 10th, 11th, and co-ruler of Aquarius ruling the 12th.

Uranus is in the chart in the 2nd house conjuncting the third in Gemini. The third house has to do with travel. The couple moved from one country to the next. Pluto has good aspects in the 5th house in Leo, and is ruler of the 8th, other people's possessions. Don't forget, the 8th house is the body and possessions of the partner.

The moon is also in good contact with Jupiter in the 6th. Jupiter is ruler of the 9th and 12th houses. Jupiter is in Virgo. Mars is opposing Jupiter. Sun, Mercury and Venus in the first is square to the moon in the 4th.

From all that information, there was a marriage. They moved house to another country.

Do not be afraid to make predictions once you have studied properly, and know exactly what you are doing. No one so far has ever told me that I am wrong. I do not make public predictions. I could, if I want to, but I just don't. I am still too full of ideas, and trying to research them, that in itself is a lot of work.

Try out some predictions on your friends and your families, and see how good you are.

29: Royal Charts

Some of these charts are lacking for accurate time; while others are spot on. I will do a Midnight wheel for those times that are not available or is hard to come by. I would have liked to have Brutus' chart, but that's not possible. King Alfred the Great birthdate is not recorded, only the year. There's no particular order with these charts.

King George III was born on 4th June 1738 at 07:30 am, London UK. His chart is showing us 00. Leo14 as the ascendant. He has the sun, Mercury, and Chiron in Gemini in the 11th house. Venus Saturn and Neptune in the 12th in Gemini. So he was a strong Gemini. He has Mars conjuncting the Mid with 15 degrees away from Jupiter also in the 10th house. Mars is making exact contact with the 9th house. Saturn in the 12th is exactly conjunct the 12th. The node is in the 1st house in Leo. There's a loop in the 12th with the sign of Cancer in it. The opposite sign, Capricorn has the moon and Uranus inside of it. Pluto is in the 4th house in the fifth house sign of Scorpio. The position of Jupiter in the 10th house shows a real king or Queen.

King Edward VII was born on 9th November 1841 at 10:48 am, London UK. His ascendant is 27 degrees and 37 minutes of Sagittarius. Jupiter is there in the 12th house in the same sign conjuncting the ascendant. Inside the first house, there's a loop with Capricorn as the sign, carrying Saturn and Mars. Saturn is holding 0 degree pointing to the same loop, and the second house which is Uranus, co-ruled by Saturn. The node is in the first house in the sign of Aquarius, the second house. Note that this Aquarius is not the second sign, but the third sign. Neptune is in the second house in Aquarius. There's a loop in the second house with the sign of Pisces carrying Uranus. Pluto is in the third house in Aries. Mercury is in the 11th house in Sagittarius. The sun is in the 10th house in Scorpio. The loop in the 7th house has the sign of Cancer there. The loop in the 8th house has Virgo carrying the moon. Venus is in the 9th in Libra. Again, we see the power of Jupiter at the angle giving kingship power.

King George VI was born 14th December 1895 at 03:05 am, London, UK. His ascendant is 27 degrees and 8 minutes of Libra. Chiron is in the 12th in Libra conjunct the ascendant. Jupiter is in the 10th in Leo conjunct the Mid. Neptune and Pluto in Gemini, the 9th house, but in the 8th. There's a loop in the 9th with the sign of Cancer. The opposite loop in the third is Capricorn. Venus, Saturn and Uranus are in the first house, in the second house sign of Scorpio. The moon is in the second in Scorpio. In the second is the sun, Mercury and Mars in the third house sign of Sagittarius. The node is in the 4th house in the 5th house sign of Pisces. You see how powerful Jupiter is in the 10th house.

There are other planets that can give leadership powers besides Jupiter. But we know that Jupiter is the biggest in our Solar System.

The Queen's mother **Elizabeth Angela Marguerite Bowers-Lyon** was born 4th August 1900 at 00:30 am, London, UK. Her ascendant is 22 degrees and 47 minutes of Gemini. Pluto is in the 12th house in Gemini conjunct the ascendant. Mars and Neptune are in the first house in Gemini conjunct the ascendant. Venus is in the first house but in Cancer, the sign of the second house. Sun and Mercury are in the third house in Leo. The moon is in the 6th house in Scorpio. Jupiter is about 21 degrees away from the 7th house, it is in the 6th in the sign of Sagittarius. The node is in the 6th in Sagittarius. Uranus and Chiron also in the 6th in Sagittarius. Saturn is in the 7th house in Sagittarius. She got married in the year 1923; took the throne with her husband in 1936; the place where she lived was bombed in 1940; husband died 1952; hip operation 1995 and 1998; In 2000 she fell and broke her collar bone. She said bye to the world in 2002, lived to be 101 years old.

Queen Elizabeth II Alexandria Mary Windsor was born 21st April 1926 at 02:40 am, London, UK. Her ascendant is 21 degrees and 24 minutes of Capricorn. There is a loop in the first house with the sign of Aquarius in it carrying Mars and Jupiter. Venus is in the first house in the sign of Pisces exalted. There is a loop in the second house with the sign of Aries in it carrying Mercury and Chiron. Pluto is in the 6th house in Cancer. The node is in the 6th house in Cancer conjuncting the 7th house. The 7th house loop is Leo carrying the moon and Neptune. The loop in the 8th house is Libra. Saturn is in the 9th house conjunct the Mid in the sign of Scorpio. The third/ninth houses holding 0 degree. The Queen has taken the title as the longest reigning monarch in British history.

She is now in her 67th year of reign. Married Philip Mountbatten Duke of Edinburgh in 1947. Her father died 1952. Took the throne in 1952 and got crowned on 2nd June 1953. 2016 had a terrible cold.

Son born in 1948, Prince Charles. Daughter born 1950, Princess Anne. Son born 1960, Prince Andrew. Son born 1964, Prince Edward. 2013 Grandchild born, George Alexander Louis. 2015 Grandchild born, Princess Charlotte. 2018 Grandchild born, Prince Louis. 2019 Grandchild born, Archie Harrison. Other grandchildren: Peter Phillips, Princess Beatrice of York, Princess Eugenie of York, Zara Tindall, Lady Louise Windsor, James, Viscount Severn, Grandchild born 1982, Prince William. Grandchild born 1984, Prince (Henry) Harry.

Philip Prince Consort Mountbatten was born 10th June 1921 at 21;46 PM, Corfu, Greece. Married Queen Elizabeth 2nd. His ascendant is 13 degrees and 17 minutes of Capricorn. There's a loop in the second house with the sign of Pisces carrying Uranus. Chiron is in the 3rd in Aries. Venus is in the 3rd in

Taurus. The sun is in the 5th in Gemini. Mars is in the 6th in Gemini. Pluto is in the 6th but in the 7th house sign of Cancer. Mercury is exactly conjunct the 7th in Cancer. The moon is in the 7th in Leo. Neptune is in the 7th in Leo. The loop in the 8th house has the sign of Virgo carrying Jupiter and Saturn. The node is in the 9th house in Libra.

Charles Prince of Wales. Charles Philip Arthur George Mountbatten-Windsor was born 14th November 1948 at 21:14 pm, London UK. His ascendant is 5 degrees and 23 minutes of Leo. Pluto is in Leo in the first house. Saturn is in the second house but in the third house sign of Virgo. Venus and Neptune in the 4th house in the sign of Libra. Sun and Mercury in the 4th in the fifth house sign of Scorpio. Chiron is in the 5th house in the sign of Scorpio. There is a loop in this fifth house with the sign of Sagittarius carrying Mars and Jupiter. Moon and its node in the 10th house in Taurus, the 11th house sign. The loop in the 11th has the sign of Gemini carrying Uranus. Prince Charles was Married to Diana Spencer.

Diana Princess of Wales. Diana Frances Spencer was born 1st July 1961 at 19:45 pm, Sandringham, UK. Her ascendant is 18 degrees and 24 minutes of Sagittarius. Saturn is in the first house conjunct the second in Capricorn. There is a loop in the second with Aquarius as the sign carrying the moon and Jupiter. Chiron is in the 2nd house but in the third house sign of Pisces. Venus is in the 5th house in the sign of Taurus. The sun and Mercury are both in the 7th in the sign of Cancer Inside the 8th house is a loop with the sign of Leo there, carrying the node and Uranus. In the 8th house is Mars and Pluto in the 9th house sign of Virgo. Neptune is in the 10th house in the 11th house sign of Scorpio. Diana got married in 1981. Children born were: Prince William 1982, and Prince Harry (Henry) 1984. Charles and Diana divorced in 1996. Her sudden death came about in 1997.

William Duke of Cambridge. William Arthur Philip Louis was born 21st June 1982 at 21:08 pm, Paddington, UK. His ascendant is 27 degrees and 26 minutes of Sagittarius. Neptune is there in the 12th conjunct the ascendant. There's a loop in the first house with the sign of Capricorn in it. A loop is also in the 2nd house with the sign of Pisces in it. Venus and Chiron are in the 5th house in the sign of Taurus. Mercury is in the 5th house but in the sign of the 6th which is Gemini. The loop in the 7th house has the sign of Cancer carrying the moon, the node and the sun. In the 8th house there's the loop with Virgo inside of it. The 9th house has Mars, Saturn and Pluto in the sign of Libra. Jupiter is in the 9th house in the sign of Scorpio, and only about 2 degrees from the MId. This shows power for kingship, or for holding a top job. In the 11th house there is Uranus in the 12th house sign of Sagittarius. Prince William is married to Kate Middleton who is now Princess Catherine, Duchess of Cambridge. They have three children: Prince George, Princess Charlotte, and Prince Louis. They were married in 2011.

Harry Duke of Sussex. Henry Charles Albert David was born 15th September 1984 at 16:20 pm, Paddington, UK. His ascendant is 11 degrees and 21 minutes of Capricorn. Jupiter is in the 12th house with an 8th degree conjunction to the ascendant. This too, is kingship power. A loop is in the 1st house with the sign of Aquarius there. The moon is in the 4th house in the sign of Taurus. The node is in the 4th house but in the 5th house sign of Gemini. Chiron is in the 5th in Gemini. The loop in the 7th house is empty, only the sign of Leo is there. Sun and Mercury are in the 8th house in the sign of Virgo. Venus is in the 9th house but in the 9th house sign. Venus anywhere around the 9th house are people who likes travelling. Saturn and Pluto are both in the sign of Scorpio in the 9th house. Saturn is in conjunction with the Mid. The Queen has this position as well. Uranus is in the 11th house in the sign of Sagittarius. Here you see, the Prince will have unusual friends from foreign countries. Universal friends. Mars is also in the 11th house making contact with the 12th, also in Sagittarius. Neptune is in the 12th, its own house, and conjuncting it, in the sign of Sagittarius. It is conjuncting Jupiter. Prince Harry married Meghan Markle, an American in 2018. They have their first child: Archie Harrison born 6th May 2019 at 05:20 am. If the prince wants to have a long marriage I advice him to read about King Alfred the great; and also the book of Annie Oakley who married an Irish man, and lived together for 50 years. Why do I give this advice? Because just like Annie Oakley, Princess Meghan, Duchess of Sussex is a lion, as an individual. You cannot tame a lion unless it wants to be tamed. The husband of Annie Oakley knew that, and they, doing the same things together, he let her to have the lead, and not stop her doing what she wants.

Princess Meghan Duchess of Sussex. Rachel Meghan Markle was born 4th August 1981 at 04:46 am, Canoga Park, California, U.S.A. Her ascendant is 24 degrees and 17 minutes of Cancer. The same ascendant as Joan of Arc. Cancer is always good for the home and the country. Mars is in the 12th house in the sign of Cancer. In the 1st house in the sign of Leo, the 2nd house sign, are the sun, the node and Mercury. Fortune and Venus are in the 3rd house in the sign of Virgo. Also in the 3rd house are the moon, Jupiter and Saturn in Libra, the 4th house sign. Pluto is in the 4th house in Libra. Here you see that she is a strong Libran. Saturn is exalted in Libra and it conjuncts the 4th house. Jupiter is in a position to hold high position. Uranus is in the 5th house and is exalted in the sign of Scorpio. Neptune is in the 5th house exactly conjunct the 6th in the sign of Sagittarius. Meghan and Prince Harry were married 19th May 2018 at 12:39 pm, Windsor, UK. Meghan was married in 2011, divorced in 2013. She gave birth to a son in 2019, Mountbatten-Windsor, Archie Harrison.

Princess Catherine Duchess of Cambridge. Catherine Elizabeth Middleton was born 9th January 1982 at 19:00 pm, Reading, UK. There is another time recorded at 08:00 am. Her ascendant for the 19:00 pm time is 19 degrees and 45 minutes of Leo. In the third house are the planets Mars, Saturn and Pluto in Libra. In the 4th is the planet Jupiter in Scorpio. Here, we have Queen power, or high position power. Uranus is in the 4th house but in the 5th house sign of Sagittarius. Neptune is in the 5th house in the sign of Sagittarius. The sun is in the 5th house in the 6th house sign of Capricorn. Mercury and Venus both in the sign of Aquarius but in the 6th house. Chiron is in the 10th house in Taurus. The moon is in the 11th in Cancer the 12th house sign. The node is in the 12th house in Cancer. Maybe this time is the right one because of the node in the 12th, and Jupiter holding a strong position in the 4th. Catherine was Married to Prince William in 2011. They have three children: Prince George, Princess Charlotte and Prince Louis. .

Princess Margaret Rose Windsor-Mountbatten. Countess of Snowdon was born 21st August 1930 at 21:22 pm, Glamis, Scotland. Her ascendant is 6 degrees and 7 minutes of Aries. Uranus is conjunct the ascendant in the first house. The node is in the 1st house in Aries. Chiron is in the 1st house in the 2nd house sign of Taurus. Mars is in the 3rd house in Gemini. Jupiter, the power planet is in the 4th house, and exalted in the sign of Cancer. She had the potential to be in a high position. Also in Cancer but in the fifth house are the moon and Pluto. The sun is in the 6th house in Leo. A loop is there in the 6th house with the sign of Virgo carrying Mercury and Neptune. Venus is in the 7th house in Libra. In the 10th house is the planet Saturn, another power planet, in the sign of Capricorn. The loop in the 12th house has the sign of Pisces in it. In her early days she fell in love with Peter Townsend but split from him in 1955. She then met her husband Anthony Armstrong-Jones who became the 1st Earl of Snowdon. They got married in 1960. A son was born: David Albert Charles in 1961, Lord Linley. Then came a daughter in 1964: Lady Sarah Frances Elizabeth. Princess Margaret divorced in 1978, the first in the Royal Family for 400 years. In 1987 she had surgery. She said goodbye to the world in 2002.

Princess Anne. Anne Elizabeth Alice Louise was born 15th August 1950 at 11:50 am, London UK. Her ascendant is 25 degrees and 2 minutes of Libra. Neptune is in the 12th house, and in Libra. Mars is in the 1st house but in the second house sign of Scorpio. Chiton is in the second house in the third house sign of Sagittarius. There's a loop in the third house with the sign of Aquarius there. In the 4th house is the planet Jupiter, a power house for holding a high position. The node is in the 5th house in the 6th house sign of Aries. There's a loop in the 9th house with the sign of Cancer in it carrying Venus and Uranus. In the 10th house is the sun and Pluto in the sign of Leo. The 11th house has moon, Mercury and Saturn in Virgo. She works for over 200 organizations. Some one was trying to kidnap her in 1973. The same year she married Mark Phillips who was then a Lieutenant. Divorced 1992. Two children: Peter Mark Andrew born 1977; Zara Anne Elizabeth born 1981. Princess Anne married Timothy Laurence 1992. She is a very good horse woman. Rode in the British Equestrian Team. She took the European Cross-country title in 1972. In 1988 she was made a member of the Olympic Committee. She is President of the British Olympic Association.

King George V. George Frederick Ernest Albert. Duke of York. Member of the House of Lords was born 3rd June 1865 at 01:18 am, London, UK. His ascendant is 2 degrees and 1 minute of Aries. Neptune is in the first house in Aries. Mercury, Venus and Pluto are all in he sign of Taurus in the first house. Taurus is the sign on the second house cusp. The sun is in Gemini in the second house but of the third sign. Uranus is in the 3rd house in the sign of Gemini. Mars is in the 5th house but in the 6th house sign of Leo. The moon is in the 6th house, in the 7th house sign of Libra. The node and Saturn is in the 7th house in Libra. There is a loop in the 6th house with the sign of Virgo. Fortune and Jupiter are in the 9th house in the sign of Sagittarius. Chiron is in the loop in the 12th house in the sign of Pisces. George was king from 1910 to 1936. His older brother was Albert. George was the son of Edward 7th and Alexandra of Denmark, grandson of Victoria and Prince Albert. His brother Albert died of influenza. In 1893, George married his cousin who was German, Princess Victoria of Teck. They had five sons: Prince Edward, Prince Albert, Prince George, Prince Henry, Prince John and a daughter, Princess Mary. Prince John when he was 13. George was behind the troops supporting them at the war in 1914. He travelled up to the front line, and visited the many hospitals. He had a serious fall from his horse in 1915. Celebrated Silver Jubilee in 1935. In 1936 he said goodbye to the world.

Prince Andrew. Andrew Albert Christian Edward. Duke of York was born 19th February 1960 at 15:30 pm, London, UK. His ascendant is 11 degrees and 32 minutes of Leo. Uranus is in the 1st house in Leo. Pluto is in the 2nd house but in the 3rd house sign of Virgo. The node is in the 3rd house in Virgo. There's a loop in the 4th house with the sign of Scorpio there, and carrying the moon and Neptune. Jupiter is in the 5th house in the sign of Sagittarius. Venus, Mars and Saturn are in the 6th house in the sign of Capricorn. Chiron is in the 7th house in the 8th house sign of Aquarius. The sun and Mercury are in the 8th house in the 9th house sign of Pisces. The loop in the 10th house has the sign of Taurus in it. The Duke joined the Navy in 1979. Became a helicopter pilot. Did 22 years service. Married 1986 to Sarah Ferguson. 1996 divorced. He served on the ship HMS Invincible which was sent to war when Argentina took the Falkland Islands. Two children were born to the Duke and to the Duchess. They were : Beatrice Elizabeth Mary, born 1988, and Eugenie Victoria Helena, born 1990. The Duke left the Navy in 2001.

Duchess of York. **Sarah Ferguson** was born 15th October 1959 at 09:03 am, London UK. Her ascendant is 18 degrees and 12 minutes of Scorpio. Jupiter is in the first house but in the second house sign of Sagittarius. Here we see Jupiter with its kingly/queenly power. Saturn is in the second house but in the third house sign of Capricorn. There is a loop in the 3rd house with the sign of Aquarius carrying Chiron. The moon is in the fourth house but in the 5th house sign of Aries. The loop in the 9th house has the sign of Leo in it carrying Uranus. Venus and Pluto are in the 10th house in the sign of Virgo. The node is in the 10th house in the sign of the 11th which is Libra. The sun and Mars are in the 11th the sign of Libra. Mercury and Neptune are in the 12th in the sign of Scorpio. Sara Ferguson was married 1986 until 1996. The two children were: Princess Beatrice of York and Princess Eugenie of York.

William III King of England. William Henry of Orange. King of England, Ireland and Scotland was born 14th November 1650 at 20:30 pm, Den Haag, Netherlands. His ascendant is 28 degrees and 11 minutes of Cancer. Saturn is in the 12th house in the sign of Cancer. The moon is in the 1st house in Leo the sign belonging to the 2nd house. Mars and Chiron are in the third house in the sign of Virgo. The sun and Jupiter is in the 5th house in the sign of Scorpio. Mercury, Uranus and Neptune are all in the fifth house in the 6th house sign of Sagittarius. Venus is in the 6th house but in the 7th house sign of Capricorn. The node is in the 10th house but in the 11th house sign of Taurus. William 3rd' father died before he was born. If you use the data, you'll see clearly what took place. His father was William 2nd, and this is how they called William the 3rd in Scotland. He was known to them as William 2nd. King Charles 1st of England's daughter, Mary, was his mother. His reign started in 1689 until his death in 1702.

Prince Edward. Edward Anthony Richard Louis Windsor was born 10th March 1964 at 20:20 pm, London UK. His ascendant is 16 degrees and 27 minutes of Libra. In his second house is the planet Neptune in Scorpio. THe moon is in the 4th house but in the 5th house sign of Aquarius. Saturn is in the 5th house in the sign of Aquarius. The sun is in the 5th house but in the sixth house sign of Pisces. Mercury is in the 5th house but in the 6th house sign of Pisces. Mars is in the 5th house in the sign of Pisces which belongs to the 6th house. Chiron is in the 5th house in the sign of Pisces, the 6th house sign. Jupiter is in the 7th house in the sign of Aries. Here we have king/queen power. Or to hold a top job. Venus is in the 7th house but in the 8th house sign of Taurus.

The node is in the sign of Cancer in the 9th house. Cancer is the sign of the 10th house. Uranus and Pluto are in the 11th house in the sign of Virgo which is the 12th house sign. Prince Edward joined the Royal Marines and left after a while. A relationship with Sophie Rhys-Jones, later got married. Two children: Lady Louise Windsor born 2003, and Viscount Severn born 2007.

Sophie Rhys-Jones. Countess of Wessex was born 20th January 1965 at 12:46 pm, Oxford, UK. Her ascendant is 12 degrees and 49 minutes of Gemini with the node there with 20 degrees and 56 minutes. In her 5th house are the moon, Mars, Uranus and Pluto all in the sign of Virgo. This is a stellium, and she is a strong Virgo. There is a loop in the 6th house with the sign of Scorpio carrying Neptune. In the 8th house are Mercury and Venus in the sign of Capricorn. The sun is in the 9th house in the 10th house sign of Aquarius. Saturn is in the 10th house but in the 11th house sign of Pisces. Chiron is in the 11th house in the sign of Pisces. The loop in the 12th house has the sign of Taurus in it and carrying the planet Jupiter. The Countess is the wife of Prince Edward and they were married in 1999. Two children; a daughter born 2003; and a son born 2007.

Zara Tindall. Zara Anne Elizabeth Phillips MBE was born 15th May 1981 at 20:15 pm, London UK. Her ascendant is 20 degrees and 31 minutes of Scorpio. The planet Uranus is in the ascendant sign with 28 degrees and 14 minutes. In the second house is the planet Neptune in the sign of Sagittarius. There is a loop in the second house with the sign of Capricorn. In the 6th house are Mars and Chiron both in the sign of Taurus, the 7th house sign. The sun is in the 7th house in Taurus. Mercury and Venus are in the 7th house but in the sign of the 8th house. The loop in the 8th house has the sign of Cancer in it. The node is in the sign of Leo in the 9th house. Here in the sign of Libra, she has a stellium. She is a strong Libtran; and also a strong Taurus. Jupiter and Saturn are in the 10th house but in the 11th house sign of Libra. The moon and Pluto are in the 11th house in the sign of Libra. Zara and Mike Tindall came together in 2003, engaged 2010, married 2011. They have a child, Mia Grace Tindall born 2014, and another name Lena Tindall. In 2005 Zara won the individual European Eventing Championship title, and went on in 2006 to get the World Eventing Champion. In the same year she became BBC Sports Personality of the Year. Got the MBE in 2007. She was selected for the British Olympic Team to go to Beijing, but her horse had trouble, so was withdrawn. She took the Silver Medal in 2012 at the London Olympics.

Mike Tindall was born 18th October 1978, Otley, UK. There is no recorded time for this birth. I will set it at Midnight. The ascendant is 5 degrees and 10 minutes of Leo. In the ascendant sign in the first house is Jupiter with 6 degrees and 42 minutes. Here we have Jupiter showing its royal power. In the second house is Saturn in the third house sign of Virgo. The node is in the third house in Virgo. The sun and Pluto are in the fourth house in Libra. Mercury, Mars and Uranus in the fourth house but in the fifth house sign of Scorpio. Venus is in the 5th house in the sign of Scorpio. Venus here shows a love of children and the person is very creative. There is a stellium in Scorpio, Mercury, Venus, Mars and Uranus. A loop is there in the fifth house with the sign of Sagittarius and carrying the planet Neptune. Fortune is in the 6th house in Capricorn. The moon and Chiron in the 10th but in the 11th sign of Taurus. The loop in the 11th house has the sign of Gemini there. Mike Tindall married Zara Phillips. They have a child, Mia Grace Tindall. Mike Tindall was in the England team when they won the 2003 Rugby World Cup. He broke a leg in 2007 and couldn't take part in the World Cup.

Camilla Duchess of Cornwall. Camilla Rosemary Shand was born 17th July 1947 at 07:10 am, London, UK. Her ascendant is 04 degrees and 53 minutes of Leo. Saturn and Pluto are in the ascendant sign in the first house. Neptune is in the 3rd house but in the 4th house sign. Jupiter and Chiron are in the 4th house but in the 5th house sign of Scorpio. Here again, you see the power of Jupiter. There is a loop in the 5th house with the sign of Sagittarius there. The node is in the 11th house in the sign of Taurus. The loop in the 11th house has the sign of Gemini in it carrying the planets Mars and Uranus. IN the 12th house is the sun, moon, Mercury and Venus all in the sign of Cancer. This is a stellium, a strong Cancer person. Lover of the home, family and country. Camilla married Prince Charles, and became his second wife.

Peter Phillips. Peter Mark Andrew Phillips was born 15th November 1977 at 10:46 am, London, UK. His ascendant is 2 degrees and 31 minutes of Capricorn. The moon is 20 degrees and 51 minutes in the ascendant sign in the first house. There is a loop in the second house with the sign of Pisces there. Chiron is in the third house but in the 4th house sign of Taurus. Jupiter is in the 7th house exalted in the sign of Cancer. The Jupiter power house again. Mars is in the 7th house but in the 8th house sign of Leo. Saturn is in the 8th house in the sign of Leo. The loop in the 8th house has the sign of Virgo in it. Pluto and the node in the 9th house in the sign of Libra. Venus in the 9th house but in the 10th house sign of Scorpio. Venus is conjuncting the Mid. You often find people with Venus in the 9th house are interested with travel and foreign peoples. Uranus is in the 10th house in the sign of Scorpio. The sun is in the 10th house but in the 11th house sign of Scorpio. Mercury and Neptune are in the 11th house but in the 12th house sign of Sagittarius. Peter is the son of Princess Anne and Mark Phillips. His grandmother is Queen Elizabeth 2nd, and his grandfather, the Duke of Edinburgh. Received a cap for rugby in 1995. Engaged to Autumn Kelly. 2008 got married. 2010 first child Savannah Phillips, the second, Isla Phillips in 2012. .

Autumn Kelly. **Autumn Patricia Phillips** was born 3rd May 1978, Montreal, Quebec, Canada. We have no proper time for her so we do a Midnight chart. Her ascendant is zero degree and 50 minutes of Capricorn. Fortune is in the second house in the sign of Aquarius. The moon is in the second house but in the third house sign of Pisces. Mercury is in the third house but in the 4th house sign of Aries. The sun and Chiron are in the fourth house but in the fifth house sign of Taurus. Venus is in the fifth house but in the 6th house sign of Gemini. Jupiter is in the 7th house exalted in the sign of Cancer. Even with a midnight chart we see royal power. Mars is in the 7th house but in the 8th house sign of Leo. Saturn is in the 8th house in the sign of Leo. Pluto and the node in the 9th house but in the 10th house sign of Libra. Uranus is in the 10th house but in the 11th house sign of Scorpio. Neptune is in the 12th house, its own house in the sign of Sagittarius. Autumn is married to Peter Phillips. Engaged 2007, married 2008. Children are: Savannah Phillips 2010, and Isla Phillips 2012.

Richard I, King of England, was born 8th September 1157 at 03:00 am, Julian Calendar, 15th September on the Gregorian Calendar, He was born at Beaumont Palace, Oxford, UK. His ascendant is 24 degrees and 5 minutes of Leo. Venus is in the first house but in the second house sign of Virgo. With Venus in the 1st house, beauty and love, Venus in Virgo is always looking for the right partner. The sun is in the second house in the sign of Virgo. You see that his individual self is here in the second house, and he was involved with money all the time. Mercury is in the second house but in the third house sign of Libra, Mercury is just entering Libra. People with Mercury in Libra are talkative, nice company and good communications. The moon and Saturn are also in Libra but in the third house. So he has three planets in Libra. Saturn, the destiny planet is exalted in Libra. The node is in the 3rd house but in the 4th house sign of Scorpio. Neptune is in the 4th house but in the 5th house sign of Sagittarius. Uranus is in the 6th house in the sign of Capricorn. Jupiter is in the 9th house, its own house in the sign of Aries. What would you think with Jupiter in the 9th house? It has a trine aspect to the ascendant, and to Venus. Richard did a lot of travelling to foreign countries. Pluto is in the 10th house but in the 11th house sign of Gemini. Chiron is in the 11th house in the sign of Gemini. Mars is in the 11th house, in the 12th house sign of Cancer. There's always enemies and isolation here. House 11th and 12th; groups and clubs and friends. Richard's father was Henry 2nd, his mother was Eleanora of Aquitaine. His brothers were: John who became King of England. Henry the young King. Geoffrey 2nd, Duke of Brittany. William, 9th Count of Poitiers. William Longespee, 3rd Earl of Salisbury. Richard was married when he was 4 years old to the daughter of King Louis of France. Her name was Alice. Richard sisters were: Eleanor of England. Alix of France. Joan of England. Matilda of

England. Marie of France countess of Champagne. Richard was 32 when he took the throne. Both Richard and Philip of France made plans to go on a Crusade. Richard got quite a lot of money raised to help him with the Crusade. From a hill, Richard saw Jerusalem but couldn't enter it. He turned back and went on home. The book of Richard 1st is a very interesting book. He was well-loved by the English people. He got shipwrecked and was captured. The English paid a ransom for him, which was a heavy one. He had a child from an unknown woman. The child name was Philip of Cognac.

Princess Eugenie. Eugenie Victoria Helena Windsor was born 23rd March 1990 at 19:58 pm, London, UK. Her ascendant is 21 degrees and 22 minutes of Libra. She has the planet Pluto in the first house but in the second house sign of Scorpio. IN the third house she has Saturn, Uranus and Neptune in Capricorn which is the 4th house sign. There is a loop in the 4th house with the sign of Aquarius there and carrying the moon, the node Mars and Venus. In the 6th house the sun and Mercury are in the sign of Aries. In the 9th house the planet Jupiter is in the sign of the 10th house, and is exalted. The sign is Cancer. Chiron is there as well, about 9 degrees from Jupiter. The loop in the 10th house has Leo in it. Princess Eugenie is the daughter of Prince Andrew and Sara Ferguson. She's the granddaughter of Queen Elizabeth 2nd. She was 6 when her parents divorced. Back surgery at age 12. 2011 dating Jack Brooksbank. 2013 move to New York, U.S.A. Back to London 2015. Married 2018. Eighth, and the third female waiting in line for the throne.

Victoria, Queen of England. Alexandria Victoria Saxe-Coburg Hanover was born 24th May 1819 at 04:15 am, London, UK. Her ascendant is 5 degrees and 57 minutes of Gemini. The sun and moon are in the 12th house conjuncting the ascendant. There is a loop in the 5th house with the sign of Virgo there. One important point here: this loop could have to do with the fact that she had extra children. And the sign Virgo has to do with servants. In the 6th house, there is a loop carrying the sign Scorpio. Uranus is in the 7th house but in the 8th house sign of Sagittarius. Neptune is in the 8th house in the sign of Sagittarius. Jupiter, the big powerhouse planet, the kingly/queenly power is in the 10th house in the sign of Aquarius. The loop in the 11th house has the sign of Pisces carrying Saturn, Chriron and Pluto. Here we find the loop showing extra friends and groups and clubs. Venus, Mars and the node are in the 12th house in the sign of Aries. The loop in the 12th house has the sign of Taurus carrying the planet Mercury. Queen Victoria is the 2nd longest reigning British Monarch 1837-1901. Empress of India from 1877-1901. She married her cousin Prince Albert of Saxe-Coburg. She is the granddaughter of George 3rd, and Charlotte of Mecklenburg-Strelitz. She was very much devoted to her husband. Prince Albert died 1861. Some attempts were made to harm her, but nothing happened to her.

She had 9 children, four boys and five girls. They were: Edward 7th, Victoria Princess Royal, Princess Louise Duchess of Argyll, Princess Alice of the United Kingdom, Princess Beatrice of the United Kingdom, Prince Arthur Duke of Connaught and Strathearn, Prince Leopold Duke of Albany, Princess Helena of the United Kingdom, and Alfred Duke of Saxe-Coburg and Gotha.

Princess Beatrice of York. Beatrice Elizabeth Mary Mountbatten Windsor was born 8th August 1988 at 20:18 pm, London, UK. Her ascendant is 11 degrees and 7 minutes of Aquarius. There is a loop in the first house with the sign of Pisces carrying the node. In the 3rd house is the planet Jupiter but in the sign of the 4th house which is Gemini. Jupiter is conjuncting the 4th house. A power house position. The moon, Venus and Chiron are all in the sign of Cancer in the 5th house but Cancer belongs to the 6th house. It can be seen that people with planets in Cancer has a love for their parents, home and country, especially if the planets are in good contact. The sun and Mercury are in the sign of Leo in the 7th house. The loop in the 7th house has the sign of Virgo in it. Pluto is in the 8th house but in the sign of the 9th house which is Scorpio. Pluto here, is in its own dark house. Saturn and Uranus are in the 11th house in the sign of Sagittarius Neptune is in the 11th house in the 12th house sign of Capricorn. Princess Beatrice is the daughter of Prince Andrew and Sara Ferguson the Duchess of York. Princess Beatrice is the cousin of Prince William and Prince Harry. She was two years old when her sister Princess Eugenie was born. She had a couple of dates that didn't work out. She's an actress.

Prince George of Cambridge was born 22nd July 2013 at 14:24 pm, London, UK. His ascendant is 6 degrees and 1 minute of Scorpio. The node is in the first house conjuncting the ascendant. Saturn is in the 12th house in the ascendant sign conjuncting the ascendant. Pluto and the moon are in the third house in the sign of Capricorn. Pluto is exactly conjunct the third. Neptune and Chiron are in the fourth house but in the fifth house sign of Pisces. Uranus is in the 5th house but in the 6th house sign of Aries. Fortune is in the 6th house but in the 7th house sign Taurus. Mars and Jupiter are in the 8th house in the 9th house sign of Cancer. Jupiter is exalted in Cancer. In the 9th house is the sun and Mercury also in the sign of Cancer. Here we see that he is a strong Cancerian, and will like his home and his country and his people. Venus is in the 10th house but in the sign of Virgo which is the 11th house sign.

Louis, Prince of Cambridge. Louis Arthur Charles was born 23rd April 2018 at 11:01, Paddington, London, UK. His ascendant is 27 degrees and 39 minutes of Cancer. The moon and its node are in the first house but in the second house sign of Leo. Jupiter is in the fifth house in the sign of Scorpio. Mars, Saturn and Pluto are in the 6th house in the 7th house sign of Capricorn. Neptune is in the 9th house in Pisces. Chiron is in the 9th house but in the 10th house sign of

Aries. Mercury and Uranus are in the 10th house in the sign of Aries. The sun is in the 10th house in the 11th house sign of Taurus. Venus is in the 11th house in the sign of Taurus.

Charlotte, Princess of Cambridge. Charlotte, Elizabeth, Diana was born 2nd May 20155 at 08:34 am at St. Mary's Hospital, London, UK. Her ascendant is 5 degrees Cancer and 34 minutes. The node is in the second house in the third house sign of Leo. Jupiter is in the third house in the sign of Leo. The moon is in the fifth house in the sign of Libra. Saturn is in a loop in the sixth house in the sign of Sagittarius. Pluto is in the 7th house but in the 8th house sign of Capricorn. Neptune is in the 10th house in its own sign of Pisces. Chiron is also in the 10th house in the sign of Pisces. Uranus is in the 11th house in the sign of Aries. The sun is in the 11th house in the 12th house sign of Taurus. Mars is in the 12th house in the sign of Taurus. The loop in the 12th house has the sign of Gemini, and carrying the planets Mercury and Venus.

30: Charts Without The Natal

It is coming up pretty soon of the anniversary of the death of Princess Diana. I decide to have a look at her chart. This chart is the progress chart. It mean that it is taken from the birth chart; you already know how it is done.

Progress chart for Princess Diana for 6th August 1961 at 19:45 pm, Sandringham, UK. . This will give us the year 1997.

23 Capricorn 56	Sun. . . 14.02 Leo
24 Pisces 23	Moon. . . 22.46 Gemini
05 Taurus 07	Mercury. . . 05.28 Leo
29 Taurus 01	Venus. . . 03.38 Cancer
16 Gemini 44	Mars. . . 23.32 Cancer
03 Cancer 18	Jupiter. . . 00.39 Aquarius R
23 Cancer 56	Saturn. . . 25.13 Capricorn R
24 Virgo 23	Uranus. . . 25.21 Leo
05 Scorpio 07	Neptune. . . 08.37 Scorpio
29 Scorpio 01	Pluto. . . 07.01 Virgo
16 Sagittarius 44	Node. . . 27.48 Leo
03 Capricorn 18	Chiron. . . 05.15 Pisces
	Fortune. . . 02.39 Sagittarius

By now all of you should know what the signs mean and what the planets and houses represent. The chart we are looking at has an ascendant with the sign of Capricorn rising. Do you know anything about Capricorn? If you don't, get cracking and look it up on the internet.

Capricorn is ruled by the planet Saturn. Again, I will ask: do you know anything about Saturn? Saturn is the ruler of the fixed sign on the 10th house: it is also co-ruler of the 11th.

So we see already that the princess would be interested in the 10th and 11th houses. The 10th is career, the outside world, and the 11th is clubs, groups and friends.

In the chart, Saturn is negative to Uranus over in the 7th house in the loop of Leo.

Positive wise, these two planets can make you to be someone who is interested in religion, philosophy, education, law, travelling and foreign countries.

Because in this chart the two planets are negative, they will bring some trouble. We already know that Uranus is disrupted, unusual and sudden. The all got a shock when we heard the news of the princess's death, because it was sudden.

It doesn't mean to say that everyone who has that aspect will go the same way. What I'm trying to make clear is: Uranus is the planet of astrology, of scientific subjects such as astronomy, physics and those subjects. Electricity. It is also the planet that rules the back and spine. We get the Aquarius/Leo signs. The heart comes in here as well. As long as you know that there'll be some sort of trouble when these two planets are negative, and yet they are there to be used in a positive way by the wise person.

Saturn is also known as the *'Destiny planet.'*

Saturn is conjunct the ascendant with about 2 degrees; but I work close with 1 degree in the progress chart.

So we have both Saturn and Uranus in exact quincux aspect. Uranus is making the same contact to the ascendant, but not exact.

Inside the first house we have a loop with the sign of Aquarius there. Jupiter is inside this loop with zero degree, and is going backwards (retrograde). This zero degree will take us to the places ruled by Jupiter. The 2nd house and the 11th house. These slow planets Jupiter and Saturn will hold the degree they are in for a long time.

The second house is her body, or possessions. Eleventh house show groups or friends.

As I have already told you I'm very busy trying to sort out this loop business. It seems to me that if a planet is in a loop, the individual will have to work it out in the sign an house ruled by those planets. And as I said, there is something extra going on, just a theory at the moment.

In this chart then, we see that in the first house there is the loop with Aquarius as the sign, and Jupiter as the planet. There's an extra personality here, and it is universal, unusual, and disrupted. But always remember, if the planet has good aspect, it will be for good.

So we have Saturn sextile the Mid, and so is Jupiter. Jupiter, the king/queen planet. The Midheaven sign is ruled by Mars and Pluto. Both of these planets are in the sign of Virgo which is the 8th sign in the chart. Mars is in conjunction with it. Mars and Pluto are in the 7th house.

Mars and Pluto then are rulers of the 9th, 10th, and the loop in the second house. This loop in the second house is showing an extra body. We already know that the sign of Aries is ruled by Mars. Mars is in the 7th house conjunct the 8th in the sign of Virgo. This is showing the public, partnership, servants, sickness etc.

In the first house we have Chiron in the second house sign. I've been working with Chiron as ruler of Sagittarius. Some think that he is ruler of Virgo and even Capricorn. Chiron is holding 5 degrees, that is an angel degree, and would point us to the 11th house if it is the ruler of Sagittarius; it would point us to the 8th house if it is ruler of Virgo; it would point us to the ascendant and the 12th house if it is the ruler of Capricorn.

To give you an idea what's going on when a planet is negative to Uranus, I myself have three planets ready to oppose Uranus. The first one was the sun. Now, I could write a book about all the things that took place, but that will take a long time. Then I have Mercury exact with uranus, then there is Venus having its go.

Uranus in Princess Diana chart is in a loop and in the sign of Leo. It is semi-sextile the 8th, and just about semi-sextile with Mars. These two planets are aggressive, and can cause upsets; but they can be used in sports to get rid of some of the energy. It is important if you have children with Mars negative to Uranus, to watch carefully, that they use these energies properly. The two planets, Jupiter and Saturn should have rescued the princess seeing that both of them are in an angular position and making good contact to the Mid. But from researches, I have seen that good aspects are in operation too, when people passes away.

I cannot pick up so well with Chiron as I could with other planets. But I know it will take some time.

In the princess chart, the progressive one that we are now looking at, Chiron is in Pisces, holding an angel degree, That mean that it is sextile exactly to the third house where the sign of Taurus is stationed. The angel degrees are telling us that something is happening in those areas. So we could say, that something has happened or is going to happen to do with travelling and communications, short journeys.

You see the crying degree at the 4th and 10th houses.

The moon is passing through the fifth house in the sign of Gemini. Don't forget that this Gemini is the third house fixed sign. While passing through this house, the moon is square to Mars in the 7th house. You see that Mars already is ruling the 9th and 10th houses and the loop in the 2nd house.

Mercury in the loop in the 7th house in the sign of Leo is exactly square the 9th.

Neptune and Pluto hold there aspect for a long time; they are both in sextile aspect to each other.

Venus is exactly conjunct the 6th house being ruler of the 3rd and 4th houses and the loop in the 8th.

Fortune is in the 10th, in the sign of Sagittarius, and semi-sextile to the 12th house.

In *Tiger Wood*'s progress chart, let's see what we can pick up for his divorce in 2010. The progressed date is 3rd February 1976, at 10:50 pm, Long Beach, California, U.S.A.

23 Libra 29	Sun	14 Aquarius 35
21 Scorpio 50	Moon	29 Pisces 46
22 Sagittarius 57	Mercury	23 Capricorn 20 st
25 Capricorn 54	Venus	11 Capricorn 03
28 Aquarius 27	Mars	15 Gemini 57
28 Pisces 04	Jupiter	19 Aries 39
23 Aries 29	Saturn	28 Cancer 19 R
21 Taurus 50	Uranus	07 Scorpio 07
22 Gemini 57	Neptune	13 Sagittarius 30
25 Cancer 54	Pluto	11 Libra 35 R
28 Leo 27	Chiron	24 Aries 01
28 Virgo 04	Node	17 Scorpio 27
	Fortune	08 Virgo 17

The first thing you notice in this progressed chart is that the planet Saturn is high in the 10th house. This let you know that the individual is someone who has a top job or is top in his career.

Saturn is about 3 degrees conjuncting the Mid. It is semi-sextile the 11th, but sextile the 12th.

We find the ascendant is ruled by Venus. Venus is in the third house in the sign of Capricorn, and is exactly square to Pluto in the 12th but in the ascendant sign of Libra.

Taking Libra=7, Capricorn=10, we get 7/10, trouble will be in these departments, and also in the 3rd and 12 houses.

Pluto is ruler of the 2nd house, Venus is ruler of the ascendant and the 8th house. So it has to do with money and legal stuff. We find the planet Uranus in the first house but is in Scorpio ruled by Pluto. Uranus is ruler of the 5th. THis has to do with romance, love affairs. The sun is there in the fourth house in Uranus sign of Aquarius. The sun is ruler of the 11th house which has to do with friendships or groups.

We see the moon crying in the 6th house in the sign of Pisces but this is only for the month of February. The divorce took place in July. The moon is conjunct the 6th house and trine to Saturn in the 10th, and semi-sextile to the 5th.

The 8th house ia also the house of the body of his wife, while the second house is his body. The planets ruling these two houses are Venus and Pluto, and as you have already seen, the two planets are not positive to each other, they are square.

Celine Dion's progressed chart for the year 2001 when she had her first child. The progressed date is 2nd May 1968 at 12:15 pm, Charlemagne, Quebec, Canada.

15 Leo 41	Sun	12 Taurus 18
05 Virgo 38	Moon	07 Cancer 13
00 Libra 51	Mercury	21 Taurus 18
03 Scorpio 07	Venus	29 Aries 14.
10 Sagittarius 40	Mars	25 Taurus 49
16 Capricorn 14	Jupiter	26 Leo 00
15 Aquarius 41	Saturn	18 Aries 46
05 Pisces 38	Uranus	25 Virg 28 R
00 Aries 51	Neptune	25 Scorpio 31 R
03 Taurus 07	Pluto	20 Virgo 22 R
10 Gemini 40	Node	17 Aries 29
16 Cancer 14	Chiron	01 Aries 41
	Fortune	10 Libra 36

Her ascendant sign is Leo with Jupiter in the first house and in the sign of Leo. It so happens that this same Jupiter is the ruler of the 5th house – the house of children. Notice that Leo belongs to the fifth house in the fixed wheel; and is also to do with children.

The angel degree is at the second house with the sign of Virgo there. The third house has zero degree. This is the house of close family.

Inside the second house is Uranus in an exact aspect, a trine with Mars up in the 10th house. Mars is ruler of the 4th and the 9th houses, Uranus is ruler of the 7th.

If you are hoping to interpret every chart for the bearing of a child like this one, you are going to be disappointed. All pregnancies are not the same. But you can look to the 5th house in every chart. And the third house as well.

The 8th house has something to say because this is the house where operations and babies are born. The house of Mars and Pluto.

Even the 12th house as well which has to do with hospital, isolation, and behind the scenes. The 10th house should tell of the birth.

Because the child was born 2001, we have the perpetual date (the cosmic year date) as 2nd May. The child was born in January. The moon as we see is in 7 degrees of Cancer, so if we take off 4 degrees, one degree for every month, we would get the moon in about 3 degrees of Cancer for January, the month of the birth. This then makes an exact sextile to the 10th house.

But don't get lost in the chart. The planet of the birth is Jupiter in the first house in the sign of Leo.

Here is the natal chart of *Emma Stone*. You are probably wondering why the natal chart when we are dealing with progress chart without the natal. Well, it is to let some of you see clearly what I mean. Emma Stone was born 6th November 1988 at 00:50 am, Scotsdale, Arizona, U.S.A.

Her progress chart for 2017 when she started courting is 5th December 1988 at 00:50 am, Scotsdale, Arizona, U.S.A.

We are here dealing with the progress chart only, but you can check the natal if you want to.

21 Virgo 29	Sun	13.24 Sagittarius
18. Libra 11	Moon	27.26 Libra
18. Scorpio 25	Mercury	15.35 Sagittarius
20 Sagittarius 25	Venus	14.32 Scorpio
23 Capricorn 08	Mars	08.05 Aries
23 Aquarius 46	Jupiter	29.25 Taurus R
21 Pisces 29	Saturn	02.28 Capricorn
18. Aries 11	Uranus	00.09 Capricorn
18. Taurus 25	Neptune	08.56 Capricorn
20. Gemini 45	Pluto	13.42 Scorpio
23 Cancer 08	Chiron	05.53 Cancer
23 Leo 46	N Node	09.20 Pisces

In this progressed chart we find her moon is in 27 degrees and 26 minutes of Libra. It is in her second house semi-square the sun and Mercury in the third house, but sextile Saturn, the ruler of her 5th house, house of romance. Placing the moon in her natal chart it would fall in the 3rd house conjuncting Mercury the ruler of the 11th and second houses. The 11th house is that of friendships. It would be sextile to both Saturn and Uranus in her 5th house.

I hope that you see clearly that the progress moon does make contact as it moves around the chart; and that the individual would fall under the influence whether it is positive or negative.

31: Who is Right and Who is Wrong?

There are many human beings on earth who doesn't know anything about the workings of astrology. Thank God, I know and have experienced personally how it works. It is not an easy thing to explain. People have tried or have said that astrology has to do with witchcraft. I don't know whether to laugh or cry. It has nothing at all to do with such things like that. I have a billion people who I am going to teach very simply how to understand what is actually happening to them down here on Earth. It is a fact, a hundred per cent fact that the planets has something to do with us. I would bet my life on that, but I do not bet, so we can forget that. After showing these people what's going on, and they, experiencing certain things in their lives, would have to finally admit that astrology is true and working. Someone wants to change the system, but I tell you now, it's not going to change until the whole solar system collapse, and is no more. I have nothing against scientists, but let them not come and try to test me about astrology. They have made claims that they have tested some astrologers and found nothing reliable.

You know, I was looking at a picture of Princess Margaret of England, and in her face, I saw that she looked just like my youngest daughter. My daughter is an Aries. Princess Margaret is a Leo by the sun, but has Aries rising with Uranus and the node there. Why is it that I am getting these insights which turns out to be correct? We do not worship astrology, nor do we bow down to it. It is just a science like all the others that we human beings study.

Let's take a man, his wife and 3 children. The man and woman wants to keep the family close and as one unit. Some families achieve this, but others not. I shall tell you right now, if you have one of your children with Mars in their fourth house, and is negative, you're going to end up with much trouble. It is best to let the son or daughter, if they are old enough, to go and make their own way in life. By doing this, you bring some peace and much understanding in your own family. Some families cause more trouble than is necessary.

Whose fault is it then? For if we close our eyes to the real truth, we are going to end up no more wiser.

Astrology, for what it is, shows clearly what is happening, and we as human beings has to act along with it positively and negatively.

You are not going to believe this: but those planets up there are inside of us. We are walking around with their energies deep inside of us.

We must not forget too, that upbringing has a lot to do with it. What the individual inherits from his parents, and also where he is living, the environment. All these affect us.

We shall take a quick look at the chart of a top celebrity. She is *Kim Kardashian* born 21st October 1980 at 10:46 am, Los Angeles, California, U.S.A.

13.43 Sagittarius	Sun	28.29 Libra
16.23 Capricorn	Moon	28.09 Pisces
23.02 Aquarius	Mercury	19.48 Scorpio
28.26 Pisces	Venus	19.36 Virgo
28.06 Aries	Mars	06.47 Sagittarius
22.21 Taurus	Jupiter	28.52 Virgo
13.43 Gemini	Saturn	03.41 Libra
16.23 Cancer	Uranus	24.12 Scorpio
23.02 Leo	Neptune	20.35 Sagittarius
28.26 Virgo	Pluto	21.58 Libra
28.06 Libra	Chiron	16.40 Taurus
22.21 Scorpio	N Node	16.17 Leo
	Fortune	03.23 Taurus

For some of you who are still struggling to read a chart, I can tell you now that it is really a hard thing, but once you master it, it becomes a piece of cake.

From experience I know that when I see the planet Saturn in the 10th house, even if it has negative contact, the individual has a chance of holding some sort of power.

In this chart, we see that that the planet Saturn is in her 10th house, the house of career; it is exalted in the sign of Libra. The sign of Libra is ruled by Venus, the planet of love. The ancients called Saturn, the planet of Destiny. It is to be seen too, that Saturn is the ruler of her second house, the house of money. Saturn is not only in the 10th house, but in the sign of the 11th house. Having then 11/2, gives money coming in now and then.

She has the big planet Jupiter in her 10th house. This is the position of a king or queen, in my books. One don't have to be in the Royal house to feel like a king or queen. And we see too, that Jupiter is the ruler of the ascendant and her fourth house. So she must have come from a big family.

The fourth house is parents and roots.

She has that strange planet Neptune in her first house. It is ruling her 4th house.

Those who can manage the affairs of Neptune are lucky, especially if it is negative. In her 10th house, she has the planet Pluto which is another powerhouse.

Her sun is in the 11th house which has to do with friends and groups.

Her Mercury is also in the 11th house in Scorpio, she thinks deep.

Venus is in Virgo, in its fall and making a square to Neptune. Venus is in the 9th, and she has the ability of much travel. Venus is asking for something that is almost impossible. Although it's in its fall, it is still asking for pure love.

Her moon is in Pisces in the third house exactly conjunct the 4th. A trine to Uranus in the 12th, and a quincunx to the sun in the 11th.

This chart is not very hard to interpret, but there are others that would blow your head.

A quick look at her progress chart for 2003 when her dad died. The progress date is 13th November 1980 at 10:46 am, Los Angeles, California, U.S.A.

18.46 Capricorn	Sun	21.33 Scorpio
28.39 Aquarius	Moon	28.42 Capricorn
07.34 Aries	Mercury	04.08 Scorpio
08.39 Taurus	Venus	17.23 Libra
03.20 Gemini	Mars	23.45 Sagittarius
25.22 Gemini	Jupiter	03.14 Libra
18.46 Cancer	Saturn	06.11 Libra
28.39 Leo	Uranus	25.35 Scorpio
07.34 Libra	Neptune	21.16 Sagittarius
08.39 Scorpio	Pluto	22.51 Libra
03.20 Sagittarius	Chiron	15.32 Taurus
25.22 Sagittarius	N Node	15.04 Leo
	Fortune	25.55 Pisces

Remember, always check the progress chart with the natal chart, and look to see what the transits are doing. If you are very good at reading the chart, you'll see quickly what you want to see in the progress chart.

Go to the fourth house and count 8 houses anti-clockwise. You're going to end up at the 11th house. The planet ruling this house is Jupiter, and is in the 8th house in the sign of Libra. Jupiter is exactly sextile to the 11th house.

One thing you must know, never try to look for the same aspects in every chart. You can look for the same house, of course. We see that the ruler of the fourth house is Venus. This planet is in the 9th house in the sign of Libra, and is square to the ascendant. Venus is also square to the descendant (7th house). Venus is ruler of the 9th house. This 9th house is the 6th house of the father.

The whole body, for some unknown reason shows the sickness that we get through the zodiac signs, and the planetary combinations. I have experienced this personally. So, I know what I am talking about.

Keep an eye open for the signs Taurus and Scorpio.

In this chart we see that the planet Mercury is in the 9th house in the sign of Scorpio, semi-sextile the 11th, and semi-sextile Jupiter.

In the fourth we find Chiron in Taurus exactly square the node in the 7th house in the sign of Leo.

The moon in her first house is exactly semi-sextile the 2nd, and quincunx the 8th.

In a woman's chart, the sun represents the man or the father, You see the sun in Scorpio exactly semi-sextile Neptune in the 11th house.

A quick look too, at her chart for when she got married, then decided after 4 months, she wants a divorce.

The progress date is 21st November 1980 at 10:46 am, Los Angeles, California, U.S.A.

27.18 Capricorn	Sun	29.37 Scorpio
08.47 Pisces	Moon	22.39 Taurus
17.00 Aries	Mercury	10.18 Scorpio
16.37 Taurus	Venus	27.11 Libra
10.29 Gemini	Mars	29.46 Sagittarius
02.35 Cancer	Jupiter	04.35 Libra
27.18 Cancer	Saturn	06.57 Libra
08.47 Virgo	Uranus	26.05 Scorpio
17.00 Libra	Neptune	21.33 Sagittarius.
16.37 Scorpio	Pluto	23.07 Libra
10.29 Sagittarius	Chiron	15, 08 Taurus
02.35 Capricorn	N Node	14.38 Leo
	Fortune	20.20 Cancer

Let's go to the ascendant where Capricorn is rising. Saturn, the ruler of the ascendant is in the 8th house. Notice here that she was born with this her destiny planet exalted in Libra, and it will stay like that for a long time. It just means that there is something good in her to do with the public and relationships, even if they go wrong.

Saturn is in a 2 degrees conjunction with the planet Jupiter. Jupiter is ruler of the 2nd and 11th houses. Money come in now and then.

Saturn isn't doing very much, but if placed in the natal, he makes a sextile with Mars who is ruler of the romance house in the natal.

But we are not dealing with the natal but with this progress chart.

At the second house we see that the axis is holding 8 degrees, this is something out of our power. The second house is her body, and the 8th house is his body.

We do find Venus in the 9th house in Libra (Libra has to do with the 7th house), square to the ascendant.

Mars is in the 11th house, house of friendships and it is crying. So too, is the sun, in the 10th house, and ruler of the loop in the 7th.

The node is in that 7th loop in the sign of Leo. And as I am working with the loop as ruler of Cancer, we see that Cancer is on the 7th house. The node is square the Mid about 2 degrees away.

Mercury, in the 9th house, ruling the 5th and the 8th houses is semi-sextile the 11th.

Chiron in the fourth house is square the node in the loop in the 7th. Chiron in my workings, as test, rules the 11th house Sagittarius.

Venus is semi-sextile Uranus. Uranus is ruler of the loop in the fist house. This loop gives an extra personality.

Then we have the moon in the 4th house, ruler of the 7th, opposing three planets in the sign of Scorpio. The opposition to Mercury or any negative contact can cause wrong decisions.

Taking 3 degrees away from the moon will give us about 19 degrees Taurus for the month of August when she got married. It falls in her 5th house in the natal chart, conjuncting the 6th, and trine to Venus.

A look at *Rihanna*'s chart. Born 20th February 1988 at 08:50 am, Bridgetown, Barbados.

15.09 Aries	Sun	01.06 Pisces
17.47 Taurus	Moon	11.06 Aries
15.40 Gemini	Mercury	13.17 Aquarius R
11.33 Cancer	Venus	12.56 Aries
08.41 Leo	Mars	28.43 Sagittarius
09.47 Virgo	Jupiter	26.38 Aries
15.09 Libra	Saturn	00.31 Capricorn.
17.47 Scorpio	Uranus	00.12 Capricorn
15.40 Sagittarius	Neptune	09.29 Capricorn
11.33 Capricorn	Pluto	12.34 Scorpio R.
08.41 Aquarius	Chiron	28.29 Gemini
09.47 Pisces	N Node	24.29 Pisces
	Fortune	25.09 Taurus

Aries is at the ascendant with three planets hanging around. Jupiter is in the first house; moon conjunct Venus in the 12th house. Mars, the ruler of the ascendant is in the 9th house in the sign of Sagittarius.

Mars is in conjunction with Saturn and Uranus, both in the 9th house. Mars is sextile the sun in the 11th house. It is square her node in the 12th house, It is trine Jupiter. Opposing Chiron in the 3rd house.

Notice that both Saturn and Uranus are in the 9th house, and both in zero degrees in Capricorn. We know that zero degrees is pointing us to where the planet is ruling. So, if we take Saturn, we get the 10th house and 11th. Taking Uranus, we get the 11th. These two planets, Saturn and Uranus, especially in the 9th house has to with genius qualities. Lots ot travelling here as well.

She is a Pisces by the sun in the 11th house . The sun has good contact with Saturn and Uranus.

Her moon sign is Aries and it is conjunct Venus in the 12th house. This Venus position here is good for romantic love, isolation, music, art, singing and dancing.

Both the moon and Venus are sextile Mercury in the 11th house; both square to the Mid, quincunx Pluto in the 7th house. Pluto is sextile the Mid.

This chart shows us that the person has the chance to do well.

Now we are onto *Shakira*. She was born 2nd February 1977 at 10:08 am, Barraquilla, Colombia.

17.38 Aries	Sun	13.40 Aquarius
19.43 Taurus	Moon	25.06 Cancer.
17.33 Gemini	Mercury	19.09 Capricorn.
13.43 Cancer	Venus	00.21 Aries
11.17 Leo	Mars	24.42 Capricorn
12.40 Virgo	Jupiter	21.44 Taurus
17.38 Libra	Saturn	13.25 Leo R
19.43 Scorpio	Uranus	11.43 Scorpio
17.33 Sagittarius	Neptune	15.37 Sagittarius. .
13.43 Capricorn	Pluto	14.06 Libra R.
11.17 Aquarius	Chiron	27.37 Aries
12.40 Pisces	N Node	28.09 Libra
	Fortune	29.04 Virgo

We find that her ascendant is Aries with Venus there in the 12th house in Aries. This is the planet of love and beauty. Chiron is there in the first house in Aries but not conjuncting the ascendant. Venus is holding zero degree and is pointing us to the 2nd and 7th houses.

Mars, the ruler of the ascendant is in the 10th house exalted in the sign of Capricorn and conjuncting Mercury also in the 10th house and the same sign. Mars is just about making a sextile aspect to Venus, but square to Chiron. Chiron is supposed to be in charge of the 9th house which is Sagittarius. Mars is trine Jupiter in the second house in the sign of Taurus. Mars is trine Fortune in the 6th house in the sign of Virgo. Mars is opposing the moon in the 4th house in the sign of Cancer.

A good opportunity is here with Jupiter in the second house. The individual has the chance to make money, or to have many possessions.

This Pluto in the 6th house conjunct the 7th is showing her husband

Pluto is sextile Saturn in the fifth, while Saturn is semi-sextile the 6th. Saturn is trine the ascendant, so that she has the chance of having children. Saturn is good at stopping the birth of children if it is badly afflicted. Saturn is trine Neptune. It opposes the sun.

What is *Taylor Swift* showing us in her chart? She was born 13th December 1989 at 05:17 am, Reading, Pennsylvania, U.S.A.

25.34 Scorpio	Sun	21.23 Sagittarius
26.21 Sagittarius	Moon	01.29 Cancer
02.14 Aquarius	Mercury	08.38 Capricorn
08.47 Pisces	Venus	01.50 Aquarius
10.04 Aries	Mars	26.41 Scorpio
05.01 Taurus	Jupiter	07.44 Cancer R
25.34 Taurus	Saturn	13.26 Capricorn
26.21 Gemini	Uranus	04.38 Capricorn
02.14 Leo	Neptune	11.19 Capricorn
08.47 Virgo	Pluto	16.29 Scorpio
10.04 Libra	Chiron	15.03 Cancer
05.01 Scorpio	N Node	19.26 Aquarius
	Fortune	15.28 Taurus

Some of you by now should know how to read your own chart, and also the progress. It is still a complicated science, but it is true.

In this chart, we see that Scorpio is rising, and that Mars is there conjuncting the ascendant. There is lots of energy here. Pluto is also ruler of the ascendant and it is located in the 12th house and in Scorpio.

Her sun is in the first house in the sign of Sagittarius conjunct the second house. Does that tell you anything? There are four planets in the loop in the 2nd house in the sign of Capricorn. They are Mercury, Saturn, Uranus and Neptune. Notice that Mercury has 8 degrees and is exactly trine the Mid. This is something that we cannot do anything about. It is out of our powers.

All the planets in the loop in the second house are in a trine contact with the Mid. We have Fortune in the 6th with a 10 degrees conjuncting the 7th.

What about Jupiter and the moon and Chiron in the loop in Cancer in the 8th house? Jupiter is exalted in Cancer, and is ruler of the 2nd and fourth houses. The moon and Jupiter makes a sextile contact to the Mid. Venus is conjunct the 3rd house, and quincunx the moon.

A look at our last chart which is *Dua Lipa* born 22nd August 1995 at 11:45pm, London England.

29.05 Libra	Sun	8.52 Leo
26.15 Scorpio	Moon	16.06 Cancer
00.20 Capricorn	Mercury	20.34 Virgo
08.57 Aquarius	Venus	29.16 Leo
12.53 Pisces	Mars	19.42 Libra
09.05 Aries	Jupiter	06.07 Sagittarius
29.05 Aries	Saturn	23.02 Pisces R
26.15 Taurus	Uranus	27.18 Capricorn R
00.20 Cancer	Neptune	23.15 Capricorn R
08.57 Leo	Pluto	27.52 Scorpio

12.53 Virgo	Chiron	27.28 Virgo
09.05 Libra	N Node	29.24 Libra
	Fortune	16.18 Virgo

This chart has Libra rising almost at its end. Venus is the ruler and is up in the 10th house in the sign of Leo, and almost at its end of the sign.

Venus holds a strong position in this 10th house. There's a chance to get to the top in their career. The position is good for artists and singers and painters.

Venus is exactly sextile the ascendant, and this has to do with beauty, and love. Venus is really solid here, being the ascendant ruler and making good contact with the ascendant. Venus is also exact sextile with the node; and the node is in Libra in the 12th which is the sign of Venus; and the 12th house has to do with Neptune which is art and music and dancing.

My study of many charts, brought me in contact with this Venus/node combination. Even when they are not in contact like a conjunction, but both in the same sign; it is showing that the person has a sort of soul love.

The sun and Venus in conjunction in the 10th is something beautiful. The sun represents life, and Venus represents love and beauty. The 10th house has to do with career and parents.

Venus is square Pluto. All sort of things can happen here. With Venus holding a strong position, Pluto is the one that will probably try to lead Venus astray. The individual may do certain things that others dare not do. From Mythology we learn that Pluto is a kidnapper; and he is empowered with the beauty of Venus.

We know that in the normal chart (fixed), Venus is ruler of the second while Pluto is ruler of the 8th. Here you have your own money, and other people's.

Pluto we see is in her second house conjuncting the second. Pluto is exactly sextile to Chiron in the 11th house. Here we have that contact of 2/11 which brings in money now and then. The 11th house has to do with friends, groups, or clubs.

Now we have the big planet, Jupiter, the planet that can make you rich, give you plenty, the expansive planet is in the second house, and in the loop of Sagittarius which is own by itself. Jupiter is conjunct with Pluto, It is semi-square Neptune in the third house. It is trine the Mid, and square Venus in the 10th. Jupiter is also co-ruler of the 5th house.

Saturn we see is in the 5th house. Saturn here, and is negative, gives no children. But as we see in this chart, Saturn has a few positives. A negative to Saturn is Mercury in the 11th house. The two planets are fighting against each other like in a tug-of-war game, which one will win. Bad decisions can be made. The moon in the 9th is good for travel, foreign countries and peoples. The moon itself, rules the 9th house.

32: Chart for the U.S.A.

We are going to really dig in deep, and see what we can get out of this chart. We're not going to rush anything. And I hope along the way, you can pick up a few important points. I'll be staying on track, but rambling my head off; still keeping on the astrological path. You won't get lost I'm sure. By now, you should know your way around.

The chart I'm working with is the 4th July 1776, 17:10 pm. Philadelphia, Pennsylvania, U.S.A.

12.21 Sagittarius	Sun	13.19 Cancer
16.04 Capricorn	Moon	27.10 Aquarius
24.53 Aquarius	Mercury	24.11 Cancer
01.03 Aries	Venus	03.06 Cancer
29.48 Aries	Mars	21.22 Gemini
22.34 Taurus	Jupiter	05.56 Cancer
12.21 Gemini	Saturn	14.48 Libra
16.04 Cancer	Uranus	08.55 Gemini
24.53 Leo	Neptune	22.25 Virgo
01.03 Libra	Pluto	27.33 Capricorn R
29.48 Libra	Chiron	20.08 Aries
22.34 Scorpio	N Node	07.35 Leo
	Fortune	26.12 Cancer

The sign of Sagittarius is rising in this chart. This sign, I associate with space, travelling, freedom, high education, foreign countries, religion, law, philosophy. The ruler is the planet Jupiter, in the 7th house holding 5 degrees, and exalted in the sign of Cancer. So there is something really big going on here. With me, Jupiter in an angular position is like a king or queen, or someone who'll be in a high position. We see that Jupiter is conjunct with Venus and the sun, it is semi-sextile the node in the 8th house. It is square the Mid, and square to Saturn in the 10th house.

Looking at the chart, you'll see that the sun is in Cancer and in the 7th house. This too, is a very strong position.

We see that Pluto the planet of the 8th house, other people's possessions, is in the second, the chart's money house.

We see also that the planet Mars, the planet of war is in the house of war, or the house of others. Uranus is in the 6th house in the same sign as Mars. These two planets together are very powerful when it comes to energy.

We see the moon in the the third house in the sign of Aquarius, the universal sign. And we see the powerful planet Saturn, up there in the 10th house, exalted in Libra.

Fortune is in the 8th house which has to do with other people's possessions. I am still trying to see what fortune is actually doing in the charts.

Mercury in the 8th house will know quite a lot. It is in the house of Pluto, and only Mercury is allowed to see and know what's going on down there. Jupiter is in the 7th house but in the 8th house sign, this is interesting because Jupiter, when he is in or around the 8th house, knows deep things.

In the third and 9th houses we have intercepted signs (loops), this could have something to do with something extra, like travelling, foreign countries, and everything that the 3rd and 9th house are responsible for. I'm still trying to pin-point these loops which are rather difficult.

The United States of America has about 18 charts, but we are not going into them. Only this one and the next we'll take a look at, and also a progressed one.

In this chart that we are now busy with, we already see that Saturn is all powerful in the 10th house, and exalted as well. Read properly what that mean. We find many individuals with Saturn in the 10th house has taken over a top job. So in this chart, we see that America has a top job. ; and it has to do with Libra. Libra is the sign of togetherness, harmony and the public. Saturn is sextile the ascendant, and it rules the second and third houses. At the second house, we find Pluto, ruler of the 12th house. At the third house we find the moon, ruler of the 8th house. There at the 8th house we find the sun, ruler of the 9th house. We find Mercury, ruler of the 7th, house, and the 9th with the loop of Virgo carrying Neptune, ruler of the loop in the third. We find at the 8th too, the planet Venus, ruler of the 10th, 11th and the 6th houses. Jupiter is there at the 8th house, ruler of the ascendant, and co-ruler of the loop in the third.

Mars in the 7th house, the house of war is very aggressive. It is square Neptune in the loop in the 9th house. This is furious. We see that Neptune is making contact to the 12th house. This has to do with strange secrets to do with the 9th house, notice that the loop is extra. Mercury is in the 8th house, ruler of the 7th and the loop in the 9th, and it is exactly semi-sextile the 9th. This contact of 7 and 9 you will find in many charts of people who has contact with foreign countries, travels a lot, or husbands or wives are from other countries. THis chart has connection with the 9th house. The ninth house is long distance travel, space, religion, philosophy, high education, law and freedom.

There is another chart with Gemini rising with 7 degrees and 14 minutes. Mars and Uranus is the first house. This time is for 02:13 am. So we have Sun, Mercury, Venus and Jupiter in the second house. THis sounds good with Jupiter there and exalted. And also Venus who is ruler of the second in its own house. Lots of riches here. But I still like the first chart with Saturn in the 10th and exalted in Libra. That is really showing that the nation is powerful; and with

Jupiter in a kingly position in the 7th, and exalted, I really go for that. But I could be wrong. There are so many charts.

Now what we are going to do is move the first chart to the year 1941. Why to that year? Because that is the year America was at war. The date is 7th December.

We get a perpetual date or cosmic date of 16th December 1776, 17:10 pm, Philadelphia, Pennsylvania, U.S.A.

04.27 Cancer	Sun	25.39 Sagittarius
24.22 Cancer	Moon	09.15 Pisces
15.48 Leo	Mercury	17.19 Sagittarius
12.13 Virgo	Venus	27.29 Capricorn
16.46 Libra	Mars	00.22 Libra
27.28 Scorpio	Jupiter	23.13 Cancer R
04.27 Capricorn	Saturn	00.51 Scorpio
24.22 Capricorn	Uranus	08.16 Gemini R
15.48 Aquarius	Neptune	27.04 Virgo
12.13 Pisces	Pluto	27.04 Capricorn
16.46 Aries	Chiron	15.40 Aries
27.28 Taurus	N Node	27.35 Cancer
	Fortune	18.03 Virgo

Looking at the chart, we see that Mars is in the house of the moon, but in the 5th house sign and holding zero degree. Mars is in the sign of Libra. It is pointing us to the 11th house which has to do with groups and friends. There, we find Chiron whom we have given the sign of Sagittarius to as a test. Sagittarius is in a loop in the 6th house carrying the sun and Mercury. The sun is ruler of the 3rd house to do with travel and communications etc. Mercury is ruling the 4th house to do with the home, the country. We find that Mercury is also ruler of the opposite loop with Gemini as the sign. Inside Gemini, we see the planet Uranus ruler of the 9th house, this has to do with foreign countries, and long distance travel. But when we were at the 4th house, we saw Neptune and Fortune there. Neptune is ruler of the 10th house which has to do with the boss. And we see the moon there, ruler of the ascendant, which is the people of the country, and the second house, is money.

In the 5th house we see the planet Saturn also holding zero degree in the house of the sun and in the 6th house sign of Scorpio. Scorpio is the natural sign of the 8th house. Saturn is ruling the 7th, 8th and 9th houses. There is an exact semi-sextile between Mars and Saturn.

Inside the loop of the 12th house, we see the planet Uranus in Gemini in the loop. Uranus is ruler of the 9th house. The 12th house we know is secret enemies; and the 9th house has to do with travel and foreign countries.

In the 9th house we see the progress moon in Pisces. This moon is square to

Uranus; and is also the moon for the month of December. Uranus is holding 8 degrees, something that is out our hands, we have no control over it.

Notice Venus and Pluto exactly conjunct in the 8th house in Capricorn. Both exactly trine the 12th house which is ruled by Venus. Venus also rules the 5th house. Pluto rules the 6th. For some of you who do not know, the 6th house has to do with services, that is the military, policemen nurses doctors and so forth. The fact that Venus is in the 8th with Pluto and is trine the 12th is showing that 8th house, other people's possessions will come to the country. 8th house also has to do with the dead.

We have the node in the second house exactly sextile the 12th. Something secret is going on. The node in my test rules the ascendant and the second house. Jupiter is there conjuncting the second. Jupiter is ruling the loop in the 6th house and also the 10th. The 10th is the president of the country. (The Boss.)

Still with the node in the second house to do with money and possessions, there's something about getting and losing here. The node is sextile Neptune in the 4th house.

Fortune in the fourth house is angular. It is square to Mercury in the loop in the 6th house in the sign of Sagittarius. Don't forget that this sign is the normal sign at the 9th house. Mercury is ruling the fourth house, and also the loop in the 12th, Gemini. So again, we have enemies.

Inside the loop in the 6th house is the sun in semi-sextile aspect with the 8th. The sun is ruler of the 3rd house.

33: Past and Future Events

I had no idea at all that there was something like astrology that can tell you things about yourself and others. I wasn't into it as yet. While I was in my camp, still a young soldier, this young girl came up to me and asked if I would take her to the flicks. I said to her, "No way! You have a boyfriend, and I don't mess around with people who are dating or are married." She said that she had finished with him, and it was okay to take her out. So I took her to the cinema. The following day, the chap came up to me and said, "You couldn't wait, could you?" There, I wanted to explain to him that I had no intention of doing what took place.

A few days later, some chaps decided to go over the border to the Netherlands which wasn't very far away. I went with them. We gathered in the first cafe that we saw, while we waited for the bus to come. Inside this cafe, the girl behind the bar, was very friendly, and was interested in me, even the guys saw that. Anyway, the bus came, and we headed to the town which was some distance away. We got there, and while we were inside a bar, this girl, who lived next door, came out, walking a little child. At first, I took a liking to her, then I change my mind because of the child, thinking she was married, and the child was hers. The barman told me, that the child belonged to her mother. After hearing that, I made my move and approached her. That girl turned out to be my first wife.

It was only after I started studying astrology that I realized that that year I would meet someone. There in the chart, I saw it clearly. That is why that girl in the camp, and that one over the border were so friendly to me. Now I understand and see it clearly in other people's chart who fell in love and got married. How do we explain that for we know that we have choices to say yes or to say no. If we don't like a thing, we just don't buy it. So then we are looking at a chart, and the event is staring back at us for some particular year. It is okay if the event is good; but what if it is bad or let's say negative. I feel not everyone can take this.

There you are then, staring at a chart in the future. It has to do with your 4th house. Let's say that Venus is the ruler, and it is in the first house in Cancer, and squaring Mars in that 4th house. Remember that Venus also rules the 11th house. Mars is ruling the 10th and the 5th. So what then would your interpretation be?

We only have two planets to play with – Venus and Mars. Venus is in the first house, and Mars is in the fourth house; both are in angular houses. I do hope you know what that mean. It is not so bad as when they are in other places, still, they are negative.

The first house is you, and the 4th house is your home and parents. There is your first interpretation.

Remember, astrology is not straightforward so that you can exactly pin-point what it is. And two charts doesn't show exactly the same thing Like I mean, one chart has other aspects for one getting married, while the other shows something else. But you can bet your life that Libra would be involved.

Venus rules Libra, and Mars is in Libra. Venus also rules the 11th house Taurus.

Mars rules the 5th house, and also the 10th house. Another interpretation for you.

You're going to be surprised at the amount of information can come from just these two planets square, and in angular houses.

You know already that Venus is ruler of the 7th house in the fixed wheel. Also ruler of the second house. Keep this in mind.

Venus is in the first house of this chart. The first house is you. Venus is in Cancer. We know that Cancer is a protective, homely and sensitive sign. Don't forget that the first house belongs to Mars in the fixed wheel.

There's something here to do with love and probably feelings. We see that Venus is in contact with Mars and the fifth house comes into play. Mars is energetic, assertive, and this could bring out love at first sight. These two planets can cause love trouble as well. Mars in the fourth house, is not a very good position for Mars, but it is strong, being in an angular position. There could be slight problems in the home or with parents or even decorating, making the home pretty. We have the fifth house also to deal with. This house rules many things, such as children, love affairs, speculation, sports, entertainment, gambling.

We must not forget the 10th house and the 11th house, they too are important.

Let's have a look at *Jennifer Aniston* progress chart for 2012. Her birthdate is 11th February 1969 at 22:22 pm, Los Angeles, California, U.S.A.

To move her chart to 2012 we have to check that there's 43 days between 1969 and 2012. . February has only 28 days for its month. We take the 17 days from February and plus them with 26 of March, giving us the perpetual date of 26th March 1969, at 22:22 pm, Los Angeles, California, U. S. A as the progress calculations for 2012.

29 Scorpio 39	Sun	06.24 Aries
00 Capricorn 22	Moon	19.51 Cancer
04 Aquarius 54	Mercury	24.11 Pisces
10. Pisces 14	Venus	25.14 Aries R
11 Aries 39	Mars	11.35 Sagittarius
07 Taurus 37	Jupiter	00.27 Libra R
29 Taurus 39	Saturn	25.45 Aries
00 Cancer 22	Uranus	01.46 Libra R
04 Leo 54	Neptune	28.31 Scorpio R

10 Virgo 14	Pluto	23.26 Virgo R
11 Libra 39	Chiron	03.00 Aries
07 Scorpio 37	N Node	00.05 Aries
	Fortune	16.12 Leo

Okay then, let's start with the ascendant rulers – they are Mars and Pluto. We find Mars in a loop in the first house in the sign of Sagittarius. Mars is exactly sextile the 11th house where Libra is stationed. Mars is also ruler of the 5th house where Aries is stationed.

The 11th house is that of friendships, clubs or groups. Fifth house is love and romance. So there we have it, and we are not even looking in the natal chart. But this you must do to get more information. The two charts work together. Mars is also square the Mid, but notice, angular positions.

We find the planet Neptune in the first house in the sign of Scorpio, and closely conjuncting the first house. Neptune is also semi-sextile the second house. Neptune is co-ruler of the 4th house. I bet you're wondering why Neptune is conjuncting the ascendant, and is ruler of the 4th?

The other ruler of the ascendant, Pluto is up in the 10th house in the sign of Virgo and is opposing Mercury which is ruler of Virgo. You see that Mercury is in the fourth house in the sign belong to Neptune. 10th and 4th are angular positions, and only slight problems can come from them. If they were stationed in other houses, there would be much trouble between them. Mercury is ruling the loop in the 7th house with Gemini there; it is also ruling the 10th house.

The second and eighth houses are holding zero degree, and are letting you know that there is something here to do with money, other people's money, her body, and her partner's body.

Mercury in the 4th house is semi-sextile to both Venus and Saturn in the 5th. Venus and Saturn are exactly conjunct in the 5th in Aries.

The moon is in the 8th house in the sign of Cancer, and is ruler of the 8th. The moon is in 19 degrees for March: her engagement took place in August. So if we add another 5 degrees bringing the moon to August, we get it in around 24 degrees or thereabouts. It would be making contact with Pluto in the 10th, Mercury in the 4th, and with Venus and Saturn in the 5th.

Look up your own chart, and that of others that you know. Do a chart for the year that they first met their loved ones, and see what you make of it.

This next chart is of *Kristen Stewart* born 9th April 1990 at 09:21 am, Los Angeles, California, U.S.A.

I think that she made it plain that she was in love with Rob around 2011.

We are going to progress her chart to 2011. She is then 21 years old, and that would give us 30th of April as her perpetual date (cosmic year).

02.10 Cancer	Sun	10.03 Taurus
23.41 Cancer	Moon	25.35 Cancer
16.35 Leo	Mercury R	15.15 Taurus
14.05 Virgo	Venus	26.07 Pisces
16.24 Libra	Mars	07.17 Pisces
26.51 Scorpio	Jupiter	06.53 Cancer
02.10 Capricorn	Saturn	25.19 Capricorn
23.41 Capricorn	Uranus. R	09.28 Capricorn
16.35 Aquarius	Neptune. R	14.31 Capricorn
14.05 Pisces	Pluto R	16.34 Scorpio.
18.24. Aries	Chiron	12.08 Cancer
26.51 Taurus	N Node	12.07 Aquarius
	Fortune	17.42 Virgo

Her progress chart is showing an ascendant of Cancer. She has finished with Gemini, and is now running on Cancer. The ruler of Cancer is the moon in the second and conjuncting the second. In the ascendant, we have Jupiter and Chiron. Jupiter is exalted in Cancer, and is ruler of the loop in the 6th house, and the co-ruler of the 10th.

The moon has rule over the ascendant and the second house. It is trine the planet of love, Venus, in the 10th house, and Venus is exalted in this sign. The moon is exactly opposing Saturn in the 8th house. Saturn is ruler of the 7th, 8th and 9th houses. Saturn is sextile to Venus. You notice here, that Venus is now in good contact with Saturn, this is good for steady, loyal love. In her natal, Venus wasn't making any contact with Saturn at all. Also in her natal we find that Jupiter is conjuncting the second house, this is always good for becoming rich, expanding. Jupiter is exalted in Cancer. I hope you have seen the three planets that she have in Capricorn. They are Saturn, Uranus, and Neptune.

Knowing what has happened in the past, you can set your chart for any year. Suppose we knew the exact year when creation started, you can take your chart right back to that year. And you see too, that we can move it forward into the future and know certain things before they take place. Astrology is true as I have said many times, and I will keep on saying so. It shows that it has to do with nature and all things created. Most of us see the sun and we know that it is there. So too, astrology is there, but not comprehended by everyone. Astrology is a science that is very good; it's like a medicine for healing once you learn what it is all about, and how to use it. The real point is accepting the positive and the negative. A bad upbringing, and negative forces does not work together, there's confusion, but later it can be put right.

I have been looking into lots of faces to see what I could find. I must admit that I cannot see the signs in every face, but most the time, I do see the signs.

Take for instance The Duchess of Cambridge. I can see the Taurus in her face. She has Leo rising with Taurus at the 10th house. I do look quite a lot at the celebrities.

Talking about celebrities, let us look at *Megan Fox*. She was born 16th May 1986 at 00:35 am, Oak Ridge, Tennessee, U.S.A.

We are going to look at her progs at the age of 18, for that is the year she fell in love with the man who became her husband.

We finish off the month of May with 15 days, then we pick up three days from the Month of June. The Progressed date is the 3rd June 1986 at 00:35, Oak Ridge, Tennessee, U.S.A.

09.54 Aquarius	Sun	12.19 Gemini
24.14 Pisces	Moon	24.24 Aries
00.51 Taurus	Mercury	25.20 Gemini
28.04 Taurus	Venus	15.05 Cancer
20.37 Gemini	Mars	22.54 Capricorn
12.50 Cancer	Jupiter	20.26 Pisces
09.54 Leo	Saturn R	05.57 Sagittarius
24.14 Virgo	Uranus R	20.43 Sagittarius
00.51 Scorpio	Neptune R	05.02 Capricorn
28.04 Scorpio	Pluto R	05.00 Scorpio
20.37 Sagittarius	Chiron	14.54 Gemini
12.50 Capricorn	N Node	27.42 Aries
	Fortune	27.49 Pisces

Her progressive ascendant is Aquarius with 9 degrees and 54 minutes. This 9 degrees is telling us that something has ended or has started. Something new. We see that the planet Uranus has rule over the ascendant along with Saturn.

Uranus is exactly conjuncting the 11th house in the sign of Sagittarius. The 11th house in the fixed wheel is ruled by Saturn and Uranus. This house has to do with friendships, hopes and wishes, clubs and groups. Uranus is an unusual planet, sudden and disruptive. I read that she saw him, and realize that he is the one, but he was not so sure, thinking about their ages. So you see how Uranus was acting here with the friendship.

Saturn is in the 10th house but in the sign of the 11th which is Sagittarius. Saturn is holding 5 degrees and is exactly sextile to Pluto in the 9th house also in 5 degrees. Saturn is semi-sextile Neptune in the 11th house also in 5 degrees. These planets are slow moving, and will be holding the degrees for sometime.

Jupiter in her first house is exactly square the 11th. Jupiter is ruler of the 2nd and 11th house.

There's no doubt in my mind that the future can be told from the chart. That is a solid fact. We must also remember, who is the individual using the chart?

This first chart is of *Dawn Walkup* who was born on 6th July 1998 at 03:45 am, Tulsa, Oklahoma. Unfortunately, she died the same month. Can we read the chart? What are we going to find? Let's have a look.

08.00 Gemini	Sun	14.05 Cancer
01.32 Cancer	Moon	04.49. Sagittarius
23.06 Cancer	Mercury	08.10 Leo
16.55 Leo	Venus	14.05 Gemini
17.06 Virgo	Mars	29.59 Gemini.
26.18 Libra	Jupiter	27.50 Pisces.
08.00 Sagittarius	Saturn	02.15 Taurus
01.32 Capricorn	Uranus. R	11.49 Aquarius
23.06 Capricorn	Neptune R	01, 14 Aquarius
16.55 Aquarius	Chiron	12.26 Scorpio
17.06 Pisces	N Node	03.51 Virgo
	Fortune	17.16 Capricorn

Straightaway you see that the ascendant is holding 8 degrees in Gemini. This does not mean that everyone with 8 degrees rising is dead. It means that this is something that is out of our power. We cannot explain it. You will find people with these degrees, they are not strange or anything like that, it's just that they have this power that is hard to explain.

The ruler itself is also holding 8 degrees in its own house and in the sign of Leo. So we have the ruler in an exact sextile to the ascendant. Many people would get lost trying to interpret this chart. The ruler is also trine to the Moon and Pluto both in the 6th house, and in the sign of Sagittarius. And the ruler is square the destiny planet.

The destiny planet is in a loop in the 12th house in the sign of Taurus. This sign Taurus is the sign that is normally on the second house, and rules the body and possessions.

Look at the 8th house, which planet is the ruler? Look at the fourth house, which planet is the ruler. Are there any contact between the two rulers? Yes, there is, if we use the 72 degrees.

In the 8th house we see that Fortune is exactly sextile the 11th. I am testing fortune as ruler of Leo, and seeing what results I get.

Pluto is holding 5 degrees in the sign of Sagittarius and is in the 6th house, and ruler of the loop in the 6th house which is Scorpio, with Chiron there. Chiron is ruler of Sagittarius, but I am keeping my eyes on Capricorn, Aquarius and Virgo.

This chart is not going anywhere for the individual. But it can still be plotted for past and for future.

Notice that the destiny planet is also ruler of the 8th, 9th and 10th houses;

and it is trine to the 8th house. The destiny planet is square Neptune in the 9th house. Neptune is semi-sextile the 8th.

We see that Mercury, the ruler of the ascendant is opposing Uranus and Neptune in the 9th house, both in Aquarius. Mercury is conjunct the fourth house, opposing the Mid.

I don't work with some minor aspects, but there are two, the Quintile and the Bi-Quintile. Quintile 72 degrees, and Bi-Quintile 144 degrees, allowing 2 degrees either side.

Saturn is about 71 degrees from the sun. About 41 degrees from Venus, and about 56 degrees from Mars.

Having the destiny planet in the 12th house, and in a loop shows something to do with isolation, prison, or hospital, or even meditation. This shows people, like Presidents and high officials working behind the scenes for others. Whatever it is, it has to do with isolation.

I read that the mother was charged, and ended up having to spend 50 years inside. I don't know if that is true.

Saturn is ruler of the 10th house which has to do with parents. As we have seen, Saturn is not in good contact with Neptune that is there in the 10th house sign of Aquarius.

Not knowing certain codes, and given this chart to interpret, I think I would have made a mess of it. I would not be seeing that there's something dreadfully wrong in this chart.

Venus in the first house is conjuncting the ascendant, and is exactly semi-sextile the sun in the second house in the sign of Cancer.

Mars, also in the first house is holding 29 degrees, and telling us that there's something wrong. Mars is ruler of the loop in the 6th house, and ruler of the sign on the 12th.

The sun is quincunx Uranus. Uranus is in the 9th conjunct the Mid. Uranus is square Chiron in the loop in Scorpio in the 6th house.

If you were to take your time and sort this chart out properly, you would come out with quite a lot of information. I must admit that sometimes I miss important things that were there staring back at me.

We must not forget that the sign Cancer has to do with the home, country, roots, parents and the grave.

If you were a very good astrologer, and someone had asked you to tell about a certain year for the individual. You would know at that time, that what they asked, was not possible.

It is only possible for past and future, but not about the individual.

I don't know if I have mentioned it already, but Mercury is opposing both Uranus and Neptune. Fortune is in the 8th house, and is exactly sextile to the 11th.

Jupiter semi-sextile the 12th. Pluto holding 5 degrees in the sign of Sagittarius, in the 6th house, and is ruler of the loop in the 6th house carrying Chiron.

The Node is square the moon and Pluto, and also square the ascendant.

Our next chart is of the lead singer of Nirvana who took his own life. Read up on the story if you have the time. Born 20th February 1967 at 19:20 pm, Hoquaim, Washington, U.S.A. His name is *Kurt Cobain*.

Our progress chart is 19th March 1967 at 19:20 pm, Hoquaim, Washington, U.S.A. Look for the codes, and take them seriously.

Start from the ascendant, and work your way around.

09.44 Libra	Sun	28.49 Pisces
05.32 Scorpio	Moon	08.12 Cancer
06.39 Sagittarius	Mercury	04.51 Pisces
12.02 Capricorn	Venus	29.39 Aries
16.33 Aquarius	Mars R	02.22 Scorpio
15.57 Pisces	Jupiter R	24.25 Cancer
09.44 Aries	Saturn	02.00 Aries
05.32 Taurus	Uranus R	22.06 Virgo
06.39 Gemini	Neptune R	24.12 Scorpio
12.02 Cancer	Pluto R	19.04 Virgo
16.33 Leo	Chiron	25.52 Pisces
15.57 Virgo	N Node	09.10 Taurus
	Fortune	00.21 Cancer

Libra is rising with 9 degrees, this means that there is something ending or starting. It has to do with himself or partnerships, the public, open enemies, others. The planet Venus is ruler of Libra, and we find it in the 7th house in a crying degree, 29 degrees. Venus is also ruler of the 8th house where we find the node holding 9 degrees in Taurus. Venus is square Jupiter up in the 10th house, but the orb is too large, we are working with 1 degree orb. Venus is semi-sextile the sun in the 6th house in Pisces. The sun is ruler of the 11th house. Venus is sextile Fortune in the 9th house but in the 10th house sign of Cancer.

In the first house we see the planet Mars in 2 degrees conjuncting the 2nd house. The 2nd and eight axis has angel degrees, and is telling us that something is happening there. Mars is quincunx Saturn in the 6th house in the sign of Aries. Saturn is ruler of the 4th and 5th houses. Mars is ruler of the 2nd and 7th houses. This contact between Mars and Saturn is not a good one, even though Mars is angular, in its own house, and sign, and is strong.

Neptune is in the second house exactly trine with Jupiter. Neptune is ruler of the 6th house.

Note: There's another time for Kurt Cobain. It is 19:38 pm, giving an ascendant of 13.05 Libra. In research we do come up against such things. But we are looking for accurate times, and we stick to the chart that corresponds with the event.

In the 5th house we find the planet Mercury. It is in the sign of Pisces which can make one psychic, and can also cause confusion. On the opposite side in Virgo are Uranus and Pluto, but the orb is too great. Mercury is sextile the 8th house. Mercury is ruler of the 9th and 12th houses.

The third house is the lower mind, while the 9th house is the higher mind or lower thinking, to the higher thinking. These two houses has to do with communications, writing, travelling, the environment. There is no other aspect to Mercury.

Inside the 6th house we have Chiron in Pisces making a trine contact with Jupiter in the 10th house. You see clearly that Jupiter is exalted in Cancer. Also in the 6th house is the sun conjunct Chiron 2 or 3 degrees apart. The sun is semi-sextile Venus. The sun is conjunct Saturn with a 3 degrees orb. The sun is square Fortune in the 9th house. The sun is in Pisces. Saturn, we find also in the 6th house in Aries, and is in a quincunx aspect with Mars in the first house in Scorpio. Saturn is conjuncting the 7th with about 7 degrees.

Later, I will do a chapter on Lilith, the asteroid. It seems to me that it is working in the charts, because while I was drawing charts, I kept my eye on it all the time.

In this chart, Lilith is exactly conjunct the 7th house, exactly semi-sextile the node in the 8th house, exactly opposing the ascendant, and square to the moon.

Venus is in the 7th house in Aries and crying. I have already given information about it because it is the ruler of the ascendant.

In the 8th house you see the North node with 9 degrees and 10 minutes of Taurus.

The 9th house has the moon and Fortune stationed there. But both are in the sign of the 10th. The moon you'll see is in 8 degrees and 12 minutes of Cancer, its own sign; and this is for the month of March. The event took place in April, so we just have to add about 1 degree to the moon's position, and we get the moon holding about 9 degrees and minutes. Then it would be exactly square the Ascendant.

Jupiter is in the 10th, exalted in the sign of Cancer. Trine to Chiron in the 6th, and exactly trine Neptune in the 2nd.

In the 12th house we see two planets, Uranus and Pluto. This is the house of isolation, working behind the scenes to help others, prisons, hospitals, meditation places, enemies. Mercury then would be the ruler of this 12th house because it rules the sign of Virgo which is there, along with the two planets. Uranus is ruling the 5th while Pluto takes charge of the 2nd.

You can look for transits on the day of the event.

34: Ceres, Pallas Athene, Vesta, Juno & Lilith

Ceres is known as the one who cares. She failed to carry out her work until she finds her daughter who was kidnapped by Pluto. Saturn is the father of Ceres while her mother is Rhea. She is known as The Great Mother. The goddess of agriculture.

Pallas Athene is the asteroid of wisdom. It is also the asteroid of war. Pallas was born fully grown from the head of her father, Jupiter.

Vesta is the asteroid of the burning flame, the vestral virgin. Her father is Saturn, and her mother is Rhea.

Juno is the asteroid of marriage. Juno was the wife of Jupiter and was loyal. She is also the sister of Jupiter.

Lilith is an asteroid. We know that it is not fiction. There are other Liliths such as the Mean Lilith, The True Lilith, and even something called Lilith, The Dark Moon. We are just interested in the asteroid, Lilith. It could mean darkness, temptation, wanting to break away. It is best to find where your Lilith falls in your chart, and see if it makes any sense at all. Lilith can be found in Hebrew and other mythologies. Funny enough, Lilith is exactly conjuncting Kurt Cobain's progress chart for 1994. There was talk that he had enough and was planning to leave his wife. Being conjunct to the 7th, it tell quite a lot.

I have been keeping an eye on Ceres in the 7th house. The partner will always portray the energies of Ceres in this house. Ceres will work here, harmoniously, showing motherly love. But be careful, because if you upset her, she'll drop everything.

My first wife was very motherly. I met a girl later, and she too was motherly, she also cared for old people. You know, I was looking at my chart, and saw that Uranus will make contact with the

11th house. I met this woman who had two children – boy and a girl, she was over the top with motherly love. Then I met a friend, but she was married, an she was awfully motherly. So I suppose that Ceres in that 7th house, could be giving those energies.

I shall report as I go along about the other asteroids; it's difficult to see how they work, you have to know people very well, so that you can get good information.

Let's take a peep into the chart of *President Trump* for 2020. His progress date is 27th August 1946 at 10:45 am, Queens, New York, U.S.A. Here, you'll find the four asteroids but God knows what we are going to make of them.

27.36 Libra	Sun	03.43 Virgo
25.38 Scorpio	Moon	13.07 Virgo
27.48 Sagittarius	Mercury	17.27 Leo
02.37 Aquarius	Venus	19.31 Libra
05.49 Pisces	Mars	11.28 Libra
04.16 Aries	Jupiter	24.32 Libra
27.36 Aries	Saturn	03.05 Leo
25.38 Taurus	Uranus	21.22 Gemini
27.48 Gemini	Neptune	07.05 Libra
02.37 Leo	Pluto	12.05 Leo
05.49 Virgo	Chiron	19.46 Libra
04.16 Libra	N Node	16.50 Gemini
	Fortune	07.00 Scorpio
	Ceres	00.39 Aquarius
	Pallas	28.02 Sagittarius
	Juno	27.56 Libra
	Vesta	05.13 Aries
	Lilith	12.40 Sagittarius

Venus is the ruler of the ascendant, and it is in the 12th house in its own sign of Libra. It is with Jupiter about a 5 degrees difference, and exactly conjunct Chiron also in the 12th house. I am working with Chiron as ruler of the Sagittarius as a test.

So, so far, we have house 1 and house 3 and also house 8.

House 1 is the individual; house 3 is communications, talking, reading writing, travelling; house 8 is other people's possessions. This is a political house.

In the first house we see that Juno is exactly conjunct the ascendant in Libra. Juno, like Venus, is ruler of the ascendant. Juno is exactly trine the 9th. Inside the first house, but in the sign of Scorpio, Fortune is there semi-sextile Neptune in the 12th house in the sign of Libra. I am working with Fortune as ruler of Leo as a test. Neptune is the ruler of the 5th house.

Pallas is in Sagittarius conjuncting the third house. Pallas is also ruler of Libra. So we have 1 and 3 again. Talking, communicating travelling. The third and 9th houses are for short and long distance travel. Pallas is sextile the ascendant and Juno.

There is a loop with the sign of Capricorn there in the third house. The ruler is Saturn up in the 10th house in Leo.

Ceres is in the third house in the sign of Aquarius, and holding 0 degree. Ceres is ruler of Virgo at the 11th house. Ceres is opposing Saturn, and square to Juno and semi-sextile Pallas.

Notice the fifth axis holding 5 degrees. A chart has to be accurate to determine these degrees. If the wrong time is given, the chart is out.

In the 6th house we see Vesta in the sign of Aries semi-sextile the 5th.

I don't know if you know this: the 5th house is the house of the sun, the house of speculation, sports, children, entertainment, romance, love affairs; and of course promotion. Vesta is ruling the 11th house where Virgo is stationed.

The node and Uranus are in the 8th house, both in the 9th house sign of Gemini.

Don't forget that this is the progress chart for 2020, and not the natal chart. For more information, you use this chart with the natal, and check the transits for the date of 3rd November 2020; the date of the election.

There is a loop in the 9th house carrying the sign of Cancer. The moon is ruler of that sign and is in the 11th house. 11th and 9th connection shows long distance travel. This moon is square Lilith in the 2nd house. Lilith is sextile Mars, and trine Pluto in the 10th house.

In the 10th house, which is the career and outside world, and parents, we have Mercury in Leo sextile the node in the 8th house. Pluto, we see, is sextile Mars in the 12th house in Libra, Mars is ruling the 2nd, 6th and 7th houses. There is Saturn in Leo conjuncting the Mid, This is a strong position for Saturn because the 10th house naturally belongs to it. Saturn is exactly semi-sextile the sun in the 10th house but in the sign of 11th which is Virgo. The sun is ruler of the 10th. Saturn is ruler of the loop in the third house, and ruler of the 4th. The sun makes a semi-sextile contact with the Mid. The sun is semi-sextile the 12th. This will give a 10th and 12th contact.

Charts with Mars in the 12th house will always have enemies, even when Mars has good aspects.

This next chart is an event chart. You are to study it and see what you make of it. You'll get the chart, and at the end, you get the information.

24.26 Taurus	Sun	08.54 Aquarius
20.19 Gemini	Moon	05.34 Pisces
11.41 Cancer	Mercury R	22.37 Capricorn
03.44 Leo	Venus	25.17 Pisces
00.58 Virgo	Mars	24.37 Capricorn
08.35 Libra	Jupiter	05.25 Aquarius
24.26 Scorpio	Saturn R	21.04 Virgo
20.19 Sagittarius	Uranus	20.17 Pisces
11.41 Capricorn	Neptune	23.22 Aquarius
03.44 Aquarius	Pluto	02.11 Capricorn
00.58 Pisces	Chiron	20.14 Aquarius
Forune	21.05 Gemini	
Ceres	12.31 Virgo	
Pallas	05.06 Gemini	

Juno	02.56 Aquarius
Vesta	05.32 Taurus

You have the sign of Taurus rising with Vesta in the 12th house, and in the sign of the ascendant. Vesta, according to some information, rules Virgo. I have not done any deep research on it.

Venus is the ruler of the ascendant. It is in the 11th house exalted, conjunct Uranus, and in the same sign with the moon. Uranus is co-ruler of the 10th house. Venus is sextile the ascendant, square Fortune in Gemini in the second house. Venus is semi-square the sun in the 10th house, semi-square the node in the 10th house. Venus is sextile Mars in the 9th house. (Notice that Mars is exalted in Capricorn.) Venus is opposing Saturn in Virgo in the 5th house.

Uranus is semi-square Jupiter in the 10th house. Uranus is semi-square the Mid. Uranus is exactly semi-sextile Chiron in the 10th house, exactly square to the 8th house. The sign there is Sagittarius. Uranus is opposing Saturn.

Should you ever get married, the wedding chart would be an event; and the ascendant would be you.

In our event chart, the ascendant is the person we are after. And the information that we have so far, is that the person is someone exalted. This is because of the ruler of the ascendant Venus, in Pisces, and we know too that his friends and groups and clubs are people who are exalted and are very compassionate, sympathetic and kind. Unfortunately, Venus is negative to the sun in the 10th house, house of career. The sun is ruler of the 4th house, Venus ruler of the 1st and the 6th houses. The 6th house is work. The 4th house is home or country.

The opposite sign of the ascendant is Scorpio, and it shows the partner or partnerships, and the public. Mars and Pluto are the rulers. Mars is exalted in Capricorn and is sextile to Venus. Pluto is semi-sextile to the Mid.

Pluto is in the 8th house, its own, and this is the house of politics and other peoples possessions. Lilith is also in the 8th house exactly conjunct Pluto, and semi-sextile the Mid.

In the second house we have Fortune exactly square Saturn in the 5th house. I am working with Fortune as ruler of Leo. Saturn is ruler of the 9th and the 10th. Notice the signs Fortune and Saturn are in. Saturn has a good aspect to Mercury in the 9th, it is a trine. Mercury is ruler of the second and the 6th houses.

Mars and Mercury are both semi-sextile Neptune in the 10th house. I don't know if I'm right, but I am seeing Neptune in the 10th as being famous. Neptune is square the ascendant.

The event chart is *Barak Obama*'s end of Presidency. The progress date is 28th January 2009, noon, Washington DC, U.S.A.

There is more information in the chart.

35: Negatives and Positives

In one chart, we find the node in the 10th house in Libra, and squaring Neptune in the second in Capricorn. The node is with me in a test as ruler over Cancer, and Cancer is at the 8th house. Neptune is ruler of the 4th. The ascendant is 9 degrees Sagittarius. Mercury and Jupiter are both in the first in Sagittarius exactly conjunct each other. Venus is in the 2nd house in Capricorn, one degree from a conjunction with the second. Uranus is in the second house in Capricorn, square the 11th house, but trine the Mid. Saturn is in the third house in Pisces trine the 12th with the sign of Scorpio there. The moon is in the 7th house in the sign of Cancer –Cancer is on the 8th cusp, exactly quincunx Pluto in the 12th in Sagittarius. Mars is exalted in Capricorn, the second sign. Mars is in the first house. It is about 98 degrees from the Mid. Mars is opposing Lilith in the 7th house in Cancer. It is also opposing the moon, but with a five degrees difference. We work close with one degree. The sun is in the first house holding 15 degrees. I have a theory about this 15 degrees, but I'm not sure yet how to explain it. At first, I thought it was strange. The sun is ruling the 9th house. By the way, Mercury is ruling the 7th and 10th houses, while Jupiter is ruling the first and the fourth. What do you think about this chart?

What did you make of it? The chart is a terrible one. Here is the birth date: 8th December 1995, 06:45 am, Hamstead (Nassau County) New York, U.S.A.

This was a birth thrown into a toilet bowl. Mother found guilty of manslaughter.

What would you say of this chart with the ascendant rising with 16 degrees of Virgo? The ruler is in the 10th house in the sign of Cancer which is the 11th house sign. The ruler is exactly conjunct with the sun, also in the 10th house and in the sign of Cancer; and in conjunction with Neptune in the same position. All three in the 10th house, in the sign of Cancer. The sun is ruler of the 12th house; Neptune is ruler of the 7th.

You remember I told you that when Neptune is in the 10th house, I get the feeling that the person could be famous? Well then!

All three planets are trine to the node down in the second house in the third house sign of Scorpio.

Pluto is in the 10th house in Gemini conjuncting the Mid, squaring the ascendant. Remember those negative planets in angular positions are not the same as in other houses.

Mars is in the 9th house in the tenth house sign of Gemini, conjuncting the Mid, conjuncting Pluto, square to the ascendant.

In the fourth house there is Uranus conjunct Lilith both in the sign of Sagittarius; both are square to the ascendant. Chiron is in the fourth house but in the sign of the 5th which is Capricorn, trine to the ascendant. Saturn is in the 5th in Capricorn. The moon and Jupiter are in conjunction in the 5th house, but in the sign of Aquarius. Jupiter is exactly quincunx the ascendant. Jupiter is sextile Lilith and Uranus. Jupiter and the moon are both trine to the Mid. Jupiter is square Venus in the 9th in Taurus, and is ruler of the 2nd and the 9th houses. Saturn in the 5th is trine Venus. Saturn is conjunct the 5th. Saturn is sesqui-quadrate to the Mid. The moon in the 5th house is holding 8 degrees and exactly trine the 2nd, it is square the 3rd. Chiron in the fourth is exactly semi-sextile the 4th.

The chart is of a woman who lived to be 97 years old. She was a sculptor and represented the United States. She was also a Fashion Designer.

Did you notice the sun, Mercury and Neptune all in 1 degree in Cancer in the 10th house? Remember, Cancer is the sign of home, parents, roots and country. And already, with Neptune in the 10th, a bit of fame.

Venus in the 9th. People with this position are interested in foreign countries and travel. Mars so close to the Mid. There's lots of energy here. I always say that the moon with Jupiter is someone special, even if the person doesn't get to be known.

There is no writing about if she was married or have children. Looking at the 5th house, I see that Saturn is there in its own sign, and is square to Venus. Jupiter is also in the 5th, and square to Venus.

What would you say of this chart with Aquarius rising, the sun being there in the 12th house in Aquarius and holding 8 degrees, and is ruler of the 7th house.

There is a loop in the first house with the sign of Pisces carrying Venus and Uranus. Venus and Uranus are in conjunction about 2 degrees.

The sun is sextile Mars in the 9th house, but in the sign of the 10th, and conjunct the Mid. The sun is also sextile Jupiter in the 10th, conjunct the Mid. The tenth house sign is Sagittarius. The sun is square the moon in the 8th house, in Scorpio, the 9th house sign. The sun is semi-sextile Venus in the loop in the first house. The sun is quincunx Pluto in the 5th house retrograde in the sign of Cancer. Neptune is on the opposite side of the sun, in the 6th house in Leo, conjuncting the 7th.

Chiron is found in the second house in Aries semi-sextile both Venus and Uranus in the loop in the first house in Pisces. Venus is exalted in Pisces. Lilith is in the 3rd house in the sign of Taurus. Pluto is in the 5th house in the sign of Cancer. Pluto is trine the moon in the 8th house in Scorpio, the 9th house sign. The node is in a loop in the 7th house in Virgo. Fortune is in the 9th house in Scorpio conjunct Mars in the 9th in the sign of Sagittarius. Fortune is semi-sextile Saturn in the 11th house in Capricorn, and exactly conjunct 11th. Fortune is square the ascendant, opposing Lilith.

Mercury is in the 11th in Capricorn, semi-sextile the Mid, and Jupiter, sextile the moon. Jupiter is in the 10th conjunct the Mid, trine the 2nd, square Uranus in the loop in the first, trine Chiron in the second.

Lilith is square the ascendant, square Neptune in the 6th house in Leo. Neptune is trine Jupiter. Pluto is quincunx the Mid. The moon is semi-sextile the Mid.

I hope you have seen the energies that the person has to work with positively and negatively. And of where things can go wrong. Sometimes you see that clearly in the natal chart. But for year after year, we have to look in the progress chart.

This woman was an actress, a real estate agent, and public relations. The sun in the 12th house holding 8 degrees shows us already, things that we have no control over. The sun is ruling the 7th house. Things went wrong here in her marriage or relationships. That is the way life works. It goes wrong, we move on.

She was engaged in 1952, they ended it 1957. She married 1959, had two daughters, divorced 1964. 1969 married a businessman, marriage annulled four weeks later. 1971 married a motel chain executive. They divorce after 3 years. She lived to be 93 years old.

Her name is *Dorothy Malone* born 29th January 1924, 08:00 am, Chicago, Illinois, U.S.A.

The following chart has an ascendant of Libra rising. Its ruler is Venus and it is in the 8th house in the sign of Gemini, the 9th house sign. It is conjunct Mercury also in the 8th, and in the same sign. Venus is sextile the Mid, square Neptune in the 10th in Virgo, retrograde. Virgo is the 11th house sign. Venus is semi-sextile the node in the 7th house but in the 8th house sign. Venus is sextile Mars in the 6th house in its own sign of Aries. Venus is trine Lilith in the 4th house in the sign of Aquarius. Venus is exactly quincunx Fortune in a loop in the 3rd house in Capricorn

In the 3rd house we have a loop with Fortune and Saturn in the sign of Capricorn. Saturn is ruler of the loop. Fortune in my test is ruling the 10th.

Saturn is square Mars and Uranus both in the 6th house in the sign of Aries. Saturn is trine Chiron and the sun in the 7th house, both in the sign of the 8th which is Taurus. Saturn is opposing Pluto up in the 9th, and in a loop with the sign of Cancer.

Fortune is trine the node in the 7th house. Fortune is trine the 11th. Fortune is square Mars and Uranus in the 6th. Fortune is trine the sun in the 7th. Fortune is exactly quincunx Venus in the 8th in Gemini, the 9th house sign.

Mars and Uranus are conjunct in Aries in the 6th house. Mars is about 112 degrees from the Mid, this could be a trine. Mars is sextile Venus. Mars is 142 degrees from Neptune in the 10th but in the 11th sign which is Virgo. A

Bi-Quintile is 144 degrees, but we don't bother much about that. Or do we?

Uranus is semi-square to Mercury in the 8th in the sign of Gemini, the ninth house sign. Uranus is sextile Jupiter in the 8th house in Gemini which is the 9th house sign. Uranus is square Pluto in the loop in the 9th house in Cancer. Uranus is sesqui-quadrate Neptune in the 10th house. Uranus is semi-sextile Chiron in the 7th in Taurus, the 8th house sign. Uranus has a semi-sextile aspect with the sun in the 7th house but in the 8th house sign of Taurus.

The sun as you have just seen is in Taurus conjunction with Chiron. The sun is sextile Pluto in the loop in the 9th.

The node is in the 7th in Taurus, semi-sextile Mercury and Venus, semi-square Jupiter. The node is square the Mid, trine Neptune, trine 11th.

Mercury and Venus is conjunct in Taurus, 8th house. Mercury is square Neptune, semi-square Pluto. It is about 144 degrees from the ascendant. Mercury is sextile the Mid, trine the 12th house.

Venus is sextile the Mid, semi-square the moon in the loop in the 9th house in its own sign of Cancer.

Jupiter is exactly semi-sextile Pluto. Jupiter has a quintile to Neptune.

The moon and Pluto are in a loop in the 9th house in the sign of Cancer; they are in conjunction. The moon is just about making a conjunction with the Mid. The moon is square the ascendant. Pluto also is square the ascendant.

Neptune is in the 10th house in Virgo conjunct the 11th, exactly semi-sextile the Mid, sextile the ascendant.

We can tell the parents of the chart that their child has the chance of becoming famous because of Neptune in the 10th house. And of course, very creative and sportive. Notice that Neptune is in 0 degrees. The 4/10 axis too.

Venus is the ruler of the chart, and it is in the 8th house in Gemini. Gemini is normally at the 3rd house in the fixed wheel. So here we have more information about communications, reading and writing and talking very much, and travelling. Well, we know that the 8th house has to do with other people's money; the energies are there in that area. Venus is conjunct Mercury also in Gemini, and in the 8th house. Again, we find much communications and other people's money. Very versatile. Mercury is in its own sign here.

The chart is of *Clint Eastwood* born 3rd May 1930 at 17:35 pm, San Francisco, California, U.S.A.

If you have time read his biography, and you'll see how he used the energies that are in the chart – positive and negative.

Venus making contact with the Mid is always good for the career. Venus is sextile the Mid. Venus is also with Jupiter but they are 13 degrees apart, well out of the conjunction range, but maybe they are still working together. Venus sextile Mars is good for the houses both planets are rulers of.

In the sixth house we see hat Mars is with Uranus. There is enormous energies here to do with work and service. These two planets can also cause problems if not handled properly. The square between them can cause harm – like someone messing about with a sharp knife.

We know that the planets have to make their way up to the Mid. The sun only finds its place there if the individual is born around noon or thereabouts. Mercury and Venus is always not far away from the sun. They don't have to make their way up to the Mid. You must always remember too, that the sun is sometimes in conjunction for a long time with the house where it is at, whether it is morning, noon or night or in between.

Jupiter in the 8th house can have deep insight; and don't forget, it is in its brother's house, the house of Pluto.

The sun is in Taurus in the 7th house, this is a good position for the public and partnerships.

Fortune and Saturn are in the sign of Capricorn, in the loop in the third house. If we are to take seriously what the ancients said about Saturn – that it is the destiny planet, then we see clearly, that there is something here to do with travelling, reading, writing, and much talking, communications. To me, the loop is showing something extra. Capricorn is an ambitious sign, slow but sure.

In the ninth house we have the opposite sign Cancer in a loop with moon and people there. In the third house, Saturn is the ruler of the loop, while in the ninth house, the moon is the ruler of the loop. Don't forget that Mercury is sextile the Mid.

I have been working for years trying to find a system that everyone could understand, and which is easy to read. But there is a lot of work to do yet before I can say anything about it. Working on many systems before, I thought I had found the one, after looking at many charts, but it didn't work out the way that I wanted it to. Anyway, you'll hear from me about it, if it stays consistent.

This next chart is of a Private Pilot born 13th August 1938 at 07:15 am, Des Moines, Iowa, U.S.A. See what you make of it, and the energies he has to work with. We are interested in the positive and negative energies. Some people have a way of making the negative energies work for them. I think earlier, I did tell you about Mars and Uranus, how dangerous they can be when negative, and even when positive, depending on how they are being used. They give out lots energy.

11.30 Virgo	Sun	20.07 Leo
05.35 Libra	Moon	16.14 Pisces
04.44 Scorpio	Mercury	12.16 Virgo
08.42 Sagittarius	Venus	04.15 Libra
12.40 Capricorn	Mars	13.53 Leo
14.11 Aquarius	Jupiter	28, 16 Aquarius R
11.30 Pisces	Saturn	17.53 Aries R
05.35 Aries	Uranus	17.46 Taurus
04.44 Taurus	Neptune	19.45 Virgo
08.12 Gemini	Pluto	00.16 Leo
12.40 Cancer	Chiron	07.04 Cancer
14.11 Leo	N Node	22.20 Scorpio
	Fortune	07.37 Aries

Some of us gets kind of scared when we talk about negatives, but life is made up of positives and negatives. You either want to know, or you don't want to know – not interested. But I can assure you that astrology is one of the main keys of knowing what's going on when things go wrong. Astrologers can tell you all the good things, but they do see negative things in the chart as well. I don't know what they tell their clients.

In the forty odd years that I have been messing about with astrology, I have seen the negatives in my progressive chart. You cannot totally get rid of it all, but you can prepare yourself, and lessen the fall. In my progressive chart, it so happens that I have three planets on one side, and two on the opposite. The two on the opposite are Saturn and Uranus. The three on the other side are the sun, Mercury, and Venus. The sun has made its contact, and I knew what to expect, and acted accordingly, had I acted another way, things could have turned out worse. And at the same time, I was still using the sun opposing Uranus for what they were worth. You'd think I was a scientist from what I now know. The sun still have to oppose Saturn. And Mercury to oppose both Saturn and Uranus, and then there is Venus to oppose Saturn and Uranus.

We know that Uranus is a very disturbing planet, sudden and unusual. If I were to tell you all the things that is happening to me now, you just won't believe it. It's like going to the town, the bus is not running, so You have to make other plans or don't go to the town at all. That can be done another day. With astrology, you have to get to your inner self, the will, the spirit or whatever you want to call it, and that's a good thing.

In our chart, the pilot can do whatever he wants. He doesn't have to be a pilot, but he has taken that path. Within the chart, we find Mars in the 11th house in the sign of Leo, and it is squaring Uranus in the 9th house in the sign of Taurus.

Mars is ruler of the 8th house, while Uranus takes the 6th house. Mars is also ruling the 3rd house. Here we have a combination of 3-6-8.

So let's get on with it. The Individual fell when hang gliding; broke up his whole body; lived for only six weeks.

The sun is also square Uranus. Pluto is 0 degree pointing to the 3rd house. There is a good aspect from Venus to the Mid. Venus is square Chiron in the 10th. Fortune in the 8th house is sextile the Mid, but exactly square to Chiron. The node in the 3rd house is square the sun in the 12th.

My aim was to let you see how Mars and Uranus can work against someone. As I have said before, I believe that it can be avoided if one takes care; but if it has to happen, there's nothing we can do about it. I see the aggressiveness of Mars connecting up with the sudden and disruptive planet, Uranus. It is the same when the destiny planet, Saturn, is negative to Uranus, we get a shock when we hear the news of someone leaving us suddenly, we never expected to hear that. I have checked many charts with these energies, and they have shown me that it is so. .

36: What Would You Say?

We know that we have got the chart before us with 360 degrees. Every house with its 30 degrees holds planets in their signs and degrees. It is not an easy task in trying to pin-point every single thing, but we can give it a good try. What I have been doing is reading up what some of the ancient astrologers have said, and then I put it to work, and see what I can find. I myself, have been digging up some strange ideas, and also putting them in the chart and studying them. Research work is hard, trying to grasp every detail. You have to look carefully, because all those planets in their signs and degrees are there, and you just have to check them out properly.

Your chart starts with let's say 2 degrees of the sign of Aries, then we say that you have at least 27 degrees to do before Aries come to an end, oh! and minutes of course. The next sign is Taurus, so you'll find yourself doing what Taurus people does. And so it is for all the signs in the wheel. You can also manage to get onto Gemini and even Cancer. This is an experience you'll have.

I progressed my chart to the year I got married. Zero degree was at the 6/12 axis, I was baffled, just staring at it. I wasn't sick that year, I had no pets, but I did have servants. And I forgot that the 6th house has to do with military. I did have a guard of honour.

Sometimes we'll find chart with Zero degree with no way of knowing what had taken place in the person's life. So you'll be without information. I'm still busy looking into the faces to pick up the signs; it is working for me well. It is hard though, to see Aquarius, Sagittarius, Capricorn. But the way they act give it away.

Looking at a chart with Saturn in the 4th conjunct the 5th, and Mars in the 4th conjunct Saturn, both in Scorpio which is the sign of the 5th house. Mars is also ruling the 10th. Saturn has rule over 7th and 8th houses. Saturn is conjuncting the 5th by 1 degree. The ascendant is Cancer with the moon conjuncting it exactly in the first house. The moon is opposing Uranus in the 6th house in Capricorn. The moon is quincunx the node exactly in the 6th house. The node is semi-sextile Uranus. Uranus is ruling the 8th house, the node has charge of the ascendant. What do you see happening here? Saturn is holding 8 degrees; and Mars is in Zero degree.

Cancer ascendant is very sensitive, homely, and because this is a water sign, they absorb everything around them. You can test this by looking in people's chart with Cancer ascendant, or planets in Cancer. Even when Cancer is negative, people are still homely.

The moon is exactly conjunct the ascendant. This can have something to do with the Mother, and the individual is really concern about members of the family.

With Mars in the fourth house and ruler of the fifth, there's lots of energy here, Hard working in the home, and sometimes problems with parents. WE see that Mars is holding zero degree, and is ruler of the 5th and the 10th houses. Mars represent the individual because it is ruler of the first house in the natural chart. And it rules where its signs are. When a baby is born, the 10th house has to announce it, along with the 5th house, the 8th, and the 12th as well.

It is quite possible that with Saturn in the 4th conjunct the 5th, that the individual comes from a poor family and have the ability to get somewhere. Saturn conjunct the 5th house could be responsible for not many children, one or two. In conjunction with Mars, this is a tough conjunction, could show energetic children. You see that Saturn rules the 7th and 8th. This is the husband and his body or possessions.

Saturn holding 8 degrees is something that we cannot do anything about. It is out of our power. The moon opposing Uranus will bring some unexpected changes, to do with the houses the moon and Uranus are rulers of, and the houses they are in, along with the signs.

Saturn has to be very well-aspected for it to act positively. I was chatting with someone who gave me their chart to look at – remember, I'm only an amateur researcher, and not an astrologer. Professional astrologers knows more than I do. I'm the one who is looking at astrologer in a different way. So I looked at this woman chart, and she had Saturn in the 5th house, exalted in the sign of Libra, but it was squaring the ascendant, and the ruler of the ascendant. She was old and had no children.

I'm already satisfied that astrology works, and it is a good science. We are all filled up with it. And it becomes rather difficult to unravel it, though we see how it works plainly in some human beings.

There are many planets going through the sign Capricorn at the moment, and I was really wondering what is going to happen. Well, I wasn't expecting that!

We shall look at a chart which I plot for midnight, 5th January 1709, Norwich, UK. This was the time of the great Frost.

As you already know, I'm trying to work the numbers of numerology into astrology. So far, I's working out okay, but rather difficult. I will give you the numbers when I'm absolutely sure that they work.

09.59 Libra	Sun	14.36 Capricorn
04.48 Scorpio	Moon	07.58 Scorpio
06.01 Sagittarius	Mercury	23.13 Sagittarius
13.14 Capricorn	Venus	04.10 Sagittarius
18.53 Aquarius	Mars	14.13 Cancer R
17.40 Pisces	Jupiter	28.40 Libra
09.59 Aries	Saturn	27.20 Gemini R

04.48 Taurus	Uranus	22.02 Leo R
06.01 Gemini	Neptune	22.57 Aries
13.14 Cancer	Pluto	26.24 Leo
18.53 Leo	Chiron	19.03 Capricorn
17.40 Virgo	N Node	22.13 Pisces
	Fortune	02.36 Leo

For a start, we want to know what sign or planet could be responsible for cold. Don't you think it could be Saturn, and the sign could be Capricorn?

Okay, so Libra is rising with Venus as Ruler. Now Venus is in Sagittarius conjuncting the 3rd house, and is in the second. Venus is exactly semi-sextile the second house. Venus is also ruling the 8th house.

Sagittarius is the sign of the 9th house natural, so a little bit of information here. Venus ruling the 8th, more information.

Jupiter in the first ruler of the natural 9th, trine to Saturn in the 9th in Gemini. Jupiter is ruler of the 3rd and 6th, Saturn ruler of the 4th and 5th.

Jupiter is opposing Neptune in the 7th in Aries. Neptune is ruling the 6th.

Mercury is in its own house in Sagittarius opposing Saturn in the 9th in Mercury's sign of Gemini. The node in the 6th house is square Mercury, and Saturn.

The node is ruler of the 10th. I think we find in the 10th house, the planet Mars in its fall in Cancer, opposing exactly, the Sun in Capricorn. Mars is squaring the ascendant. Mars is ruler of the 2nd and the 7th houses.

Venus is squaring Pluto, and Pluto is co-ruler of the second house. Pluto is sextile Saturn. Uranus conjunct Pluto in Leo. Uranus sextile Saturn.

The moon is semi-square Mercury. The moon is semi-sextile the 3rd. The moon is conjunct Jupiter, conjunct the 2nd. The moon is square Fortune in the 10th in Leo.

The sun is square the ascendant. Mars is conjunct the Mid. The moon is trine Mars and the Mid. Neptune in the 7th trine Uranus and Pluto in the 11th

The sun is conjunct Chiron in the 4th house. Chiron is conjunct the 4th in Capricorn, semi-sextile the 5th, sextile the node, square Neptune.

In Virginia Woolf's 'Orlando' she wrote how cold it was.

Once you have your correct chart, you must examine it properly, noting down all the negatives and positives, where the planets are, in the houses, and in the signs, Note carefully the planets that are making aspect to the ascendant. Note the houses the planets are rulers of. It so happens that a house in astrology carries many interpretations, so be very careful how you examine the chart.

It is very interesting progressing the chart year by year. Inside this progress chart, you are able to see where the moon is, and how it is moving, and how long it will stay in one house.

The Solar System, created by the powers of God dishes out energies that are taken on waves or rays, and come down to everything that is upon the earth. These energies within us human beings gives us the drive we need to carry out our work here on earth.

We know that God is Spirit, and we were made in His image, so we too, have a spirit within us. Some people call the Spirit the soul, and make the two as one. But I prefer to have the body, soul, and spirit.

We are told that the soul can die. So it is plain that the spirit is most powerful. The spirit doesn't care about material things, yet it knows how everything works.

The planets in our solar system each has a function. The sun as giver of life to everything. The scientists has told us that there are other suns. From this we know that our sun is responsible for our earth. The sun gives a spark of life to everything. Everything has already been arranged by the Creator, and only a fool will deny the workings of the solar system.

We cannot change anything; only that which we ourselves have created. Changes takes place within ourselves; and we act accordingly. I read in the book of Ezra that the solar system is there to serve us.

Each human being has an individuality, and this is from the sun. You can have billions and billions of human beings with the same individuality, but with different moods and feelings, and intellectual capacities. Also with with different love energies, endurance, kindness and justice and patience and so forth.

Some people are born to be stinking rich, it shows clearly in their chart. Others are born to be beggars, and living poorly. Some are born to be lovers, loving only one person, with a love that is highly exalted. Then too, you'll find someone who has so much energy, he wants to take on the whole world. And that is all because of our solar system, brought into being by the Creator. And there's also that individual who would take up arms and go make war with the Creator. I have seen very clearly many charts with a certain aspect that keeps them away from believing in God. But if they get into the spirit, that's another thing.

You are going to find that in the first progressive year, you natal moon has moved, but it hasn't actually moved – only progressively. Your natal moon will always be in the same position throughout your whole life. Year by year, your progressive moon is taking on degrees, moving into signs and houses. These you must note down carefully Especially important are the aspects the moon is making to the rest of the chart; that is: the natal and progressive charts.

Let us say that the progress moon is in the 4th house, in the sign of Gemini; and let's say that it is in 23 degrees of Gemini.

You have to check the progressive chart to see if the moon is making any aspect anywhere. The moon is ruler of the 6th house. We find that it is exactly square to Mars in the 7th house in the sign of Virgo.

Suppose we have a progress chart with Aquarius rising, and Pisces in the first house intercepted, with Aries on the second cusp.

Some of us start to count taking Aries as the second house which it is; but we must not forget that it is the third sign from the ascendant of Aquarius. This mean that Mars is ruler of the third sign, and of the second house.

In the progressive chart, we see that Scorpio is on the 9th cusp. Mars is the ruler of that sign.

In astrology, this is serious business, it depends on how the individual behaves themselves in accordance with this moon square Mars aspect.

We know that Mars is in the 7th house, and the moon is in the 4th. Mars is in Virgo, and the moon is in Gemini.

So we have house 7, and house 4; sign 6, and sign 3; Mars ruling third sign, second house, and 9th house. Moon ruling 6th house.

Any astrologer, good astrologer, will tell you that there is trouble here. The 7th house is the house of war – partnerships, and the public. The 6th house has to do with work, pets, servants, sickness, health.

The third sign of Gemini has to do with travel, it could be long or short, has to do with people who are close, the environment, and the signing of papers. Most of all, it has to do with the way you are thinking at the time. Mars and the moon negative, is not a good thing.

There's going to be problems with servants. travel, thinking, foreign countries (9th house Scorpio). The 4th house is the home, the country, parents and the grave.

Once the astrologer has warned you not to travel for at least three months (this is the period when the moon is in contact with Mars. It would start at least when the moon is in 22 degrees, it become exact in 23 degrees, and it is leaving when in 24 degrees. The moon is the fastest body.

We have in the same progress chart, Mercury in the 6th house in the sign Leo, opposing Jupiter in the 12th house in Aquarius. Mercury is ruler of 4th and 5th, and the loop in the 7th. By the way, Mars is in this loop of Virgo in the 7th house. Mercury is square Neptune in the 8th house, but in the 9th sign Scorpio.

Neptune is ruling the second sign from Aquarius, but this sign is in a loop in the first house. So we have something extra here to do with the individual.

There are more negative aspects in the progress chart, and I'm now thinking, can we tell the individual exactly what's happening? The mind is a very tricky part of the body. If a person doesn't know, they do not care, and if they know, it probably will be there on their mind all the time.

Remember, do not forget to check the progress chart with the natal.

With the progress moon then, you have to keep a check on it. The time will come when it is passing through the 12th house which is ruled by Jupiter and

Neptune. Thank God when it gets out of that house and into the first. Receiving good aspects while passing through the 12th house is lucky for you, but still with something strange. Of course, you know what the 12th house is?

Make sure that you look after your health before the moon goes into the 6th house. Again, if it has good aspects, things could work out good; but when the moon leaves the 6th house and enters the 7th, that is really good.

Check for negative aspects, and do something about it, and not to get into trouble. This goes for yourself and your whole family.

Some people don't understand that when they are born, the whole solar system on that day stays the same throughout theirs lives. It is the progress chart or other progressive systems that shows what energies you have to work with. There should be no conflict between astrology and religion. It is through the higher powers that astrology came into being. From the energies of astrology, men and women can become religious or ignore it.

Seeing your progress moon passing through the 9th house, there's always the urge for higher education, and travel. Then your moon is about to enter the 10th house. This is very good even with negative aspects, it brings popularity.

In the progress chart, the moon is always travelling anti-clockwise, while the planets are going clockwise.

Having an accurate time of birth would give you accurate information, and so you should check carefully all the contacts that the moon and the planets make to the cusps of the chart. You also have to check what they do to each other.

Keep away from arguments with people who have never studied astrology. It is like talking wisdom to a fool. They don't understand you.

Be careful how you look at a positive aspect, and whose chart it is in, and where the planets are. You can give wrong information about a positive aspect.

Looking at a chart, a progressive one, I see Neptune in the first house in the sign of Virgo, the second house sign. It is exactly trine to Uranus in the 9th house in the sign of Taurus. Neptune is co-ruler of 7th and 8th house; Uranus is co-ruler of the 6th. Neptune is about 2 degrees away making conjunction with the 2nd house. Uranus is also about 2 degrees away making conjunction with the Mid.

The ascendant sign is Virgo, its ruler in the 12th house in Leo, squaring Uranus; exactly squaring the Mid.

The sun is in the 11th house holding zero degree, and in the sign of Leo. The sun is in a close conjunction with Pluto. The sun is 00.29 Leo, Pluto is 01.03 Leo. Both sun and Pluto are in the 11th house. Sun ruler of the 11th, Pluto co-ruler of the 4th.

Saturn is in the sign of Taurus in the 9th house. Taurus is the sign on the 10th. Both sun and Pluto are square to Saturn. Saturn is ruler of the 5th, co-ruler of the 6th.

In the 6th house is Lilith in the sign Aquarius, opposing Mercury in the 12th, and square the Mid. (I'm still trying to find out the sign Lilith is ruler of).

The chart has a loop in the 4th house with the sign of Sagittarius there, and Fortune is there. The loop in the 10th house is Gemini having Mercury as its ruler.

Mars is crying in the 5th house, holding 29 degrees, and in the sign of Capricorn, exalted. It was from Ivy Goldstein-Jacobson that I got that information about Mars.

Mars is about 110 degrees to Uranus. We work very close so that we could get good information. I do not know if Mars would be working at that distance, almost 10 degrees.

Anyway, in the 8th house is Jupiter in the sign of Aries which is the 9th house sign. Jupiter is holding 8 degrees.

The ascendant is 3 degrees Virgo and Mercury by the way, is quincunx the 8th house, semi-sextile the 2nd.

Chiron is in the 11th house in Cancer quincunx Fortune in the 4th house in the loop of Sagittarius.

The dragon's tail in the 9th house in Taurus is sextile the ascendant. Its opposite, the Node, is in the 3rd house in Scorpio sextile the ascendant.

Now we have the progress moon. It is in the 3rd house in the sign of Scorpio. It is in 10.26 of Scorpio. The event took place in June. The perpetual date we have is July. Knocking 1 degree off the moon, we get 09.26 degrees, and that would give us a quincunx aspect with Jupiter in the 8th house.

There is Pluto in the 11th house in Leo, semi-sextile the 11th house with Cancer as the sign there. And we have Venus in the 11th in Cancer square to the 3rd house of Libra. Square to the 9th house of Aries.

So now you have a progress chart for a certain year with all the aspects. Hope you'll be able to get some information on what is actually going on here.

As a researcher trying to find out what the planets are doing in the charts, natally and progressively, and for other methods that are used, I do not predict the end of a person's life. Even if I was good at seeing it, I would keep it to myself. And I can tell you, I have tested many charts, and have seen carefully what is happening.

It becomes very hard to understand what is going on because every chart is different. What keeps cropping up most is the Taurus/Scorpio axis. Either planets are in Scorpio and going over to Taurus; or they are in Taurus going over to Scorpio.

The chart we are now looking at has an ascendant of 3 degrees Virgo. The ruler is in the 12th house in Leo. The ruler is exactly square the Mid. There is something wrong here. The ruler is not in an angular position where it would be more difficult to interpret. The Mid is 23 degrees and 38 minutes, the ruler of the ascendant is 23 degrees and 42 minutes of Leo. The tenth house sign is Taurus. This is the sign of the second house which has to do with money, possessions and the body.

The sun is in zero degree in Leo in the 11th house square to Saturn in 0 degree in the 9th house in Taurus. Although Saturn is in the sign of the 10th, it is not in the tenth, therefore, not in an angular position. Both the sun and Saturn are not in angular position.

Mars, we said is crying, it is ruler of the 4th and 9th house. I will not waste time telling you what the fourth house is all about, you should know this by now. Oh! And the fifth house has to do with many things. But do you know that it is the house of life? The sun is the ruler.

Anyway, the whole chart is unfortunate when it comes to the individual and the romance. Venus in the 11th square the 3rd and 9th is telling you of travel and friendship. The square in astrology we know is not good, for even when angular, it is still negative, but not as bad as when both planets are not angular. So this progress chart shows clearly, when it is looked at properly, interpreted properly, gives the answer of what happened that year. I have not even looked at the transits or the natal chart. That shows you how much information you can get from one chart.

37: Madeleine McCann's Astrological Case

I am sure that every one has heard about the case of the young girl who disappeared in Portugal 2007. I have found a time for her birth which is given by a top site. Let us just hope that it is correct. What we are going to do is look at the birth chart – this will show the energies that she has to work with.

The information I have is this: *Madeleine McCann* 12th May 2003, 18:14 pm. Leicester, UK.

Then we would look at the progress chart for 2007.

25.56 Libra	Sun	21.34 Taurus
22.35 Scorpio	Moon	03, 21 Libra
26.15 Sagittarius	Mercury	13.10 Taurus R
05.05 Aquarius	Venus	25.28 Aries
09.24 Pisces	Mars	12.07 Aquarius
05.52 Aries	Jupiter	10.16 Leo
25.35 Aries	Saturn	27.17 Gemini
22.35 Taurus	Uranus	02.33 Pisces
26.15 Gemini	Neptune	13.10 Aquarius
05.04 Leo	Pluto	19.19 Sagittarius R
09.24 Virgo	Chiron	17.57 Capricorn
05.52 Libra	N Node	00.03 Gemini
	Fortune	07.43 Pisces

Taking the time to be correct, hopefully, we can say that with an ascendant of Libra, she would turn out to be very harmonious, seeking peace and togetherness.

Her ruler Venus is in the 6th house in the sign of Aries, exactly conjuncting the 7th. This shows her partner as well. This is a very good contact Venus is making with the 7th only that it is in Aries, and a little bit negative for being in Aries. Remember, Venus rules Libra. Aries rules the head. Venus is sextile Saturn in the 8th house but in the 9th house sign of Gemini. Venus is also sextile the 9th house. She has contact with the 9th house, and could be that her partner would have bee from another country. Venus is trine to Pluto in the second house in the sign of Sagittarius Pluto is in the sign of the third house. The second house is ruled by Mars and Pluto, and is ruled natally, by Venus. I don't think she would have been short of cash. And she would love deeply. It can be seen, too, that Venus has rule over the 8th and 12th houses as well. It is not very good to have this position where the ruler of the ascendant is also ruler of the 12th. But there are many of us who are born with that position, and have to live with it. The 12th house is the past, enemies, isolation etc.

Venus has a distance of about 71 degrees to the planet Neptune in the 4th house in the sign of Aquarius. This is a Quintile aspect. Venus makes also a

Quintile aspect with Mars in the 4th house in the sign of Aquarius. Neptune is co-ruler of the 5th house along with Jupiter; and Mars rules the second house, the 6th and the 7th.

SATURN SHOULD BE IN THE 9th HOUSE CONJUNCTING THE 9TH (My mistake, I have it in the 8th). LILITH TOO IS MISPLACED, IT SHOULD BE 10.08 TAURUS in the 7th house.

So we have seen that apart from Venus being ruler of the 12th, it is not bad off in the chart. Only that it is in the sixth house in Aries.

Scorpio is on the second cusp: the rulers of Scorpio are Mars and Pluto. Mars is in the 4th house, while Pluto is in the second. This shows an interest in money or the body or possessions with Pluto in the second house. Now with Mars in the fourth house, that is something else. First, let us see what aspects Mars has. Mars is conjunct Neptune also in the fourth house; Mars is square Lilith in the 7th house; Mars is square Mercury in the 7th house; Mars is square the sun in the 7th house.

Quite a lot of energy here! Because Mars is co-ruler of the second house, money could come from real estates or from parents. But if the individual is old enough, it is wise to let them go and live away from the family. We see that the aspects are all from angular to angular, so that the energies can be used without much harm; and it depends again, on who it is that is using the energies. Mars will cause trouble in the home.

Mars in conjunction with Neptune can cause quite a lot of rouble, deception, confusion within the family. Neptune is co-ruler of the 5th house. Mars is ruler of the 6th and 7th houses. Mars is opposing Jupiter in the 10th house in Leo. Again, we are dealing with angular positions, and have to do with career and parents, and the outside world.

We see that Pluto is in the third house sign of Sagittarius, and this has to do with the 9th house, and other people's possessions.

There is a quintile aspect between Pluto and Uranus. A quincunx aspect between Pluto and the sun. The sun is ruler of the 10th house.

There is a loop in the third house carrying the sign of Capricorn with Chiron inside. At the moment, I am still working with Chiron as ruler of Sagittarius. Sagittarius is at the third cusp, having Jupiter as its ruler. Capricorn in the loop is ruled by Saturn in the 9th house in Gemini.

So far, the third and the 9th houses are at the fore. But don't forget, this is the foundation chart, and will remain so all the life. It is showing that the individual is connected to the houses of travel.

Chiron has an aspect with Uranus, and this is a semi-square. A trine aspect to Lilith, Mercury and the sun in Taurus in the 7th house. Chiron is Semi-quadrate to the node in the 8th house in the sign of Gemini. The node rules Cancer in the loop in the 9th.

I am still pondering over the intercepted signs (loops) in a chart. I'm still sticking with – there's something extra going on. In this chart, we have third and ninth house.

I have already mention Mars in the 4th house in the sign of Aquarius. Neptune is there and has the same aspects as Mars. We find Uranus in the 4th house in the sign of Pisces conjunct the 5th, conjunct Fortune also in the 4th and in Pisces. An aspect from Uranus to Lilith is about 67 degrees, just leaving the sextile aspect. To Mercury, we get about 70 degrees, this could be a Quintile. To Saturn in the 9th, we get a trine. Both Saturn and Uranus are rulers of the 4th house. Uranus is trine to the ascendant. Now we find the moon in the 11th house in the sign of Libra is quincunx Uranus.

The moon is negative to Uranus, and this can cause some problems, in fact disturbing ones. The aspect can also be used for scientific subjects.

Fortune is in the 5th house in Pisces conjunct the 5th. It is in conjunction with Uranus, semi-sextile to the 4th, semi-square Venus in the 6th in Aries. Fortune is sextile Lilith in the 7th in Taurus; and just about making a sextile to Mercury in the 7th in Taurus, with a Quintile to the sun, just about making a square to the node in the 8th in Gemini. It has about 147 degrees to the Mid, close to a quincunx. And to Jupiter, well, this is a quincunx. Jupiter is in the 10th in Leo. I am working with Fortune as ruler of Leo, but I still have to find out if that is so. Fortune to the moon is about 153 degrees.

Venus, we have already dealt with because it is the ruler of the ascendant.

In the 7th house we have Lilith in Taurus. Note that the 7th house is ruled by Mars. There are many stories going around about Lilith. She is supposed to have been the first wife of Adam, but didn't want to be bossed by him, and so ran away. Supposed to be terrible when it comes to children, and is called a demon. I have been looking at where Lilith is placed in charts, but there is not much that I can say because you have to know the person of the chart, or have a good biography before you.

The 7th house is the house of war, partnerships, the public, business partners and open enemies. Note that the ascendant, the secret enemies, and open enemies are all ruled by Venus. But we take Lilith, Mercury and the sun because they too, are in the 7th house.

Lilith is square the Mid, it is conjunct Mercury, ruler of the 9th and 11th houses. A long time ago, I told you to watch out for this contact, 9/11, because it has to do with travel. Short, or long distance. Lilith is exactly square Jupiter in the 10th houses. Lilith is trine the 11th.

We are getting here from Lilith, travel, a group or friends or a club. The 7th house and the 10th houses. The 10th represents parents, outside world, but as we see, Lilith is in an angular house, and so is Jupiter. There will be some sort of conflict, but not as much as when the planets are somewhere else. I don't know how Lilith is going to act in that 7th house. WE know the sign it is in, is Taurus, and we know a lot about Taurus. By the way, I almost forgot to mention the 5 degrees that is at the 4th and 10th houses; and also at the 6th and 12th houses.

Lilith is semi-square Saturn in the 9th house in Gemini. Mercury is conjunct the sun with about 8 degrees. It is semi-square Saturn. Mercury is square Jupiter in the 10th house.

The sun is conjunct the 8th house, just about a conjunction with the node. The sun is Quintile the Mid.

The node is in the 8th house in the sign of Gemini along with Saturn in the 9th. It is sextile the Mid. Quintile Jupiter. Trine the moon in the 11th house in Libra.

Saturn is in Gemini in the 9th house conjunct the 9th. Saturn is semi-square Jupiter. Saturn is square the moon, but trint to the ascendant. Pluto is on the opposite side of Saturn.

Jupiter is in the sign of Leo conjunct the Mid, semi-sextile the 11th. The moon is in the 11th in the sign of Libra conjunct the 12th, sextile the Mid

What have I got from the chart? It is very complicated with all the aspects. I am picking up something to do with travel. Something to do with a group, a club, or a group of friends. Something extra to do with the third house, and of course we have Saturn in the 9th trine the ascendant. This is only the natal chart. But sometimes we can see certain things clearly. The fact that Saturn is trine the ascendant and is ruler of the loop in the third house, points to travel, and extra close family. Should Chiron be ruler of the Sagittarius, then we see the third house comes into play for travel. I don't like the fact that Lilith is in the 7th and making a negative contact with Jupiter in the 10th. Jupiter is ruling the third and fifth houses. It is the same with Mercury square Jupiter. But because the planets are angular, I have to be careful how I interpret them. .

Mercury is ruler of the 9th and 11th houses, and Jupiter rules 3rd and 5th. There's something not true here, some sort of falseness, and miscalculations. It seems to me that it had to be that the girl had to go to a foreign country, but I'm sure it could have been prevented for another time.

The moon has a nice aspect to the Mid, and is ruler of the loop in the 9th house. The moon is also ruler of the 4th house in the fixed wheel. In Libra, the moon is harmonious, and popular. Works well with others.

I think that the girl would have had a nice life working with others and the partner. Jupiter holds a very strong position, and she would have held a top job.

What we are going to do now is look at the progress wheel for that is the chart that shows the energies year by year.

Adding four years to the 12th of May, we get 16th of May as the perpetual date (cosmic birthday). She would have been 4 years old on the 12th of May 2007. So our calculations are 16th May 2003, at 18:14 pm, Leicester, UK. This would give us a progress chart for 4 years old, but the moon will decide for the months. And you will see that the progress moon is for the month of May which makes her 3 years old.

28.39 Libra	Sun	25.25 Taurus
25.38 Scorpio	Moon	03.28 Sagittarius
29.51 Sagittarius	Mercury	11.36 Taurus R
08.56 Aquarius	Venus	00.18 Taurus
12.58 Pisces	Mars	14.21 Aquarius
08.59 Aries	Jupiter	10.43 Leo
28.39 Aries	Saturn	27.45 Gemini
25.38 Taurus	Uranus	02.37 Pisces
29.51 Gemini	Neptune	13.11 Aquarius R
08.56 Leo	Pluto	19.13 Sagittarius R
12.58 Virgo	Chiron	17.51 Capricorn
08.59 Libra	N Node	29.50 Taurus
	Fortune	06.42 Taurus

The ascendant in the chart is Libra, and notice that Venus is now in the sign of Taurus, in zero degrees in the 7th house. It is telling us something. Pointing us to the 1st, 8th and 12th houses.

Still in conjunction with the 7th house, but square the Mid. It is sextile Saturn in the 8th house in Gemini. *Note: the square to the Mid is about 8 degrees, and the sextile to Saturn is about 3 degrees orb.* I normally try to keep within 1 degree. The wider degree is for natal charts; but maybe the wider degrees are working. Venus is conjunct Fortune in the 7th house in Taurus about 6 degrees.

The moon, we see, is in 3 degrees and 28 minutes for the month of May when the event took place. The moon is in Sagittarius in the second house, and is square to Uranus in the fourth house in the sign of Pisces. Uranus is co-ruler of the 4th, the moon is ruling the loop in the 9th house.

Mars is conjunct Neptune moving away 1 degree within the 4th house. Mars is ruler of the 2nd, 6th and 7th houses; Neptune is cor-ruler of the 5th. 8 degrees are at the cusp of the 4th and 10th houses. They are also at the 6th and 12th houses.

In the 7th house, Mercury in Taurus is in a close conjunction with Lilith, and both of them are square to Jupiter in the 10th. The sun is in the 7th and exactly conjunct the 8th.

It is interested to find that this progress sun is exactly semi-sextile Venus in the natal chart; and is exactly semi-sextile the 7th house cusp in the natal chart. It is also quincunx the ascendant of the natal chart.

Mercury in the 7th house in the sign of Taurus is sextile the 5th house with the sign of Pisces there. Mercury is also trine 11th house with the sign of Virgo there. We must not forget that the girl travelled with her parents and a group to another country. The chart shows this clearly.

One thing we must not forget: from the ascendant to the loop in the third house, there are four signs – and Capricorn is that 4th sign. Capricorn is normally at the 10th house in the Zodiac wheel. And Saturn is the ruler. WE find Saturn in the 8th house conjuncting the 9th with about 2 degrees, and trine the ascendant.

The node is crying in the 8th house in the sign of Taurus, exactly semi-sextile the 9th; and is quincunx the ascendant.

What we shall do now is have a look at the chart where the girl's mother went to check. This was at 22:00 pm. The chart should be: 3rd May 2007 at 22:00 pm, Lagos Portugal.

03.05 Sagittarius	Sun	13.02 Taurus
04.45 Capricorn	Moon	29.05 Scorpio
10.38 Aquarius	Mercury	13.53 Taurus
16.38 Pisces	Venus	25.02 Gemini
17.20 Aries	Mars	21.04 Pisces
12.06 Taurus	Jupiter	18.36 Sagittarius R
03.05 Gemini	Saturn	18.19 Leo
04.35 Cancer	Uranus	17.41 Pisces
10.38 Leo	Neptune	21.54 Aquarius
16.38 Virgo	Pluto	28.41 Sagittarius
17.20 Libra	Chiron	15.31 Aquarius
12.06 Scorpio	N Node	13.09 Pisces
	Fortune	17.02 Taurus

After checking many charts I now see how difficult it is to make a decision, especially when it comes to missing or kidnapped children. With other cases I've checked, they had not been to another country. The chart in this case (the girl's chart, shows travel). And that makes it a bit hard to separate those aspects.

The mother's chart for 3rd May at 22:00 pm is a transit chart which we call an event chart only for that moment.

Sagittarius is rising with the ruler Jupiter in the first house with Pluto at a distance of about 10 degrees. Some will like to call that a conjunction, but for me, it is too far out. This ascendant is showing the mother, and any planets in or around the ascendant. Jupiter has an exact trine to Saturn in the 9th house in Leo. This will bring the first, second, third and fourth houses into operation. WE must not forget that the third house has to do with close relatives and neighbours.

Jupiter is a big planet. It is 1300 times that of the earth. That's pretty big. In angular positions, Jupiter acts as a king or queen. Here we find Jupiter angular and in its own sign.

Jupiter is sextile the 11th. This has to do with friends, clubs or a group. Lilith is there in the 11th house, but I haven't a clue as yet what it is doing. Jupiter is square the Mid. Jupiter is sextile to Neptune in the third house in Aquarius, aslo sextile to Chiron in the same house and sign. Jupiter is square Uranus and Mars in the fourth house in the sign of Pisces. Talking about Mars, this is the ruler of the sign on the 5th house which is Aries, and represents her first child.

Every astrologer should know that house 4 and house 8 represents one's departing, and it should be made known by the 10th house. Not forgetting the first house and the fifth and 6th houses. The opposite sides come into force as well. But astrologers know as well, it is not that easy. I see with my eyes, but I say nothing.

So then if Mars is the ruler of her child, it is in the 4th house conjunct Uranus. This is not a good position. Uranus is a disruptive and sudden planet, and with Mars this could cause trouble. I have seen it in many charts, and read what happened to the individual of that chart.

Uranus is the co-ruler of the third house, pointing to travel or neighbours. WE have Uranus exactly semi-sextile the 5th, exactly sextile Fortune in the 6th house in the sign of Taurus. Uranus is quincunx Saturn in the 9th house. Uranus is conjunct the 4th house, and is quincunx the 11th. Mars is exactly semi-sextile Neptune in the 3rd house in the sign of Aquarius. Neptune is ruling the 4th house. WE see that Jupiter in the first house is trine to the 5th.

Okay, we are at the 5th house. Start counting anti-clockwise around the chart until you come to the 8th house. Why the 8th house? This is the house we call the death house or the otherworldly. There at the 8th house for Aries, we see the sign Scorpio. And inside this house we see the moon there and crying.

I have gathered that the crying degrees are just what they say – but there is some sort of power behind it. I had Neptune crying where they pulled out my toe nail without anaesthetic. Later. I did quite a lot of athletics.

The moon in the mother's 22:00 pm chart is in the 12th house which would be the 8th for her first child; and it rules the 8th house of the 22:00 pm chart.

Lilith in the 11th house in the sign of Libra is exactly trine to Neptune in the 3rd house in Aquarius. But Lilith is Quincunx Mars exactly in the 4th house.

What I'm getting is something to do with closeness to do with friends and neighbours. There's also something to do with water and trees (Gemini). Sorting this chart out properly, we are going to get secret enemy (12th house). Open enemies (7th house). There we find Venus in Gemini. Venus is ruling the 11th and 6th houses. Mars in the 4th house is ruler of the 12th and 5th houses.

It can be seen that something quite suddenly and accidentally has happened.

I have been looking into some charts of people who were kidnapped, and who came back years after. Like the case of Jacee Dugard. She was kept in for 18 years, and then she was free. I looked at her chart very carefully to see what was happening.

We have to look very carefully at the rising sign. The ruler of that sign, and where it is located in the chart. Then you have to check the aspects the ruler makes to the whole chart.4 and 8 are some clues, and as I have said before, the Mid should be telling us something. Planets should be exact with the Mid. In the girl's progressive chart for 16th may 2003, There is the sun in the 7th house, exactly conjuncting the 8th house. The sun is ruler of the 10th carrying Jupiter. The sun is Quintile the Mid.

Back to the 22:00 pm chart when the mother went to check. As you have already seen in the fourth house, Uranus is causing some upset being semi-sextile to the 5th, and Quincunx to Saturn in the 9th. Uranus exactly sextile to Fortune. This Uranus is ruling the third house. Inside the 6th house we see the sun and Mercury exactly in conjunction, and both conjuncting the 6th. This 6th house is the child's body, counting anti-clockwise from the 5th. The sun is ruling the 9th, Mercury is ruling the 7th and the 10th houses. There in the 7th house we find Venus ruler of the 6th and 11th houses. It is terrible to say, but Venus is opposing Pluto in the first house, both are angular. Pluto is ruling the 12th house.

Fortune we find in the 6th house in the sign of Taurus, and is square Saturn in the 9th in Leo. Fortune is ruling the 9th and Saturn the 2nd and the 3rd. Fortune is trine the Mid. Fortune is Quincunx the 11th house where the sign Libra is stationed. Saturn in the 9th house is sextile the 11th.

Lilith is in the 11th house in Libra sextile Jupiter in the first in Sagittarius. Lilith is trine both Chiron and Neptune in the third in Aquarius. Chiron probably has rule over the ascendant, Neptune has rule over the 4th.

We have already dealt with the moon in the 12th house in Scorpio.

I wanted to give Sagittarius to Lilith, but being the daughter of the underworld, I was thinking of Scorpio, but that too, I am not sure. It seems that Lilith doesn't like children. And according to her aspects in a chart, could be dangerous.

Should we get to no more about Lilith, it would explain quite a lot to us. he chart is showing Lilith in good contact with Neptune in the 3rd, yet it is quincunx Mars in the 4th house – Mars being ruler of the 5th and 12.

Well, anyway, let's move on a bit. The girl's natal moon is exactly sextile our chart ascendant. Her progress chart's moon is exactly conjunct our chart's ascendant.

I do hope that you have seen by taking time, and examining all the charts, you can get enormous information. But you have to work them out.

38: The Astrological Case of Joanna Yeates

You can read up quite a lot about this case which took place in Bristol in 2010. A young man was sentenced to 20 years for the murder. We haven't got the time of birth of Joanna, but we shall concentrate on the 12:00 pm time; and also on the date when she went missing.

Joanna was born on 19th April 1985, Hampshire, UK. (Use the 12:00 pm time.) I have taken Portsmouth as one of the towns in Hampshire. The degrees will not be far off. But it would have been more accurate if we had the time. Remember, the sun's position is not to be interpreted, only its aspects, and the sign it is in. Below is the progressive chart for the event. 14th May 1985, 12:00 pm, Portsmouth.

21.48 Leo	Sun	23.35 Taurus
10.46 Virgo	Moon	24.19 Pisces
05.45 Libra	Mercury	00.33 Taurus
08.25 Scorpio	Venus	12.20 Aries
17.30 Sagittarius	Mars	12.27 Gemini
23.21 Capricorn	Jupiter	16.14 Aquarius
21.48 Aquarius	Saturn	24.55 Scorpio R
10.46 Pisces	Uranus	16.54 Sagittarius R
05.35 Aries	Neptune	03.13 Capricorn R
08.25 Taurus	Pluto	02.47 Scorpio
17.30 Gemini	Chiron	07.35 Gemini
23.21 Cancer	N Node	18.04 Taurus
	Fortune	21.47 Gemini

So this is the chart that is progressed from her natal chart. Let's have a look around quickly. 5 degrees are at the 3/9 axis. Uranus is conjuncting the 5th house. Jupiter in the 6th house in Aquarius is sextile Uranus in the 5th house. We see the moon in 24 degrees of Pisces in the 8th house. The event took place in December, and the moon is for May, the perpetual date. We need to add about 7 months to the moon which gives us about 1 degree in Aries. The moon is still in the 8th house but now in the 9th house sign of Aries. It is Quincunx Pluto in the 3rd house in Scorpio. Venus is in the 9th house ruler of the third and 10th houses, Lilith is there with about 15 degrees away from Venus. At the Mid, we see 8 degrees, also at the fourth. Venus is exactly sextile Mars in the 10th house, but in the 11th house sign of Gemini. Mercury is zero degree, and is ruler of the 2nd and 11th houses. The sun is in Taurus exactly sextile to the 12th. The sun is ruler of the ascendant. You notice that the sign at the 12th is Cancer. Chiron in the 10th in the sign of the 11th Gemini is semi-sextile the Mid. Fortune is in the 11th in Gemini and exactly sextile the ascendant. The node in the 10th house in Taurus is semi-sextile the 11th. And we go back to Jupiter and find it trine to the 11th.

That was quick, and I hope you got the information out of that. The reason why I did that quick is because I want to show you quickly, some more charts.

The next chart we are going to look at is an event chart. This is far different from the natal or the progressed charts. In the event chart, the sun is there in the same degree. The moon in its sign stays there for a long time depending on the degree its in. This chart is for when she left her friends after spending some time with them at the pub. It is the 17th December 2010 at 20:00 pm, Bristol, UK.

13.29 Leo	Sun	25.46 Sagittarius
01.10 Virgo	Moon	13.05 Taurus
24.13 Virgo	Mercury	01.01 Capricorn R
25.36 Libra	Venus	11.02 Scorpio
05.22 Sagittarius	Mars	07.28 Capricorn
13.42 Capricorn	Jupiter	24.55 Pisces
13.29 Aquarius	Saturn	15.52 Libra
01.10 Pisces	Uranus	26.43 Pisces
24.13 Pisces	Neptune	26.22 Aquarius
25.36 Aries	Pluto	04.49 Capricorn
05.22 Gemini	Chiron	26.57 Aquarius
13.22 Cancer	N Node	03.03 Capricorn
	Fortune	26.10 Pisces

Have a good look around the chart. You see the moon is in a loop in the 10th house in Taurus. Jupiter is exactly conjunct the 9th house. 5 degrees are on the axis 5/11. The moon in the loop is exactly sextile the 12th, and exactly square the ascendant. Venus is in a loop in the 4th house in Scorpio. Mercury in Capricorn in the 5th house is exactly trine the second house. The sun in the 5th house in Sagittarius is square the 9th, square Jupiter, square Uranus, square Fortune. The sun is sextile Neptune and Chiron in the 7th house in the sign Aquarius. The sun is conjunct the node in the 5th house in Capricorn. The sun is conjunct Pluto in the 5th house in Capricorn. And the sun is conjunct Mercury in the 5th house in Capricorn. The sun is exactly trine the Mid. Jupiter is semi-sextile the Mid. Uranus is semi-sextile the Mid. Fortune is semi-sextile the Mid. Fortune and Uranus are exactly semi-sextile to Chiron and Neptune in the 7th. While Chiron and Neptune are sextile to the Mid.

This is not a progress chart where we keep to the 1 degree either side.

Saturn in the 3rd house is quincunx to the moon; it is also sextile to the ascendant. Venus in the loop in the 4th house is square the ascendant. Venus is sextile Mars, and we see that it is opposing the moon.

Keep an eye on the group in Pisces, and the group in Capricorn. The sign

Capricorn is cold and freezing. Notice that her body is ruled by Virgo and Mercury. The second house has to do with money as well; one's possessions.

We move on quickly to the next chart. She is still alive because at 20:30 pm, she phones her best friend. She's on her way home.

Here is the chart:

18.45 Leo	Sun	25.47 Sagittarius
07.06 Virgo	Moon	13.21 Taurus
01.09 Libra	Mercury	00.59 Capricorn
03.29 Scorpio	Venus	11.03 Scorpio
13.02 Sagittarius	Mars	07.29 Capricorn
19.53 Capricorn	Jupiter	24.55 Pisces
18.45 Aquarius	Saturn	15.52 Libra
07.06 Pisces	Uranus	26.43 Pisces
01.09 Aries	Neptune	26.22 Aquarius
03.29 Taurus	Pluto	04.49 Capricorn
13.02 Gemini	Chiron	26.57 Aquarius
19.53 Cancer	N Node	03.03 Capricorn
	Fortune	01.12 Aries

In this chart, we see that the moon is out of the loop, and is exactly semi-sextile to the 11th house. Chiron in the 8th house is exactly trine to the 12th; it is also quincunx the ascendant. The node in the 5th house is exactly trine to the Mid. Mars in the 5th house is sextile the 8th. Pluto in the 5th house is trine the Mid. Mercury in the 5th house has moved into 0 degree, and squaring Fortune, and the 9th house. Fortune is exactly conjunct the 9th house.

We need not worry, she's still alive. And we mustn't forget that we know how this case turned out. The friend said that they talked for about 7-15 minutes. The next chart is for 20:40 where she is seen on CCTV buying a pizza.

20.31 Leo	Sun	25.48 Sagittarius
09.05 Virgo	Moon	13, 26 Taurus
03.28 Libra	Mercury	00.59 Capricorn R
06.04 Scorpio	Venus	11.03 Scorpio
15.32 Sagittarius	Mars	07.30 Capricorn
21.55 Capricorn	Jupiter	24.55 Pisces
20.31 Aquarius	Saturn	15.52 Libra
09.05 Pisces	Uranus	26.43 Pisces
03.28 Aries	Neptune	26.22 Aquarius
06.04 Taurus	Pluto	04.49 Capricorn
15.32 Gemini	Chiron	26, 57 Aquarius
21.55 Cancer	N Node	03.03 Capricorn
	Lilith	19.17 Pisces
	Fortune	02.52 Aries

Looking around the chart again, we see that Saturn in the 3rd house in Libra is making a trine aspect with the 11th house. Saturn is exalted and is ruler of the 6th and 7th houses. Fortune is still in conjunction with the 9th. 9 degrees is at the second house, so something is happening there. Maybe her paying out money to get the pizza. But why is Saturn trine the 11th? Lilith is quincunx the ascendant. Venus still in Scorpio in the fourth; Mercury still in 0 degree retrograde; and the node is exactly square the 9th.

I always find 15 degrees strange, and I can't explain why. We have to now guess that after buying the pizza, she's on her way home. And that's where we start looking carefully in the charts to come.

The following chart is for 20:50 pm.

22.16 Leo	Sun	25.48 Sagittarius
11.04 Virgo	Moon	13.31 Taurus
05.47 Libra	Mercury	00.58 Capricorn R
08.39 Scorpio	Venus	11.03 Scorpio
17.59 Sagittarius	Mars	07.30 Capricorn
23.56 Capricorn	Jupiter	24, 55 Pisces.
22.16 Aquarius	Saturn	15.52 Libra
11.04 Pisces	Uranus	26.43 Pisces
05, 47 Aries	Neptune	26.22 Aquarius
08.39 Taurus	Pluto	04.49 Capricorn
17.59 Gemini	Chiron	26.57 Aquarius
23.56 Cancer	N Node	03.03 Capricorn
	Lilith	19.17 Pisces
	Fortune	04.32 Aries

In this chart we see that 8 degrees are at the 4/10 axis. 5 degrees are at the 3/9 axis. 22 degrees: I have been checking these degrees for sometime now. Something disruptive or masterful, not very sure here. Jupiter in the 8th house is trine the 12th. Fortune in the 8th house is exactly square to Pluto. Mars in the 6th house is trine the Mid. And we have Venus in the 4th house in Scorpio exactly sextile to the 2nd. Note that Venus is ruling the 3rd and 10th houses.

Something is happening to do with her neighbour, and her body or her possessions.

At 21:00 pm, the landlord said he saw three people on the path to the flat. The chart for that time shows quite a lot.

24.01 Leo	Sun	25.49 Sagittarius
13.03 Virgo	Moon	13.37 Taurus
08.05 Libra	Mercury	00.58 Capricorn R
11.12 Scorpio	Venus	11.04 Scorpio
20.24 Sagittarius	Mars	07.30 Capricorn

25.56 Capricorn	Jupiter	24.55 Pisces
24.01 Aquarius	Saturn	15.52 Libra
13.03 Pisces	Uranus	26.43 Pisces
08.08 Aries	Neptune	26.22 Aquarius
11.12 Taurus	Pluto	04.49 Capricorn
20.24 Gemini	Chiron	26.57 Aquarius
25.56 Cancer	N Node	03.03 Capricorn
	Lilith	19.17 Pisces
	Fortune	06.13 Aries

Notice that he planet Venus have moved from out of the loop in the fourth house, and was in the fourth house. Now it has moved from the 4th house into the 3rd, and is ruler of the 3rd and 10th houses. Venus is exactly conjunct the 4th.

The moon in the 10th in Taurus is exactly trine the 2nd house, and exactly sextile the 8th.

Lilith is square the 11th. Note the 11th sign as Gemini, and its ruler is Mercury. Lilith is in the 8th house.

Jupiter in the 8th house is trine the 12th, and is exactly quincunx the ascendant. Jupiter is ruling the 5th and 8th houses. Uranus in the 8th house is trine the 12th.

We have both Chiron and Neptune in the 7th both quincunx to the 12th. Mars in the 5th is square to the 9th. Mars is exalted in Capricorn, and is ruler of the 4th and 5th house.

The sun, ruler of the ascendant is trine the ascendant; and quincunx the 12th. Fortune also in the 8th house is square Mars. Fortune ruling the ascendant.

Earlier in one of the charts, we saw that Saturn in the third house, exalted in Libra made a trine aspect to the 11th house. I am still wondering what that could have been. Saturn is ruling the 6th and 7th houses. Saturn, to astrologers, is old, cold, steady, patient; but in the exalted sign of Libra, it is very friendly and helpful. The 6th house has to do with pets, and she did have a pet. I think it could explain the time when she bought the pizza. 7th house, and 11th house Gemini. Maybe! Her landlord was an exalted person, and seems to have been a friendly person – I am just guessing. Anyway, I heard that the man who was responsible for killing Joanne, said that it was an accident, he never meant to do so.

So you see now, how astrology can help. It is not the only key there is. There are many more ways, but it is from the workings of the solar system that everything gets its power. The spirit, as we already know is more powerful. God is spirit. And it was God who created the solar system.

39: Observations

The three numbers 11, 22, and 33 in numerology, I've been trying to get them to work in astrology. 33 is out because no one is born on 33. And the degrees only goes up to 30 degrees.

A Leo woman is not going to stand any nonsense, and she's not going to be overpowered. Still, she'll be a good wife.

People with Neptune in the 1st house are strange either for positive or for negative. They like music very much; and if they don't get off the drink or drugs, they could ruin their lives.

The planet Saturn in the 5th house, even when exalted, and square the ascendant or the ascendant ruler will find it hard to have children. Yet they are very nice people, and kind and helpful.

Mars in the first house is like walking round with a bomb ready to go off.

Mars was always messing about with Vulcan's wife. If Mars is negative with any of the outer planets, one need to be in good control.

Look at this chart, and see what you make of it.

31st May 1923 at 14:25 pm, Petersburg, Indiana.

13.58 Libra	Sun	09.20 Gemini
11.21 Scorpio	Moon	01.46 Capricorn
12.24 Sagittarius	Mercury	05.12 Gemini R
15.55 Capricorn	Venus	12.18 Taurus
18.59 Aquarius	Mars	00.38 Cancer
18.44 Pisces	Jupiter	10.58 Scorpio R
13.58 Aries	Saturn	13.34 Libra R
11.21 Taurus	Uranus	17.21 Pisces
12.24 Gemini	Neptune	15.43 Leo
15.55 Cancer	Pluto	09.55 Cancer
18.59 Leo	Chiron	19.49 Aries
18.44 Virgo	N Node	16.21 Virgo
	Lilith	26.52 Aries
	Fortune	06.24 Taurus

Before we start at the ascendant, did you have a good look around the chart to see if you can pick up anything? Okay! The ascendant sign is Libra, the 7th sign of the zodiac wheel. This sign is supposed to be harmonious and good relationship. The ruler, Venus, is in the 8th house. This is a dark house. Venus is in the money sign of Taurus, and is conjuncting the 8th, exactly semi-sextile the 8th, quincunx the ascendant, and Saturn, semi-sextile the 7th, square Neptune in the 10th.

It' is not looking so nice for the ascendant Libra. People might still be friendly, but there's something wrong here. Don't be led astray by the exaltation of any planet; check out their aspects properly.

Saturn is square Pluto in the 9th in Cancer. It is trine the sun and Mercury in the 8th house in Gemini. Don't be fooled too, with the good aspects. The trine of Mercury and Saturn is a good aspect; here, we find Mercury is retrograde, losing some of its power. Saturn is also trine the 9th house. We can get just about a quincunx between Saturn and Uranus in the 5th house in Pisces. Saturn is sextile Neptune in the 10th while Neptune is exactly semi-sextile the Mid. Saturn is opposing Chiron in the 7th in Aries.

This house is war, the partner, the public or business partnerships, and open enemies. Chiron, I am still using as being ruler of Sagittarius which is on the 3rd cusp. This third cusp, is normally ruled by Mercury, the lower mind. Jupiter is ruler of Sagittarius and is in the first house in Scorpio, conjunct the second. Jupiter is trine the Mid, and Pluto. It is quincunx the sun. Opposing Venus and Fortune. Jupiter is trine Uranus.

Jupiter in Scorpio is very deep thinking, and there is something here to do with money. Notice that Jupiter is not very good with the sun. If you have anyone with the sun and Jupiter negative, do not let them run your business. They don't know how to go about with money. They just use it up. Something might work out if both planets are angular, but still, you should be careful. Jupiter is square Neptune.

We see that the moon is in Capricorn, and is in the 3rd house which is the house of Mercury. The moon is about 153 degrees from Mercury in the 8th house, and in its own sign of Gemini. The moon is opposing both Mars and Pluto up there in the 9th house. It is Sesqui-quadrate Neptune. It is trine Lilith in the 7th in Aries, and trine Fortune in 7th in Taurus, the 8th house sign.

Uranus in the 5th house is opposing the node in the 11th house in the sign of Virgo. Uranus is sextile Venus, semi-sextile Chiron, trine the Mid.

I need to start looking more deeply into Lilith, its sign, house-placing, and its aspects to see what I could find. It is in about 7 degrees with Chiron, semi-square the sun, and Quintile with Pluto, sextile with Mars.

I am sure that you have found certain things that would lead you to say that the individual is not all there. And why? Because we are human beings, and we do make mistakes. It is at a certain time in life that we find ourselves doing strange things, or sometimes good. These future things are called progressions, and it is up to the human being, how he or she work them out. It is not an easy thing. The astrologer cannot do anything but to tell you of a certain year, and what he sees there. He does not control the solar system. No one does, but the Creator. So it would be pointless giving the astrologer a hard time for telling you what he see, whether its good or bad.

This individual is a murderer, and a thief. He likes to make love choking the woman he's with. He was married and had two children. He tried doing the same to his wife. Notice Venus in the dark house of Pluto and conjunct the same house. It doesn't mean that everyone who has that position will go around and do the same thing. It has to do with early upbringing, and the environment, and heredity. If one cannot use the energies of the planets, whether they are positive or negative, properly, then things will definitely go wrong.

I had a couple of friends, women, who had Saturn exalted in Libra, very nice and helpful and kind, looks after old people. But Saturn is negative to their ascendant, and both of them have no children. My own mother has Saturn in the 5th house exalted in Libra, and she only has me as her child. And I have seen other charts with Saturn in the 5th house, and it gave problems with bringing children into the world, sometimes it gives you one or two, not many more.

Let's have a look at another chart of a murderer, and see what you can pick up.

This one is of *Dennis Whitney* born 15th August 1942 at 11:00 pm, Riverside, California, U.S.A.

09.01 Taurus	Sun	22.44 Leo
08.43 Gemini	Moon	11.45 Libra
02.04 Cancer	Mercury	05.46 Virgo
24.40 Cancer	Venus	28.55 Cancer
20.51 Leo	Mars	09.24 Virgo
25.24 Virgo	Jupiter	14.46 Cancer
09.01 Scorpio	Saturn	11.07 Gemini
08.43 Sagittarius	Uranus	04.19 Gemini
02.04 Capricorn	Neptune	28.16 Virgo
24.40 Capricorn	Pluto	05.52 Leo
20.51 Aquarius	Chiron	19.14 Leo
25.24 Pisces	N Node	04.48 Virgo
	Fortune	20.00 Pisces
	Lilith	28.43 Gemini

This chart is showing a Taurus ascendant. The ruler is Venus. We find Venus in the fourth house in the sign of Cancer. So here, we have a Taurus/Cancer. Taurus are stubborn, but of course they still love strongly. Love money and possessions. Cancer is a homely, sensitive sign. Venus has a very strong position there in the fourth house. It is also ruler of the loop in the 6th house where Libra is the sign, and the moon is there. Why is the moon in the loop. The moon is ruler of the third and fourth houses. The moon in Libra should be showing a harmonious, togetherness person.

Venus, the ruler of the ascendant is conjunct the dark planet Pluto also in the fourth house in the sign of Leo. Venus is exactly sextile with Neptune in the 6th house in the sign of Virgo. Neptune is ruler of the 12th house.

Venus has a Quintile aspect with the moon in the loop in the 6th house in Libra. This shows us that something is wrong here, even though we came up with some good aspects.

Venus is exactly semi-sextile Lilith. Venus is semi-square Saturn in the second house in Gemini. Lilith is also in Gemini, and in the second house. Saturn is ruling the 9th, 10th and 11th houses.

With Uranus in the first house, it is hard to overpower the individual. Their mind is set on doing something, and they will carry it out, no matter what. Uranus is in Gemini, and it is conjunct the second house. Uranus rules the 11th house with Saturn. Uranus is conjunct Saturn. Saturn too, is conjunct the second house. Uranus is sextile Pluto, but this is a long term aspect, we could only take the houses and signs that both planets are in.

Venus we see is also conjunct the 4th and opposing the Mid. This chart has Jupiter in the 3rd exalted in Cancer, sextile the ascendant, semi-sextile Saturn, in the same sign with the ascendant ruler, sextile Mars in the 5th house in Virgo, Quintile Neptune in the 6th house in Virgo.

Saturn is square Mars, this aspect can bring trouble if used wrongly. Saturn is square Mercury, this is the destiny and the intellect in conflict for those who are not tune in properly. Saturn is trine the moon.

Jupiter is square the moon. Pluto in the fourth house is exactly semi-sextile Mercury in the 5th. Mercury is in the 6th sign of Virgo.

Over in the 11th house we see that Fortune is in Pisces and conjunct the 12th Friends who are enemies, and the chance of isolation, whether through the self our from others.

We see that Mercury in the 5th house has a trine to the ascendant, but Mercury is holding 5 degrees, and is ruler of the second and the 6th houses. You notice that Pluto is also holding 5 degrees, and that Mercury is exact with Pluto.

Mars is exactly trine to the ascendant, and is ruler of the 7th, and the loop in the 12th.

I hope you have read what he has done, and can see that he had the chance to act otherwise; but we don't know anything about the early life. You see that the ascendant and Mars are both in 9 degrees. Something to think about!

Our next chart is about a woman who was described as being the Number one astrologer of the United States. She has a book entitled *"Outrageous Fortune."* She died in 1996 at the age of 99. This is also for some of us to think about; why people live to be such an age; even an astrologer!

Her name is *Myra Kingsley*, born 1st October 1897 at 16:15 pm, Westport, Connecticut, U.S.A.

06.23 Pisces	Sun	08.56 Libra
23.20 Aries	Moon	21.19 Sagittarius
24.25 Taurus	Mercury	23.38 Virgo
17.21 Gemini	Venus	06.18 Virgo
08.12 Cancer	Mars	24.24 Libra
01.48 Leo	Jupiter	24.42 Virgo
06.23 Virgo	Saturn	27.21 Scorpio
23.20 Libra	Uranus	26.27 Scorpio
24.25 Scorpio	Neptune	22.32 Gemini R
17.21 Sagittarius.	Pluto	14.40 Gemini.
08.12 Capricorn	Chiron	13.37 Scorpio
01.48 Aquarius	N Node	02.38 Aquarius
	Lilith	03.00 Gemini
	Fortune	18.46 Taurus

From what I have gathered, there was always a top astrologer in New York. Evangeline Adams was the one when Myra's mother took her for a reading. Myra was told that she is very good in music, and that she would turn out to be a top astrologer. Can you see that? Of course!

The planet Venus in and hanging around an angular house is always know to make one to be interested in music or art. In our chart, you see that Venus is exactly conjuncting the 7th house. That's easy isn't it?

Okay! Let's look at her chart properly. The ascendant is rising with 6 degrees and 23 minutes of Pisces. It is a water sign ruled by Jupiter and Neptune. We find Jupiter in the 7th house in the sign of Virgo in conjunction with Mercury also in the 7th house, and in the same sign. Jupiter is exactly semi-sextile Mars in the 8th house in the sign of Libra. Mars is ruler of the 2nd and 9th houses. Jupiter is also ruler of the 10th. Jupiter is sextile Saturn and Uranus both in the 9th house in the sign of Scorpio. Both planets rule the 11th and 12th houses. Jupiter is semi-sextile the 8th house, and exactly sextile the 9th. Jupiter is square the moon (note that both planets are in angular positions). They still produce some negative effect, but are strong in angular position.

Neptune is co-ruler of the ascendant, it is in the 4th house in Gemini, and is sextile the 2nd house. It is in conjunction with Pluto in the 3rd house, also in Gemini. These two planets were around in the 1800s, and they have brought out quite a lot of secrets and new inventions. Even Hitler had these two planets in his 8th house – the dark house. Neptune is square both Mercury and Jupiter in the 7th house, the house of partnerships. They both hold strong positions, bit still can cause problems. Neptune is trine the 8th house, and Mars in that house. Neptune is Quincunx Uranus in the 9th house in the sign of Scorpio. Uranus rules the 12th house along with Saturn. Neptune is opposing the moon in the

10th house in the sign of Sagittarius. Again, we find these two planets holding strong positions. The moon is ruler of the 5th house. Neptune, of course, is conjuncting the 4th house.

Fortune in the second house, well, what can I say. She wrote that book *"Outrageous Fortune."* I am still trying to pinpoint what exactly Fortune is doing in the charts.

Pluto in the house of Mercury which is the third house. The intellect is deep, and their could be writings on deep subjects. Remember that Pluto is a dark planet. Whatever house it is in, that house is dark positive or negative. You must always keep in mind too, that if there was no Pluto, the third house is ruled by Venus, and we find Venus in the 6th house exactly conjunct the 7th, and in the sign of Virgo. This sign of Virgo is known to be critical, analytical, looking for all the small details. Well Venus in Virgo is someone who is looking for the perfect partner.

Pluto is opposing the moon, square Mercury in the 7th house, trine the sun in the 7th house, and Quincunx Chiron in the 8th house, but in the sign of the 9th.

Here at the 7th house, it looks good with Venus exactly conjunct, Mercury and Jupiter placed there. She got married in 1921 and divorced in 1927. It seems to me that she was married to someone very religious because Jupiter is sextile Saturn in the 9th house. These two planets are good for religion.

Mercury has a semi-sextile to the 8th and to Mars in the 8th. It is sextile both Saturn and Uranus in the 9th. It is square the moon in the 10th both planets angular. In the 7th, we see the sun. This is a good position, if aspects are good. The chance of marrying someone high, and dealing with the public. Notice that the sun is holding 8 degrees, and is exactly square the 5th and the 11th. These two cusps holding 8 degrees. There's no mention of children.

Mars is in the 8th house in Libra conjuncting the 8th. It is ruler of the opposite sign Aries, so there's a loss of some of its energies. It is exactly semi-sextile the 9th. Semi-sextile both Saturn and Uranus in the 9th. Mars is sextile to the moon in the 10th house.

Chiron is in the 8th house in the 9th house sign of Scorpio, I am still working with Chiron as ruler of Sagittarius until something solid shows up. Chiron is opposing Fortune in the 2nd house.

Now in the 9th house we see the two planets Saturn and Uranus in a close conjunction in the sign of Scorpio. In this house, as far as I have experienced, these two planets can do great things. I suppose they do as well in any house, and in the signs that they are in. People are very intellectual, and we see that the sign is Scorpio, so that gives us more information. Saturn is square the ascendant, while Uranus is just about doing the same with 99 degrees. What do you think? Both planets are sextile to the node in the 12th house.

The moon in the 10th house in the sign of Sagittarius shows publicity. Help comes from women and those in high positions. Remember, the moon represents the mother, the emotions and the feelings. Sagittarius is the sign that is normally on the 9th house, and has to do with freedom, higher learning, and travel. The moon rules the 5th house, and this is the house of creativity and entertainment etc. As I said before, there's nothing said about children, but I bet she loved children. I have met many people who cannot have children themselves, and are great lovers of children. The moon is about 74 degrees away from the ascendant, this is close to a Quintile which is 72 degrees.

The node is in a Universal sign which is Aquarius, and is normally at the 11th house. The node is in the 12th house about 44 degrees from the Mid which works out as a semi-square. The node is conjunct the 12th house. This could be a position of people who are working behind the scenes for the benefit of others; it could also be people who like to be alone for a while to recuperate; or imprisoned or hospitalized according to what the node is doing in the chart.

Should your 12th house sign be the same as your ascendant sign, take care.

Should your 5th house sign be ruled by Saturn or Saturn is in it with negative aspects, then you could expect trouble in that area. There could be other planets in the house with good aspects, so check carefully.

The moon with Mars is rude, gets angry quickly, unless good aspects are coming to them.

In the astrology that I have been researching, there are 12 stages of life. They are known to us as houses. Let us take Venus in her exalted sign of Pisces. This is love at its best, compassionate, and kind, helpful. Even when the planet is negative. So we only need to place Venus in every stage of life, and we see the energies that are there to work with. If Venus is hitting any one of the angular points, you can bet your life that this is good for music, beauty, art, singing or dancing.

I have found, and I don't know why that is so, that when Venus is negative to the ascendant, the person is more prettier.

Should you have Jupiter in the second house with good aspects, get cracking, you could become very rich.

Mars at the angles gives very much energy. Saturn in the first house can set you off in life very early.

Let's have a quick look at the chart of a cult leader. She is *Anne Hamilton-Byrne*, of '*The Family New age group.*' Children were tortured after being stolen through strange adoptions schemes. She lived to be 97 years old. Born 30th December 1921 at 12:07 pm, Melbourne, Australia.

03.49 Aries	Sun	07.51 Capricorn
00.38 Taurus	Moon	17.33 Capricorn
01.13 Gemini	Mercury	09.16 Capricorn
04.18 Cancer	Venus	27.59 Sagittarius
07.17 Leo	Mars	02.06 Scorpio
07.34 Virgo	Jupiter	17.02 Libra
03.49 Libra	Saturn	07.18 Libra
00.38 Scorpio	Uranus	06.32 Pisces
01.13 Sagittarius	Neptune	15.31 Leo
04.18 Capricorn	Pluto	09.01 Cancer R
07.17 Aquarius	Chiron	09.29 Aries
07.34 Pisces	N Node	13.46 Libra
	Lilith	29.25 Aquarius
	Fortune	13.32 Aries

The ascendant Aries is ruled by Mars. We find Mars in the 8th house in the sign of Scorpio. conjuncting the 8th. I always call this house a dark house, the same as I do with Pluto. It could be positive or negative, but it is still dark. Mars is sextile Venus in the 9th house in Sagittarius. Mars is sextile the Mid and the sun in the 10th house in Capricorn. Mars is also sextile Mercury in the 10th house also in Capricorn.

We have to do with a strong Capricorn person, and you know what Capricorns are like. They have this urge to get to the top. Mars is semi-sextile the 9th house, trine Uranus in the 11th house in Pisces. Mars is Quincunx the ascendant, trine Pluto in the 4th house. You see that Mars is in its own sign Scorpio which is also ruled by Pluto, and Mars has good contact with Pluto. But as we see, Mars is not good to the ascendant. That doesn't stop the person from functioning, and enjoying their life. It shows what type of person they are.

In the first house, we have Chiron in Aries conjunct Fortune also in the first, and in Aries. Chiron is conjunct the ascendant, and is exactly square Mercury in the 10th house in Capricorn. Chiron is also square the sun in the 10th house in Capricorn. Chiron is exactly square Pluto in the 4th house in Cancer. Chiron is semi-sextile Uranus in the 11th house in Pisces. Chiron is trine Neptune in the 5th house in Leo. Chiron is opposed to Saturn in the 7th house in Libra. Chiron is also opposing the Node in the 7th house in Libra.

Fortune in the first house should be ruling the 5th house in my test. Fortune is square Pluto in the 4th house; it is trine Neptune in the 5th; exactly opposing the node, opposing Saturn and Jupiter all in the 7th house. Fortune is semi-square Lilith in the 11th house in Aquarius. Fortune is square the Mid, the sun, the moon, and Mercury, all in the Capricorn.

Pluto is in the fourth house in Cancer. Pluto is co-ruler of the 8th house. It is square the ascendant. Squaring Node, Jupiter and Saturn in the 7th house, trine Mars in the 8th house. Pluto is opposing sun, moon, and Mercury, all in the 10th house.

I never like to see Neptune in the 5th house. If it is well aspected, the individual can be very creative to do with dancing, singing, and music. Being the ruler of the 12th house natural, it has a connection with 12/5, something that is secret, or to do with children.

Neptune is conjuncting the 5th house, sextile the node and Jupiter in the 7th, quincunx the moon in the 10th.

In the 7th house we see the node, Jupiter and Saturn there in the sign of Libra. Saturn is exalted in Libra, and Jupiter works well in Libra. Saturn is square the Mid, the sun and Mercury. The node is square the moon, and the sun, and Mercury. Jupiter is square the moon. Notice that Saturn is exactly trine the 11th, exactly quincunx the 12th. Saturn is conjunct the 7th, quincunx Uranus in the 11th.

Up in the 9th house we see that Venus is there in the sign of Sagittarius. With Venus in this position, you could say that the person is interested in travel and foreign countries, they are also interested in high education or some sort of philosophy. Sagittarius is at its own place here. Well, in fact, as we see, the chart has the first sign Aries as the starter.

Venus is conjunct the Mid, sextile Lilith in the 11th in Aquarius. Venus is square the ascendant, quintile the node in the 7th house, sextile Mars in the 8th. Venus is ruler of the 2nd and 7th house.

In the 10th house we see the sun in Capricorn – this is her sun sign. The sun is in this angular house because she was born around Midday. It holds a strong position, and is good for the career. The moon too, is in this same house in the same sign, so is Mercury. We have a strong Capricorn here. The sun is conjunct Mercury which is good for the intellect, and writing or teaching. The sun is exactly semi-sextile the 11th house. It is exactly sextile the 12th. Sextile Uranus, square the ascendant. Opposing Pluto in the 4th house.

The moon in the 10th house is good for publicity, help through people in high office and from women. The three planets in Capricorn in the 10th house is good for the career, depending on the aspects they make.

In the 11th house we see Lilith in Aquarius conjunct Uranus in the 11th and in Pisces. Uranus is conjunct the 12th, semi-sextile the 11th, sextile the Mid, trine Pluto.

I do hope you get a lot from reading different charts. And as you can see, I do try to give as much information as I can. It is also up to you, if you are good at it, to sort out certain things that I might have missed.

Let us now have a look at *Joe Biden*'s progress chart, and see what we think.

He was born 20 November 1942 at 08:30 am, Scranton, Pennsylvania. U.S.A. Remember, it is the progress chart we are about to look at. Progress details for 2020: 6th February 1943 at 08:30 am Scranton, Pennsylvania, U.S.A.

22.32 Aquarius	Sun	16.51 Aquarius
11.05 Aries	Moon	08.12 Pisces
15.04 Taurus	Mercury	24.58 Capricorn st
09.17 Gemini	Venus	06.25 Pisces
00.05 Cancer	Mars	07.48 Capricorn
22.10 Cancer	Jupiter	16.57 Cancer R
22.32 Leo	Saturn	05.35 Gemini st
11.05 Libra	Uranus	00.34 Gemini R
15.04 Scorpio	Neptune	01.45 Libra R
09.17 Sagittarius	Pluto	05.51 Leo R
00.05 Capricorn	Chiron	26.56 Leo
22.10 Capricorn	N Node	25.34 Leo
	Lilith	18.09 Cancer
	Fortune	13.53 Pisces

Having a quick look at President Trumps's progressive chart, we have already seen that he has Saturn in the 10th and conjuncting the 10th; semi-sextile the sun in the 10th; and the sun itself is semi-sextile the Mid; and is ruler of the Mid. WE have Venus in the 12th exactly conjunct Chiron also in the 12th. Venus is ruler of the ascendant and the 12th and the 8th. Chiron we give as ruling Sagittarius in the 3rd house. Juno is exactly conjunct the ascendant while it is in the 1st in Libra, and making a trine to the 9th. Mars in the 12th is sextile Pluto in the 10th, and Mars is sextile too, to Lilith in the 2nd. The moon is in Virgo in the 11th, semi-sextile Pluto in the 10th. The moon is ruling the loop in the 9th house, while Pluto is ruling the 2nd.

Now all this sounds great, and there are more that I didn't go into. For it would be too much work. But Saturn and the sun in the 10th house are powerful positions; and Saturn is just right, in its own house for power. I think we need to look at the transit for 3rd November 2020, and see what's happening. The fourth house, if he's going to move, should be showing us something. Saturn up in the 10th is conjunct the MId, and is ruler of the 4th. so we have 10/4 in operation. I think this is a tough one.

Let's see what the Vice President Joe Biden's chart is showing. In his chart we see he has quite a few planets in exaltation. There is Venus in Pisces which is very good. Mars in Capricorn exalted, also good for energy. Jupiter in Cancer which is very, very good; and Pluto in Leo exalted for political energy.

We see that 9 degrees is at the axis 10/4. The 9 we know has to do with something ending or starting. Inside the third house we see Uranus holding 0 degree – Uranus is ruling the ascendant. In that same third house we see Saturn holding 5 degrees – Saturn is also ruler of the ascendant, the 11th, and 12th houses. We see Pluto also in the 6th house holding 5 degrees, and is ruler of the 9th house. Chiron and the Node are in conjunction in the 7th house. Chiron would be the 10th, and the node 5th and 6th houses.

This is a real fight between the two men, and it has given me a headache.

There's a loop in the first house with the moon, Venus and Fortune all in the sign of Pisces. The moon at the moment is square to the Mid, but in November it will be in 17 degrees of Pisces thereabouts. And it will be trine to Jupiter in the 5th house, bringing the 5th and 6th houses into play, and also the loop in the first house, the 10th house will come into play as well.

The sun in the 12th house is square to the third. The sun being ruler of the 7th. The sun is Quincunx Jupiter

Venus in the loop, is squaring Saturn in the third house. Venus ruling 3rd and 8th, Saturn ruling 1st, 11th and 12th.

Transit Jupiter in November is conjunct the 12th, semi-sextile the ascendant. Transit Mercury is in the 8th house square Mercury in the 12th, sextile the node in the 7th, and Chiron also in the 7th. Transit moon falls in the 4th house, square to Fortune in the loop in the 1st. It is sextile the 2nd. Transit Saturn falls in the 12th, quincunx the node and Chiron in the 7th. Transit Uranus falls in the 2nd house, semi-sextile the 4th, trine Mars in the 11th, quincunx the Mid. Transit Neptune falls in the loop in the 1st house conjunct the transit moon, trine Lilith in the 5th. Transit Pluto falls in the 12th house exactly conjunct the 12th. Pluto is ruling the 9th house. It is exactly semi-sextile the ascendant. Transit node falls in the 4th house, trine the ascendant, quincunx the 12th. Transit Lilith falls in the 2nd quincunx Neptune in the 7th. Transit Chiron falls in the 1st house semi-sextile Venus in the loop in the 1st, exactly sextile Saturn in the third.

A good aspect that I see is Jupiter exalted in Cancer in the 5th trine the 9th. Notice that Jupiter is in the 5th but in the sign of the 6th. The node and Chiron conjunct in Leo in the 7th. Chiron has rule over the 10th, the node over the 5th and 6th houses.

In President Trump's chart I see Juno is exactly conjunct the ascendant (progress chart), exactly sextile the 3rd. Pallas is in the 3rd conjunct the 3rd. So we could see plainly that something to do with the 3rd house is happening in both charts.

President Trump has 5 degrees at the 11/5 axis: Vice President Biden has 0 degree. Fortune is in President Trump first house, while it is also in the first house of Vice-President Biden' chart, in the loop of Pisces.

Jupiter is conjuncting the ascendant from the 12th house in President Trumps's chart – this is also a powerful position.

The trine of the moon in November to Biden's Jupiter is a very good aspect; and Jupiter is ruling the 10th house in the progress chart.

The battle is really between the sun ruling the 10th house in President Trump's chart, with Saturn up there, the sun as well; both are semi-sextile to each other, and to the Mid – and to Vice President Biden's chart with Jupiter ruling the 10th house. Biden has a good aspect in November with the moon trine Jupiter, but I see he has the sun quincunx Jupiter.

I let you professional ones get on with it, and sort that out. There is lots more information in the natal charts still to be checked.

In the mythological stories, Jupiter was more powerful than Saturn. The progress chart of Trump is powerful with the sun up there, and then that Powerful Saturn too, in Leo. Awesome in power.

Biden has Jupiter exalted in Cancer and is ruler of the 10th, I don't know what's going to happen there...

40: When People Are Put Off Astrology

I personally know that astrology is true. Many people are asking for proof which is a hard thing to ask for. The fact that the solar system is functioning within us, is one of the things that can't be explained at the moment. Maybe, later generations will understand. We don't know how long it will last, but as long as it last, we have to live with it. A good astrologer never tells everything that he sees in the chart. It is not good to be telling things that the individual doesn't want to hear, and even if they do, it is not a good thing to tell. It plays on the mind. But the astrologer is good at what he do. And he must be good, because if he makes a prediction, and it does not come about, it is not good for himself and astrology.

We do tend to ignore things that are true, and there is call for proof. But there are some things that cannot be explained to certain human beings. Not everything is there to be explained to us. I read about physics, I know nothing about it, only from what I read about other human beings who are good in it. I do not go asking for proof – that would be utterly stupid of me. I know nothing of it, haven't studied it, so how can I go and asked for proof?

There are some charts, I mean natal charts, that are stamped with some negative energies. Anyone who has studied astrology would now as soon as they see that stamp, what it entails. Example: Sun opposing Neptune. To me, this is a stamp of some scandal that will come about in the individual's life. This gives us a 12/5 contact. For even if the person has a secret love affair, it is still a scandal. Another example: The sun square Saturn. This is something that is telling us that the individual has come through hard times, and possibly from poor family.

Let us look at this chart of *Babara Hutton*, a millionaire, has to do with the Woolworth fortune. At the end of her life she was worth about 100 million. She had 7 marriages.

Born 14 November 1912, at 14.25 pm, New York City, NY, U.S.A.

01.20 Aries	Sun	22.04 Scorpio
12.29 Taurus	Moon	28.50 Capricorn
09.11 Gemini	Mercury	13.36 Sagittarius
00.42 Cancer	Venus	25.50 Sagittarius
22.20 Cancer	Mars	19.03 Scorpio
19.28 Leo	Jupiter	18.57 Sagittarius
01.20 Libra	Saturn	01.18 Gemini R
12.29 Scorpio	Uranus	00.04 Aquarius
09.11 Sagittarius	Neptune	25.56 Cancer R
00.42 Capricorn	Pluto	29.42 Gemini R
22.20 Capricorn	Chiron	06.25 Pisces
19.28 Aquarius	N Node	10.13 Aries
	Fortune	08.06 Gemini

She only had the one child.

Her ascendant is Aries early in the sign. The ruler is Mars in the 8th house in Scorpio, its own sign. The 8th house is known as the goods of the dead, other people's possessions, legacies, inheritances, and things that are deep and hidden from us. The node is in the first house in Aries, and is ruling the 4th and 5th house. Land and estates, speculations and entertainment. Mars in the 8th is conjunct the sun, the ruler of the 6th. Work, health, sickness, servants Her sun sign then is Scorpio, and is in the 8th house. So we have a strong 8th house in operation. Mars is square Neptune in the 5th house, ruler of the loop in the 12th. Mars is semi-sextile Jupiter in the 9th, ruler of the 9th and the loop in the 12th. Mars is square Lilith in the 11th house in the sign of Aquarius.

The moon sign is Capricorn in the 11th conjunct 11th, semi-sextile Venus in the 9th in Sagittarius. The moon is conjunct Uranus in the 11th house, in Aquarius, its own sign. The moon is sextile the ascendant. There is a quintile aspect between the moon and the node in the first house. A trine aspect between the moon and Saturn in the 2nd house in Gemini. Notice that there is a connection here of 2/11, this brings money in. Between the moon and Pluto, we get a quincunx aspect. Pluto is ruling the 8th house. Even with this aspect we have both planets, one in 11th, and the other in 2, can still bring money in with slight problems.

Moving to the second house, Venus is the ruler, and the sign there is Taurus (the money sign). What about the Arab part – Fortune? Well we could speculate that the person will get money. Fortune is in Gemini, and conjunct the third house. Saturn and Pluto is also in the second house in Gemini. Fortune is conjunct Saturn, and Saturn is ruler of the 10th, 11th and 12 houses. The ruler of the and house, Venus is in the 9th house. Money comes through some sort of institution, or in connection with foreign people or countries, also from trading.

The ruler of the third is Mercury, and Mercury is in the 9th house. Here, we find something to do with travelling. The individual is very intellectual, and contact with foreigners.

Taking the sign Cancer at the fourth house, we know that the ruler is the moon. We find the moon in the 11th house in the sign of Capricorn, So we have a 4/11 contact. Should the two planets, moon and Saturn be in good contact, then the individual's hopes and wishes should be positive, and with many friends, clubs and groups. The same goes for the contact 5th house and 11th, This would work out fine with entertainment, speculative, romance, friends and groups.

At the sixth house is the sign Leo. The sun is the ruler of the 6th house, and is in the 8th, conjunct with Mars, the ruler of the first and the 8th. Mars is in its own sign. There's a lot going on here with other people's money, legacy, inheritance, and all deep dark things that cannot be revealed to ordinary people.

The sun conjunct Mars gives a lot of energy, but it is negative. The sun with the moon or Venus is more easier. Remember, Mars is ruling the ascendant. The 6th house not only represents servants, pets, work, health, sickness, colleagues, but it also represents the body and possessions of the children. Turning the wheel, you find that the 8th house is the end of life, or the home for the children. The combination of 6/8 gives you much more information.

I went pass Neptune in the 5th house. It is making a trine contact with the ascendant about 113 degrees. Neptune is square to Venus in the 9th house. Venus is ruler of the 2nd and 7th houses. Neptune is co-ruler of the loop in the 12th. We know that she only had the one child. Neptune is opposing the moon in the 11th house. Neptune is also opposing Uranus in the 11th house, and Uranus is co-ruler of the 12th along with Saturn. Saturn is in the 2nd house. Neptune is conjunct the 5th house.

When I first started researching astrology, my pet name for Neptune was "*strange*." In this chart you see that there's something strange going on with speculating.

Inside the 6th house there is the loop with the sign of Virgo there. Virgo is ruled by Mercury, and Mercury is in the 9th house. There are lot of talk about these loops. Some say they have to do with the past, while I theorize that they have to do with "*something extra*." Should they have to do with the past, that would be really interesting. We need something solid to go on.

Her 7th house has the sign of Libra there. Libra is ruled by Venus, and Venus is in the 9th house conjunct Jupiter, both in Sagittarius. Venus in mythology is the daughter of Jupiter by Dione.

Venus is square to the ascendant.

Venus is quincunx Neptune in the 5th.

Venus is conjunct the Mid.

Venus is opposing Pluto in the 2nd house. .

The connection of 7 and 9 shows that she has contact with people from the 9th house.

From my research I find that people with this contact often marry someone from another country.

At the 8th house is the sign of Scorpio. I have already mention Mars ruling both the ascendant and the 8th house.

The sun is there in Scorpio as her sun sign. It must be said here that you can see in the chart where the sun is – what sign it is in – what house it is in; and the aspects it is making to the rest the chart.

Notice that Pluto is in the 2nd house, and is co-ruler of the 8th; and don't miss that it is holding 29 degrees. There's something to cry about, and at the same time, powerful.

We find ourselves at the 9th house. Sagittarius is the sign there; it is ruled by Jupiter, and Jupiter is in its own house – the 9th.

Many things can happen in this house. This is the house of high education, and foreign countries.

People with this contact can be religious, philosophical, in contact with foreign peoples, interested in freedom and justice.

Jupiter is in conjunction with Venus – a very powerful combination; it is also in conjunction with Mercury. So we have three planets in the 9th house. Mercury, Venus and Jupiter. With Mercury, the mind is very active, and there is interest in travel and higher education. People with Venus in the 9th house do like to travel a lot. Interest in music, and art

The sign of Capricorn is on the 10th house, the ruler is Saturn in the 2nd house in conjunction with Fortune. Saturn is exactly sextile the ascendant. Inside the 11th house, is the moon which I have already told you about. There in the 11th we see Uranus holding 0 degree. Saturn and Uranus are rulers of the 12th house. Uranus is sextile the ascendant, and square Saturn. INside the 11th we see Lilith in Aquarius conjuncting the 12th. At the 11th house is also the sign of Capricorn, At the 12th house is the sign of Aquarius. There is a loop in the 12th with Pisces as the sign in it. Pisces is ruled by Jupiter and Neptune.

Remember, a professional astrologer will give you more details than I do. I run through the chart very quickly You can get to see certain things in a natal chart, but be very careful. The progress chart is packed with more information of the years passed, and those to come.

Should you be a young person and you have the time on hand, I would advise you to start from the very beginning, if you take an interest in astrology. This means that you will have to know a bit about astronomy, and of course those horrible maths, and all those questions that will pop up into your head wanting to know what makes astrology work. The answer is right there, but for some unknown reason, you still don't understand.

The astrologer would tell you that you are going to fall in love next year. You can bet your life that it will be so. If the time is not accurate, it could be earlier, or later. But with an accurate time, the astrologer knows what he is saying. One of the things I am always thinking about are the progressions. I am sitting there staring at me own chart, at a certain year, You see all the energies there, and you know before hand, how they are going to work out, positively or negatively.

Before the year 2018 came along, I had already seen in my chart three planets opposing two. One was the sun opposing Uranus. Well, we all know what Uranus is like. Suddenly, unusual, and disruptive. These things actually happen because I had to move out of my house suddenly because they were coming to fix it up. There were no heating in the house, and now it has heating, and a nice new kitchen. They did it up very well. All my stuff are still in boxes – all my books on astrology and philosophy and history.

I am at the moment going through what I call a burn up. That is my sun and Mercury are very close to each other. It is good, and at the same time dangerous, if it is not controlled, and that is exactly what I'm now trying to do. But it is strange. My memory is sharp, and I am seeing things that has happened long time ago. The other opposition is yet to come. The sun opposing Saturn. It is amazing, for I have already gotten a taste of what the energies are, and acting accordingly. We must not forget, we are not living on the earth all by ourself. Other people are involved, and that's what makes astrology so mysterious.

People turn away from astrology if they get the wrong information. Then they say it is not true because it failed to convince us. It is very hard to try to make people to understand that the energies of the solar system are there inside of them, and is working. We cannot tear you apart to try and get to the energies. They are absolutely there within every individual and everything.

41: Western Astrology

The other systems from other cultures, I have tested, but the Western system goes deep, with lots more information, leading to the progressive state of the individual. Many people are confused because they have only read the sun signs in the papers, and do not know that 'real astrology' is really a complicated system. Should you get to master it, and understand how it works within the human being, then you have done well.

We shall look at the chart of *Oprah Winfrey* born 29th January 1954, at 19:51 pm, Mississippi, Mississippi, U.S.A.

10.28 Virgo	Sun	09.38 Aquarius
06.57 Libra	Moon	12.32 Sagittarius
07.02 Scorpio	Mercury	20.16 Aquarius
09.09 Sagittarius	Venus	09.39 Aquarius
11.16 Capricorn	Mars	23.56 Scorpio.
11.58 Aquarius	Jupiter	16.37 Gemini R
10.28 Pisces	Saturn	09.03 Scorpio
06.57 Aries	Uranus	20.17 Cancer R
07.02 Taurus	Neptune	26.03 Libra R
09.09 Gemini	Pluto	24.08 Leo R
11.16 Cancer	Chiron	23.38 Capricorn
11.58 Leo	N Node	23.12 Capricorn
	Lilith	14.48 Libra
	Fortune	07.34 Scorpio

Taking a quick look around the chart, we see a few important things. We see that Fortune is in the third house, and it is making contact with the second. I am now beginning to pick up some information on Fortune, but still a long way to go. THis information tells us that the individual will be fortunate when it comes to money. Jupiter in the 10th house shows the possibility of holding a top job in the career. Then we see that Saturn is in the third house, and holding 9 degrees, is ruler of the 5th, and squaring both the sun and Venus in that house. We know that when Venus is in the 5th house, people love children no matter what. I think that the node exactly conjunct Chiron in the 5th house has to do with entertainment, groups of people and friends, some that are unusual. And because of Gemini at the 10th house, this has to do with communications. Okay let's start at the ascendant.

The 6th sign of the zodiac, Virgo is on the ascendant. What does that mean? The individual is critical, analytical, searching for small details to get the story right. Young children who are Virgos see everything that goes on around them, but hardly ever say anything. But they look back on it in later life. It affects them very much.

Mercury is the ruler of the ascendant sign. It is in the 6th house in the sign of Aquarius. This shows that the individual is interested in all the 6th house energies. There could be something universal here about the individual. Dealing with groups of people and friends, and we see too, that Mercury is also ruler of the career. Mercury is with the sun and Venus, these two planets are in the 5th house, and in the same sign as Mercury. Mercury is trine Jupiter in the 10th house, and this is a good aspect because it shows that the person is honest, intentions are very good, thinking clearly, and very serious.

Mercury, unfortunately, is quincunx Uranus in the 11th house, some difficulties through the houses ruled by the planets, and the signs that they are in. Uranus, is ruling the sign that Mercury is in, the 6th house. genius energies can come from this contact, critical, sometimes impulsive.

Mercury has a square to Mars in the 3rd house. Mars is in the sign of Scorpio, and is co-ruler of that sign. The other ruler is Pluto, and we find it in the 12th house in the sign of Leo. I don't have to go into all the details, but if you are good in astrology, you will know what the energies are. And what difficulty they could bring. Mars is also ruler of the 8th house.

Mercury has a good aspect with Neptune in the second house. This is a trine. It also has a good aspect with Lilith, in the second. This too, is a trine. I've got my eyes on Scorpio as the sign Lilith rules, but I am not so sure as yet. Neptune rules the 7th, and Lilith would take the third. Mercury opposes Pluto in the 12th.

WE know that she is a Virgo, and have checked her ruler Mercury for its position and aspects in the chart. Her sun sign is Aquarius. She has sun, Mercury and Venus in Aquarius, and these will show more in her personality than the ascendant.

Aquarius people are friendly, and are interested in groups and clubs. They are shy, but not as shy as the Virgo. They sort of hold back, not getting too attached.

The moon sign we see is in Sagittarius. And I get the feeling that these people are from space, intelligent, likes freedom, education, travel, foreign countries. The moon is responsible for our feelings and emotions. It also has to do with women and the mother.

Libra we see is on the second cusp. The ruler of this house is Venus. Venus is in the 5th house holding 9 degrees, in the sign of Aquarius. It is exactly conjunct with the sun also holding 9 degrees. They both are in conjunction with the 6th house. And are both trine the Mid. Semi-sextile the 7th house, quincunx the ascendant. They are both square Saturn in the third house. I don't know if I have told you this before, but Saturn, in the mythology stories, doesn't want children to live. Rhea his wife had to hide Jupiter, and give Saturn a stone for the child. After looking through many charts, I found that it is so. Many women lost children through the bad position of Saturn in the chart, or they fail to have children.

In this chart, you'll see that Capricorn is on the cusp of the 5th house, and Saturn is the ruler, and is in the third house holding 9 degrees. So the square from the two planets in the fifth to Saturn could cause problems.

Venus the ruler of the second and 9th houses makes a trine to Jupiter in the 10th house in Gemini. It is sextile the moon square Fortune, trine Lilith, and quincunx the ascendant. This Venus, I've been checking, when it is negative to the ascendant, the individual can be very beautiful. Hedy Lamaar has Venus negative to the ascendant, and she's very beautiful.

Inside the second house we see the planet Neptune, and there is Lilith there as well. Neptune has a square to Uranus in the 11th, and Lilith has also a square to the same planet. Neptune is sextile the outer planet Pluto in the 12th house. These planets stay long in their signs and house, and hold their aspect for a very long time. Both are retrograde. Neptune is semi-square the moon in the 4th house. Lilith is sextile to it. Neptune is square the node and Chiron in the fifth house.

At the third house, the sign of Scorpio is there. Mars and Pluto are the rulers. Mars is in the third in Scorpio, and Pluto is in the 12th in Leo. Saturn and Fortune are in this third house, and in conjunction. Fortune is in this third house, and is exactly conjunct the third, with a semi-sextile to the second. So we could definitely say that she would be well-off, not short of a bob or two, and interested in travel and talking, writing, and communicating.

Sagittarius is at the cusp of the fourth house. Jupiter is the ruler, and it is in the 10th house in the sign of Gemini conjunct the Mid. It is square the ascendant. Don't forget that we are dealing with two angular positions, so the square won't be that bad. The moon is in the fourth house in the sign of Sagittarius, square to the ascendant, sextile Lilith, semi-sextile Saturn, sextile sun and Venus in the 5th.

Capricorn takes the cusp at the 5th house. The ruler is Saturn. Saturn is in the third house in the sign of Scorpio, conjunct the third house, conjunct Fortune, sextile the ascendant. Inside the 5th house we have the node and Chiron exactly in conjunction in the sign of Capricorn. The sun and Venus is exactly conjunct in the sign of Aquarius.

Aquarius takes control of the 6th house carrying three planets – sun and Venus in the 5th – the ascendant ruler, Mercury in the 6th. Saturn and Uranus are rulers of Aquarius. Saturn is in the third, Uranus in the 11th

The sign Pisces is at the door of the 7th house. The two planets ruling are: Jupiter and Neptune. Jupiter is in the 10th, and Neptune is in the second.

Aries is at the 8th house with Mars as ruler, and is in the third house.

Taurus we see at the 9th cusp, with Venus as its ruler in the 5th house.

The 10th house has Gemini there. The ruler is Mercury, and is in the 6th house. It is also the ruler of the ascendant. . The biggest planet in our solar system Jupiter, is in this 10th house.

The 11th cusp has the sign of Cancer there. The moon is the ruler of this sign. The moon is in the 4th house. Uranus is in the 11th house.

The last house of the chart has the sign of Leo, and its ruler is the sun in the 5th house. Inside this 12th house you see the planet Pluto which is a slow moving planet.

I have quickly run through this chart, and I do hope you have picked up some info. When you shall settle down and do your own chart or of your family and friends, more information will come to you, especially if you take your time, and understand what it is all about. Reading the chart is very important, and in doing so, you must bear in mind that you are dealing with energies that comes from the solar system, and believe it or not, some scientists doesn't know how that is possible. Take your time, read the chart carefully. If you can, get to know some things about the individual, like how they were brought up, and what education they have. This will help you along. Later, when you become really good, you can set up a business in astrology. With astrology, you cannot lose, because you are dealing with the solar system, and with human beings.

42: Digging A Bit Deeper …

This astrology stuff came to be my hobby. It actually kept me out of trouble, and got me thinking. I was asking myself many questions, and not really getting the answers. But I kept on with my research. Then I found out that it was going to be hard getting answers from this astrology business. As I told you before, I avoided some of the maths, and only got to the ones that are important.

Prince Philip, the Queen of England's husband, was very old. Let's have a quick look and see what happened in his chart. He was born 10th June 1921 at 21:46 pm, Corfu, Greece.

13.17 Capricorn	Sun	19.20 Gemini
25.05 Aquarius	Moon	22.15 Leo
05.58 Aries	Mercury.	13.31 Cancer
07, 09 Taurus	Venus	05.43 Taurus
00.59 Gemini	Mars	24.35 Gemini
21.41 Gemini	Jupiter	10.47 Virgo
13.17 Cancer	Saturn	18.20 Virgo.
25.05 Leo	Uranus	09.38 Pisces
05.58 Libra	Neptune	11.36 Leo
07.09 Scorpio	Pluto	07.55 Cancer
00, 59 Sagittarius	Chiron	13.24 Aries
21.41 Sagittarius	N Node	24.29 Libra
	Lilith	06.49 Aquarius
	Fortune	16.12 Pisces

A quick look, and we see that the ascendant is Capricorn. The ruler is in a loop in the 8th house conjunct with Jupiter there, both in the sign of Virgo. We've got some information here. Why is the ascendant ruler in a loop? And why in the 8th house, and in the sign of Virgo?

We know that Capricorn is the sign in the fixed wheel at the 10th house. This is the career, and the outside world, the parents, the boss. Capricorns like to be in a good position in their lives. Of course, not every Capricorn would get the chance of being right up there in a top job, but they are thinking about it. The 8th house has to do with other people's possessions, inheritance, legacy and so forth. This house has to do with things that are hidden, and not known to everyone. It is political, underground, doctors and surgeons. The 8th house is ruled by Mars and Pluto. It is the house of the dead, transformation, renewal.

Virgo, as far as I can see, has to do with service, servants, health, pets, colleagues and work. So having Saturn in that sign could give the possibility of the individual having servants, and be in some way serving others. The whole of the 6th house should come into force. Saturn, being joined with Jupiter in that

8th house could show some power here, maybe to do with religion and other peoples's possessions. Something political here, too.

Both Saturn and Jupiter are trine to the ascendant, and this could be one reason why he made it to old age. But there are quite a lot more to why we live to old age. Astrology shows the energies that can take you there, if you take good care of yourself.

Lilith is in the first house in the sign of Aquarius. In the loop in the second house, we see the planet Uranus along with Fortune in the sign of Pisces. At least, so far, Fortune is giving us some good information. Again, being in the second house, we can say that the individual has the chance to be rich. And I haven't even check the aspects.

We shall move on very quickly so that we can see more charts.

Venus is in the third house close to the fourth. This sometimes is good for comfort in the home.

The sun is in the 5th, Mars in the 6th, Mercury and Pluto in the 6th in the sign of Cancer. Note this properly, because Cancer is the sign of the home and the country. There's always some connection here. The moon and Neptune is in the 7th house. Jupiter and Saturn are in the 8th house in the sign of Virgo.

There are quite a lot of aspects in this chart. I think it is right to say that this prince had been brought up well, so he can handle some of the negative in his chart. In his chart, we see that the sun is square Jupiter. In an undisciplined individual chart, this is someone who cannot deal properly with money. They squander it. Another aspect we find in the Prince chart is the sun square Saturn. But we must remember, both Jupiter and Saturn are trine to the ascendant. There are over 51 aspects in the chart – positives and negatives. A very interesting chart.

Another chart to look at is: *Evan Rachel Wood* born 7th September 1987 at 13:24 pm, Raleigh, North Carolina, U.S.A. Married 2012 to Jamie Bell, divorced 2014. The progs for the marriage is 2nd October 1987. For the divorce it is 4th October 1987.

I saw Fortune in the 6th house exactly conjuncting the 7th. Fortune is ruler of the 9th. So I said to myself, her husband should be someone from the 9th house, and sure enough, when I checked, Jamie Bell, her first husband is from the UK.

04.30 Sagittarius	Sun	14.33 Virgo
06.01 Capricorn	Moon	14.05 Pisces
11.51 Aquarius	Mercury	00.14 Libra
17.37 Pisces	Venus	18.46 Virgo
18.18 Aries	Mars	10.07 Virgo
13.13 Taurus	Jupiter	29.08 Aries R
04.30 Gemini	Saturn	14.50 Sagittarius
06.01 Cancer	Uranus	22.44 Sagittarius

11.51 Leo	Neptune	05.15 Capricorn R
17.37 Virgo	Pluto	07.52 Scorpio
18.18 Libra	Chiron	28.15 Gemini
13.13 Scorpio	N Node	03.16 Aries
	Fortune	04.02 Gemini
	Lilith	02.16 Leo

She is an actress, model and musician. Talking about a model, well…

Venus has a high position conjuncting the Mid. And don't forget the Mid has to do with the career. So there is something beautiful going on, music, art or even singing, decorating. Venus is the planet of beauty.

Right, let's go to the ascendant. Sagittarius is rising, and Jupiter is the planet ruling. Jupiter is in the fifth house in Aries. Notice, Jupiter is crying.

Saturn and Uranus are both conjunct and in Sagittarius. These two planets can make one into a genius if the energies are used properly. Saturn is semi-sextile the 12th, and both Saturn and Uranus are square to the Mid. I do hope by now that you have a hold on this square aspect coming from angles. They can still cause problems, but not as bad as when they're not in angles. Saturn is exactly square the sun in the 9th house in Virgo. Saturn is square Venus, so does Uranus. Saturn is square Mars. Saturn is exactly square the moon in the third house in Pisces. Notice that the moon is conjunct the fourth. Neptune is in the first house in Capricorn, and is in conjunction with the second house. Neptune in the first, – *My God!* – quite a lot of things can happen with this position. It can lead to music, art, dancing, singing, and it can get you drunk and hooked on drink. Best to keep away from drugs. Neptune is square Mercury in the 10th house. Again, you have two planets in angular positions. Neptune is sextile Pluto, and this is a long term aspect. But you can use the houses and the signs. Neptune is square the node in the fourth house, but in the fifth house sign of Aries.

Neptune is trine Jupiter in the 5th house In Aries. Normally, Jupiter is good for teaching children, and good for creativity and entertainment. Neptune is quincunx Fortune, and is also opposing Chiron.

Chiron, you see, is in the 7th house in Gemini. We give Chiron as ruler of Sagittarius until something better comes along.

Lilith is in the 9th house. I still do not know for sure what sign Lilith rules. At the very beginning, I started out with Sagittarius. Then after hearing what Lilith was like, I picked Scorpio. Now I have just read an astrological book, and it said that Aries ids the sign for Lilith – strange, don't you thinK/ I have to start doing some serious check.

Her sun sign is Virgo, and it is with Venus and Mars – all three conjuncting the Mid. So this is a treble, and will come out to the fore, followed by the two planets in the ascendant. Saturn is the nearer to the ascendant, so life could have started out early for her. With heavy responsibilities, probably for the family. Then we have Uranus in the ascendant. It is not easy to overpower someone with Uranus in the first house. There's something that they want to do, and nothing will stop them from doing it.

You notice too, that Venus is exactly semi-sextile the 11th. Mercury has just entered Libra, this is a nice position to have Mercury. In Libra, Mercury can talk its head off. People are friendly, and likes togetherness, very sociable. Pluto is in the 11th house. One of my pet names for Pluto was: the dark planet, not meaning anything bad. It is the underground planet where there is no light, you have to feel yourself around to get where you want to. Pluto is in its own sign of Scorpio, and the energies that come from this to help the individual to achieve great things. Pluto here has some good aspects from the sun, mars and Neptune. Hopes and wishes can definitely come to the fore. We must not forget that Pluto is ruling the 8th house in the fixed wheel.

Our next chart is of *Walter Koch* born 18th September 1895 at 06:25 am Esslingen, Germany.

In astrology, he is responsible for the Koch house system.

29.07 Virgo	Sun	25.02 Virgo
22.24 Libra	Moon	15.52 Virgo
22.25 Scorpio	Mercury	17.35 Libra
27.38 Sagittarius	Venus	26.42 Virgo R
03.03 Aquarius	Mars	02.36 Libra
03.26 Pisces	Jupiter	02.27 Leo
28.07 Pisces	Saturn	04.49 Scorpio
22.24 Aries	Uranus	17.07 Scorpio
22.25 Taurus	Neptune	18.03 Gemini
27.38 Gemini	Pluto	12.45 Gemini R
03.03 Leo	Chiron	12.09 Libra
03.26 Virgo	N Node	12.04 Pisces
	Lilith	09.57 Pisces
	Fortune	18.57 Virgo

We see that Virgo is rising. By now you should know what the Virgo is like. The ruler is Mercury, and we find it in the first house but in the second house sign of Libra. with Mars and Chiron. Mercury is conjuncting the second house. It is exactly semi-sextile Uranus in the third house in the sign of Scorpio. Uranus is ruler of the 5th house. Mercury is also ruler of the 10th. His sun sign is also Virgo. The sun is in the 12th house along with the moon, Venus and Fortune.

Saturn and Uranus are both in the sign of Scorpio in the third house. These two planets are known to make people to become very intellectual. And we see also that Jupiter is in the 10th house in Leo. Here, he has the chance to hold a top job in his career. And then we see the two planets that were around in the 1800s that brought about lots of inventions. They are Neptune and Pluto in the 9th house in the sign of Gemini. Venus is square the Mid, semi-sextile the ascendant. Hitler had Neptune and Pluto in Gemini in the 8th house. In this chart we see that the node is in the 6th house conjunct Lilith in the sign of Pisces.

There are many things that the individual will do that we won't be able to predict. He has a hereditary line through his mother, and also one through his father. This goes back into the past. We don't know how he has been brought up. But what we do know, is what we are seeing in the chart. The energies that has been allotted to him. And in our Western astrology, we can see by the moon's position, what sort of soul he has.

We can ask questions about astrology. Is it a science? Yes, it is because it deals with human beings. And as I have already said, I see clearly the signs of the zodiac in the faces of human beings. Some human beings show their signs better than some. I would not bet with anyone that I could see the signs in a certain face. But believe me, I do see these things. Can astrology tell us about the science of the stars? We depend upon astronomy for the positions of the planetary bodies. Astrology is not interested to be telling you about the makeup of the solar system – that is done by astronomy. Can astrology tell about your love life. Yes, it can. According to the planets in your chart, where they are, the aspects that they are making with the rest of the chart, a lot of information can be told to you, about yourself, your money, your thinking, your home, your creativity and romance, your work and health, your partnerships and the public, dealing with other people's money, inheritance and legacy, education, religion, philosophy, foreign countries, your career, your boss, your parents, your friends and groups, and your enemies, and isolation and meditation. These are facts and not made up by astrologers to fool anyone. You are the one who has the key, and with this, you can use free-will. You have the choice to pick and to chose. Just like when you see someone, and you like them. It is you who have to decide in the end. But you must also know that the astrologer can tell you things that will definitely come to pass from the future. He looks in the chart for years ahead from your birth, and it is amazing! But he sees the energies there for a certain year. It might be the year when you get divorce, or meet a new partner. It could also be the year when you move to another country. Or when you find yourself with more money. Believe me, astrology is not a fool's game. It is true.

43: More Charts ...

In this chart of *Angela Merkel,* former Chancellor of Germany, you will see clearly that she is a Cancer, having the sun in Cancer, Mercury in Cancer, Jupiter in Cancer, Uranus in cancer, and Fortune in Cancer; all in the 7th house.

She was born on 17th July 1954 at 18:00 pm, Hamburg, Germany. I don't know if I have given this chart before, so you will have to excuse me.

16.30 Sagittarius	Sun	24.33 Cancer
27.24 Capricorn	Moon	15.27 Aquarius
16.29 Pisces	Mercury	09.17 Cancer
21.38 Aries	Venus	04.59 Virgo
14.42 Taurus	Mars	26.34 Sagittarius R
01.46 Gemini	Jupiter	12.12 Cancer
16.30 Gemini	Saturn	02.44 Scorpio.
27.24 Cancer	Uranus	23.26 Cancer
16.29 Virgo	Neptune	23.19 Libra
21.38 Libra	Pluto	23.42 Leo
14.42 Scorpio	Chiron	25.55 Capricorn.
01.46 Sagittarius	N Node	14.16 Capricorn
	Fortune	07.23 Cancer
	Lilith	03.42 Scorpio

She has Sagittarius rising, and Mars is there in the first house. The ruler of Sagittarius is Jupiter. Jupiter is in the 7th house exalted in the sign of Cancer. The seventh house is partnerships and the public. Jupiter is also ruler of the 12th house, co-ruler of the third. Jupiter is in a stellium group with the sun, Mercury, Uranus and Fortune.

Jupiter is conjunct Mercury and Fortune, opposing the node in the first house, in the second house sign of Capricorn. If I had told her mother that her child would become famous, I would have been right, on the simple fact of the chart having Neptune in the 10th house. I do not know if this is solid, but so far, it has not failed me.

Jupiter is just about making a square to the Mid. Up in the 10th house Is the planet Saturn in Scorpio, and it does give power in the career. But it also can bring you crashing down to the ground, if the power is not used well. Lilith is up there in the 10th house and in the sign of Scorpio. I'm only now beginning to get a grip on Lilith, but it will take time. Does Lilith gives power when she's in the 10th house?

Mars in the first house gives lots of energies. It is semi-sextile the second house, sextile the Mid and Neptune, trine Pluto in the loop in the 8th house. Her moon is also in a loop in the second house in the sign of Aquarius. It is semi-sextile the third house, sextile the ascendant, trine the Mid. Opposing Pluto. Saturn up in the 10th is conjunct with Lilith. It is strange, because someone has given Aries to Lilith, that would bring the fourth house into being. And in the very beginning, I used to work with Sagittarius as belonging to Lilith, then I changed to Scorpio; I just don't know why?: But we will get a clear picture of which sign belongs to Lilith in later researches. Both Saturn and Lilith are sextile to Venus in the 8th house; and both are trine to Fortune in the 7th house. Neptune is sextile Pluto, both planets are slow, but they show the houses and signs that they are in. Pluto is sextile the Mid, trine the ascendant. It is semi-sextile the sun.

This chart shows a sun sign of Cancer. A moon sign of Aquarius, and an ascendant of Sagittarius.

The next chart is that of *Katy Perry* born 25th October 1984 at 07:58 am, Santa Barbara, California, U.S.A. She is a singer-songwriter. Married 2010, divorce 2012, engaged 2019.

10.46 Scorpio	Sun	02.22 Scorpio
09.56 Sagittarius	Moon	17.57 Scorpio
12.18 Capricorn	Mercury	11.59 Scorpio
16.31 Aquarius	Venus	06.32 Sagittarius
19.05 Pisces	Mars	14.24 Capricorn
17.13 Aries	Jupiter	07.28 Capricorn
10.46 Taurus	Saturn	17.05 Scorpio
09.56 Gemini	Uranus	11.25 Sagittarius
12.18 Cancer	Neptune	29.12 Sagittarius
16.31 Leo	Pluto	02.04 Scorpio
19.05 Virgo	Chiron	07.37 Gemini
17.13 Libra	N Node	28.42 Taurus
	Fortune	26.21 Scorpio
	Lilith	05.37 Aries

This chart has Scorpio rising, and its rulers are Mars and Pluto. Mars we find in the 3rd house exalted in the sign of Caprcorn. There'll be much energy flowing. Pluto we find in the 12th house, in its own sign conjuncting the ascendant. There are five planets in the sign of Scorpio plus Fortune. This is a stellium. This is a real Scorpio. The sun is in Scorpio, the moon, Mercury, Saturn, Pluto and Fortune. The nearest planet to the ascendant degrees is Mercury. Mercury rules the 8th and 11th houses. It is square the Mid conjunct the moon and Saturn in the first house. Exactly semi-sextile Uranus in the second house. It is semi-square Neptune in the second house. Sextile Mars in the third house, and Jupiter in the second.

Inside the first house we see that the moon is exactly conjunct with Saturn. The moon has to do with women, the mother, feelings, emotions, and don't forget it rules the fourth house in the natural chart, and is ruler of the 9th in this chart. You do the same with Saturn, and all the rest planets that are about her ascendant. Get the information from these planets, and don't get lost with the interpretation. Sometimes Saturn shows an early start in life when its in the first house. The ancients said that Saturn is the destiny planet. . Fortune in the first house could mean that the person is fortunate through their own effort.

Venus is in the first house, but in the sign of Sagittarius, the 9th sign ruled by Jupiter. Venus is conjunct the second house its own house. This gives us some information that the person would not be out of money, and that there's something beautiful going on here. Remember, Venus is in an angular house, It is also ruler of the 7th and 12th houses. It is conjunct Uranus in the second house also in Sagittarius. Having Venus in a good position, and with good aspects, all the good energies can flow; to do with singing, art, dancing, and being in the public eye. Venus is the planet of love and beauty.

Venus is opposing Chiron, both in angular position. Uranus in the second house can be unusual when it comes to money or the body. Neptune in this house is crying It is ruler of the 5th house. Jupiter is here in the second house in the sign of Capricorn; it is in its fall. Mars in the third house is in conjunction with Jupiter, and Mars is exalted here in Capricorn. Jupiter is getting help. Jupiter is sextile the ascendant. It is semi-sextile Venus, sextile sun and Pluto. Jupiter has many good aspects, so even though it is in its fall in Capricorn, its energies in the second house can still bring in the money. It has a square aspect to Lilith, and a quincunx to Chiron.

We see that Lilith is in the 5th house but in the sign of Aries which is the 6th house sign. Then we have the node in the 7th house. Chiron is also in the 7th house in Gemini, the 8th house sign.

A quick look at *Brad Pitt*'s chart. He was born 18th December 1963 at 06:31 am, Shawnee, Oklahoma, U.S.A.

11.53 Sagittarius.	Sun	25.51 Sagittarius
14.30 Capricorn	Moon	22.49 Capricorn
21.20 Aquarius	Mercury	16.06 Capricorn
26.58 Pisces	Venus.	23.28 Capricorn
26.40 Aries	Mars	10.01 Capricorn
20.47 Taurus	Jupiter	09.50 Aries
11.53 Gemini	Saturn	19.08 Aquarius
14.30 Cancer	Uranius	10.04 Virgo R
21.20 Leo	Neptune	16.48 Scorpio
26.58 Virgo	Pluto	14.13 Virgo
26.40 Libra	Chiron	10.34 Pisces
20.47 Scorpio	N Node.	12.04 Cancer
	Fortune	14.55 Scorpio
	Lilith	29.03 Scorpio

Looking quickly around the chart we see that the biggest planet, Jupiter is in an angular position, in the fourth house. It is in the 5th house sign of Aries. Jupiter is ruler of the ascendant and of the 4th house. The person here, could be like a king, if a man, and like a queen, if a woman. But we are dealing with a male chart.

The ascendant is Sagittarius with the sun there in the first house. The sun is ruler of the 9th house. It is square the Mid, sextile the 11th. Mars is in the first house exalted in the sign of Capricorn which is the second house sign. There is enormous energy here. Even if Mars wasn't exalted, being in the first house is enough. It is conjunct Mercury in the 2nd house also in Capricorn. This is very clever. Mars is semi-sextile the ascendant. Mars is sextile Neptune and Fortune in the 11th house. It is exactly trine Uranus in the 9th house, trine Pluto also in the same house. Mars is exactly sextile Chiron in the thirde house, but square Jupiter in the fourth. Notice that both Mars and Jupiter are in angular positions, so watch out for the interpretation of negativeness. Of course, there is some there, but not as strong as when the planets are out of the angular positions. Mars is opposing the node in the 7th house. Notice that the node is conjunct the 8th house, and is ruler of that same house along with the moon which is in the opposite sign, and in the second house.

There are four planets in Capricorn and this is a stellium. This makes a very strong Capricorn. There are moon, Mercury, Venus and Mars all in Capricorn. And they follow each other in order. Within the 10 degrees, they all conjunct the second house. The house of money and possessions. Venus alone would show that the person could be well-off.

Saturn is in the second house in the third house sign of Aquarius. Saturn is the destiny planet, and Aquarius is the sign that is normally on the 11th house in the fixed wheel. So it is easy to say, that the person is busy with may friends and groups and clubs. Saturn is square Neptune and Fortune in the 11th house. It is square the 12th house. About 142 degrees from the Mid. Remember, there's that 144 degrees aspect.

Uranus and Pluto are two planets which are very powerful. Pluto having rule of the 8th house naturally, but ruling the 12th in this chart. Uranus has rule of the 11th house naturally, and is ruler of the third in this chart. They are both in the 9th house, both sextile to Neptune and Fortune in the 11th house, and sextile the node in the 7th house. Opposing Chiron in the third house, They are trine to Mercury in the 2nd house. Pluto is exactly trine the second house.

We take a look at *Alicia Sacramone*'s chart. She's an Olympain gymnast. Born on 3rd December 1987, at 018:39 pm, Boston, Massachusetts, U.S.A.

16.38 Cancer	Sun	11.16 Sagittarius
05.41 Leo	Moon	25.23 Taurus
27.34 Leo	Mercury	00.39 Sagittarius
25.34 Virgo	Venus	07.20 Capricorn
01.53 Scorpio	Mars	06.26 Scorpio
12.02 Sagittarius	Jupiter	19.59 Aries R
16.38 Capricorn	Saturn	22.10 Sagittarius
05.41 Aquarius	Uranus	25.58 Sagittarius
27.34 Aquarius	Neptune	06.45 Capricorn
25.34 Pisces	Pluto	11.07 Scorpio
01.53 Taurus.	Chiron	26.53 Gemini
12.02 Gemini	N Node	28.39 Pisces
	Fortune	02.30 Aquarius
	Lilith	12.00 Leo

Cancer is rising and the ruler the moon, is in the 11th house. This is the house of friends, clubs and groups. The moon is in the sign Taurus. So she is stubborn, loyal and loving. The moon is opposing Mercury in the 5th house. It is quincunx to Uranus in the 6th. Her sun sign is Sagittarius, and it is in the 5th house. Remember, there are many things happening in this 5th house, and sports is one of them. Also you must know that the 5th house is the house of life. It is ruled by the sun in the fixed wheel. There are four planets in the sign of Sagittarius which is a stellium. The sun, Mercury, Saturn and Uranus. Don't forget too, that Saturn and Uranus has energies to make one into a genius. Sagittarius will take over from Cancer, it will show her personality more, while Cancer is at the back. Funny, enough, when I looked at some pictures of her, I could hardly make out Cancer. And Sagittarius, for me, was hard to pick out. But I did see a bit of ram and Scorpio.

Mars and Pluto is in Scorpio in the 5th house. Having Mars here is good, it gives energy for the sport. Mars is semi-square Saturn, sextile Venus and Neptune. Conjunct Pluto with a trine to Chiron. Venus and Neptune are in the sign of Capricorn in the 6th house. The sun in the 5th house has a trine to Jupiter up there in the 10th house. Jupiter is in Aries, and in this 10th house, can help the person in their career. The ability to come top, or be a leader is there. Jupiter has good aspects like trine to Saturn and Uranus but with a square to the ascendant. The node is in the 10th house in the sign of Pisces. This is also a good position for the node.

44: Tricky Interpretations

Looking at a chart, I saw clearly the 7th house in good aspect with the ruler of the ascendant. Of course, you could easily say that this has to do with partnership, and you'll be correct. It doesn't have to be a personal partnership, most the time it is. If you check the 5th house as well, which is the house of romance, you'll get more information.

You have a chart with Uranus conjuncting the 4th house with a difference of 1 degree, Uranus is ruler of the ascendant. Of course, this has to do with the person of the chart, the home or parents or country, and let"s not forget the roots, the grave. You know that there is something disruptive. How do you know that? Because of the planet Uranus.

Some of us are very hasty. We want things to happen right away. With astrology, that is not going to happen. We have to wait. Everything is in motion in time and space, well, and even matter. Astrology shows you clearly that there is motion taking place. The planets are moving. In your chart, they all have to get up to the 12 pm point. I remember that when I was a soldier, a group of us had to walk 85 kilometres, when we get there, we would get a reference to take us to the next place. Arriving late would be disastrous.

In charts, you can see the planets in different places. Those that are near the 12 pm point will do so in a certain time. By the way, that 12 pm point is the Midheaven (the Mid). So you see too, you can set the chart at its correct time.

Looking at President Trump's natal chart, you'll see that he was not born with Saturn in the 10th house like Hitler was. Trump's Saturn took time to get there, and a good astrologer could tell you when it would enter that house.

It was very tricky trying to determine who will take the Presidency between Trump and Biden. But having read some mythological stories, and learned that Jupiter, the biggest planet in our solar system, is the planet of Justice, law and order; and seeing that Biden had Jupiter exalted in Cancer, and Sagittarius was on the 10th house, I realized that he had a very good chance of winning.

Some charts are really tricky, and hard to interpret, but you must not give up. Sort it out, starting very slowly from the ascendant.

This chart we are now going to look at is of *Jacki Cisneros* born on the 28th September 1970 at 02:52 am, Whittier, California, U.S.A. This woman is Vice-President of the Gilbert and Jacki Foundation. On May 5th 2010, her luck was in. She won the lottery of 266 million dollars. So we shall also look at the progress chart of 2010.

15.32 Leo	Sun	04.51 Libra
08.51 Virgo	Moon	10.48 Virgo
06.40 Libra	Mercury	17.01 Virgo
09.07 Scorpio	Venus	17.06 Scorpio
13.30 Sagittarius	Mars	16.00 Virgo
16.09 Capricorn	Jupiter	07.32 Scorpio
15.32 Aquarius	Saturn	22.07 Taurus R.
08.51 Pisces	Uranus	08.54 Libra
06.40 Aries	Neptune	28.45 Scorpio.
09.07 Taurus	Pluto	27.30 Virgo.
13.30 Gemini	Chiron	08.14 Aries.
16.09 Cancer	N Node	00.58 Pisces
	Fortune .	09.35 Virgo
	Lilith	02.46 Virgo

This chart is not so tricky, even a child could interpret it. The Leo ascendant with the sun as ruler in Libra in the second house. The sun is conjunct the third and Uranus in the third. There is a semi-square between the sun and Venus in the 4th house. The sun is opposing Chiron in the 9th house. In the first house we see Lilith in the second house sign of Virgo. Lilith is conjunct the second house, and also conjunct the moon in the second house. It has a conjunction with Fortune in the second house.

In the second house we see the moon, Mercury, Mars, Pluto and Fortune. They are all in the sign of Virgo. This gives a stellium. Did you remember we did a chart of Myra Kingsley who was number one astrologer in New York, and she wrote a book called outrageous Fortune, we did saw in her chart, Fortune in the second house. In this chart, we also see Fortune in the second house. I think that we are now getting some good information on Fortune or it might be too early to say. The moon is conjunct Fortune, Mercury and Mars. Mercury is conjunct Mars and Fortune. Mars and Fortune are in conjunction. Pluto is conjunct the sun. Uranus in the third house in the sign of Libra is conjunct the third and exactly conjunct the second. Our code of 8 degrees shows that there is something out of our control. But we can see that it has to do with her possessions, and we take the opposite house, which has to do with other people's possessions. Uranus is ruler of the 7th house.

The moon in the second house is trine the Mid, quincunx Chiron in the 9th house. It has a semi-sextile contact with Uranus in the third. It is sextile Jupiter in the third in Scorpio. Mercury is semi-sextile the ascendant, sextile the 12th house, trine the Mid, exactly sextile Venus in the 4th house. Mars is semi-sextile the ascendant, trine the Mid, sextile Venus in the 4th house, trine Saturn in the 10th house. Mercury is also in contact with Saturn in the 10th house. Uranus in the third house is semi-sextile the 4th house, and it has a semi-sextile contact with Jupiter in the third house.

You see Jupiter in the third house in the sign of Scorpio. This is someone who has energies for deep thinking. Good for getting down to the core of mysteries. Occult energies, Kind and active. Jupiter is conjunct the 4th house, and this is a placing for someone like a queen. Jupiter is sextile to the second house, and semi-sextile the third.

Venus is holding a strong position in the 4th house which is angular. Venus is in the sign of Scorpio. Some energies are lost here because of the sign Venus is in. But in this fourth house, Venus can still shine. There could be a love of luxury and pleasure. Don't forget that Venus is the ruler of the second and the 7th house in the natural wheel. Venus is square the ascendant, but people can be really beautiful with this negative aspect of Venus. Venus is trine the 12th house, just about conjuncting the 4th, and opposing Saturn in the 10th.

Neptune in the fourth house is strange. Something to do with Parents, toots or family. Neptune is square the node in the 7th house in the sign of Pisces, the 8th house sign. It is square Saturn in the 10th. Quincunx to Pluto in the 3nd. Chiron is in the 9th house in the sign of Aries semi-sextile the Mid, and exactly semi-sextile the 8th. Chiron is semi-square Saturn.

Now we come to Saturn in the 10th house in Taurus, and is retrograde. It is square the ascendant. She is Vice-President of a Foundation.

Now let's tackle the progress chart for 2010. Remember that the moon in this chart moves about 1 degree per month. The cosmic year (perpetual date) is 7th November 1970 at 02:52 am, Whittier, California, U.S.A.

01.00 Libra	Sun	14.37 Scorpio
28.15 Libra	Moon	26.38 Aquarius
28.43 Scorpio	Mercury	21.18 Scorpio
01.00 Capricorn	Venus	19.18 Scorpio
03.27 Aquarius	Mars	11.25 Libra
03.53 Pisces	Jupiter	16.04 Scorpio
01.00 Aries	Saturn	19.29 Taurus R
28.15 Aries	Uranus	11.20 Libra
28.43 Taurus.	Neptune	00.01 Sagittarius
01.05 Cancer	Pluto	28.52 Virgo
04.27 Leo	Chiron	06.34 Aries
03.53 Virgo	N Node	28.50 Aquarius
	Fortune	18.58 Gemini
	Lilith	07.12 Virgo

This progress chart is a bit tricky. You have to examine it carefully. And if you want good information, there's a lot of work to do. First, you have to use the progress chart with the natal one. Then you have to check the Transits for the day in question. Not the perpetual date, but the actual date she won the money. Her natal chart shows her as a Leo ascendant. She has been through all of

Virgo, and now she is into Libra. This is a beautiful period for her with Venus having rule over her ascendant.

I told you some time ago that I was trying to fit some numbers in numerology into the chart. It is not an easy task. In this chart then, we have Venus as the ascendant and is in the second house in the sign of Scorpio, conjunct Jupiter, conjunct the sun and Mercury. It is square the moon in the 5th house, also the node in the same house, both in the sign of Aquarius. Venus is exactly opposing Saturn in the 8th house in the sign of Taurus. Venus is ruler of the ascendant, the second house and the 9th house.

So we find in the first house Mars and Uranus exactly conjuncting in Libra. Both holding 11 degrees which I call *"masterful"*. We see that Mars is ruler of the 7th house which has to do with the public or partnerships. It rules also the 8th house which has to do with other people's money. Mars is co-ruler of the third house. Now Uranus is co-ruler of the 5th house. This 5th house has to do with gambling, speculation, romance, children, sports, entertainment. From these two planets alone, Mars and Uranus in the first house, we know that something speculative took place. Actually, these two planets are rather dangerous, but they are in the sign of Libra. They give lots of energy, active and forceful. So she was set into action to get something done.

Going into the chart for the first time, You will see that Neptune is in zero degree oF Sagittarius, and in a loop in the third house. In the natal chart Neptune is ruling the 8th house while it is ruling the 6th house in the progs chart. Neptune is a planet that moves very slow, so we shall not waste time here. In the progs chart we see that there are four planets in the second house. They are: Sun, Mercury, Venus and Jupiter. Venus is in her own house, and ruler of the ascendant, second house and 9th house. You will later come to understand that the 9th house is an institution, just like the 12th house is also an institution. Money can come from these contacts. Jupiter in the second house we know if the person is wise, they can become rich, or over do things by too much spending. The sun in the second house, but it is ruler of the 11th, so we have a contact of 11/2 which brings in money. You have to be careful when checking some charts. The planets of 11/2 were negative, and yet, there I was baffled. They brought in money for the individual. And as I already said, be careful when dealing with planets in angular houses.

Fortune up in the 9th house in the loop of Gemini has a trine aspect with Mars and Uranus in the first house. We have the natal Neptune exactly conjunct the progs 3rd, and semi-sextile the progs second. The node in the progs is exactly square the third in the progs, and sextile the second in the progs.

Because I have been doing some strange research, I had to throw quite a lot out the door, this had to do with time, and I just could not make sense of it. I have my eyes on the 19 degrees. They are a part of the 10.

Check carefully the natal chart with the progs chart, and look also for transits on the day. Notice that the moon is in the 5th house for the month of November in this progs chart. We should bring it back to the month of May. Knocking about 6 degrees off (1 degree for a month) we get the moon for the month of May with about 20 degrees, and it would be in trine with Fortune, square to Mercury and Neptune. Notice that the node is quincunx Pluto, and that Pluto is conjuncting the ascendant.

This next chart is for an exercise. You are to check it carefully. See how much information you can dig out.

29.28 Gemini	Sun.	16.53 Pisces
18.12 Cancer	Moon	02.47 Leo.
07.39 Leo	Mercury	06.55 Pisces
01.32 Virgo	Venus	02.51 Aquarius
04.32 Libra	Mars	27.05 Capricorn
18.08 Scorpio.	Jupiter.	01.00 Cancer
29.28 Sagittarius	Saturn	22.42 Capricorn
07.39 Aquarius	Uranus	09.00 Capricorn
01.32 Pisces	Neptune	14.08 Capricorn.
04.32 Aries	Pluto	17.42 Scorpio R
18.08 Taurus	Chiron	10.36 Cancer
	N Node	16.16 Aquarius
	Fortune	15.22 Scorpio
	Lilith	13.46 Scorpio

This is not an event chart.

Each one of the zodiacal signs has a description about it. For example: Leo rising at the ascendant, we say this is the Lion sign, and the person can be like a lion.

In this chart, Gemini is rising with 29 degrees, with Jupiter in Cancer in conjunction with the ascendant. Jupiter is exalted in Cancer. Because Gemini is rising, we say that the person is like twins, double personality.

Okay here is the information: The chart has to do with the *Hensel twins – Abigail and Brittany* born on 7th March 1990 at 11:29 am, Buffalo, Minnesota, U.S.A.

The 29 degrees should be plain to you now once you know that the time is correct. I never asked questions about twins or other strange conceptions. I go and look for the information. Jupiter you see is in the first house, exalted in

Cancer and is conjunct the ascendant. Chiron is conjuncting the second house. Mercury, the ruler of the ascendant is up there in the 10th house with the sun, both in Pisces. Mercury is semi-sextile the 9th; semi-square Saturn in the 8th house in its own sign of Capricorn. You see the 22 degrees, don't you? Mercury is sextile Uranus in the 7th house in Capricorn. Neptune in the 7th house is conjunct the 8th house.

The Moon is in Leo in the second house. I am still trying to find out what the 7 degrees mean, and also Mars with its 27 degrees in the 8th house. The Moon is semi-sextile the ascendant. It is opposing Venus in the 8th house in the sign of Aquarius. Lilith in the 5th house is sextile Uranus and Neptune. . Lilith is conjunct Pluto, and Fortune all in the 5th house in Scorpio. And all conjunct the 6th house. Pluto is conjunct the 8th house, and square the node in the 9th house in the sign of Aquarius. Lilith is also square the node, Fortune as well. You will notice that Fortune is in 15 degrees. Seeing these degrees, I said to myself, there is something strange with this chart – not strange like Neptune, but sort of out of the ordinary. I have been looking at many charts with the 15 degrees, and I still have to make up my mind what they are saying.

This next chart is done for Midday. Let's see what information we could get from it. The chart is for Heather Mills born 12th January 1968, Aldershot, UK.

In 1993 she was hit by a police cycle, and lost half of her left leg. She met Paul McCartney in 1999. They got married in 2002. She brought forth a daughter in 2003. And in 2008 she was awarded 30. 9 million euro from Paul McCartney. We shall look at all the charts.

13.32 Taurus	Sun	21.21 Capricorn
12.13 Gemini	Moon	14.37 Gemini
01.05 Cancer	Mercury	00.19 Aquarius
18.44 Cancer	Venus	12.42 Sagittarius
10.00 Leo	Mars	02.24 Pisces
13.36 Virgo	Jupiter.	05.07 Virgo R
13.32 Scorpio	Saturn	06.40 Aries
12.13 Sagittarius	Uranus	29.11 Virgo
01.05 Capricorn	Neptune	25.56 Scorpio
18.44 Capricorn	Pluto	22.46 Virgo R
10.00 Aquarius	Chiron	25.53 Pisces
13.36 Pisces	N Node	23.23 Aries
	Fortune	06.49 Libra
	Lilith	12.25 Taurus

Quick look around. The ascendant is Taurus with its ruler Venus in the 8th house exactly conjunct the 8th. Lilith is there in the 12th conjunct the ascendant. I still don't know for sure which sign goes with Lilith. Aries is in a loop in the

12th. Scorpio is at the 7th cusp. Sagittarius is at the 8th cusp. WE will get to know as we go along.

Do you see Mercury in the 10th house in zero degree of Aquarius, the 11th house sign? Mercury is ruling the second house. 11/2, money comes in. Mercury also rules the 6th house. The Moon is conjuncting the second and is ruler of the third and fourth houses. The Moon is semi-sextile the ascendant, square the 12th. Lilith is sextile the 12th, trine the Mid. Venus is square the 12th, quincunx Lilith. Uranus is in the 6th house with 29 degrees; the opposite sign is Pisces, the feet. Pluto is 22 degrees also in the 6th, both planets in Virgo Fortune is in a loop in Libra in the 6th house. Fortune rules the 5th house. WE expect the sun to be in the position it is in because it is around noon. The sun is ruling the 5th house. We are now going to look at the Progress chart for 1993.

She was 25 years old, so we add this to 12th January 1968. There are 19 days left for January, so this gives us 6th February 1968 at Midday, Aldershot, UK. This is the Perpetual Date.

17.42 Gemini	Sun	16.46 Aquarius
06.01 Cancer	Moon	16.37 Taurus
22.54 Cancer	Mercury	02.16. Pisces
12.27 Leo	Venus	13.10 Capricorn
10.08 Virgo	Mars	21.49 Pisces
24.54 Libra	Jupiter	02.40 Virgo R
17.42 Sagittarius	Saturn	08.36 Aries
06.01 Capricorn	Uranus	28.43 Virgo R
22.54 Capricorn	Neptune	26.24 Scorpio
12.27 Aquarius	Pluto	22.23 Virgo R
10.08 Pisces	Chiron	26.54 Pisces
24.54 Aries	N Node	22.03 Aries
	Lilith	15.11 Taurus
	Fortune	17.33 Virgo

It is good if you understand the signs of the zodiac, and the planet or planets ruling those signs. There is that part which is called Medical Astrology, and is very complicated. I spend some time just studying the basics, and it did me good. For an example: Aries is the first sign of the zodiac, and it rules the head. Having troubles with the head will show in the chart.

In this chart, we see that Gemini is rising. Mercury is the ruler and is in the 10th house in Pisces. It is opposing Jupiter in the fourth house in the sign of Virgo. We know that from experience two planets in angular positions are strong, but they are still negative. The sun is in the 10th house, in Aquarius. It has to be around this position because of the time. The Moon is in a loop in the 12th house in the sign of Taurus. For the month of February, it is in 16 degrees of Taurus exactly square the sun. The Moon is ruler of the second house and the third house. The sun is ruler of the 4th.

Lilith is in that same loop with the Moon, and in conjunction with it. Lilith is square the sun. The sun is trine the ascendant. Chiron in the 11th house in the sign of Pisces is trine Neptune in the loop in the 6th house in Scorpio. Chiron rules the 7th, Neptune co-ruler of the 11th. The third house is holding 22 degrees, and Pluto in the 5th house in Virgo is also holding 22 degrees. The node in the 11th house is in 22 degrees. Notice that Saturn is in the 11th house in 8 degrees and is ruler of the 8th house, the 9th, and co-ruler of the 10th. Mars in the 11th in Pisces is opposing Pluto. Semi-sextile the node, trine the 3rd house. Fortune is exactly square the ascendant

To get our progress Moon at the right place, we must add about 1 degree per month, starting from March. The accident took place in on 8th August. So if you want to get information there's lots of work. Her Progress Venus in 13 degrees Capricorn is sextile her natal 12th exactly; and trine her natal ascendant exactly. Saturn rules the knee, so is Capricorn. Check the transits for 6th August 1993. Now I will push on to the next chart.

The progressive date is 12th February 1968 at 12:00 pm, Aldershot, UK. This date represents the year 1999. It will end in February 2000. She met Paul McCartney in 1999.

23.50 Gemini	Sun	22.50 Aquarius
11.07 Cancer	Moon	00.38 Leo
28.02 Cancer	Mercury	29.21 Aquarius R
18.24 Leo	Venus	20.31 Capricorn
17.52 Virgo	Mars	26.26 Pisces
04.09 Scorpio	Jupiter	01.55 Virgo R
23.50 Sagittarius	Saturn	09.11 Aries
11.07 Capricorn	Uranus	28.32 Virgo R
28.02 Capricorn	Neptune	26.28 Scorpio
18.24 Aquarius	Pluto	22.16 Virgo R
17.52 Pisces	Chiron	
04.09 Taurus	N Node	21.44 Aries
	Fortune	01.38 Sagittarius
	Lilith	15.51 Taurus

Friendship and romance you will find comes from the 11th and 5th houses. It can also come from the 7th house. Notice Mars and Chiron in Pisces in the 11th house. Notice Mercury crying and being powerful, and is ruling the ascendant and the 5th house. Inside the 5th house we see Pluto holding 22 degrees in Virgo, and is square the ascendant. It is exactly quincunx the sun in the 10th house in Aquarius, the sign that is normally on the 11th house. Mercury is semi-sextile the 9th house. Some contact here with the 9th. We pick up Venus in the 8th house in Capricorn, and squaring the node in the loop in the 11th house in the sign of Aries. This has to do with extra friends, as I myself have experienced in the year 1986.

Neptune in the 6th house in Scorpio is trine Mars and Chiron in the 11th house. Neptune is co-ruler of the 11th house.

Let's put Chiron, Lilith, Fortune, the North Node, and the three outer planets, Uranus and Neptune and Pluto out of the chart; you still have Mercury up in the 10th house conjunct the sun, trine to the ascendant, and sextile the 7th. Mercury is ruling the ascendant and the 5th house. There at the fifth house we see the Moon and Jupiter. Jupiter rules the 11th and the 7th. The moon rules the second house. Notice at the 6/12 axis, you have 8 degrees. This is something we have no control over – out of our power. She got married in this chart 11th June. For that month, the Moon would be about 15 degrees in Virgo in the fourth house, with about 6 degree conjunction to the fifth, but we work always close with 1 degree. Bringing Lilith back in, the Moon would be making a trine aspect. Does Lilith rule Scorpio, Sagittarius or Aries. I am still trying to get it spot on. Anyway, she was pregnant in this chart, the following chart we are going to look at is when she brought forth a daughter. Let's take a look. Don't forget to look up the transits for 11th of June 2002.

This last chart is for when she gave birth to her daughter on October 28th 2003. We add another day to the 15th February which gives us another year. One day equal one year. So the perpetual date then would be 16th February 1968 at 12:00 pm, Aldershot, UK.

Please excuse any mistake that I should make. I do try to be precise, but as you know, we humans, still make mistakes. And at the moment, I am going through what I call a 'burn up.' Having the sun and Mercury one degree apart. What an experience that is. I will explain to you later on.

27.39 Gemini	Sun	26.52 Aquarius
14.26 Cancer	Moon	25.39 Virgo
01.27 Leo	Mercury	25.00 Aquarius R
22.25 Leo	Venus	25.26 Capricorn. .
23.04 Virgo	Mars	29.30 Pisces
10.02 Scorpio	Jupiter.	01.23 Virgo R
27.39 Sagittarius	Saturn	09.35 Aries
14.26 Capricorn	Uranus	28.24 Virgo R
01.27 Aquarius	Neptune	26.29 Scorpio
22.25 Aquarius	Pluto	22.10 Virgo
23.04 Pisces	Chiron	27.24 Pisces
10.02 Taurus	N Node	21.31 Aries
	Fortune	26.26 Capricorn

I was suppose to say Mercury in Aquarius, but I keep saying: Mercury in Pisces. Anyway, the ascendant here is Gemini. As soon as you hear the name, you should know what it is all about, even if you are just starting out. Well, the ruler of Gemini is Mercury, and it is in the 10th house in Aquarius (I got it right this time). You'd see too, that it is in conjunction with the sun also in the 10th and in Aquarius. Mercury is trining the ascendant, and it is doing so with about 2 degrees. We work with one. But no harm done if it should work with 3 or even four and more. Mercury is exactly semi-sextile Venus in the 8th house in Capricorn. Mercury is semi-sextile Fortune in the 8th house in Capricorn. There is a square between Mercury and Neptune. Neptune in the 6th house in Scorpio. Mercury is exactly quincunx the Moon in the 5th house in the sign of Virgo. Notice, that the moon is holding its degrees and sign for the month of February. To get it to October, the month of the birth, you have to add about 8 degrees to those of the Moon. This will bring us to about 3 degrees of Libra. This is my quick way of doing it, but to get it absolutely right. you have to go back a year and see where the Moon was, then do some subtraction, and then division by 12. Sometimes the Moon reaches up to about 13 degrees per year, and when divided, can turn out to be about 1 degree and some minutes.

So the progress Moon at the time of the birth would be in about 3 degrees of Libra, and in the loop in the fifth house. We'll come to that again when we finish with the sun, and planets before it. The sun is semi-sextile Venus, and exactly semi-sextile Fortune. Exactly square Neptune. It is semi-sextile Chiron in the 11th house in Pisces. And this Chiron, is exactly square the ascendant. Chiron is sextile Fortune, and Trine Neptune. Both Mars and Chiron are still opposing Uranus in the 5th house.

Pluto in the 4th house is conjunct the 5th, and is co-ruler of the 6th house. Jupiter is semi-sextile the October Moon in the loop in the 5th house. Uranus is in conjunction with it with about 4 degrees. Jupiter is exactly quincunx the 9th. Pluto is quincunx the Mid. The Node in the loop in the 11th house in Aries is sextile the Mid.

I do hope you got through that chart without losing your way. The third house is also that of close relatives. The 8th and 12th house will also come into contact, and so does the 11th which is opposite the 5th. The 10th house announces the birth. The 6th house shows that the person is sick, not that there is something wrong with you, but you are having a baby. Join me on the next chapter where I'll be talking my head off.

45: Are You Still Baffled?

I said to you sometime ago that you must make a book; and you do this when you have an accurate time. Within the family, this is good, and especially for children, and your friends. It is a lot of work, but it is also fun. You draw before hand every year the progress wheel, So, if you just have a child, and you have to make the progress, you will know what the energies are in the charts, and be able to direct the child in certain ways. This really helps.

Let's say for an example, you see that the child has Mars in the first house. Already, you know that the child will be energetic, and you could start by directing it in some sort of sports which would be good for the child. You also need to know what sign the Planet Mars is in. It could be the ascendant sign, it could be in a loop sign or it could be in the second house sign. At least you know that you are dealing with the planet Mars.

There are also the aspects to think of, but I won't go into them because not everyone would be able to accept them. Like I said earlier on, Mars is a dangerous planet, but good comes from it as well.

Suppose you see the planet Venus in the first house. We all know that this planet has to do with love and beauty. Here you see that the child would have a lovely personality, and you can feed it more while the child is young. Venus is also good for art, painting, singing, dancing and all sort of lovely things. I have seen that when Venus is negative to the ascendant, the individual is very beautiful, that is baffling. Why more beautiful when negative?

Look for some planets like Jupiter, Saturn, Uranus, Neptune or even Pluto in the 11th house. They are all slow, and takes time to reach the 12 pm mark. This is the highest point in the chart. We call it the Midheaven (MC) Mid. Jupiter will get there first, so knowing this, you can see from the book of progress charts when it will arrive. Jupiter is the biggest planet in our solar system, it is big. Do you find Earth a big planet? Well Jupiter is 1300 times bigger. My God, that's big! Getting at the Mid point, Jupiter is boss. You will find your child, at this time or this age in some high position.

Saturn does the same, but it takes a very long time. Joan of Arc had it in the 11th house, and finally, when it arrived at the Mid, she was given charge over the soldiers in her company.

Should your child have Venus in Pisces, start feeding it with good things, music around the house and such likes. Venus is exalted in Pisces, and love and beauty will be at its best.

Let us have a look at the chart of Elijah Wood, the actor. He has Mars in the loop in the first house in Aquarius. He was born 29th January 1981, at 06:46 am, Cedar Rapids, Iowa, U.S.A.

26.27 Capricorn	Sun	09.32 Aquarius
13.15 Pisces	Moon	24.16 Scorpio
22.59 Aries	Mercury	27.14 Aquarius
20.58 Taurus	Venus	22.50 Capricorn
12.45 Gemini	Mars	23.20 Aquarius.
02.59 Cancer	Jupiter	10.21 Libra R
26.27 Cancer	Saturn	09.40 Libra R
13.15 Virgo	Uranus	29.34 Scorpio
22.59 Libra	Neptune	23.59 Sagittarius.
20.58 Scorpio	Pluto	24.20 Libra R
12.45 Sagittarius	Chiron	13.25 Taurus
02.59 Capricorn	N Node	11.00 Leo
	Fortune	11.43 Aries
	Lilith	03.24 Scorpio

Note: if you are a lover of Philosophy, then try to read Vesalius and Pomponazzi. There was a big heated debate going on in the middle ages, and astrology was being talked about.

In Elijah Wood's chart, Capricorn is rising, and Venus is there with about 4 degrees conjunction. Saturn is the ruler of the ascendant, and it is in the 8th house exalted in Libra, conjunct Jupiter, and having Pluto in the same sign, but in the 9th house. Saturn is sextile the node in Leo in the loop in the 7th house. Saturn is semi-square the Moon in the tenth house in the sign of Scorpio. There is an exact trine from Saturn to the sun in the loop in the first house in Aquarius.

The conjunction of Jupiter and Saturn is good for religion and philosophy. Charts with Jupiter in good contact with Saturn shows this. It is known that Saturn in this 8th house can bring out some magical stuff. And Jupiter in this, his brothers house, will have deep insight. Saturn is opposing Fortune in the second house. Talking about Fortune here in the second house, we have picked up that this Fortune in this house can make one become rich, is that really so? Well, the owner of this chart is very rich. We need lots more chart with this position of Fortune before we can definitely say that it is so.

Venus is in the 12th house and is ruler of the 4th and 9th. It is semi-sextile Mars in the loop in the first house. Venus is semi-sextile Neptune in the 11th house in the sign of Sagittarius. There is a sextile aspect between Venus and the Mid. Also a sextile aspect with the Moon in the tenth house in the sign of Scorpio. There is a square between Venus and Pluto in the 9th house in the sign of Libra. Notice that Pluto is in Venus's sign.

Inside the first house, there is the loop of Aquarius with three planets: Sun, Mercury and Mars. This makes him a strong Aquarian, and also a strong Libran with three planets in Libra.

The sun, as we know, represents life, Mercury the intellect, the thinking power, and Mars the energy. The sun is ruler of the loop in the 7th house with the Node there. Mercury is ruler of the fifth and eighth houses. Mars is ruler of the third and tenth houses. In the Queen of England's chart, she has Mars and Jupiter in the loop of Aquarius. I just read somewhere that Interceptions has to do with a past life, and we have to sort it out in this life. Whether that is true or not, I do not know. At the moment, I am going through another loop, and when it is over, I will have more information on what was going on.

There are lots of information in this chart, and I do hope that you will be able to see them. Venus conjunct the ascendant in Capricorn; The moon in the 10th in Scorpio; Uranus in the 10th in Scorpio; The three planets, Jupiter, Saturn and Pluto in Libra.

Do you know we just had Jupiter, Saturn and Pluto in Capricorn? Now Jupiter and Saturn are in Aquarius, and Pluto is left alone in Capricorn. But it wont be long before he makes his way into Aquarius. Pluto is a slow planet.

46: Into Astrological Deep Waters

Back home when I was just a little boy, I saw many things happening in my community. Now I am a Virgo, and Virgo people are very critical, analytical, wants to get all the fine details so that they could understand what's going on. I am like that. I am a strong Virgo. No one told me anything about dangerous fishes in the sea. I just dash in without any bother. Then later, I was told that there are sharks and other dangerous fishes. From that time on, I stayed along the sea shore, and kept my eyes open.

I've been keeping my eyes open with Astrology. It is a beautiful hobby for me. I have learned quite a lot, but not enough. The one thing that we must not forget is, that astrology is not the only thing that has to do with our existence here on Earth. It is one of the main things that has to do with us. The one reason why many people do not understand it is because they are walking around, filled up with the energies of the heavenly bodies within them. Reading a bit of what Pomponazzi said, I come to realize that it makes sense. It is through these cosmic forces, that we get the energies to become what we want to be with good and proper training. There's no way that a person can become President of America or Prime Minister of UK if they have not got the proper energies given to them.

You know, I have been talking my head off to a certain person about religion. I found out later, that I was wasting my time. You can talk for a million years, that person won't pay any attention to you. I found out from some careful study and research that when Jupiter is negative to Saturn, the person tends to go the other way. There's no God, there's no this, and there's no that. They stick to their own way of seeing things. Nothing is wrong with that. We all have our choices, and way of doing things. But astrology is making a lot of sense to me.

It is wise to have a chart done, and to see the energies that you can work with. Some people are disciplined by their families, and so they make it in life quite easily. Some of us can take chances, and get away with it. Others get into trouble.

I am still heading out into deep waters, throwing fear aside, but being careful. For I was told that there are fishes that will come along and take away your private parts. I didn't want that to happen to me, but still I didn't let it get to me.

I was down the bay, and I saw these fishermen preparing their nets, I walked along, and watched them patching up nets. I was a bit nosy when I was young, but not in a bad way; just wanting to know how things work. Then when they were finished, I gave them a push to get the boat down to the shore and into the water. I heard a lot about these fishermen, and so I knew when they would be back from sea; and I was there. Some came back with their boats empty, others came back loaded down. So I found out later, some of the fishers had nets laid, and they would just go and haul them up with a great catch. In the astrological chart, it is almost the same. Some people are lucky being born at a time when the planets are in good positions. Others are a bit unlucky with hard aspects, but this must be a lesson for them. It is so complicated when I set my mind in thinking that way. We are mortals, and those planets up there are set in motion, and no one can disturb them. What ever we say or do, we just have to live with them. Sometimes it seems as if things are already planned, but I keep away from that area. The human being, along with what he has been given, has a bunch of astrological keys to open many doors. They can make a mess of it, but it is their choice. Astrology has shown clearly that you cannot avoid everything. Some things are fixed. Just like the sun comes up every morning running along the Ecliptic with a 1 degree every day. Who is going to change that?

We see the sun almost every day depending on where we are. Some of us don't know it, but the sun is a dangerous star. Scientists have been trying for a long time to find out what goes on down in the core of our sun. It's like a bomb, God knows how it stayed together. Every time I look up and I see it, I smile to myself because I know, or I must say, that I feel that there is some great power behind the sun. We are told that it is God, and that I do believe. Reading how it all came to be is rather interesting. Now I have found myself into deep scientifical waters, and that too, in my old age.

Astrology is responsible for my dive in these deep waters. To make it clear, I must say the energies that come from the planets and down into us, depending on when we were born, gives us the chance to pursue certain subjects, and to behave in a certain way. They are not telling us what we have to do. The choice is ours. And knowing the human race, everyone to his or her own way. Sometimes we can act too early or too late, or don't act at all.

I was in a book shop, and I saw a book that I became interested in. I said to myself, I will get it tomorrow. I got back, and found that someone else had bought it. I could have taken the book straight away, but I did not make up my mind properly.

I'm absolutely amazed when I look through some charts. I see the action there. I'm thinking, how does that person go about it. Then I get the chance to read about the person, and how they themselves went through life, not knowing anything at all about astrology. But I know what is happening. Astrology is there and working all the time whether a person knows of it or not. Some people feel within them what they want to do. But all this feeling – is energy. Our sun pours out a lot of energy, and we must not forget, if it wasn't there, we would not be here. It is the great supplier of life.

In my community, when I was young, I saw how the people on a Friday after work, would all go the center of the town where the cinema was situated. All along the streets, there were people sitting with trays selling all sorts of things to eat. I noticed how they reacted when they were given something that was not good. Then I got the shock of my life when my mother said that I should go out with a tray, and try to sell as well. I made sure that what I had was first class, so that no one could moan. Believe it or not, it all went down well. Every week, I became confident that I'll be able to get customers. If you are going into business, no matter what it is, make sure that your customers are looked after properly, you cannot go wrong. A good customer service goes down well.

We shall now have a look at *Zipporah Dobyns* chart. She was an astrologer, did a lot in her life, married with four children. She was born 26th August 1921 at 21:48 pm, Chicago, Illinois, U.S.A.

24.23 Taurus
20.01 Gemini
10.42 Cancer
01.56 Leo
28.21 Leo
06.09 Libra
24.43 Scorpio
20.01 Sagittarius
10.42 Capricorn
01.56 Aquarius
28.21 Aquarius
06.09 Aries

Sun 03.19 Virgo
Moon 11.08 Gemini
Mercury 06.57 Virgo
Venus 24.26 Cancer
Mars 15.12 Leo
Jupiter 23.37 Virgo
Saturn 24.53 Virgo
Uranus 07.50 Pisces R
Neptune 14.14 Leo
Pluto 09.41 Cancer
Chiron 13.17 Aries
N Node 20.23 Libra
Lilith 15.28 Aquarius
Fortune 16.34 Leo

We are starting right at the ascendant with the rising sign of Taurus in 24 degrees and 23 minutes. The ruler of the rising sign is Venus. We find Venus in the third house in Cancer. This shows that the woman is very sensitive, protective and home loving. The third house represents travelling, writing, talking, communications, close relatives, neighbours. Venus is exactly sextile with the ascendant. This shows a lovely personality. Venus is sextile Jupiter, and is exactly sextile Saturn in the 5th house in the loop. This is much creativity and entertainment, and children. There is about 85 degrees between Venus and the node in the 6th house. Notice that the node is in the 7th house sign of Libra. This aspect is a square, and could bring some problems in the houses and signs.

Because the planet makes contact with the ascendant, it is also making contact with the Descendant. Keep that in mind.

Inside the first house, but in the second house sign, we see the moon in the sign of Gemini. . Do you see what is happening here? Venus in the moon sign, and the moon in the first house ruled by Venus. The moon has a contact with Chiron in the 12th house in the sign of Aries. This could have to do with study or meditating, and with Aries, a lot of ideas. Because of the moon in Gemini, her emotions and feelings are double, versatile, intellectual. Notice that the moon is making a semi-sextile contact with the third house, and also with Pluto.

The moon is sextile to Mars in the fourth house in Leo, sextile to Neptune in Leo, and sextile to Fortune also in Leo. The moon rules the third house Mars rules the 7th and 12th houses. Neptune rules the loop in the 11th house carrying Uranus in Pisces retrograde. Fortune rules the 4th and 5th houses.

Talking about loops, we see that up in the 11th house, Uranus is in the loop of Pisces, and Uranus rules the 10th and 11th houses. So according to my theory, there's something extra going on to do with the 10th and 11th houses. And she has to deal with friends who are not her close friends. And don't forget the sign Uranus is in. The moon also has contact with Lilith, the contact is a trine. Lilith is in the 10th house, but in the 11th house sign of Aquarius. Again, we see here, that she has to do with friends, groups and clubs in her career. According to one astrologer, Lilith rules Aries. If that is true, then the 12th house comes into operation with Chiron there. Chiron is ruling the 8th house, other people's possessions, legacies, and hidden things. Notice too, that Mercury is the ruler of the second house, and is in a loop in the 5th house in its own sign of Virgo. Here, we see again, she's very intellectual, very creative, critical and analytical. This loop in the 5th house is very interesting because it has four planets there. This is a stellium, and makes her to be a strong Virgo.

Now the ruler of house 1 is in house 3; and the ruler of house 3 is in house 1. This is something that will definitely come about in the life of the individual. We see that Mercury is the ruler of the second house, and is in the loop in the fifth. There are lots of energy here for creative work, travel, writing, and talking. You see too, that Pluto is in the second house in Cancer conjuncting the third. Pluto is co-ruler of the 7th house. The sign of Leo is at the 4th house. Inside that house we see Mars, Neptune and Fortune all in Leo. Mars is conjunct Neptune and Fortune. Neptune is conjunct Fortune. All three of them are sextile to the node in the 6th house in the sign of Libra. In astrological interpretations, we are told that Mars in the fourth house can cause upset in the home and family. Mars is very positive. It has a trine to Chiron in the 12th house in the sign of Aries. With a negative to Lilith in the 10th house. I think even with positive aspects, there must have been some sort of unrest at some time in the home. Many charts with Mars in the fourth house shows this. She got divorced in 1958, and Mars is co-ruler of the 7th, and ruler of the 12th.

Neptune in the fourth house – my interpretation – something strange to do with family and roots whether it is positive or negative. Neptune holds a strong position because it is in an angular house. You know when I first started looking into astrology, I had the one word for Neptune – strange. The planet is trine with Chiron in the 12th house, opposing Lilith in the 10th house. Fortune is also opposing Lilith. We notice that the sun is ruler of the fourth and fifth houses, and itself, is in a loop in the fifth house in the sign of Virgo. Her sun sign is Virgo just like all the others who are Virgo by the sun. There are other types of Virgos. But you must also bear in mind that everyone has a touch of every sign in their wheel. And it s time and place that decide where it is. Talking about time, that is one of the things that run astrology along with space. It is too complicated for me, even though I try to understand how it works. Even the scientists themselves have trouble understanding 'time".

So we have house 4 in house 5; house 5 in 5. Don't you know by now your houses, and what they mean? Like you count 1, 2, 3, you should know from the beginning what your houses mean, this will really help you understand how the planets work within the signs and houses and aspects.

In the 5th house, in the loop of Virgo, are four planets. The sun, Mercury, Jupiter and Saturn. She has Mercury close to the sun. If it was closer, about one degree, then she would have been in a burn up phase. I will talk on that later. The sun and Mercury are good for the intellect. Writing and communicating ability is here, Some of us keep forgetting that the fifth house is the house of light. It is the natural house of the sun, house of life. We see too, that the sun itself is ruler of the 5th. It is very important when doing a chart to get the aspects right, and from where they are coming from. In this chart, the sun is about 98 degrees away from the ascendant. A bit far out I would say. Some even go as far as 10 degrees orb. I prefer a much closer one. The sun should function well in its own house, the house of creativity, entertainment, children, speculation etc. Being in the sign of Virgo, it will be searching, wanting to get things right. Her sun hasn't got any real bad aspects. It is conjunct the 5th house, and semi-sextile the 6th. It opposes Uranus in the 11th house.

Mercury is ruler of the sign in the loop in the 5th house. It also rules the second house. This is good for teaching, travel, and fifth house matters. Mercury makes a sextile aspect to Pluto in the second house. It is exactly semi-sextile with the 6th, and Bi-Quintile the Mid. Mercury opposes Uranus in the 11th house, semi-square the node in the 6th house. Uranus is ruling the 10th and 11th houses. This is a tug-of-war between the two houses. Their energies could come out as being scientific.

Within that same loop, we have the planet Jupiter, the biggest planet in our solar system. Jupiter is in Virgo, and is ruler of the 8th house, co-ruler of the loop in the 11th house. Jupiter is trine with the ascendant, having a sextile from Venus in the third house, and is trine the Mid. Jupiter is conjunct Saturn. This conjunction is good for religion, but the sextile and trine aspects are more solid.

Because Jupiter is co-ruler of Pisces, and Uranus is in that sign, and is ruler of 10th and 11th houses, we can say that something scientific is playing out in her career, and has to do with groups, clubs and friends. As we have already seen, Jupiter is well-aspected in the loop in Virgo in the 5th house.

This position of Jupiter in the fifth house is good for working with children, for teaching. Energies here are critical, and good for literature and travel. It expand the 5th house. No wonder she had four children. The children were born 1949, 1950, 1952 and 1955. She was married 1948 and divorced 1958. 1999 an operation.

Saturn is in the 5th house in the loop of Virgo. It is ruler of the 9th, co-ruler of the 10th and 11th houses. It has the same aspects as those of Jupiter. What is interesting here is, that Saturn in or around the 5th house, or even ruler with bad aspects causes problems in the fifth house, and the houses that it rules. But in this chart, Saturn has good aspects, so you can see why she was able to have so many children.

I have an ex-girlfriend who has Saturn in the fifth house, exalted in Libra, and have no children. Saturn is holding the code of 8 degrees. I have another friend who has Saturn in the fifth house, exalted in Libra. Saturn is in conflict with her ascendant ruler. She too, is in her 60s, and have no children.

I first got the idea from the mythological story of Saturn, Rhea and Jupiter. Saturn was in power, and every time a child was born he would eat it up. So when Jupiter was born, Rhea hid Jupiter in a cave, and gave Saturn a stone instead.

After checking many charts of women who had miscarriages, and of those who have no children, I found that Saturn was either negative to the ascendant or the fifth house ruler, especially if Saturn was in the fifth house or ruler of the fifth house. But it is not Saturn alone that does that. We do not take one aspect, and make an interpretation for the event. We examine the complete chart.

I found a book that I have here written by Zipporah Pottenger Dobyns. It is called: Progressions Directions and Rectifications.

Okay, back to her chart. As we have seen, the 5th house is packed with planets, and shows much creativity.

The ancients told us that Saturn is the destiny planet, and I have been doing some research in that area. In this chart, Saturn is in the fifth house in a loop in Virgo, Exactly trine the ascendant, exactly sextile Venus in the third house in Cancer, trine the Mid, conjunct Jupiter, and having Uranus on the opposite side.

47: Time and Space

While the planets up above are turning around the sun in their different cycles, we below hardly know what is actually going on. Information comes to us from the astronomy scientists, and we use that information in our astrological system. I would like to get hold of time, and have words with it. "What the devil are you playing at?" And space? Well, we all have a good idea what that is.

There is a law that has been given to us: As above, so below. If the sun is negative to Mars, it's going to happen below.

We know that our fixed chart starts with the first sign of Aries with Mars as the ruler. From the time I started playing around with astrology, I have these strange things that I always say. For instance, I say that Mars is the pusher out of the belly and into this world. He is the first energy. *"Out you go, all you babies!"* And of course, little babies start to cry. Some of them, much too young to know what's happening, won't even make it. Why did this happen?

Our astrologers gives us the answer after he has checked mother's chart. He sees clearly what is wrong. Of course, he cannot do anything about it, only to try and explain it as simply as he can. To some people, it sounds rather weird. Are you telling me that the planets have power to do that? Can I explain? The astrologer would say. It is not the planets that is doing that. It is the energies that the planets gives out at a certain time that caused such things to happen. No one is going to understand properly what the astrologer is trying to say. But the astrologer is right, just like Jesus was right when he spoke of *"It's the spirit that gives life. The flesh counts for nothing."* But even though he was right, some of his disciples found it too hard to accept, and went away from Jesus.

Whenever you have time it is good to check out Plato's Parmenides – space and time.

Einstein on time.
Aristotle on time.
Newton on time.
What the Physicists have to say about time.
What the Philosophers have to say about time.
And here's a book by Carlo Rovelli: *"The Order of Time".*

Having done so, it will give you a good idea what we are dealing with. Newton believed that time still flows if there are no events.

You have to understand your subject. Break it apart. Know what you are dealing with. It is truth we are after, and astrology is full of truth.

When I was in the Army, I had to check the notice board to see when I would be on guard duty, and all the other soldiers as well. I make a note of it. I could start planning certain things. But the notice on the board could change, and all my plans too. Not so with the planets, you can bet your life, they'll come just like they should.

I am staring at my progress chart for a certain year – four years to come. I see what Mars and Venus are doing. My Mid, and its ruler. My ascendant, and planets making aspect to it. I know a hundred percent what is going to take place. Well, let me say, I know what the chart is telling me. And I start to prepare myself. Can I avoid what the chart is saying? It is speaking to me in a language that not everyone understands. It is possible to use my free will, and make a choice, and avoid certain things. But I am not on my own. There are other people who have made decisions that will affect me. Some things that I can't prevent. So we are definitely caught up in a circle of events. I think that there are things that are fixed, and we have to accept them and get on with our lives as best we can. And I also think that what we have been given from our birth – planetary combinations and aspects – will work themselves out positively or negatively whether we like it or not. It is just the way life is.

Let us have a quick look at *Serena Williams'* chart. I don't know if I have done this before, I hope not. She is a top tennis player was born 26th September 1981 at 20:28 pm, Saginaw, Michigan, U.S.A. World number 1 in 2002 for the first time. Knee surgery 2003. Surgery on foot 2010. Surgery 2011. Engaged 2016. She was 8 weeks pregnant, won Australian Open 2017. Birth to a baby girl 2017. Got married 16th November 2017. We shall take a peep in her progress book, and see if we could spot the energies.

03.09 Taurus
05.00 Gemini
27.05 Gemini
17.18 Cancer
10.29 Leo
13.16 Virgo
03.09 Scorpio
05.00 Sagittarius
27.05 Sagittarius
17.18 Capricorn
10.29 Aquarius
13.16 Pisces

Sun 03.48 Libra
Moon 20.33 Virgo
Mercury 29.39 Libra
Venus 16.19 Scorpio
Mars 15.34 Leo

Jupiter 17.02 Libra
Saturn 11.42 Libra
Uranus 27.14 Scorpio
Neptune 22.14 Sagittarius
Pluto 23.27 Libra
Chiron 22.24 Taurus
N Node 28.16 Cancer
Lilith 00.20 Sagittarius
Fortune 16.34 Taurus

We all know our houses and what they represent. Some people still can't understand how they came about; and find them to be rubbish and make no sense at all. I have taken time, and check carefully; and to me, they make sense. The same with the planet energies. I hope that when you yourself check, you shall find it to be true. Jesus said: *"The truth will set you free"*. Once you know that something is true, you'll feel good within yourself. We do tend to like only the good part of things, but I can assure you, there's a negative side of astrology that will upset most people. I try always to keep on the positive side even though I see the negative side. I am a researcher who likes to see how the entire chart works. That is okay. It is really hard to see how it works within the human being. But I can assure you, it does work.

This chart we are going to look at, is the chart of a great champion. One who has energy, discipline and determination. Not knowing whose chart it was, I would have given the same interpretation; and I do this from what I see.

The sign of Taurus is rising (on the east). Its planetary ruler is Venus. We find Venus in the 7th house in the sign of Scorpio. Scorpio is the sign that is normally on the 8th house, and has to do with legacies and other people's possessions. The seventh house is owned by Venus, so we see that Venus is in its own house. Of course, you must understand that Venus is the ruler of the 7th house in the natural chart. Mars and Pluto has rule in this chart. This 7th house has to do with the public, partnerships – private or personal. It has to do also with open enemies. In an event chart, it is the house of war. The sign and the planets in this 7th house shows a bit about the partner.

Uranus is with Venus in this 7th house, bit not in conjunction. I still believe that they are working together, both in the same sign of Scorpio. Scorpio is ruled by Mars and Pluto. Some people has give Pluto total rule over Scorpio. I cannot do that just now. I need to be absolutely sure.

Venus while in the 7th house is sextile to the Mid. This is a fantastic aspect to have. The Mid is the outside world, shows the energies for the career, and has to do with the boss, or parents. I've got lots of charts with celebrities having Venus conjunct the Mid, and is in or hanging around the tenth house.

Her Venus is semi-square the sun in the 6th house in the loop, in the sign of Libra. Venus is semi-sextile Jupiter in the 6th house in the loop with the sign Libra. Venus is sextile the moon in the sixth house conjuncting the sixth house, in the sign of Virgo. Again, we find this aspect to be a good one. For if the sun represents the father, and the moon, the mother, it shows clearly, the positive side here.

Venus is square to Mars in the 5th house in the sign of Leo. This is a tough aspect, and can only be controlled by a disciplined person. It is good too, that Venus has a strong position by being angular in the 7th house. Venus is opposing Chiron and Fortune in the first house, both in Taurus sign. The first house would be empty if we had not brought in Chiron and Fortune.

So far, we see that the person has the opportunity to make it in their career, and with the public and partner.

Gemini is at the second house, the ruler is Mercury in the loop in the 6th house. The sign in the loop is Libra. Mercury is crying, but it has power behind it. Gemini is also at the third house, and its the mathematics that caused this to happen. So we have a 2/6, and a 3/6. Remember that the 6th house is that of work and service and colleagues and sickness. Mercury is the ruler of the 6th house in this chart. The loop has Venus as the ruler, and Venus is in the 7th house.

Let's go back to the first house. Taurus is rising, and Chiron and Fortune are in conjunction in Taurus, in the 1st. I do not know much about Chiron as yet, but I think that it is the ruler of Sagittarius. This sign is at the 8th house. And of course, you know the 8th house has to do with other people's money which is given to you, or inherited. Lilith is there in the 7th house conjuncting the 8th. If Chiron is ruler of Aries, we see Aries in the loop in the 12th house. This is something behind the scenes like meditating, or working behind the scenes for others. In the beginning, I had Lilith as ruler of Sagittarius, and then I changed to Scorpio, but in the end, we'll find what sign it really rules. With Fortune, there's not enough information about it. I think in the first house, the individual is responsible for creating opportunities for themselves. Fortune rules the sign of Leo, and this we find at the 5th house, the house of entertainment, and creativity and children.

At the fourth house is Cancer. Inside the fourth house is the node, and is also ruler of Cancer. Having Cancer here at the 4th house shows that people do care about their homes and families and country. The node has to do with associations, groups and clubs. It is sextile Chiron. The fourth house ruler is the moon, and is in the 6th house in the sign of Virgo. We have a 4/6 contact. One must take good care in securing their possessions, do not give the thief the chance. Also against servants. The node is square to Mercury in the loop in the sign of Libra. This is something that is upsetting. Notice that the node is in

Cancer, the opposite sign is Capricorn. We tend to ignore the opposite signs. But they tell a lot. Capricorn has to do with the knees, and people can catch colds. Mercury is in Libra, ruler of 2nd, 3rd, and 6th houses. The moon is conjuncting the 6th house, in the 6th house, and in the sign of Virgo. We all know what the sign of Virgo mean. The node has a trine to Uranus in the 7th house.

In the fifth house in the sign of Leo we see the planet Mars. It is conjunct the fifth house. Mars here is action, energy, assertive. The 5th house is sports and entertainment and children. Mars rules the 7th and the loop in the 12th house. Mars has a square to Fortune in the first house. Fortune rules the fifth house. Fortune holds a strong position. You will always find planets like this, one in an angular position, and the other not. For anyone who thinks that astrology is easy, let them think again. It is complicated. There'll be some problems with this position, but nothing to worry about. Mars is square Venus. How often have we heard the story about Mars and Venus? Quite often. So we know what they represent. Again, we see Venus in a strong position, and Mars not. It is wise not to be led astray. Be wise. Another thing I would like to say is that Mars is in the house of the sun. To me, it mean that this is the house of light, energy, powerful, the house of life. And we know that Mars is the natural ruler of the first house. And the sun, well, it is actually ruling the fifth house. So there is much to do with sport and creativity. You also find Mars hanging around the angular positions, you can tell straight away that the person is very energetic, and can take up any sport that suits them.

Mars is Quincunx the Mid. It is strange here because the sign at the Mid is Capricorn, the sign Mars is exalted in. So there is enormous energy here, and should be used for good. Mars is sextile Jupiter in the loop in the 6th house in Libra. This is positive, and will work out in the 7th, 8th, 9th and 12th houses. Mars is sextile Saturn in the 6th house in the loop of Libra. This too, is positive, working itself out in the 7th, 10th, 11th and the loop in the 12th house. Mars is trine Neptune in the 8th house in the sign of Sagittarius. But notice that Neptune is conjunct the 9th, and is ruler of the 12th.

We go to the 6th house, and we get a contact of 6/6. This all has to do with work, sickness, health, pets, colleagues. The ruler is Mercury in the loop in the 6th house in the sign of Libra. People with Mercury in Libra makes good company, harmonious, very communicative. The loop of Libra is packed with planets, a stellium. The ruler of the loop is Venus and is in the 7th house in Scorpio. The work has to do with partnerships and the public. We have the sun, Mercury, Jupiter, Saturn and Pluto. Saturn is exalted in Libra, and is ruler of the 10th and 11th houses. Some good should come out of that.

The only thing that can be said with so many planets in Libra is that she is a strong Libran, and it will come out more than the Taurus Ascendant, and even the sign that the ascendant ruler is in. But they are all there within, and working according to the individual's choice.

The 7th house ruler is Mars and Pluto. Mars is in the 5th in the sign of Leo, and Pluto is in the loop, in the 6th house in Libra. Lilith is in the 7th house in the sign of Sagittarius. It is supposed to be ruler of the loop in the 12th house, Aries.

Don't forget that when you first look at a chart, look to see if there's any planets holding zero degree, also the cusps. They give information of the house that they are in, the sign that they are in, and the sign that they rule. Notice Lilith in the 7th house in Sagittarius in zero degree. And probably the loop in 12th, or 7th sign Scorpio, or 8th and 9th sign Sagittarius. Remember that Scorpio is the 8th sign, and it has to do with other people's possessions that come to you including legacies and insurance. Sagittarius is the sign of the ninth house, and has to do with travel, freedom, other countries, something that is moving through space, high education. Ares has to do with the self, and being assertive and energetic.

Now Neptune is an outer planet, and I have to admit that I do not know it as good as I know Jupiter, or one of the inner planets. But my eyes being looking at it in charts. In this chart, it is in the 8th house in the sign of Sagittarius. It is co-ruler with Jupiter of the 12th house. It is exactly quincunx Chiron in the first house. If we don't work with Chiron, then there's no contact there. Neptune has good contact with Mercury, Jupiter and Pluto, all in the loop in the 6th house in Libra. It is easy to see that there is some contact with work and foreign countries. We mustn't forget the square Neptune has to the moon; and the trine to Mars. Enormous energy and power here. People should be very careful when Neptune is in this position, to check financial dealings. There's always something strange to do with other people's possessions.

We have seen how complicated it is when we come to interpret a chart. This is really the hardest part. I now see how difficult it is for astrologers, but let them not give up, even with all the foolish talk against it. In the old days, everyone used to take part in it, then suddenly, astronomy came from it. The two then separated, and astrology went into the dark, almost blotted out. It came back because it is true. For all those who will pursue it, especially those who are young, let them understand a little about time and space, for the intellectuals are still baffled.

Here's the chart of *Raymond Jean Abescat*, France's oldest veteran who lived to be 109 years and 348 days. He was born on the 10th September 1891, 06:00 am, Paris, France. He died on 24th August 2001.

21.59 Virgo
15.31 Libra
14.55 Scorpio
19.52 Sagittarius
25.42 Capricorn
26.40 Aquarius
21.59 Pisces
15.31 Aries
14.55 Taurus
19.52 Gemini
25.42 Cancer
26.40 Leo

Sun 17.12 Virgo
Moon 03.00 Sagittarius
Mercury 23.07 Virgo R
Venus 14.56 Virgo
Mars 03.32 Virgo
Jupiter 12.27 Pisces R
Saturn 20.01 Virgo
Uranus 29.06 Libra
Neptune 09.03 Gemini
Pluto 08.51 Gemini R
Chiron 13.00 Leo
N Node 29.51 Taurus
Lilith 26.23 Virgo
Fortune 07.46 Sagittarius

I'll give you a quick story of a Dutch friend I had who had six daughters. He was born on the same day as this chart. He told me a story about a German ship that was in port and he swam out to it with the bayonet in his mouth, climb up and over in the ship. It was in the night time. He did what he had to do, and got back off.

Before I go to the ascendant, I want to have a look around the chart. Uranus is holding 29 degrees, and is ruler of the sixth house. 15 degrees is at the axis 2/8. I have been looking at these degrees for some time, and I just found 15 degrees rather strange, still can't explain why?. Twenty six degrees, I'm trying to get a hold on. You notice Neptune and Pluto in conjunction in Gemini. Quite a lot of changes took place in those days. The planet of old age, Saturn, is in the 12th conjunct the ascendant. And then there is the sun and Mars. I get the feeling that these two, gives the chance of living long. A person might have the chart for living long, and do not make it. We all know why this is so. As we run through, I will try to give the aspects, so that you can see the contacts they make.

Every time I see a bus – I know that it is a passenger bus – and I know which route it is going to take. The same with a tree, I know what tree it is. It doesn't bear apples or cherries, it bears oranges. When we see the sign Virgo, we know exactly what it means. It is the same with all the signs, we know what they represent.

Virgo is rising with 21 degrees and has not far to go before the sign of Libra takes over. I always find that when the sign of Libra takes over the ascendant, this could turn out to be a good period indeed. Even with negative aspects. The sun is in Virgo, but in the 12th house conjunct the ascendant. Mercury is in Virgo in the first house conjunct the ascendant. Venus is in Virgo in the 12th house conjunct the ascendant. Mars is in Virgo in the 12th house. Saturn is in Virgo in the 12th house conjunct the ascendant, being the nearest to the ascendant. Lilith is in Virgo in the first house conjunct the ascendant. The sun is conjunct Mercury, Venus, Saturn, and with about 9 degrees to Lilith. Mercury is conjunct Saturn and Lilith. Venus is conjunct Saturn. Saturn conjunct Lilith. The planets here form a stellium.

The 21 degrees and 59 minutes of Virgo rising can be read in certain books that are mainly for the degrees. Some are interesting, but I don't find anything that is solid. The ruler, Mercury, is in the first house, and in its own sign. Interested in the self and others. Mercury is also ruler of the 10th house, and there, we see the two planets, Neptune and Pluto in Gemini. They don't come around every day. Lilith is also in the first house, and if Aries has to do with it, then this is a 1/8 contact – to do with other people's possessions. Do not forget that Mars and Pluto are rulers of the 8th house. Mars is in the 12th, and Pluto is in the 9th.

We have to take the planet Saturn as the nearest planet to the ascendant. It is in the 12th house, the house of Jupiter and Neptune. This is the house of behind scenes, mediating, working for others secretly. This is also the house where one can get into high office, depending on the aspects from the planet. Saturn is the destiny planet, and being so near to the ascendant shows that he must have started life early. I have seen this when Saturn is in the first house. Saturn is square to the Mid. Mercury takes second place to be nearest to the ascendant. Then the sun takes third place. Saturn is ruling the fifth and sixth houses. The sun rules the 12th house where Chiron is stationed in the 11th house in Leo. Chiron is ruling the 4th house.

The sun in the 12th has to do with away from the crowd, sometimes for a while. Some people love to be by themselves. Again we find that this could be for working with hospitals and such like Giving your individual self to help others. Lilith takes fourth place as nearest the ascendant. Venus in the 12th house takes 5th place. Venus rules the second and ninth houses. The planet of love in Neptune's house. The planet of love in the secret house, this could be romantic, seclusion, mysterious partnerships, sympathetic. Also a love of helping others and animals. The aspects of Venus are: Venus opposing Jupiter; Venus conjunct Saturn; Venus semi-square Uranus; Venus square Neptune; Venus square Pluto; Venus semi-sextile Chiron; Venus conjunct ascendant; Venus square Mid.

I didn't know he had his leg amputated until I read the biography. Sometime I don't read the biography. I just get into the chart, and see what I could find. It would take a lot of work to do 109 charts of his progress life. For a child just born, that's not too bad. You can progress years ahead and see what the planets are doing.

The aspects of the sun are: Sun conjunct Mercury. Sun conjunct Venus; Sun oppose Jupiter; Sun conjunct Saturn; Sun square Neptune; Sun conjunct ascendant; Sun square Mid.

Keep your eyes open, and see what the aspects are doing. Don't forget that some people can use negative aspects for good according to their upbringing and hereditary influences, not forgetting the environment. When you check your own chart, and those of your family, you would see what I mean.

With so many planets in Virgo, he'll be functioning as a strong Virgo. I should know, because I too, am a strong Virgo. Very critical and analytical. Seeing almost everything that goes on around me. But it is all for good and not bad.

His moon is in Sagittarius. I saw the moon also in the chart of Einstein. And I started straight away to think up how that moon is working in that sign. The moon in this chart is in the third house in conjunction with Fortune. Here are the aspects for the moon: Moon square Mars (this aspect could work out terribly bad for an undisciplined person. Moody, bad-tempered, and always in arguments. The moon is square Jupiter. The moon is Quintile Saturn. Opposing Neptune, opposing Pluto, opposing the node, Quintile the ascendant, trine Chiron.

Mercury is the ruler of the ascendant and the 10th house. The aspects are: Mercury conjunct Venus; Mercury conjunct Saturn; Mercury conjunct Lilith; Mercury conjunct the ascendant; and Mercury square the Mid.

I have been reading bits and pieces about astrology. What certain people say. Who say that astrology wants to give information about how the universe works? What astrology is actually doing is to tell us how the energies of the solar system is affecting things on earth. I am not a physicist or a scientist or any of the high subjects, but one thing that I can say is, that astrology works. And let me just say again, it has nothing to do with magic like some people say. I was looking at a chart of someone, I saw that the face was a bit long, but the cheeks were well formed. Straight away, I said to myself, this has to do with Aries and the opposite sign which is Libra. The cheeks, I knew had a bit to do with Taurus and cancer. I was right when I did check it. But I do not bank on certain faces, that is not my research. I have this knack of seeing the zodiac in certain faces. That in itself tells you that astrology is true. Dealing with human beings, that has to be a science.

We see the planet Mars in the 12th house, and is ruler of the third and 8th houses. Mars is opposing Jupiter; Mars is sextile Uranus; it is square Neptune, square Pluto, square the node, and Quintile the Mid. Mars is in the ascendant sign while it is in the 12th house. This position gives quite a lot of energy to the individual. They don't have to be just soldiers, but can be adventurers, and also sports people. The 12th house has to do wit secret enemies. And I have often seen Mars in that house in many charts, where they have had problems with enemies. We can see that Mars is in Neptune's house. These two planets doesn't really see eye to eye, unless they are well aspected. Mars square Neptune could cause problems. The fact is: there are certain planets that doesn't feel good in certain houses, even worse, if they have negative aspects.

Jupiter we see, in this chart is in the 6th house, in the sign of the 7th which is Pisces. . Jupiter is kind and sympathetic here, often ready to help the underdog. The aspects of Jupiter are: Opposing Saturn; Sesqui-quadrate Uranus; square Neptune; square Pluto; quincunx Chiron; opposing the ascendant, and square the Mid.

The aspects of Saturn: conjuncting the ascendant, square the Mid. This square of the Mid can give a high position in the career, according to who the person is, and it can also give a great fall.

Uranus in the second house is quincunx the node, trine the Mid. Neptune conjuncts Pluto, sextile Chiron. Pluto is sextile Chiron. Lilith is conjunct the ascendant.

48: Progressive Charts

Progressive charts are not the same as the natal chart. The natal chart is fixed – it is not going anywhere – but it can be moved into the future. The planets in the natal chart are moving daily, some fast and others very slow. In my chart, for example, I am nearly 79 years old, and the planet Jupiter has only moved 5 degrees.

The interpretation of the natal chart is far different than that of the progressive chart.

The first chart we are going to look at is that of a homicide child, killed by its mother with gas. The child was born 23rd March 1923, 21, 30 pm, Nobitz, Germany. Progressive date is 27th March 1923, 21.30 pm, Nobitz, Germany. The child was four years old. Here is the **natal chart**.

05.32 Scorpio
03.35 Sagittarius
08.53 Capricorn
17.50 Aquarius
21.01 Pisces
16.16 Aries
05.32 Taurus
03.25 Gemini
08.53 Cancer
17.50 Leo
21.01 Virgo
16.16 Libra

Sun 02.11 Aries
Moon 11.05 Gemini
Mercury 17.28 Pisces
Venus 20.13 Aquarius
Mars 13.56 Taurus
Jupiter 18.25 Scorpio R
Saturn 17.53 Libra R
Uranus 14.36 Pisces
Neptune 15.41 Leo R
09.05 Cancer R
Chiron 16.02 Aries
Lilith 19.11 Aries
N Node 20.00 Virgo
Fortune 14.26 Libra

08.17 Scorpio
06.44 Sagittarius
12.41 Capricorn
21.51 Aquarius
24.39 Pisces
19.24 Aries
08.07 Taurus
06.44 Gemini
12.41 Cancer
21.51 Leo
24.39 Virgo
19.24 Libra

Sun 06.09 Aries
Moon 02.25 Leo
Mercury 24.36 Pisces
Venus 24.53 Aquarius
Mars 16.43 Taurus
Jupiter 18.11 Scorpio R
Saturn 17.36 Libra R
Uranus 14.49 Pisces
Neptune 15.37 Leo R
Pluto 09.05 Cancer
Chiron 16.16 Aries
Lilith 19.38 Aries
N Node 19.47 Virgo R
Fortune 12.01 Cancer

Whenever I look at a progress chart, I see what I want to see without checking
with the natal or transits. But it is good to do so for you get more information
that is more solid. First, we see that this chart has 8 degrees rising with the sign
of Scorpio. I have already explained to you all about the 8 degrees. Well, the sign
Scorpio should be no problem to you. There are some points that will remain the
same as in the natal, the child is only four years old. Lets go to the sun because
that is the giver of life. We find it in 6 degrees of Aries in the fifth house which is
its own house in the natural wheel. It is exactly sextile the 8th house Gemini. It
is interesting to find the ruler of the 8th in the fourth which is Mercury, and it
is exactly conjunct the fifth house, which is the house of the sun, in the natural

chart, and is the house of life. Notice the sign there, it is Pisces ruled by Jupiter and Neptune. We see too, that the sun is square Pluto in the 8th house in the sign of Cancer. The sun rules the 10th house, while Pluto rules the ascendant sign with Mars. Mars is in the 7th house in Taurus. Mars is square Neptune in the 9th house. Neptune is in the sign of Leo, the tenth house. Mars is quincunx Saturn in the 11th house. Saturn is ruler of the 3rd and fourth house. Mars is ruler of the 6th. Mars is semi-sextile Chiron in the fifth house, the aspect is exact. Chiron rules the second house, the body of the child. Chiron is in a trine aspect with Neptune, and opposing Saturn. Pluto in the 8th is trine the ascendant. Fortune is exactly conjunct the 9th house, and is ruler of the 10th. Lilith is in the 6th house exactly conjunct the 6th, quincunx the node in the 10th in the 11th sign of Virgo. Lilith is quincunx Jupiter in the first house in Scorpio. Jupiter rules the 2nd and 5th houses, Lilith rules the 6th, still in research. In the fourth house, we see the planet Venus in Aquarius, exactly semi-sextile Mercury, and the fifth house. Venus is ruler of the 7th and 12th house. The node is semi-sextile the 12th.

This next chart is for *Sandra Bullock* born 26th July 1964, 03.15am, Arlington, Virginia, U.S.A. She got married in 2005, and we shall look at her progress chart. The perpetual date is 5th September 1964, 03.15am, Arlington, Virginia, U.S.A.

Natal chart

26.23 Gemini
17.07 Cancer
08.20 Leo
03.44 Virgo
06.58 Libra
17.41 Scorpio
26.23 Sagittarius
17.07 Capricorn
08.20 Aquarius
03.44 Pisces
06.58 Aries
17.41 Taurus

Sun 03.19 Leo
Moon 21.57 Aquarius
Mercury 28.24 Leo
Venus 24.05 Gemini
Mars 26.59 Gemini
Jupiter 22.13 Taurus

Saturn 03.44 Pisces R
Uranus 08, 07 Virgo
Neptune 15.03 Scorpio R
Pluto 12.35 Virgo
Chiron 18.16 Pisces
N Node 01.47 Cancer
Fortune 15.11 Capricorn

Progress chart for 2005

00.52 Leo
21.35Leo
16.25 Virgo
17.25 Libra
23.43 Scorpio
29.43 Sagittarius
00.52 Aquarius
21.35 Aquarius
16.25 Pisces
17.25 Aries
23.43 Taurus
29.43 Gemini

Sun 12.44 Virgo
Moon 01.11 Virgo
Mercury 07.08 Virgo R
Venus 27.02 Cancer
Mars 23.48 Cancer
Jupiter 25.58 Taurus
Saturn 00.48 Pisces R
Uranus 10.35 Virgo
Neptune 15.29 Scorpio
Pluto 13.56 Virgo
Chiron 16.37 Pisces
N Node 29.15 Gemini
Fortune 19.19 Cancer

I am wondering why she could not have children of her own. It is a great thing she has done adopting children. I see in her natal chart that Venus is the ruler of the 5th house and is in the 12th conjunct the ascendant.

Dealing with the progress chart, zero degree of Leo is rising. This can tell you of your own birth, a partnership or something is happening between you and others. The sun is ruler of the ascendant, and is in the 2nd house in the sign of Virgo conjuncting Pluto. Pluto is co-ruler of the 5th house, house of romance. Neptune is there, and is ruler of the 9th house carrying her destiny planet Saturn, in the 8th house, in the sign of Pisces, and holding zero degree. Notice that Saturn is quincunx the ascendant. Saturn is ruler of the loop in the 6th house, co-ruler of the 7th and the 8th. This 8th house is the body and possessions of the partner. And don't forget that houses one and two are really one sign which is Leo. The mathematics have split them into one and two.

Why the loop in the 6th house? That's still a mystery to me. Still working to get it right. Notice that in the second house there are four planets in the sign of Virgo. A very strong Virgo indeed. Inside the other loop which is in the 12th house is Cancer carrying the planets Venus and Mars, and Fortune. Notice that Mars is also ruler of the 5th house, house of romance. And Mars is exactly sextile the 11th house, house of friendships, and Jupiter is there, the big planet. The node is in the 11th house, ruler of the loop in the 12th, and is exactly conjunct the 12th. The node is semi-sextile the ascendant. It is sextile the moon in the second house in the sign of Virgo. The moon is also ruler of Cancer. I do hope that you have taken note that Mars is in its fall in Cancer. Chiron in the 9th house in the sign of Pisces is exactly conjunct the 9th, and semi-sextile the Mid. Chiron rules the 6th house giving us a connection of 6/9 In the fourth house we see the planet Neptune in the fifth house sign of Scorpio. It is trine the 9th house and Chiron.

Don't forget you have to work with the natal chart as well. It is a lot of work, but it is worth it.

Before I go to the next chart, I did promise to tell you about 'the burn up'. This is having the sun and Mercury very close together. It can drive you crazy, if you're not aware of it. Being aware, you have to try to control it. It will go away when Mercury moves away, but that will take some time. It is strange, because I get a lot of pictures of places where I have been. I just see them, and suddenly they go away. At the same time, the burn up has a trine to Pluto. I will tell you more later.

We are going to look at the progressive chart of *Jerry Seinfeld* who got married in 1999. I will give you the natal chart first, and then the progressive one. He was born 29th April 1954, 06.00 am, Brooklyn, New York, U.S.A.

Natal chart

07.39 Taurus
07.55 Gemini
00.09 Cancer
21.09 Cancer
15.36 Leo
19.42 Virgo
07.39 Scorpio
07.55 Sagittarius
00.09 Capricorn
21.09 Capricorn
15.36 Aquarius
19.42 Pisces

Sun 08.32 Taurus
Moon 20.04 Pisces
Mercury 27. 63 Aries
Venus 00.36 Gemini
Mars 05.16 Capricorn
Jupiter 24.57 Aries
Saturn 05.50 Scorpio R
Uranus 19.28 Cancer
Neptune 24.18 Libra R
Pluto 22.32 Leo R
Chiron 28.38 Capricorn
N Node 18.28 Capricorn
Lilith 24.49 Libra
Fortune 26.08 Gemini

Remember that the N Node goes backwards. Here we have in this chart, Fortune in the second house.

Progressive chart

29.09 Gemini
19.13 Cancer
10.05 Leo
05.25 Virgo
08.59 Libra

20.22 Scorpio
29.09 Sagittarius
19.13 Capricorn
10.05 Aquarius
05.25 Pisces
08.59 Aries
20.22 Taurus

Sun 21.51 Gemini
Moon 17.08 Scorpio
Mercury 15.20 Cancer
Venus 24.54 Cancer
Mars 05.50 Capricorn
Jupiter 04.27 Cancer
Saturn 03.04 Scorpio R
Uranus 21.24 Cancer
Neptune 23.24 Libra R
Pluto 22.53 Leo
Chiron 27.45 Capricorn
N Node 16.05 Capricorn
Lilith 29.52 Libra
Fortune 24.27 Scorpio

Before I start on the progressive chart, I read that our Solar System came into being from a passing cloud of gas and dust. There were other Solar Systems before ours started to form. Where were we then? I went into some deep thinking trying to see which planet would be first. I took Jupiter to be the first to break away. A few days ago, I read that it was Jupiter which came out first from the mass.

We all know that some charts are easy to read than others. This one is easy. I will go straight over into the 7th house and pick up Mars holding 5 degrees, and exalted in Capricorn. Mars is opposing Jupiter in the first house, and as we see, Jupiter is exalted in Cancer. Mars is co-ruler of the 6th house, and ruler of the 11th. So we have a 11/7, and 11/6. At the 6th house, there's the Moon, Saturn and Fortune. Jupiter is ruling the 7th house, and is co-ruler of the 10th. The Moon is in the 5th house in Scorpio conjunct the 6th house. We see also that Mars is exactly sextile the Mid. The 11/5 axis is in 8 degrees, so we know that something is going on there. The Moon, while in the 5th house is sextile the node in the 7th house, both of them rules the second house. There, we pick up Mercury. Around April, The Moon would have been exact with Mercury. Don't forget that the Moon is the fastest in this chart, and moves around about 1 degree per month. You can check the Moon monthly by the contacts it will make.

We are going to peep in *Ryan Gosling* chart to see if we spot anything. He got his jaw broken in November 2013. He was born 12th November 1980, 14.34 pm, London Ontario, Canada.

Natal chart

19.42 Pisces
05.03 Taurus
03.17 Gemini
24.48 Gemini
15.26 Cancer
10.24 Leo
19.42 Virgo
05.03 Scorpio
03.17 Sagittarius
24.48 Sagittarius
15.26 Capricorn
10.24 Aquarius

Sun 20.34 Scorpio
Moon 16.21 Capricorn
Mercury 03.59 Scorpio
Venus 16.12 Libra
Mars 23.02 Sagittarius
Jupiter 03.04 Libra
Saturn 06.05 Libra
Uranus 25.32 Scorpio
Neptune 21.14 Sagittarius
Pluto 22.48 Libra
Chiron 15.35 Taurus
N Node 15.07 Leo
Lilith 24.42 Libra
Fortune 15.39 Taurus

The progressive date is 15th December 1980, 14.34 pm, London, Ontario, Canada. This date is for 2013.

Progressive chart

15.16 Taurus
13.20 Gemini
04.23 Cancer
24.55 Cancer
19.39 Leo
25.20 Virgo
15.16 Scorpio
15.20 Sagittarius
04.23 Capricorn
24.55 Capricorn
19.39 Aquarius
25.20 Pisces

Sun 24.00 Sagittarius
Moon 03.38 Aries
Mercury 15.20 Sagittarius
Venus 26.57 Scorpio
Mars 18.12 Capricorn
Jupiter 07.58 Libra
Saturn 08.46 Libra
Uranus 27.32 Scorpio
Neptune 22.26 Sagittarius
Pluto 23.49 Libra
Chiron 14.06 Taurus
N Node 13.22 Leo
Lilith 28.24 Libra
Fortune 24.55 Leo

Here's a very good book to get: *The Rulership Book* by Rex E, Bills.

I do not know why this is: but when the planet Mars is going through the signs, it affects my body. I know now that the planets have something to do with the body. But medical astrology, I find, is rather difficult.

In this progressive chart for Ryan Gosling it is easy to see that his rising sign is Taurus ruled by Venus. Taurus rules the jaw and the second house in the fixed wheel. The second house in this wheel is ruled by Mercury.

Over in the 7th house, we see that the planet Venus is in a close conjunction with Uranus, the planet of disruption, suddenness, and unusualness. Notice that Venus is also ruler of the loop in the 6th house carrying Lilith, Jupiter, Saturn and Pluto. We find the sun in the 8th house exactly semi-sextile the Mid, and it is square the 12th house, exactly trine Fortune in the 5th. Fortune is semi-sextile the 6th, quincunx the Mid. Chiron in the 12th conjunct the ascendant. Notice that Chiron is ruling the 8th house with three planets there. The 8th house is known as the house of operation, and you find that it comes up in the charts when women are having babies. Also the 12th house comes into play. For this is the house of isolation, hospitals etc. The moon is in a loop in the 12th house in the sign of Aries. It is square the 9th house. Mars in the 9th house in Capricorn exalted is semi-sextile the 11th. Pluto in the loop in the 6th is square the Mid, sextile to Fortune. By the way, the upper jaw is ruled by Aries. The node in the 4th house is exactly sextile the second house, square Chiron. Chiron is quincunx Mercury in the 8th house in Sagittarius. Lilith in the loop in the 6th, is semi-sextile Uranus in the 7th.

You can meet me on my next project:
Conception–Soul–Astrological Charts